THE SINAI
PROPHECY

THE SINAI
PROPHECY

JOHN SKRABACZ

ARPress
ILLUMINATING IDEAS
EMPOWERING VOICES

ARPress
45 Dan Road Suite 5
Canton, MA 02021

Hotline: 1(888) 821-0229
Fax: 1(508) 545-7580

Ordering Information:

Quantity sales. Special discounts are available on quantity purchases by corporations, associations, and others. For details, contact the publisher at the address above.

Printed in the United States of America.

ISBN-13:	Softcover	979-8-89330-131-1
	eBook	979-8-89330-132-8

Library of Congress Control Number: 2024901487

TABLE OF CONTENTS

PART THREE

PART FOUR

PROLOGUE

This is a fictional story, ending in the truthful account of how an extensive transformation of a human being may occur. Although parts are fiction which is similar to a science fiction story, the truth of the "Good News" is fact. What I wish to leave you with is the truth. I have heard people say, "That is the pure and simple truth." But I believe that truth is really never pure, and very rarely simple, unless it comes from an infallible source. This will come from that source because truth is a person. Enjoy this fictional account of how the message of "The Truth" will be delivered, but beyond enjoyment, it is my most fervent prayer that you accept the "Words of Truth" that are given. They are the way and the truth to eternal life! And that part of this tale is the gospel truth!

****

"Once, I thought my life had been forever planned. I never would have guessed that all I thought and believed could so drastically change. But let me explain how this all came about......."

Hiram (Ace) Walker

To God be the glory. Great things He hath done!

PART ONE

CHAPTER 1

In 1932 I can distinctly remember at age twelve going to work with my father. He was my hero. Some of my boyhood friends idolized Babe Ruth and some Jim Thorpe, but my father William J. Walker of the "Dover Herald Press," was in my eyes, the champion of the world. My adolescent brain argued that informing the world of the most important events in history, as they were occurring, was far more important than hitting a home run or scoring the next touchdown. It's not like I never liked sports because I did; but I just simply idolized my dad. You see, he was the editor of our newspaper's department of foreign affairs, and he wrote his columns about places that boggled my youthful imagination. He wrote about exotic places with authority because he had actually been to those places. He practically invented the term "War Correspondent," because he was the first person to have received that title for his escapades during World War I. He both wrote about and photographed the devastations that he witnessed in "The Great War" at places like Marne France, and the battles at the Somme and Verdun. He lived with our troops in the poison gas filled trenches on the "Western Front". His photos and stories were printed in newspapers and magazines throughout the world.

My dad loved four things in life. He loved my mother, Agatha. He loved me. He loved "Monte Cristo" cigars, and he also truly loved "Canadian Club" whiskey, and during prohibition he purchased many cases of it illegally. In fact, he loved it so much that he named me, his only child Hiram..... after Hiram Walker, the original founder of the Windsor, Ontario distillery. But people call me "Ace" which is the nickname that was coined for me by my paternal Uncle Robert.

There were some things that my father did not like. No, that was a bad choice of words, because there were a few things that my father despised. Those were, in no particular order, churches and their preachers, the New York Yankees, and Democrats. My father was a devout agnostic, a fervent St. Louis Cardinal fan, and a staunch Republican.

I was born in Rehoboth Beach, Delaware on November the 2nd 1917. In my childhood life I enjoyed fishing with dad on our "Cape Hatteras" boat, the beach life, and baseball. I also liked the forty-five-mile train rides, when I was allowed to accompany my father from Rehoboth to his newspaper office in Dover.

It seemed I was destined from birth to be a newspaper man. I was sure that it was providentially ordained for me to follow in my father's footsteps, because I started in the business at the tender age of twelve, delivering copies of the Dover Herald Press to the families of my hometown. Although dad was often away from home on assignments, when he was home, he devoted much of his time to me. Life was wonderful.

In 1934 the greatest event happened in our family. A novel that dad had previously written was published. It was entitled "My War." It instantly became a best seller, and in two years' time he was awarded the "Nobel Prize for Literature." Then things started to go downhill. He was diagnosed with leukemia, and a year later he died. Needless to say, drastic changes in life befell me and my mother, but fortunately because of his book, royalties kept coming in to supplement the already substantial nest egg that was in our coffers. The great void in our lives, because of his death, seemed at first insurmountable to us. My mother eventually cultivated new pursuits in her life such as gardening and card parties with her girlfriends. In 1938 I was becoming the well -built, tall, brown-haired, blue-eyed, handsome devil that the girls thought I was. ("Pride Cometh Before the fall") At that time in my life I was attempting to enroll in college and was finally accepted at "Delaware University" in Newark, Delaware. This of course was my father's Alma Mater and it enabled me to remain close to home, and to take Journalism as my major course of studies. I will now identify myself with the school's team mascots. Go Blue Hens!

CHAPTER 2

(1938)

The day I was to depart for school, my mother, bless her soul, saw me off on the train and she cried. At this time in my life, I imagined myself too grown up, and rather too sophisticated to shed tears. As you will discover, I wasn't socially inept, I was just immature. My new adventure begins on a short ninety- mile train trip when I meet the two men who would become, for better or worse, my best friends.

Andrew Harrison and Roger Sutcliffe were both from Lewes Delaware and were enrolled, as I was, as freshmen at the U. of Delaware. Andrew was a rowdy, outgoing and tall red-headed kid with freckles, and Roger was the exact opposite. He was of average height, had a pimpled face, was somewhat porky and shy, but always smiling. When we meet for the first time the male pecking order instantly came into play. Andrew's father was a prominent attorney, and Roger's dad was the mayor of Lewes Delaware. I trumped them both because of my father's "Nobel Prize." We first discussed our selected studies. Andrew was interested in engineering, and Roger sought a degree in the liberal arts. I didn't know it then, but thirty years later I would discover, that a person who becomes an engineer would look at a problem and ask, "How does it work?" A person obtaining a degree in journalism would ask, "What will I write?" And a person with a degree in the liberal arts would ask, "Do you want fries with that?" But nevertheless, I liked them both and we soon hoped that we could room together. Our conversation soon advanced past the mundane issues of academics and evolved into the incredibly important issues of the four B's. Since you probably don't know what those are, I'll explain. They are Booze, Baseball, the Big Band Sound, and Broads! It was quite evident that the three of us were ready for the college experience, and in our minds, the rite of passage to party! We were so ready to party that we immediately pushed our way through an untold number of passengers into the train's club car. We were dressed to kill in new suits and cocky fedora hats on our heads. We now considered ourselves, for the first time, as adult men ready to conquer the world. At the bar, my two new friends ordered gin, but I my father's son, ordered "Canadian Club" on the rocks. We lit up cigarettes and delighted in our newfound freedom, however we delighted ourselves entirely too much, because when the train arrived at the Newark station we could barely stagger off.

We were met unfortunately by Miss Amelia Lockhart a teacher at the U. of D. She could be best described as a cross- eyed and withered old spinster. When she smelled the alcohol on our breaths, she snubbed her nose up and frowned upon us. I could picture her walking with axe in hand along with Carey Nation of the "Women's Temperance Union" through the streets of Philadelphia and playing havoc upon the local drinking establishments. Miss Lockhart was simply disgusted by our inebriated condition. She never looked at us. She never talked to us. She simply drove us to the school's admissions office and then departed without saying one word to any of us.

After signing our admissions forms, we were happy to discover that we were being billeted together in the dorm on the Laird campus, and in a drunken haze we meandered the hallways of the "Dupont Hall" dormitory eventually finding room 22B on the second floor. We discovered that each dorm room housed four students. We only ascertained this because as we entered the room the body of another student was loudly snoring on the top bunk of a bed in a corner of the room. He was fully dressed and still wearing his black dress shoes. I instantly knew what this situation demanded! Without knowing the dormitory rules pertaining to smoking, I remove a cigarette from my pack of "Lucky Strikes." I strike a match, light my cigarette, tear off another match, and wedge it between the toe of his shoe and its sole. Andy and Rog both look at me smiling, while shaking their heads in the affirmative. I then light the match, now stuck on his shoe with my cigarette, thus giving our new roomie a proper hot foot. The three of us, now partners in crime, stand back, gleefully watch, and chuckle to ourselves. It takes less than a minute for our victim to loudly scream, fall from his perch on the top bunk, and land with a loud thud on the floor. As he slaps at the source of his misery, he gives us the evil eye. I thought at first, he was going to charge us, but when I notice that he is only about five-foot-four and skinny as a rail; I knew that he wouldn't.... but then he did! He threw a punch at me landing on my jaw, kicked Andy in the area where men least want to be kicked, tackled Roger to the floor, and while on top of him proceeded to pummel him with his fists. While Andy remained frozen on the floor holding his privates in agony, I finally pulled him off Rog, and yelled, "Stop now! You stop it now! It's all over! It was just a joke! He looks at me smiling, with wild red eyes and says, "Shore and be'gora, an' I be Patrick Michael O'Brien. You may call me Paddy, and it's a joy to be a meetin ya!"

The door to our room bursts open and a tall middle-aged man with graying hair wearing only a white t- shirt and boxer shorts says, "What in the world is going on here? Have you idiots been fighting?!"

Paddy answers him saying, "Oh no Mr. Jensen! We were just a playin' don't ya know!"

Jensen says, "Well quit your playing "grab-ass". It's almost 10:00 pm and time for lights out! You three must be Walker, Sutcliffe, and Harrison am I correct?"

"Yes sir," we answer, and introduce ourselves as Ace, Rog, and Andy.

Jensen says, "Well you three really know how to make a first impression. By the way, I smell smoke. Have any of you been smoking in this room?"

"I have sir," I answer.

He says, "There is no smoking allowed in this building men, or should I call you boys. I want you to read the "List of Rules" posted on this door. Walker let me smell your breath."

I walk up to him and allow him to smell my breath. He says, "You stink! Really…. you've already started Walker? Let me just say this, I am Mr. John Jensen, and I am not only the athletic director of this university, but this building's monitor as well, and that means that I am your commander and chief. I want you to know that this is a very distinguished school. It is one of the oldest in our nation, having its roots back to 1743. Three graduates in the first class of this institution were signers of the "Declaration of Independence." Another man was a signer of the "Constitution." In addition, it boasts a faculty of internationally known authors. One of its most honored graduates has won the "Nobel Prize for Literature." I believe Mr. Walker that person was your father, and I'm not so sure he would have been so proud of you today. Let me finish by saying this. By all rights I should write an incident report pertaining to you three, but since it's your first day here I won't. And you O'Brien should have known better. That's all. Breakfast is at 7:00 am. You three can put away your things tomorrow. Right now, it is lights out!"

The next morning, we wake up with hangover difficulty, and go to the dining hall for breakfast. Our newly found roommate Paddy is already seated at a table by himself. We side- step through the breakfast line, collect our food, and join Paddy. Our conversation begins with Paddy saying, "Well good mornin' to ya lads. And it is a wonderful day it tis!"

"Everyone's entitled to their own opinion Paddy", I answer.

Roger says, "I'm so nauseous I don't know if I can get this food down. I really feel bad. I think I might die."

Andy answers, "You think you might die Rog? Well, I'm not afraid to die. I just don't want to be there when it happens."

I add, "I don't believe in an afterlife, but just in case, I'm going to bring an extra change of underwear. Oh, and by the way Paddy, I want to apologize for the prank we played on you last evening. We were drunk and not thinking clearly. Would you accept our forgiveness?"

Paddy says, "Forgive? Well, I'll not do that, but I want a' thank ye laddies, cause I love a good donnybrook, and ye gave me a proper one don't ye know. I should be a thankin' ye."

Andy laughs and says, "We didn't know that we were awakening the Tasmanian Devil Paddy. Your fierceness certainly surprised the three of us."

Then Roger asks, "Paddy, your speech suggests an Irish brogue. How long have you been in this country?"

Paddy answers, "Ye are correct me new mate, me family and me self, come from county Cork in the land that the saints ave' truly blessed, and that would be St. Patrick's Ireland! We ave' been in this land of your'n for three years now. And Mother McCrea I still miss the old country of me birth."

"What do you think of Mr. Jensen who reprimanded us last evening?", I ask.

Paddy responds with, "Since I've been here a week before ye at this beloved place, saints be preserved, I have had the occasion to speak to his highness thrice. Mr. John Jensen is a saint of a man. Shor' and be'gora, he be a man that requires our greatest respect mates. He's not only in charge of our dorm, but the bloke teaches mathematics and coaches the rounders team that ye call baseball. He did his fightin' in the "Great War" don't ye know?"

I ask, "What subjects will you be studying Paddy?"

Paddy relates, "I am interested in the business side of this country laddies, and will select classes about that. Me family owns a grocer's market in the city you call "The City of Brotherly Love." I be callin' it "The City of Brotherly Shove". I'll be a wishin' to help them with it. Business will be me major and me minor will be pints of "Guinness stout."

I recount, "Andy is going to study engineering, Rog the liberal arts, and journalism for myself. I understand that we'll be selecting our major area of studies tomorrow at the "careers workshop". My father told me once that there is wisdom in a multitude of counselors, and I suggest that we help each other. Synergy is a group effort and a powerful method of achieving our goals. Let's help out each other as best we can and let us never forget we must diligently come to the aid of the fairer sex! We may now be the fighting Delaware Blue Hens, but I like the hens of any color, especially the pretty ones."

CHAPTER 3

Today is the first day that classes are scheduled. Rog and I have an English Literature class.

It is in the "Center for the Arts" building. No sooner did we take our seats than our teacher walks in, and to our dismay it is our chauffeur of the previous evening, Ms. Amelia Lockhart in all her dull glory. We glance at each other in horror. It seems that my short tenure at this school will make me infamous! I looked around and counted twenty-nine students in this class. Ms. Lockhart is looking at none of them except me and Rog. She begins saying, "It is my pleasure to have the majority of you here today." She then turns around to write on the blackboard. "This is "English Literature 101, and your proper textbook for this class is "The Medieval Period". I am Professor Amelia Lockhart. The first course in our studies will be Chaucer's "Canterbury Tales."

I whisper to Rog, "Do you know what happens to a cross-eyed teacher Rog......? You don't? Well......they can't control their pupils!" Roger tries to stifle his laugh but the girl sitting in front of me laughs aloud.

Immediately Ms. Lockhart whirls around, points at the girl and says, "Did you just laugh Miss Adams?"

"Yes, ma'am I did."

"Well by all means please tell me what is so funny?"

"It was something that the student behind me said."

"Well Mr. Walker would you like to share your humor with the entire class?"

"I said the Canterbury tales sounds like it would be pornographic." The entire class laughs loudly.

Ms. Lockhart says, "Have you been drinking again this morning Mr. Walker?"

"No ma'am I haven't."

"Well, it wouldn't surprise me any. I'm sure you are your father's son. He was also in this class a few decades ago. I would advise you sir, that I refuse to tolerate any abject behavior in this room. If you continue to do so, I promise I will remove you."

I shut up.

I meet my friends at lunch time. "Hey guys it looks like it's meatloaf today."

Andy says, "My mother was such a terrible cook! She made only one of two dishes for every meal, meatloaf, or cherry pie. I always had to ask, "Which one is this?"

Rog says, "Really Andy? Well, the most remarkable thing about my mom, is that for twenty years she served us nothing but leftovers....... The original meal was never found!"

I join in with, "Did you hear about the guy who was half French and half pygmy? He was a great cook but couldn't reach the grill."

Paddy jumps in with, "Okay blokes, what is fifty meters high and made of dough? Gotcha?......The leaning tower of pizza."

We all laugh at our attempts at comedy. I think it's our great stress reliever!

As we move forward in our new collegiate endeavors, we begin to settle into the routine of our daily activities. But after three steady months of it, the old truism that says, "All work and no play makes Jack a dull boy" starts to ring true. We're overjoyed when reading in

11

our dorm's bulletin board that a dance is scheduled in the "Jefferson Auditorium" for the coming Saturday night. We are excited about getting opportunities to party with the ladies. Andy says, "I wonder if refreshments will include any alcoholic beverages?"

Paddy answers, "Now you should be a knowin' lads, if they don't I will."

I say, "Paddy, I want you to listen to me. "All of us have been into trouble since our arrival here, and we shouldn't be getting into it anymore. Come Saturday night at the dance you need to behave yourself. You need to be displaying your best manners."

Paddy laughs and answers, "Ace, there be only one substitute for good manners, and that be fast reflexes."

I think to myself, here we go again!

The auditorium is decorated with streamers and banners. As we walk in a band is playing a Glenn Miller tune, which is telling everyone waltzing on the dance floor, that everything is wonderful "Somewhere Over the Rainbow." We strut over to the refreshment table, grab some snacks, and fill our glasses from a punch bowl. The four of us have a sip and Paddy says, "There be no booze in this bloody drink!" He then immediately takes a large bottle of vodka out of the inside of his jacket, looks cautiously around, and pours the entire contents into the bowl.

I say, "Be careful Paddy, there are two campus security guards over near the band." We look around, pour our drinks back into the bowl, and refill them with our self-made cocktails.

Paddy proudly smiles about his mischievous deed, takes a drink, and says, "Hey boyo, I've always been a man of the drink!"

Andy tells him, "Now Paddy behave yourself. Do not get drunk."

Paddy answers, "Oh come now laddies, a man isn't drunk until he lies on the floor, and he can't hold on!"

We go to chairs which are lined in single rows with their backs against three different walls of the auditorium. One row is occupied by all men, another by all women, and the third with mixed genders. We find four chairs next to each other in the male section. I look around and estimate that there are about eighty people including faculty chaperones in attendance. Fortunately, Witch Lockhart isn't present. We sit there, and rather than conversing, we watch silently, and with great rapture and admiration we study the parade of women waltzing by. I am intent on singling out my prey, in order to petition her for the next song that the band will perform. That is when I spot a pretty blonde in a black dress. I decide that she is my target. "Over the Rainbow" ends and the dance floor is vacated. Only minutes later it starts up again and a female vocalist starts singing and telling everyone that she has "Georgia on Her Mind." I take this as my cue, walk over to the ladies' row, and both arrogantly and confidently walk up to this young lady and ask, "May I have this dance ma'am?" She answers, "No thank you sir." Dejected and somewhat embarrassed, I turn away, and as I take my first step towards my seat, I hear the girls giggling behind me. My friends are laughing at me as I join them.

"Andy says, "Nice job Ace."

"Shut up Andy. I think what you lack in intelligence, you make up for in stupidity."

Rog asks, "Why did you pick a blonde?"

In order to negate my embarrassment, and to regain some dignity, I answer, "Gentlemen prefer blondes, because blondes know what gentlemen prefer."

As the evening progresses Andy, Paddy, and myself all ask a number of ladies to dance and on each occasion, we are denied. Oddly, Rog never tries to dance. Andy says, "The last one I asked said she didn't dance with freshmen." We look at each other knowingly.

I say, "That's what the problem is. We are freshmen. We are scum. We are unworthy. We are contagious. We may as well have leprosy, and we may as well stop asking them to dance any more this evening. Let's just have a couple more drinks and enjoy the music.

It is getting close to the witching hour, and we notice that the crowd is starting to get a little tipsy from the punch bowl. The three of us had three drinks each. That's right I said the three of us, because when I look at our fourth, which is Paddy, he appears to be loaded. I ask, "How many drinks have you had?"

"I don't know," he says.

I ask, "What makes you drink so much Paddy."

He says, "There be nothing, saints be blessed, to <u>make</u> me drink this much......I <u>am a volunteer!</u>"

The band strikes up the song "Happy Days Are Here Again" and Paddy is certainly happy. In fact, he has become the booze comedian of the party. I can tell he is frustrated by the numerous rejections he's received from the women, and he is angry as well. When a smiling couple comes jitterbugging by us, Paddy gets up, staggers over to them, taps the man on the shoulder, and asks, "May I be a' cuttin' in sir?" The man tells him, "Get lost shorty." And those were the wrong words to be telling our drunken friend at this time, because Paddy immediately hits him in the face with a hard- right cross! The man falls backward onto another couple causing them to both fall to the floor. The falling woman's partner stands again, helps her up, and thinking that the ruckus has been caused by the wrong man, proceeds to fight him. Paddy, filled with his love for an Irish donnybrook, grabs the empty vodka bottle from under the table and breaks it over the head of a faculty member who was attempting to stop the altercation.

Then all hell breaks loose. Everyone is fighting each other. The band continues playing "Happy Days Are Here Again" as the brawl continues. Andy and I are forced to join in the melee' when two men rush at us. The two of us start swinging our fists at them, while Rog is seen running into the bathroom. This free-for-all continues for a full five minutes.

Finally, an authoritarian voice booms over the loudspeakers saying, "Stop this nonsense immediately! I say stop your brawling or the guards will arrest you. The Newark police have been notified and they will arrive here soon! Cease and desist! Cease and desist!"

It takes a while before men start backing off each other. Then the fracas slowly comes to a stop. I look up on the stage and see that it was Mr. Jensen who ordered the fighting to stop. Andy wipes some blood off his face and says, "Look at Paddy!" I watch as a guard is handcuffing our friend. Then I see Rog returning from the bathroom. He comes over and stands by me. I say nothing to him. Loud sirens announce the presence of the police and ambulance. EMT's carrying stretchers come racing into the building followed by two police officers. The police haul Paddy out of the building, and the medics put Mr. Leonard, the teacher that Paddy hit with the bottle, onto a stretcher and carry him out to the ambulance. Most of the remaining crowd go to the university dispensary.

CHAPTER 4

The next day I skip my "Written Communications Class." My two remaining roommates have no classes scheduled. Both Andy and I are licking our wounds, and of course Rog has no wounds to lick, unless he cut himself shaving in the auditorium's bathroom. We decide that later in the day that we'd visit Paddy in the Newark jail. We have already been notified that tomorrow the "Dean of the University" has scheduled a speech about the events that happened during the dance. All students that participated in the event are required to attend and all classes have been cancelled. Before leaving for the jail, Andy phoned his attorney father to ask him if he'd handle Paddy's bail.

The Newark Transit Authority operates a bus that makes a stop at the college, and we board it at 5 p.m. Upon arriving at the police department, we are escorted to a visitor's meeting room. Paddy remaining in handcuffs is brought in shortly, and he says, "It is a joy to see ye laddies and I'll be a thankin' ye for a comin'. What d' ye do? Bunk offen' school?"

We say we did, and Andy asks him, "What did they charge you with Paddy?"

With his two swollen eyes Paddy answers, "These blokes are sayin' I 'ave been charged with a disorderly conductin', incitin' a riot, and how's it said…… the aggrava…… I forget the words.

Andy finishes the words for him, "Do you mean aggravated assault?"

"Aye! That'll be the one. I tell em...... "The whole thing was just a bit of shomozzle on the edge of the court!"

Andy tells him, "Don't try to laugh this off Paddy. But as serious as this is, I have got some good news for you; I called my father, and he has arranged for your bail. You will be going back to our dorm with us today." Andy calls a guard over, we go to the front desk, and Paddy signs his release papers.

The next morning, everyone from the dance is in the assembly hall waiting to hear from Dean Michaels. He arrives with a somber face and begins, "Ladies and gentlemen, if that is what you really are, I wish you to know that I am appalled at the behavior you displayed two nights ago. I am ordering everyone here today to compose a letter of apology, sign it, and hand carry it to my office. Mrs. Stewart, my secretary will accept them. I have all of your names, and if any of you fail to do this, you will be placed on probation. I want you to know that Mr. James Leonard, the head of the Chemistry Department, has acquired a severe concussion, and has received several stitches to repair the damage done to his scalp. I am disgusted by this incident; therefore, I will make this message short. Your actions were certainly not indicative of the teachings nor the spirit of this hallowed university. Is Mr. Patrick O'Brien in this room? (Paddy raises his hand.) You sir are to report to my office immediately! That is all."

We all exited the hall fully chastised. Paddy goes directly to the Dean's office, and Andy, Rog, and I go to our dormitory.

Three hours later a tearful Paddy enters our room. "Me mates I suppose I've made a holy show of me self. I am as thick as a plank and have been given the boot from this here academy. I 'ave also me date of me trial for the fightin', and Mr. Leonard is pressin' his charges agin' me."

I say, "You were expelled Paddy?"

"Aye! I was boyo. I be here to get me things and say me goodbyes."

I tell him that we will be present at his trial. We hug him, and as he stands by the door, he gives the room one last glimpse, shakes his head, and leaves.

The next day begins as if nothing has happened. We abandon our room and head to our scheduled classes. I find that a foreign language class is an alternate recommended course for my Journalism degree, and as unusual as it sounds, but because my father was fluent in the ancient language, I add Hebrew as an additional study. During my first foray into this ancient language, I find it interesting, and I have faith in my ability to master the spoken word, but I am also convinced that I could never be able to cipher its written vocabulary. My goal is to master the language in order to speak it fluently.

A week later we are sitting in court at Paddy's trial. It is a civil trial; there is no jury. The presiding judge will decide all matters. Paddy has a public defender representing him. During the previous arraignment he pled guilty to "disorderly conduct" and "inciting a riot," and not guilty to "aggravated assault with a deadly weapon." In his summation attorney Joseph Brannigan pleads, "We have since pleaded guilty to the lesser charges your honor, but the charge of aggravated assault with a deadly weapon, we feel, is too strong to hold my client accountable for. He did not premeditate to strike Mr. Leonard, but during the confusion of the fighting at that scene, he thought he was defending himself. My client was simply caught up in the confusion around him. We want the court to acknowledge that Mr. O'Brien is an immigrant from Ireland where fighting is almost considered a normality. He does not understand all the laws or customs of our country. We acknowledge that the victim has suffered, and we also want the court to know that Mr. O'Brien is truly sorry for his actions, and he has since been expelled from the University of Delaware. That in itself should be punishment enough.

We ask for the court's leniency, and for its consideration of a charge of "simple assault" rather than aggravated.

Judge Sutherland looks down upon Paddy and says, "You sir are responsible for severely injuring a man. You have also been rightly convicted of starting the fiasco at the U. of D. I will however consider and accept your plea for the lesser charge if financial restitution is paid to Mr. Leonard. Therefore, this court finds you guilty of simple assault and sentences you to six months in the state correctional center in Sussex County. Bailiffs remove this man into custody. This court's session is closed."

We say our goodbyes, and Paddy just nods his head and is taken away.

We are now well into our freshman year. Andy and I are doing well in our studies, but Rog is doing poorly. The longer I know Rog, the more I'm confused about him. He seems to be becoming more subdued, or maybe a better choice of words is that he seems depressed. I know he feels embarrassed about running away from the fight at the dance, but I believe that there is more to it than that.

CHAPTER 5

We come to the time of the year that every student strives for, and that is......spring break! I suggest, "Guys, I think we should all go to Rehoboth beach and take the "Miss Minerva" out!"

Rog asks, "And what pray tell is the "Miss Minerva?""

I explain, "She is one beautiful forty- foot Cape Hatteras boat. She was my fathers and now she is mine. We'll stock her with food and beer, do some swordfish angling, and maybe pick up some girls for company. We can even sleep on her. Whittaya say?"

Andy says, "Great idea Ace. What do you think Rog?"

Rog answers, "As long as I can still visit my parents, I'll go."

My mother meets us at the train station and showers me with hugs and kisses. She asks, "Did you boys want to come to our home for something to eat first, or do you want to go straight to the marina?" We all agree to depart directly to the boat. I thank mom when she drops us off and tell her that I'll see her soon. I turn to the guys and say, "Let's go over to Hansen's Market. It's right here at the end of the pier. We'll load up on food and beer and take "Miss Minerva" out today!" I'm so happy guys! You know I believe that every man has a key to happiness...... you just have to pick out the right lock. Well, the "Miss Minerva" was me and my father's key!" We grab our provisions and head over to the bait shop.

Andy asks, "What are we fishing for Ace?"

"We are going after swordfish guys! If you get one on your line, you'll never forget it! These fish grow up to fourteen feet long and can weigh up to 1,400 pounds. I have all the fishing tackle we'll need already stored on the boat. We just need to buy some Mahi or Bonita bellies for bait. When we walk into the shop, Ron Pederson the owner looks up at me, smiles, and says, "Hi Ace! Long time no see! Your mom told me you've been away at school. It's good to see you again."

"Thanks Ron these are my friends Rog and Andy. We're going out for a monster, so we'll be needing some bellies. Can you give me any news where they've been hitting."

"Yeah Ace, a couple were caught about two miles from the Indian River outlet. The weather is looking good, and the seas are fairly calm. You should have a good time. Good luck."

We carry all of our purchases to the boat, and I say, "I can't tell you how happy I am to be back on my girl, there were times in the past that I took her out almost every summer day. Mom has an old friend that captains her when she takes her girlfriends out. I just wish Paddy could be with us today."

We head out of the marina, and I am a happy man. I tell the boys never put off happiness......because there's no time like the <u>pleasant</u>.

Rog asks, "Why are there seat belts on these swivel chairs?"

"Rog," I say, "When you get one of these fish on, if you're not strapped onto that chair that fish is going to take you swimming." Andy laughs. We bait the hooks and cast the lines.

I put Andy and Rog on the fighting chairs at the stern while I remain at the helm trolling the boat at slow speed. After three hours and six beers each, we hooked nothing, although we are extremely happy and very buzzed. Then when we least expect it, Andy's line starts to whiz. His pole bends and a fish is running! Andy yells, "What do I do now Ace!?"

I tell him, "Keep the tip of your rod up, and when he slows start reeling in." Ten minutes later our prey treats us with one of the most exciting spectacles in nature. It breaches and explodes up high over the water, its body twisting, dancing, and displaying its splendor in glittering silvers and blues! Andy is constantly tugging his pole up and turning the reel. Another ten minutes pass before Andy shouts, "I'm getting tired Ace. I don't know how much longer I can hold him!"

"Don't you dare quit on that fish! I'll never forgive you if you let that fish win!" I grab the gaff hook and position myself over the transom in readiness to spear the fish.

Rog says, "There he is. I see him!"

I strike the swordfish with the gaff, tell both men to help me pull it onto the loading platform, and we slide it into the boat! We all happily dance and laugh! "This is amazing," Andy says.

I say, "We'll be the talk of the town tonight! Let's motor in and have him weighed and measured. He's really a big one guys!" I'm extremely excited and I go to the helm and gun the throttle as hard as it will go. The boat lunges forward, and Rog, who is still standing against the transom, falls backward into the ocean. Neither Andy nor I notice that Rog has fallen overboard. Andy pulls three beers out of the ice chest, gives me one, turns to hand one to Rog, and notices that Rog has disappeared. He turns to look at me and says, "Where's Rog?"

I turn around and as I look aft, I see Rog floundering in the water! "Oh no!" "Rog!" I turn the boat around and race it to our friend who is screaming, "I can't swim! I can't swim!" Andy throws him a life preserver, but Rog doesn't go for it, instead he keeps yelling that he can't swim. I dive into the water, swim to him, and he grabs me in panic pulling us both under. As we bob up, I punch him in the face and take him from behind. Then I put my "Boy Scout Merit Badge for Swimming to good use and with one arm under his chin, I drag him by side-stroke back to the boat ladder. We board the "Minerva" and Rog is furious. "I thought

I was going to drown you fools! Get me off this death trap! I just want to go home!"

After we moor the boat in its slip, Rog leaves us to call his parents to pick him up. Andy and I laugh. I tell Andy, "He's acting like an idiot. Did he think we were going to leave him there in the water? Come on Andy let's weigh in your fish." We happily have our pictures taken with our 9ft 7", 1,059lb prize in the background.

That evening at home mom cooked us up some lasagna, and we devoured it. It's funny how sun and saltwater increase your appetite, and mom is pleased that we stuffed ourselves. After some conversation she takes her leave. That's when I take my little black book out of my pocket, toss it on the table, look at Andy, and grin like the "Cheshire cat."

"He asks, "And what is that?"

"That my friend are the names and phone numbers of twelve; you can count them, twelve girls from my high school who wouldn't balk at dating a freshman in college. In fact, I think that any of them would love a phone call from us "Romeo". One or two may recently have been attached but most will still be available...... Watch this! Let's see. The first one on my list is Becky Roberts. She looks just like the girl next door, which is if you live next door to a movie studio. She's a beauty Andy and I remember her as being very smart at school. She's tall, has long black hair, rich brown eyes, and is outrageously top heavy, if you catch my drift!"

Andy says, "You can stop right there, no need to tell me about the others. What you just described to me is the girl of my dreams. I'm tall, and I like 'em both tall, and abundant in the department that you just described! If she's smart that's a plus. Let's call her!"

I answer, "No way Andy, we don't call her. We'll have more success if we get another girl to call her. I'm going to phone the girl I took to the prom, her name is Ginger Gable, and we were sweet on each other before I left for college. First let's see what picture show is playing at the "Majestic Theatre" tomorrow." I picked up my mother's copy of the "Herald Press" and found that a film called "Lost Horizon" will be shown at the "Majestic Theater" at 2:00pm. I tell Andy that it stars Ronald Coleman and Jane Wyatt. I add, "You know Andy I think that this is a screen adaptation of a book that I've read by James Hilton. It's about a plane crashing in the snow- covered mountains of Tibet, and the passengers are rescued by a group of sherpas who take them to the valley of the Blue Moon where they find a tropical-like place called Shangri- La. The people there live to be very old. I'll call Ginger and try to set us up a double date." A half hour later Andy and I have our dates.

We take my dad's "1930 Ford model "A" roadster convertible" to pick up the girls at Ginger's house. I am happily greeted by Ginger with hugs and kisses. Andy politely shakes Becky's hand, although he rudely and hypnotically stares at her breasts. She says, "Nice to meet you Andy, and by the way, my eyes are up here." She laughs and Andy blushes.

I'm driving, Ginger is in the passenger seat, and Andy and Becky hop into the rumble seat. Ginger says, "I'm excited to see this movie because I love Ronald Coleman. What's it about Ace?" I answer, "I don't want to spoil the movie for you, let's just say it's an adventure story."

During the film Andy and I play the old "Let's see how far we can get with the girls" game. Arms start cuddling necks and shoulders. Ginger and I do a little necking, but we have a history of doing this. Poor Andy tries and is rejected, but he is committed to keeping his arm around Becky even if it feels that it's about to fall off.

After the movie we go to "Rudy's Soda Shop" for ice cream and give our critique of the film. I say, "Don't judge a book by its film. The movie was okay, but I thought the book was better." Becky says, "It was like they were held captive there. No matter how wonderful a place is I wouldn't want to be a prisoner."

Ginger adds, "The scary part was when the girl left with the two of them, and she turned so old and decrepit."

All in all, we really enjoyed ourselves, and the very next day, we call the girls again and invite them for a cruise on "Miss Minerva". They eagerly accept. I tell Andy, "We'll cruise down to Fenwick Island, lay on the beach, catch a bunch of blue crabs and dig a few clams. That night we'll have ourselves a beachcomber's clam bake! We'll stay overnight on the boat. The girls can have the bottom berths and we'll sleep on the top deck."

Andy asks, "What about the girl's parents? You think they'll mind an overnighter for their daughters?"

I say, "Hey, we're all over eighteen. Nobody needs permission, but we'll leave it up to the girls. My intentions are honorable, how about yours?"

"I got to tell you Ace, I really like that Becky. She really trips my trigger, and if she would make a forward advance, I don't think I could say no!"

It's a wonderful eighty- degree day as we pilot the lovely "Miss Minerva" out of the Rehoboth Beach marina. Andy and I are happily having our first beer, and Ginger and Becky are giggling as they sip wine from long stemmed glasses. After cruising to our destination, we anchor, and dive into the sea. I look over towards Andy and Becky and their faces are joined in a prolonged kiss as they bob up and down in the water. Ginger grabs me and we do the same. What a glorious day! Life can't get any better than this. Although as happy as I am, and as privileged as I am, it seems that there still remains a part of me, I don't know if I can explain it; but there is part of me that is hollow, or a better word would be unfulfilled, and that there is something missing in my life. These feelings always seem to seep into my soul when I'm experiencing the best of life.

After our long swim we load up the boat's dinghy with beach towels, a large umbrella, more drink, a spade for clam digging, crab catching paraphernalia, and motor to shore. We find the small beach vacant of all people. Andy and I start a fire, and we set up our small cabana. The girls join us clam digging and crabbing until we fill one bucket with longneck clams and a bushel full of blue crabs. We cook it all over open flames, and then eat, drink, and make merry until 7:00 pm.

That's when Ginger looks at me smiles, and says, "Thank you Ace." Then she takes my hand and says, "Let's take a stroll down the beach." As we separate ourselves a good distance away from Andy and Becky, we take a seat on a boulder just outside the reaches of the encroaching surf. Ginger says, "I want you to know that I have enrolled at the U. of Delaware. My parents wanted me to go to Temple in Philly. My dad graduated from there."

"Why didn't you go to Temple," I ask?

"Because I wanted to be near you Ace. If you remember we were really a thing in high school, and after you left for college, I missed you more than I could have imagined. I have some deep feelings for you Ace, and I thought you had some for me. Am I wrong?"

"No, you're not wrong Ginger. I care for you a lot, but my mind is focused on school right now, but that doesn't mean we can't continue our relationship and see where it leads."

She says, "Fine, we'll do that. Right now, lead me down this beach. I want to watch the sunset alone with you."

We watch the sun melt into the sea, then head back to the boat, have one nightcap, and separate ourselves for sleeping.

CHAPTER 6

It's my sophomore year and I'm back at school chasing my journalism degree. After reading some of todays printed news, I am starting to believe that journalism is for people who can't write, interviewing people who can't talk, for people who can't read. Nevertheless, I love it. I have started this semester doing two things of great importance to me. I joined the university's newspaper staff, and I started to try out for the school's baseball team. Andy and Rog joined me for our first practice, and we all hope to make the team. Practice always starts after my three classes of English Literature, Written communications, and Oral interviewing. I take my Hebrew lesson later in the evening.

Our first baseball practice starts with our coach Mr. Jensen giving us the history of Blue Hens baseball. Our school has previously won four championships in the NCAA (Colonial Athletic Conference). He explains that Delaware State U., and Maryland U. are our bitter enemies, and that this rivalry extends back to the middle of the 19th century. He explains, "Our team will have no prima donnas. No superstars. In order to win we need to adhere to a team concept. We will have a strict practice schedule. It will consist of group calisthenics, loosening up by playing catch, and then individual groups of infielders, outfielders, and the batteries of pitchers and catchers, will practice their required drills. Practices will be at 5:00 pm Monday through Friday, and there will be a 1:00 pm extended practice on Saturday. A list will be posted daily on the athletic bulletin board outside my office, as to who remains on the team. If your name doesn't appear on this list then you have been cut. Cuts will occur until the roster reaches twenty-five men."

We all respect this man. He was an Army Master Sergeant, leading men into battle, and we're confident that he can lead us on the baseball diamond.

The school's newspaper is dubbed "The Hen's Voice" and is published weekly. I have been assigned a reporter's role. Besides the usual dribble of "New Piece of Equipment Arrives for the Dining Hall," and "Mrs. Bligh Awarded Teacher of the Month," the biggest story is about the war starting to heat up in Europe. It appears that their new leader Adolf Hitler has conquest on his mind and has constructed an incredibly large and powerful war machine. I will write weekly updates on this story.

Ginger has arrived on campus and is assigned a room in the Laird's complex girl's dormitory. With my busy schedule of three classes during the day, and another in the evening, baseball practice, and my duties on the newspaper, we've only been able to spend time together on Sundays. Soon that will be limited because I'll have games on Sunday, and she can only attend them when we're playing at home.

We have received a new roommate to replace Paddy. He is a first-year student named Michael Collins. He's a good- looking guy with coal black hair and of average height. His father is the pastor at the Wilmington First Baptist church. He seems like a nice guy, but I am already distrustful of him. I just don't understand how anyone can seriously get wrapped up in a religion, or any of that god stuff. I find myself both cautious and uneasy around him. I think he's a real Jesus freak because he keeps a bible on top of his dresser and reads it daily.

This semester, more than the last few, I have become more comfortable with the repetitious routine and monotony of my daily schedule. One new addition has been added to this routine. We have discovered a local watering hole in town called "The Hen's Nest." It is the typical college town bar frequented mainly by students. Although the legal drinking age in the state of Delaware is twenty-one, no one seems to care here, and IDs are never checked. This establishment always allows the three of us to relax and let our hair down after baseball practice. The owner of the bar, Mr. Louis Agnew, always comes over to say hello. He claims that he is our biggest fan, and we'll see him at all home games. After a few beers and some of the best pizza on the planet, we regularly check the "baseball cut list." After two weeks of practice the names on the list have been whittled down from 48 to 35. The three of us remain on it.

One Sunday morning as I fight waking up, I twist my blankets around myself in an attempt to drift back off to sleep, but I spot Michael already dressed in a sport coat and combing his hair in a mirror. I ask, "Where are you going this early Mike?"

"I'm going to church Ace. Don't you go?"

I answer, "No way Mike. I hope you're not offended but I don't believe in that stuff. Although I do believe that the more you complain about things…. The longer some god lets you live."

"Mike laughs and says, "I'm not offended Ace, but I will pray for you. I got to go. Dad's picking me up in ten minutes. You have a good day Ace."

Andy gets out of bed while Rog continues sleeping. He says, "I really miss Becky Ace. She's all I ever think about. I've never felt this way before. I actually think I love her. I'm taking the train to her parent's house in Rehoboth for dinner today, and I'm a nervous wreck. Do you think they'll like me?"

Oh, come on Andy, why wouldn't they like an overly tall, red headed and ugly guy whose sole ambition in life is to make passionate love to their sweet little girl?"

"Gee, thanks a lot Ace!"

CHAPTER 7

(MAY 3rd, 1939)

Headlines at the "Hen's Voice" announce, "Professor Nichols Receives Tenure." This article continues extolling the professor's virtues. The most important article of this copy of our newspaper is penned by me and reads: "U.S. contributes arms and other war materials to France in the face of Germany's continued accelerated aggression in Europe. Prime minister Neville Chamberlain of England is criticized for signing the "Munich Agreement" surrendering parts of Czechoslovakia to Germany. After meeting with Adolf Hitler, he assures England that (quote) "Germany is not hostile towards our Kingdom."

I'm having a good spring training with the baseball team. After three weeks of intra-squad games, I'm batting with a .363 average and have hit four home runs, while playing a good defensive third base. Andy is playing well also, and it appears that he'll be our starting first baseman. Rog is faltering. He consistently makes errors at second base and strikes out more often than making contact with the ball. Today will be our first pre- season home game against the University of Rhode Island, and we get to experience nepotism at its finest. After almost four weeks of practices a new pitcher is warming up in the bullpen. The new face is none other than our new roomie, and Christian boy Mike Collins. Before the game Coach Jensen explains, "Gentlemen this is highly unusual, since it is so late in our spring training sessions, but I'm adding a new player to our current try-out roster. I would like to introduce to you Mike Collins. Mike is the son of Pastor George Collins of the First Baptist Church of Wilmington. The pastor is a good friend of mine and I attend his church regularly. The reason that I'm allowing this is because Mike has started school late here at the U. of D. due to a recent death in his family. I don't believe that he should be penalized for this. Mike has had an excellent high school career as a pitcher. I want you all to welcome him and make him feel at home. Let's have a winning game."

I'm somewhat annoyed by Collins' addition to our team, and also upset with Coach Jensen.

The game progresses and Rhode Island is winning 8 to 2 going into the top of the eighth inning. Coach brings Collins into pitch. He strikes out the sides in the eight and the ninth to close out the game. Any pitcher striking out six batters in a row deserves to get noticed. The final score remains at 8 to 2.

After Collins' strong performance, some of the guys invite him to the "Hen's Nest" for beer. He politely declines, but we go......and stay......too long. After our usual excess at the tavern, we head to check on the current roster list. Rog's name does not appear. He has been cut. I feel sorry for him, but more than that, I worry about him. The news of this failure is apt to drive him further down the rabbit hole of depression.

When Andy returns from visiting Becky, he bursts into our room all full of himself and tells me, "Her parents liked me Ace! They actually liked me! Oh Ace, I love this girl, and I believe that I want to marry her!"

I say, "Whoa, slow down Andy. What about school? What about your dream of getting your engineering degree? Be careful man. You know it has been said that "I am" is the shortest sentence in the English language, but "I do" is the longest."

31

"Oh no Ace, I mean I'll marry her after graduation. What I am planning to do is to get her an apartment here in Newark. I have some savings and I can afford it. She could get a job to help supplement our finances."

"You mean that you want to shack-up."

"Call it what you want, but I don't think I can stand being apart from her. I can't thank you enough for introducing her to me!"

"All I'm saying Andy is take your time. Love makes time pass…… but time makes love pass." …… And Andy, oh my dear brother Andy, love is the tie that blinds. And love conquers all……except for maybe poverty and toothaches."

Then I think to myself; love is really two people being stupid, and Ginger and I are advancing that theory, although I'm not being as stupid as Andy is.

CHAPTER 8

When crime stops paying, gangsters and politicians will do something else. Until then crime exists; even on the glorious campus of Delaware University. A rumor that a theft has occurred at the school library has me, the ace reporter that I am, to investigate. Upon arriving at the scene of the crime I see the "Chief of Security Guards" Mr. Arnold Boswell standing by a desk interviewing the school's librarian Ms. Jean Justin. I remember that Officer Boswell was the one who handcuffed Paddy at the dance. I casually walk over to them, notebook in hand, and attempt to listen to their conversation. That's when I learned two things. One, that you never attempt to initiate an interview while appearing with pen and pad in hand, which says you are ready to immediately write, and two never attempt to interrupt an ongoing conversation. Boswell gives me a dirty look. I pocket the notepad.

He says, "Can I help you sonny?"

I answer, "Yes sir Officer Boswell, I'm Ace Walker from the "Hen's Voice." I was hoping to get my newspaper some information about a possible theft that may have occurred here."

"Look sonny, I will not disclose details to anyone about an ongoing investigation!"

I smile within myself and say, "Well sir, if there is as you say, an ongoing investigation, then the rumor of the crime must be true." I am smugly proud of myself, and I say, "I apologize for interrupting you. I'll return later." I turn around and enter the E through G section of fictional books. I think that I could have pushed the issue by citing my first amendment rights, freedom of the press, or maybe some other idea that my devious mind could have concocted, but why win the battle and then lose the war. I realize that Boswell has a self-inflated opinion of his importance. There is truth in the statement that "Power corrupts, and absolute power corrupts absolutely." Also, Boswell is reputed to be a stubborn man. He should be treated as you would treat a cat. You see, you should never try to out stubborn a cat. You will always lose and simply just bore the cat. My next plan of attack is to patiently wait until the guard leaves and get what I want from the librarian herself.

Jean Justin does not look like the typical head of a library. She is a young, pretty, petite, and pony-tailed blonde, that wears horned rim glasses. The saying of "Men don't make passes at girls who wear glasses", does not apply to Ms. Justin. She receives her share of appreciative stares wherever she roams on campus.

After the school's great protector leaves, I walk up to her desk and introduce myself. She says, "I know who you are Mr. Walker, how may I assist you?"

I say, "I believe that the students and faculty of this, our hallowed institution, have the right to know about any incident of crime on campus. Don't you Miss Justin?"

"Yes of course I do Mr. Walker. What would you like to know?"

"Were books actually stolen ma'am?"

"Yes, a complete twenty-nine volume set of Encyclopedia Britannica is missing from our library. This was a 1911 edition and has become somewhat valuable, therefore the volumes are never allowed to be taken from this building."

Do you have any clue as to when they were taken?"

"I'm not certain, and I didn't even realize that they were missing, until a student came to me asking as to why they weren't in their usual place."

"When was that ma'am?"

"Two days ago. We are now conducting a complete inventory to ascertain whether any other material has been lost."

"May I ask who the student was that first discovered the theft?"

"Certainly." Then she digs through a metal file box, removes one card, and says, "Here it is. The student was Michael Connery, a junior majoring in the arts."

I thanked her and returned to my dorm.

Two of next week's stories read, "Theft at Jefferson Library Under Investigation." "Blue Hens lose first scheduled game of season to Maryland 6-4".

That evening after my Hebrew lessons, I meet Ginger at the Hen's Nest. We begin discussing the theft. I ask her, "What do you think amazing girl teenage detective Miss Nancy Drew? Want to help me solve the crime of the century?"

"Always ready to join you Mr. Sam Spade. Do we need the assistance of Lamont Cranston because only "The Shadow Knows!?""

"No, I think we two sleuths will be sufficient to solve the mystery. The first question that comes to my mind is if the thief has finished stealing books? If not, what other manuscripts would he be interested in?"

"He? Have you already conceded that a male is the culprit? It certainly could have been a female. We have to ask ourselves, who would be most likely to want their own personal set of encyclopedias, and do they want them for their own personal use, or do they want to sell them for profit?"

"I don't believe a student that is living in a campus dormitory would want them for personal use. Where would he or she put them?

They obviously couldn't place them on a bookcase in their room. If a student is the thief then money was the motive. Remember a 1911 set of Britannica, first edition, is valuable. Also, I don't believe that a faculty member would commit such a crime."

"We are forgetting another group of people Ace."

"Who would that be Ginger?"

"That would be school employees. For instance, someone like a dining hall worker, or a janitor, or even a security guard. These folks are generally low wage earners who would possibly need some extra cash."

As we sit and contemplate our ideas another song comes on the jukebox. The jukebox here is always flooded with nickels, and after about a dozen songs Ginger's tune finally comes up, and we hear:

"You must remember this, a kiss is just a kiss, a sigh is just a sigh.

The fundamental things apply "As time goes by."

And when two lovers woo, they still say I love you. On that you can rely. No matter what the future brings, as time goes by.

Moonlight and love songs never out of date. Hearts full of passion jealousy and hate. Woman needs man, and man must have his mate, there's no one can deny.

It's still the same old story. A fight for love and glory. A case of do or die. The world will always welcome lovers, as time goes by."

As the soul stirring song plays, Ginger stares into my eyes and asks, "Where do we go from here Ace?"

I say, "I think you may have a great idea about an employee doing this crime."

"No Ace, where do we go from here?"

"I knew what you meant the first time Ginger. My answer is I'm not yet sure."

"I love you Ace. I truly love you."

"Ginger, you must know how I feel about you. But we have these obligations that must be satisfied. Besides, your parents would never forgive me, or you if you didn't finish college."

"I just know that I never want to be apart from you ever again. I feel as though a half of me is missing when you're not around Ace."

"As Time Goes By" starts to end we continue to hold hands and gaze into each other's eyes.

I break up our own little mutual admiration party and announce. "It's getting late Ginger, and you have an early class tomorrow. We better be leaving."

CHAPTER 9

In this week's headlines I write: "Germany Amasses Great Troop Build Up Along Polish Border. Tensions of War Escalate in Europe!" Page three reads, "Blue Hens lose fourth straight game to Ryder college 7-1"

I meet Ginger again the next evening in the Laird courtyard. We kiss passionately and then sit by a small fountain. I tell her, "I've a couple ideas on how to proceed next in solving this amazing, unfathomable, and utterly remarkable mystery my dear Doctor Watson. It seems elementary to me Watson. Just elementary."

Ginger laughs and says, "Well my dear Sherlock, please inform me of your plans."

I add, "I will assign you to interview Mr. Michael Connery. He is a person of interest since he was the first to reveal that the books were missing. Also, I feel as you do, that a school employee other than one on the teaching faculty could be sufficiently motivated to steal the encyclopedias. It has also occurred to me that a 29- volume set of books would be both heavy and awkward to carry, and therefore difficult to smuggle out during the library's normal hours of operation. Therefore, I also need you to make a visit to the "Administration Office" and record the names of all of the cleaning staff that are assigned to duty in the library. Make a note of janitors, maids, or any other personnel that have access to the building."

Ginger says, "I'll do that Mr. Holmes. And what will you do?"

"Again, it's elementary Watson. After you provide me with the required information, I will conduct an after- hours evening stakeout of the facility, in an attempt to catch the thief <u>red</u>-handed."

Ginger chuckles and says, "If catching this culprit is <u>red</u>-handed, then this must be "A Study in <u>Scarlet."</u>

It's Sunday morning and Rog is up early. He first proceeds to wake up Andy, and then comes over to rouse me out of bed. He announces, "Hurry up and get dressed you two clowns. We got a bus to catch to Wilmington. The Delaware State Hornets are anxious to give you your fifth loss of the season! I want you to meet your new teammate. Coach Jensen has officially hired me as the "Team Aide." I guess he figures it won't hurt any, since so far, you're just a bunch of losers anyway."

Andy asks, "What in the world is a Team Aide?"

Rog answers, "The team aide is the most important cog on the team, oh uneducated ones! I am tasked to bandage cuts, clean your spiked shoes, and serve as both water and bat boy. Most importantly, it allows me to check out the pretty co-eds at the other schools."

Andy says, "I don't know why, because you never ask any of them out. You must be the opposite of "Jack the Ripper." Every time he came home his mother would ask, "Jack, why do you always bring a different girl home each time"?

I wipe the sleep out of my eyes and ask, "Where is Mike?"

Rog answers, "He went to church early, and his dad is taking the family to the game. Mike has his first start pitching today."

In the first inning of the game Andy led off by hitting a single. Our left fielder Jay Meadows strikes out. I come to the plate and work the count full. On the next pitch, an inside, belt high, fastball, I connect solidly and watch the ball sail over the left field fence! We lead 2 to 0. The score remains the same in the top of the seventh inning. Mike Collins is pitching a one-hitter, while striking out ten batters. On the first pitch in the seventh, I put another ball into the left field bleachers. We ended up winning our first game 3 – 0. Collins gets his first win, a complete game one-hitter.

The bus drops us back off in Newark at the Hen's Nest and Coach takes us all in for celebratory beers. Even Collins joins us, but he's drinking Cokes.

Next Fridays edition of the "Hen's Voice" reads: "American Sentiment is Against U. S. Entering a War in Europe!" President Roosevelt claims, "There will be no involvement by the United States."

Page 3: "Collins pitches one-hitter. Walker hits two home runs; goes four for four. Hens win first game."

CHAPTER 10

Ginger has done her homework. Two days after the game we meet in the courtyard. She informs me, "I sat down by your person of interest Michael Connery in the dining hall yesterday. He was so shy he could barely talk to me, and his face blushed bright red the entire time. He knows nothing about the library theft Ace. He is so milk-toast that he wouldn't have the nerve to steal anything. As for library personnel, there are a number of students that assist Ms. Justin, but none are in the building after hours. Two employees clean the building. One is a young local woman named Alice Antonelli, and the other is the main school janitor Mr. Javier Alvarez. The library closes at 5:00 pm and they both come in at 6:30 pm. Besides Ms. Justin, Mr. Alvarez is the only other person with a key to the building. What are you planning next?"

"As you suggested I will employ my "Study in Scarlet." Meet me tomorrow after your last class in the library."

It's a rainy day in Blue Hen land. Under my umbrella Ginger meets me on the library's front steps. I explain, "We'll go in separately. You will go and browse the books near Miss Justin's desk, and I will take a notebook and walk over to the reference section, select a history subject, take a seat at a study table, and pretend to make notes. When you see that she is gathering her things and ready to leave, walk over to her and start a discussion. Get her mind occupied with anything that you believe will divert her attention from me, and then walk with her out the door. I will hide near the closet that says, "Janitorial Supplies."

After taking my espying position only a few minutes go by before I hear Ginger and the librarian leave.

The lights go out and I hear the door lock. The large room becomes as quiet as a tomb. A dim ray of light is projecting through a small window behind me, and it allows me to look at my wristwatch. At 5:40pm I hear a rustling, no; it would be better described as a scuffling noise, and I see a mouse scurrying across the floor in front of me. I watch its antics for a while, until the quietness and solitude of my surroundings make me drowsy, and I drift off to sleep.

I'm not sure how long I slept, but I am startled awake by the sound of boots traipsing across the hardwood floor and echoing throughout the room. As I peek up over the desk that I've been hiding behind I see two people. It takes a moment for my eyes to adapt to the bright lights, but when they do, I can identify one as a young lady dusting furniture and emptying wastebaskets. The other is the janitor sweeping the floor near the entrance. Neither is talking.

I observe their activity for at least a half hour until the woman says, "Goodnight Mr. Alvarez."

He returns with, "Goodnight Alice. I hope your young son gets to feeling better."

"Thank you sir," she answers.

After the woman departs, Alvarez walks over towards the supply closet door, leans his broom against the wall, and then goes down the aisle to where the manuals of Geography, History, Dictionaries, and other books of that genre are shelved. As I contemplate his movements, I see him take a rather large selection from a shelf. He opens the book and pages through its contents. Then he turns, book in hand, walks over to the closet, steps in, and closes the door. Moments later he comes out without the book. I believe I have just witnessed a theft in progress.

I remain silent and continue to scrutinize his actions until the mouse once again manifests itself and scampers back towards me. It runs under my desk, and I feel it trying to enter my pants leg. I feel a bite and jump up and scream, "Get out of there," as I shake my leg!!.......OUCH!!

The janitor hollers, "Who's that?!" He grabs his broom in self-defense. The mouse hurries off and Alvarez reverses his defensive stance to one of aggression. To thwart off an attack by him I throw both of my arms up in surrender and shout, "No! No! Don't. I can explain. I can explain!

He stops and stares at me, then shouts, "Quien eres y que haces aqui!!!?"

I reiterate, "I can explain Mr. Alvarez. I'm Ace Walker from the school's "Hen's Voice" newspaper. Then I lie saying, "The newspaper sent me to investigate the theft that has happened here in the library." His angry face turns expressionless, and then morphs into one of guilt, and then one of sadness. He just stands there holding his broom and saying nothing. We stand there, for the longest time, facing one another, until I see a tear flowing down his cheek. I say, "Please, let's both relax and sit down. We need to talk."

We take opposing chairs at a small study table. I look down and roll up my pants leg to see what damage "Mighty Mouse" has done.

In English Alvarez starts by saying, "I knew this would happen. I am so stupid. I knew I would be discovered."

"You knew what would be discovered Mr. Alvarez?"

"That I am a thief. But you must believe me Mr. Walker I have never stolen anything in my life until now."

"Did you take the encyclopedias sir?"

"Yes, I did. But before you hate me, let me explain why, because I didn't do it for money. I didn't do it for myself."

"Then why sir?"

"Three weeks ago, on Saturday night a man knocks on my door. He tells me he is from "The Encyclopedia Britannica Company", and they have a special offer for me. I told him I could not afford what he was selling. He says that's alright because he gets credit for showing them to me. So, I let him in. I want you to know Mr. Walker that I and my wife Angelina have three children. Rosa she is three, Jose he is six, and Pablo is eight. The man shows us his books and how wonderful they are. He tells us they will help our children in school to become better students. He says they will get better grades in order to qualify for college. My children are so excited, and they plead for me to buy the books. My wife tells me they need them. Since I cannot afford them, I tell the man no. After he leaves, Angelina and the children cry. They all cry, and then they cry some more. I feel terrible. I feel I am a bad father. Pablo says I don't love him."

"Is that when you decided to take the books sir?"

"Si, Mr. Walker. Now if you tell the school I will lose my job, maybe go to jail. What will my family do. I am truly sorry."

"What did you just take into the closet sir?"

"I took a dictionary for their use."

"Let's make a deal Mr. Alvarez."

"What kind of a deal?"

"Go get the dictionary that you just took and replace it where you found it."

The poor man does what I ask and then sits back down.

"I want you to know Mr. Alvarez, that if by tomorrow night you return all of the books, I will tell no one about what you did."

"Madre mia! I will do so Mr. Walker! Thank you. Thank you so very much!"

We leave the building together.

Three days later the same encyclopedia salesman knocks again on the Alvarez household's door. "I have a present for you Mr. Alvarez. This is a new set of Britannica complete with dictionary. Someone must really like you. These were purchased as a gift for your family."

CHAPTER 11

Hen's Voice headlines: "Missing Set of 1911 Britannica's Found at School Library". The librarian claims, "They were simply misplaced." Page 3: Collins pitches second shutout for Blue Hens.

Over beers at the Hen's Nest Ginger laughingly tells me, "That is the funniest story I have ever heard! If that mouse would have run up my leg I would have died on the spot! But that gift to the Alvarez family was really sweet. You're just an old softy Ace. You have a heart of gold, and I think that's why I love you so much." As soon as Ginger expelled those words Andy and Becky came bouncing in the front doors. They are all smiles and filled with exuberance. They come and join us at our table.

Andy says, "We did it!"

I ask, "Well what did you do?"

"We Eloped!"

I say, "Congratulations! Drinks are on me!"

"Ginger asks, "What do your parents think Becky?"

"Well, they're not happy about it, but Andy and I are thrilled! We got an apartment on Baldwin Street. Oh, and I got a job at the Dupont company as a secretary! I'll be taking the train back and forth. Really, it's only fifteen miles away."

Andy says, "Oh, there's Rog over at the bar. I want to tell him about it. I think he's doing better now isn't he Ace?"

"I suppose so. Some days he wakes up happy, and other days he acts like he's in an asylum and it's not worth chewing through the leather straps."

The months roll by, and the old routine starts to take over again, although I miss Andy being in our room, I'm getting excellent grades in all my classes except Hebrew. The odd language has been a struggle for me. Professor Abramowitz tells me that I need to spend some time in Jerusalem to truly master the dialect. The baseball season is over. Our record ends up at 11 wins and 21 losses. Andy, Mike Collins, and I performed well. Collins pitched us to all our wins, Andy received the leagues gold-glove award for his slick fielding at first base, and I led the league in home runs, batting average, and total bases. It seems that the rest of the team just didn't play up to par.

CHAPTER 12

And then catastrophe happens, and life totally changes in our small world. The sounds of sirens awaken me on an August Wednesday morning. I look out my window and see in the distance, police cars and an ambulance racing down Chestnut Street Hill. I quickly dress, grab my notebook, and exit the dormitory. I hop into the old Chevy coupe that some well -wishing soul donated to the newspaper, and follow the screeching sounds of the emergency. It ends up at the Hen's Nest tavern where a large crowd has gathered. The ambulance has pulled into the tavern's alleyway, and three police cruisers are parked about the building. Police yellow do- not- cross tape surrounds the perimeter. News reporters and their photographers are all present from the tri-county area. I make my way through the crowd to join them as I hold up my press card and I belly up to the tape. I ask a man with a Dover Herald Press card inserted in his fedora what has happened.

He says, "There has been a murder. The body was found this morning in that alley."

I ask, "Do we know who the victim is?"

A cop standing just inside the crime tape heard me and says, "You with the press?"

I answer, "Yes the college newspaper."

He says, "A young woman has been knifed. It looks like she might have been one of yours."

"Do you mean a co-ed from our campus officer?"

"That's what I mean."

I ask, "What is her name."

The officer says, "That information won't be disclosed until the next of kin are notified."

I watch the horror of this event closely, until her body is brought out on a stretcher and carried into the ambulance. I then talk to a few other bystanders without gleaning any useful information. It was only 9:00 am and the bar wasn't opened for business in order for me to interview any of their employees. But I probably would have been denied closer access to the scene anyway.

I draft the story for the Hen's Voice. The headlines will read: "Young Woman Found Dead by Hen's Nest tavern; Police Mum About Details." That same evening, I pick up a copy of the "Newark News." Its headlines read: "WOMAN MURDERED IN NEWARK." The article goes on to read: "Nineteen-year-old Miss Jane Evans was found dead Wednesday morning by an employee of the Hen's Nest tavern, 112 Sycamore Street, Newark, Del. Ms. Evans was a sophomore student at the University of Delaware. Police confirmed the murder but gave no other details. Detective John Wilson of the City of Newark police department leads the investigation into the death of the woman."

I feel a chill run through my body. I didn't know Jane Evans personally, but I had seen her occasionally at our ballgames, and most recently at the tavern just this past Monday night. The paper never mentions what type of weapon the killer used.

Dean Michaels posts a bulletin declaring the Hen's Nest tavern to be off limits to all students and faculty members. He declares that violating these orders will result in expulsion from the university. I immediately go to the administration office seeking an exemption from the Dean's orders, by claiming a reporter's freedom of the press. My requests are granted. My first thoughts are to seek out and interview the person who discovered the body.

I waited two days for things to calm down at the crime scene. Since I know the owner of the bar, I leave after classes in hopes of talking to him.

When I arrive at the bar the crime scene tape was removed, and the place is open for business. But there is a problem, because when I walk in, there is no business to be opened for. The once boisterous tavern is now empty of all patrons, except for one older man hunched over the bar, protecting his mug of beer. I see the owner, Mr. Agnew, in a corner sweeping the floor. He looks up, smiles at me, and says, "Hi Ace, how are you doing."

I answer, "Alright Mr. Agnew, how about you?"

"Not so good son. Not since the tragedy. As you can see this place is empty because ninety percent of our business was from the college. I'm afraid if Dean Michael's ban isn't lifted soon, I'll have to close down permanently."

I say, "As soon as the murderer is caught things will be back to normal."

"I hope so Ace. I don't know how long I will be able to hang on. I'd like to kill that murderous thug myself

"There I go again. I can never keep my big mouth shut. The police told me not to say anything about the crime. I don't know why, but they're trying to keep things hush about everything."

Please Ace, don't write in your paper that I talked to you. It would get me into trouble."

"I promise I won't Mr. Agnew. Can you tell me who found the body?"

"Well......I did."

"Do you mind if I look in the alley where you found her?"

"Sure. I'll take you there, but I don't know why you would want to. The police investigated the entire area thoroughly."

We walk out the back door of the bar together and Agnew stops next to the dumpster.

"He says, "I found her lying right there against the brick wall. Blood was everywhere. I could see that it was caused by a gash in her throat. Follow me Ace."

We walk about twenty feet down the brick cobblestone alley, and he stops and points at the uneven surface. He says, "The police found a tiny amount of more blood here."

"That far away from the body?"

"He says, "It wasn't her blood. The detective also found a small piece of blue cloth. I overheard him say that it looked like a fragment from blue jeans. He assumed that the killer fell here and scraped his knee on the rough surface of the bricks."

I circle around the area and see a small sliver of white stuck deep within the crack of a brick. It would have been invisible except for the exact angle that I had approached it from. I bent down and scraped it up with my pocket- knife. It looks like just a piece of white ceramic material. It is probably nothing, but I stick it my pocket anyway.

Mr. Louis Agnew is one worried human being. His business is his life. I try to reassure him that everything will eventually be alright, and that his business will jump start again, but I'm not sure that he believes me. We say our goodbyes and I return to my dorm.

The next day my mind wanders during every class. I can't get the murder out of my mind. The whole school is shocked, and a dark gloom seems to have settled in over the campus. I look at the small unknown fragment I found at the crime scene. As I study it inside the clear plastic bag that I put it in, I decide I'll take it to Professor Leonard the head of the Chemistry Department. This small sliver may mean nothing, but

I'm curious to know what it is. Maybe the Professor can determine that. I drop it off later in the day.

That evening Rog, Mike, and I are studying in our room. Mike asks, "Do you think we'll be given another roomie to replace Andy?"

Rog says, "I hope not. I thought that it was too crowded before."

I add, "We probably won't see another until next year. By the way Mike, what's your take on the murder of Miss Jane Evans?"

Mike asks, "What do you mean what's my take? It was horrible. There is a tremendous evil in this world today."

I say, "I'm confused Rog, aren't you?"

"About what Ace?"

"Well Mike says that God is love. He says that he is the creator of our entire world. He says he is all- powerful. If God is all these things, then why does he allow all these evil things to happen? I believe, since God lets evil reign, then he is complicit in all things evil. I think he's actually an accomplice in Jane Evan's murder."

Rog answers, "Don't get me involved in this discussion. I never talk about religion or politics."

Mike says, "It wasn't God's fault that Adam and Eve sinned Ace. But sin entered into this world through that first sin. Now man's nature is one of sin. In fact, the bible says, "All have sinned and come short of the glory of God." And he loved us so much Ace, that He sent His Son to die for the forgiveness of our sins. Satan is the evil one Ace, not God."

"I have just one word for that Mike...... "Hogwash." I agree with Russian novelist Fyodor Dostoevsky. He wrote, "I think the devil doesn't exist, but man has created him, he has created him in his own image and likeness."

Rog says, "Stop it you two. You're going to make me nuts with your bickering. I'm glad to be going home for a few days. I need some peace and quiet away from you both."

CHAPTER 13

My next goal is to talk to both Detective John Wilson of the Newark Police, and then the county coroner. Saturday morning finds me driving to the Newark Police Station. I walk in and ask the desk sergeant to see the detective. A half an hour later a middle-aged man with a short crew- cut, and wearing a well-worn suit comes out from behind a door. He looks at me and asks, "Are you from the college newspaper?"

"I am sir."

"Follow me." And we walk into a very small office that is terribly disheveled. Papers and folders are scattered throughout the room. "Have a seat kid." I sit down, and as I look at him, I can see a blank look in his eyes. My uncle Robert told me it was called "The thousand-yard stare." Some WW1 veterans would have that stare. Anyone who constantly witnesses the atrocities of this world have that stare. Detective Wilson has that stare.

He starts by saying, "There are certain things I can tell you about Miss Evans death. Others I cannot. For the record, she was stabbed several times. We don't know why, because we can't find any motivation for her killing. There was no theft. There was no sexual molestation. She had no angry boyfriends. She didn't owe money to anyone. The why of her death remains a complete mystery to us. I want to say this; and this is off the record. If you print what I say next I will personally come after you and beat you so many times that you'll think you're surrounded...... It is this lack of motivation that really scares us badly. Any unmotivated crime is the hardest to solve."

I ask, "Why, do you really expect more killing?"

"That's the point kid. When an unmotivated crime like this occurs, usually, and I mean usually, others may follow. We are on high alert. If another one happens the FBI will be called in. Like I said, this last comment is off the record. I don't want you to print it. If you do, you may cause a panic throughout all of the Delmarva Peninsula. People will surmise that a serial killer is on the loose, and it's way too early to think that. The only reason that I'm mentioning this is because I want you to share this information with Dean Michaels. He needs to make any precautionary rules that he feels are necessary to protect the student body. You tell him not to disclose what I just told you to anyone else. Not even his wife."

I thank the Detective for his confidence in me and assure him that I will follow his directives.

My next newspaper clip reflects what He told me. I also honor his statements that were "off the record", and I did not print them.

Later that day I go to see Professor Leonard in his lab and ask, "Were you able to make a material identification of the sample I brought you Professor?"

"Yes, I have Mr. Walker. It is not man made. It is bone."

I ask, "What kind of bone, I mean from a human or an animal?"

"That I can't say. But if you take it to Professor Simmons in Biology, he may be able to pinpoint the exact species of this specimen."

When I arrive at the Biology Department, Professor Simmons treats me cordially. He's a great fan of our ball club. He studies my finding and says, "Just looking at it with the naked eye I would agree with Jim. It does look like bone. You say you want to know what kind of animal it came from Ace?"

"Yes sir, I do."

"I'm afraid that's going to take a while. I'll need to run a few tests. What's this all about?"

I answer, "I can't say right now Professor, but I promise to tell you in the future."

He laughs and says, "That's okay Ace, I'll help anyone that hits with a .361 average."

My request to see the coroner is refused. No one in the county, neither in the coroner's office, nor in any other department will talk to me. They act like I have the plague.

CHAPTER 14

Friday, September 1, 1939, the "Newark News" headlines: "GERMANY INVADES POLAND, NAZI'S TAKE DANZIG WITHOUT WARNING; BATTLE RAGES!

Our president, Franklin Delano Roosevelt, continues to assure Americans that, and I quote; "We will not get involved with the conflict in Europe."

That is his fervent message to the country, and I put his statement in the "Hen's Voice." However, after all of his assurances, you can sense that the country is still tense. No, a better word would be nervous.

Andy joins Rog and me for lunch at the dining hall.

"She's pregnant guys." "Becky's pregnant." Rog and I congratulate him.

He continues with, "It looks like I'll have to drop out of school. I need to get a job to support us."

I ask, "Do you have your parent's support?"

"Yes, I do guys, and they aren't pleased that I'm quitting school. But I have no choice, we need the money. By the way, what do you think about this war in Europe?"

Rog says, "As long as we don't get involved, I could care less. I hope they blow each other up to pieces."

I add, "Nice attitude Rog. We're talking about human beings here. Personally, I think that this Adolf Hitler is a war monger and a complete maniac. I don't believe he'll stop with Poland. I think France is next."

Three weeks have passed since the murder and I'm studying hard for my final exams. Ginger and I seem to be getting more serious about our relationship. Andy lands a position with a tool and die shop in Wilmington and seems to be happy. Rog is his same old moody self.

It seems that things are starting to settle back down on campus when the "Newark News" headlines read: "TWO BODIES FOUND IN LEWES DELAWARE!" The article continues with:

"TWO DEAD WOMEN were discovered in the Lewes Delaware area. Two men came across the body of Ms. Beatrice Stone while deer hunting on farmland near the town of Lewes. Later that same evening, a moviegoer called the police after finding a young thirteen- year -old girl lying in the back alley of the Lewes "Bijou" theater. Her name has been withheld by the police. Police admit similarities exist between both deaths and also one that has recently occurred in Newark."

A darkness has fallen upon us again, and I think of my past conversation with Detective Wilson. Unmotivated murder can be the worst, because it means that the killer is killing for no reason except for the desire to kill. It appears that a psychopath is active in our part of the world.

The next day I pay my second visit to Professor Simmons. When I walk into the Biology Lab, he is talking to Professor Leonard. They both greet me, and I ask, "Do we have the results on my article?"

Simmons says. "Yes, we have Ace. In fact, we both agree that the splinter of bone that you brought us is from a ruminate animal."

"What's that?" I ask.

Again, Simmons answers, "A ruminate is an animal with more than one stomach, usually four. It's commonly said that it's an animal that chews its cud. We have actually determined that it is most likely from a deer."

I say, "How would a sliver of bone from a deer end up in that bar's alley? Mr. Agnew doesn't serve venison at the Hen's Nest."

Leonard says, "You're on your own there, Ace. Does this have anything to do with the murder that happened there?"

'I'm not at liberty to say." I thank the two men, take my piece of deer bone, and leave the premises.

Even with all the turmoil embittering, us we're looking eagerly for the summer break.

CHAPTER 15

Weeks go by and turn into months. After a long hiatus from the college, I am eager to start my studies again. I am also ready for the new baseball season. The only thing that has kept me in constant touch with school since the start of 1940, has been the duties I maintain at the newspaper. Becoming a junior is turning a curve; a curve on the upward spiral to graduation. I'm especially excited about a new subject I'm enrolled in called "Printed Communications."

Thankfully, no other murders have happened in our area, although The FBI is actively investigating the three that have already transpired.

Our ball club has a good start with 4 wins and 0 losses, as we prepare to play an out of conference game against the Temple Owls in Philadelphia. Our new first baseman, replacing Andy, is Don Jankowski, one of our bench men. Jankowski has proven to be a great hitter. We win 5-0 with Don going 4 for 4 and Mike Collins getting the win. Mike is becoming the premier pitcher in the league, and major league scouts are now coming to our games to look at him.

Ginger and I meet on a Sunday afternoon at our usual place in the Laird courtyard.

I ask her, "Want to take in the matinee at the "Warner Theater?"

"What's playing?" she asks.

"It's called "Casablanca," and it stars Humphrey Bogart and Ingrid Bergman."

"Let's go. I love Bogart and Bergman."

"I take the newspaper's jalopy to the theater. At the ticket counter we run in to Andy and Becky. She is three months pregnant now, and starting to show around the middle. We go in and sit together, eat popcorn and snickers bars between kisses, and enjoy an excellent movie.

Walking out after the movie both Ginger and Becky have tears in their eyes. I comment, "That was a great film. Why, may I ask, are you girls crying?"

Becky says, "Because at the end Ilsa leaves with Victor on the plane and denies her true love Rick."

Andy adds. "That's nothing to cry over. The movie was a great story, and I loved the way they portrayed the Nazi's as evil." Everything is looking brighter in our world, except for the threats of war in Europe.

"Hen's Voice" headlines June 12, 1940. "GERMANY INVADES FRANCE; NAZI'S ESTABLISH VICHY GOVERNMENT."

Then it happens again. This time it didn't make the front -page headlines, but the Newark News reports: "Woman found murdered outside of bar in South Philadelphia." Ms. Allison McKenzie was found dead outside of a South Philly tavern. Police say that the modus operandi were similar to recent crimes in the Delaware area. The FBI is investigating."

Because of the distance from Newark to Philly, I make no mention of the crime in the Hen's Voice. But I start to backtrack in my mind as to where the murders have occurred. Our team had just made the long bus ride to Philadelphia. Is it only coincidental that a murder happened there? There also was one here in Newark. And one in Wilmington where we had just played a game. No, this kind of thinking makes no sense, because two deaths happened in Lewes, and we certainly played no games there.

But finally, government officials of the Federal Bureau of Investigation give a story to the Newark News: "FBI CLAIMS TO BE

LOOKING FOR SERIAL KILLER." Officials say the recent murder in South Philadelphia has been linked to the killings in the state of Delaware."

Detective Wilson had once told me, if this kind of news got out, the public would be horrified. I believe it was put in print to serve as a precautionary warning. I want to talk to him, and I meet him the next day at the Newark police station. I ask, "I thought you said that the authorities would never mention the possibility of a serial killer; that they didn't want to cause a panic situation.

He says, "Let me tell you kid, this one is terrible. This madman is stabbing and gutting his prey. These are anger killings. The worst kind. It has gotten to the point, where the public has a right to know and beware."

I say, "There has to be a common denominator in these murders. Something that ties everything together and points us in the direction of the killer.

Wilson says, "That is exactly what we are trying to do."

I thanked him for his input and decided to go to my dorm.

As I leave the station my mind wanders over an endless number of possibilities. I keep going back to the places that the women were killed. There has to be a connection to these venues. And again, I can place our ball team everywhere except for Lewes Delaware.

And then it hits me!

I remember that Rog went back home to Lewes to visit his parents. When I arrive back at my room, I look at our wall calendar in order to check the dates. Rog, Mike, and I all make notes on this calendar. I discover that the dates of Rog's going home, and the dates of the murders coincide. I dismiss this as coincidence. Why am I being suspicious of Rog? He is so meek and shy that he wouldn't be capable of hurting a fly. But then I recalled some words penned by my favorite author Nathaniel Hawthorne. He was quoted as saying, "There is evil in every human heart, which may remain latent, perhaps, through the whole life; but circumstances may rouse it to activity."

I can't fathom that I could actually suspect Rog of anything so heinous. I look at my watch. Rog will be in his "Renaissance Art" class for another hour. I know that he keeps his things in a large duffle that he stores under his bed. I guiltily pull the duffle bag out and open it. I am ashamed of myself as I go through his things, until I find a knife in its sheath at the bottom of the bag. I take it out, unsheathe it and study it. My heart starts racing and pounding as I discern that it has a bone handle and a seven- inch blade. And then, a chill goes through my body when I see that a small piece of the bone handle is broken off. I go to my desk drawer and remove the bone fragment that I found at the murder scene, and to my horror, it perfectly matches the crevice in the handle. There is no doubt my piece of bone came off this knife. I stare it this blade in disbelief, but then both nervously and hurriedly, I replace it and the other items back into Rog's duffle. What should I do next?

After regaining my composure, I realize that there is really only one thing to do, and I call Detective Wilson and ask him to meet me at "The Soda Shoppe" on Dewey Street.

When he arrives, I give him the fragment of bone, and explain where Mr. Agnew and I found the piece. I then tell him of the matching knife handle in Rog's duffle bag.

He tells me to, "Get your other roomie, and then the both of you find another place to stay, until I am able to confront Roger in your room."

Mike and I go to a friend's room, and we watch as three police cruisers pull up and park in front. Detective Wilson leads three uniformed cops into the building. It takes only a short time when we see them bringing a tearful Roger outside in handcuffs. I look at Mike and say, "I can't believe this. Do you really think he killed all those women?" Mike just stares at me. He says nothing.

The next morning, I go to the facility where Rog was being jailed. As I walk in, I see Detective Wilson talking to two other cops. He ceases his conversation immediately and looks at me. I ask him, "What's the news?"

He walks over to me and says, "He confessed to all the murders, and knew details about the killings that only the killer would know. He's actually laughing about them. If he ever had a cloak of innocence about him, if he ever had the appearance of "Mr. Nice Guy"; that facade has diverged into one of evil. I have witnessed many terrible things in my life Ace, but when I peer into his eyes his whole persona is one of pure evil. He is hiding nothing from us now."

A part of me wants to talk to Roger. But I don't believe that I could look him in the face. Instead, I go back to my room. Mike is sitting at his desk. He looks up at me and says, "Satan is the evil in this world Ace. When are you going to believe it?"

I answer, "Joseph Conrad, the great American author once said, "The belief in a supernatural source of evil is not necessary; men alone are quite capable of every wickedness."

CHAPTER 16

Roger is found not guilty at his trial, due to reason of insanity. He is incarcerated in Philadelphia at the "Byberry Asylum" for the criminally Insane." Everything else that is happening in my junior year at school seems unimportant and watered down. Ginger and I grow further apart, and this one event has made me lose my enthusiasm for all that was important to me. I even start to blame myself for the deaths of the women that Roger killed. What if I never jumped into the ocean to save him the day that he fell off my boat? What if he drowned? Those women would still be alive. None of us can believe that someone so close to us was a cold-blooded killer. We continue to question ourselves as to why we didn't notice. That's why I decided that nothing in my life will ever be the same again unless I see him face to face. I must ask him why. Why Rog? Why?

On a Sunday I take the train to Philadelphia and then a cab to the "Byberry Asylum." This facility consists of about twenty buildings, and my driver takes me to the "Visitors Center." An orderly at the front desk informs me that I would need a doctor's permission slip in order to visit Roger.

After waiting an hour, a man approaches me and says, "I'm Doctor Lewiston. I understand you wish to see Mr. Roger Sutcliffe."

I answer, "Yes sir I do. I am Hiram Walker from the University of Delaware. I represent the school's "Hen's Voice" newspaper." I then lie and continue with, "Both the University staff, and Mr. Sutcliffe's attorney wishes me to present these papers to him."

"I'm afraid that is impossible Mr. Walker. Mr. Sutcliffe resides here under constant sedation. I am afraid that he would not even acknowledge your presence."

"I am under orders to see him doctor. I will determine if he acknowledges me."

"I am sorry Mr. Walker, but I must deny your request."

"Doctor, I am exercising my rights under the "Constitution of the United States of America", specifically under the "Freedom of the Press." I'm sure that you have heard of this manuscript before. I will honor your doctor-patient privileges, but if you deny me access to your patient, I will immediately contact Mr. Sutcliffe's attorney and furthermore, I will report this incident to your city's newspaper the "Philadelphia Inquirer." When may I ask did they last visit your facility?"

"Oh, very well sir! But there will be no photographs allowed! I will consent to a fifteen- minute meeting. Please follow me."

We leave the building and I walk with the doctor to a large multiple story building. We enter and take an elevator to the 3rd floor. When the lift's doors open, I am instantly repelled by the stench. Patients are lying naked in the hallways, locked in devices the doctor euphemistically calls restraints. But they are nothing more than thick leather handcuffs and restraining sheets. The floors are sticky with the smell of old urine and feces. As they lay in this sewer of human waste, they reach their arms out for me to help them. I pass dark doorless rooms with no beds. Voices inside cry out echoing their despair. I am appalled. I am speechless. I want to cry out to this person who calls himself a doctor, but I can't. I'm not able to find any words that would express the horrors that I am witnessing. We walk to the end of one long hall of rooms that are closed with heavy wooden doors containing small- barred windows. Williamston says, "This is Mr. Sutcliffe's room. I'll leave you here. Do not wander off. It could be dangerous for you. I'll return shortly."

As I peer into the opening, I see that it is a padded cell. In the far corner a male figure is sitting and sucking his thumb. As my eyes adjust to the dim light, I realize that it's Roger. I try to speak but only a whimper comes out. I make another attempt and I say, "Roger it is Ace Walker."

He stands and looks up at me. I cannot believe his visage. His hair is long and unkept. His face is bearded and dirty. His hospital attire is soiled. Again, I say, "Roger it's Ace Walker."

He walks over to me and puts his face in the window. He stares at me...... He just stares at me...... Then he smiles...... He stares and he smiles...... Then he opens his mouth, and with a deep demonic voice, with a voice I have never heard before, he utters, "Roger isn't here anymore!" Then he laughs. He laughs a loud ear-splitting maniacal laugh! I turn and run...... I run and I run. I race through the halls of stinking decaying humanity. I find the elevator. When it stops and opens, I exit, and continue to run until I am outside of the facility. I make my body fall at the base of an old oak tree and grasp for fresh air. I take deep breaths and then start sobbing. I can't remember ever crying so hard or so loudly. I try to maintain my composure but find it impossible. I want to blot out the horror of this experience, and I can't. I know that this will be forever etched in my mind.

After I find my way back to the college, I go to my room and sleep. It is a fitful sleep, full of frightening nightmares. Purple demons are attacking me. They are pulling me down into the slough of despair. I am fighting them, until I am roused awake by Mike Collins. He asks, "What's the matter Ace? Are you having a bad dream?"

"Mike, I say, I have just witnessed a bad dream. A real one, one that actually exists." I explain to him the terrors that I experienced at the asylum, and I add, "I can't comprehend the evil that is in this world."

He adds, "You say when Roger spoke it wasn't his voice."

"No, it wasn't Mike, it actually sounded otherworldly, like nothing I ever heard before."

"Ace, the bible has a few incidents of people becoming possessed by satanic demons. You may have witnessed this with Roger. All of us couldn't believe that he was capable of killing. If possession actually occurred, then it wasn't Roger who committed the murders."

I contemplate what Mike has said, but what he is suggesting goes against my belief in the existence of the supernatural. I understand that if I believe in a devil, then I also must believe that a God exists. I ponder about what he has said.

CHAPTER 17

I need closure from all the events pertaining to Roger, and I seek it with the camaraderie of my friends. Although it is difficult to totally erase a chapter in your life, I realize life still must go on.

Becky has given birth to a son, and he is named Brian after Becky's father. A christening has been scheduled on campus at Blair Hall. A dinner party is planned after the affair. All of our friends including the entire baseball team have been invited, and Mike and I go together to the event. After Mike's father, the good pastor, performs the ceremony, we assemble for dinner.

Mike and I are assigned seats with Andy, Becky, Ginger, and a few other members of the ball club. Mike stands and announces, "I have been offered a contract with the Chicago White Sox. My father and I have accepted their offer, with a clause stating I do not report to their farm club in Sarasota Florida until the beginning of the 1942 season. My father wishes for me to graduate from school first. This is my dream come true." We all happily shake his hand and offer our congratulations. I stand and make a toast, "Here's to the best pitcher ever to wear a Blue Hen's jersey. We wish you good luck Mike, and are glad you'll be pitching for us in our senior year! We have had a good season this year, but next season let's give Mike a proper going away present and bring the championship trophy home to the U of D!" Cheers go up around the room, and laughter ensues when Becky holds up her newborn son and says, "And here's to the future great pitcher of our beloved school, this is Mr. Brian Harrison class of 1963!" More laughter and applause saturate the room.

Afterwards I reason that this happy gathering was sorely needed. It has helped me recover from the recent dire events in my life. Ginger and I leave together, and drive to an area outside of town to an overlook affectionately called "lover's lane." We spend time there trying to renew our love for one another. But we both know that it has diminished. So far, our relationship has been one of on- again- off- again.

In the winter of '40 I was elected as "Chief Editor" of the newspaper, and I have the idea to expand our editions while relieving the school of their financial responsibilities. My idea is to sell advertising spots to Newark companies. Mike and Ginger accompany me in soliciting local businesses to place weekly ads in the paper. We are encouraged by the good responses that we have received, by signing up a large number of stores and restaurants. Mike is becoming a good friend in spite of the differences of our beliefs. The "Hen's Voice" has grown from a three -sheet paper to six, and our circulation has doubled.

One day in December Mike and I go together to the dining hall for dinner, and as we amble through the buffet line, we run into an old friend serving the fried chicken. It is Patrick Michael O'Brien! He greets us with,

"And a fine day that it tis boyos, and it's a pleasure for me to be a' seein' ye agin! I can't be able to gab with ye now. But I'll be joinin" ye at your table dont'cha know!

We are about halfway through with our meal when Paddy comes and joins us. I introduce him to Mike, and explain that he's the one who took over his bunk.

Paddy says. "Well now laddies, I've been told If I keep me job here on the chow line, and behave me self, I might be readmitted to the school!"

"As time goes by" is not only a song but it is the veritable truth. 1941 has arrived and so has our senior year. I have a 4.0 grade average in all my classes and have mailed out "feelers" to several newspapers seeking employment in the field of journalism. I started to get letters back from several small- town newspapers, but in March I received one from the "Philadelphia Inquirer" requesting that I come in for an interview. I telephone the assistant editor, a Mr. John Jacobs, and am told to report to his office on March 21, at 11:00 am. I am excited about my prospects working for a large printing company, and I take the train on that date to meet with him.

Upon arriving I am escorted to room 303 where I nervously but patiently wait, resume' in hand for my interview. As I sit, I find myself enthralled with a young secretary sitting at her desk and typing. She maybe the most beautiful woman I have ever had the pleasure to glower over. She eventually stops typing, removes the paper from the typewriter, looks at me, and while smiling says, "Are you Mr. Hiram Walker?"

"Yes, ma'am I am."

"Mr. Jacobs is just finishing a conference call; he should be right with you sir."

I must have been mesmerized by her long blonde hair, red lips, and bright blue eyes, because I say, "Pardon me?"

She smiles, gives a slight giggle, and says, "Mr. Jacobs will be right with you."

I answer, "Thank you," and I realize she could have said that the roof is falling in and I still would have been thankful. I remember a word of wisdom my father once told me. He always said, "A beautiful woman is a blessing to the soul, a paradise to the eyes, and a curse to the purse."

The opposite door abruptly opens, and a very fat man comes bursting out. He asks, "Are you Hiram Walker?" My mind hesitates. It still is preoccupied with the beauty before me. I am so entranced that for a second, I even forget why I'm in this room. I finally admit, "Yes sir. I am."

"Well then come on in." I gawk at her as I pass her desk and enter the editor's office. Mr. Jacobs squeezes his great girth into a chair behind his desk that appears to be too small for him.

He says, "Please have a seat young man. I'd like to ask you if you were somehow related to Mr. William Walker, the Nobel Prize winner from the Dover Herald Press?"

"Yes sir Mr. Jacobs. He was my father."

"Great man your father. I worked with him in Dover for a short time. You may not believe this, but I saw you when you were just a toddler. He used to bring you to work with him on occasion."

"Yes sir, he did. My mother and I continue to miss him. By the way sir, I brought you my resume'." I hand the papers to him.

"I understand that you were involved in that serial killer escapade that started in Newark Delaware."

"Yes sir, I was. Unfortunately, the person convicted of the crimes happened to be an acquaintance of mine. I really prefer not to talk about that sir."

"Well unfortunate or not, we in this business must discuss issues that are sometimes unpalatable to us. I have done some checking on you son and I know most, if not all of that story. It appears to me, in your case, that the apple doesn't fall far from the tree. Your father was the best reporter I have ever known. Give me a minute please." He then picks up my resume' to read. He pages through my short biographical notes while pausing at a page occasionally. He looks up and says, "It says here that you've done some wonders for that college rag you call a paper."

I take offense and say, "I wouldn't call it a rag sir. We on the staff are pretty proud of our "Hen's Voice". We have kept our university well informed on most of the important issues of today and have also been helpful with our local police department."

"I know that damn't. I have talked to a number of people in your area, including Detective John Wilson about you. This is a very busy newspaper young man, and I'll have you know that I'm not normally accustomed to sending invitations to students for interviews. It seems that you are an exception to the rule. Now, let's get down to the nitty gritty. The way I see it is that you're not looking for full-time employment until you graduate. Am I correct?"

"That is correct Mr. Jacobs. The reason I'm here is to make you aware that I would be honored to write for the Inquirer. I hope that you would consider me for joining your staff as a journalist after I receive my degree."

Jacob's puts his hands together, looks down at them, and rolls his thumbs. Minutes go by that seems like an hour as he says nothing. He is deep in thought. Finally, he says, "I think I would like to take this a step further Mr. Walker. I believe that you indeed would make a great addition to our staff. Your college grades are excellent. Even at your young age you have had some real- life issues on which you have reported; and your profound athletic ability has been known by some members of our staff. Especially when your Hens beat our beloved Temple Owls. Hell son, when you graduate, you'll probably be able to write your own ticket. What I'm afraid of is that you might get overly ambitious and apply at "The New York Times." Therefore, I would like to make you a proposal. I think that once you come aboard here, you will like our people and the way that we do things. I know that your family is fairly well off, but we always strive to improve our position financially. Therefore, I want to offer you something that we have never done before. I want to offer you a part time position starting right now. In exchange for your services "The Philadelphia Inquirer" will pay your senior year tuition at the University of Delaware and guarantee you a position here as a staff reporter upon your graduation. You would have to, of course, agree to a five- year contract with us. I'm offering you a unique opportunity. What do you think son?"

"What type of reporting would you expect from me?"

"Right now, with war raising its ugly head in Europe, we would like to take the temperature of the young people in our country. We want to know how they feel, how they perceive this war. Do they want to get involved in it? Do they want to avoid it? What do they want our country to do? It is this kind of information that we're seeking. I know that you already have a busy schedule young man, therefore we would only expect one weekly report from you. Also, we would expect one monthly visit from you here on these premises. Do I make myself clear?"

"Yes sir, you do. I want you to know that I am extremely happy about your offer. I would like a little time to mull this over, if I may sir; and may I ask a question?"

"Of course, you may."

"What is the name of the young lady serving as your secretary?"

Jacobs laughs and says, "Her name is Irene Jacobs. She is my daughter."

"You have a lovely daughter sir."

He says, "Thank you. She is my pride and joy. Let's leave this offer on the table for now. But don't take too long mulling things over Mr. Walker. I expect a call from you by the end of this week. You have a good day son. Goodbye for now." I thank him again and we shake hands.

As I leave, I thank Ms. Jacobs and say, "It looks like I might be seeing you again. May I ask, are you ever available for dinner? I would trade a dinner for someone to show me around this city." She says, "I must warn you Mr. Walker that I have very expensive tastes when it comes to food."

I answer, "And I have great expectations when it comes to guide services. By the way just call me Ace. Have a good day ma'am." I start to walk out the door but instead I make an about face, walk back to Mr. Jacob's door and knock. A voice inside says, "Enter." I stick my head in and say, "Mr. Jacob's there really isn't anything I need to mull over. Thankfully, I accept your offer sir. Please mail me the contract. I'll sign and return it to you in good order." I am ecstatic as I ride the train back to Newark. This is what I have always dreamed of. Things are heading my way, and I intend to scoop them up! But yet inside of me I still feel that unexplained emptiness. When I arrive back in Newark I call Andy, and we meet at the Hen's Nest. The tavern is filled with students again now that the ban has been lifted.

I ask, "How are Becky and the newborn?"

He says, "They are both fine Ace. How's things with you?"

I tell him, "You won't believe it Andy, but I've taken a job as a reporter for the "Philadelphia Inquirer."

"You're right Ace, I can't believe it. I thought for sure you were going to finish school first."

"Oh, I am. I was offered a part time position with the newspaper, and they're actually paying my last year's tuition."

"That's incredible. "

"By the way I met the assistant editor's daughter. She's a knockout! I hope to be seeing a lot of her."

Andy says, "Guess who I saw here the other night?"

"Who?"

"I saw Paddy O'Brien. He's working at the University."

"Yeah, he's working in the dining hall. Mike and I ran into him. He told me he has a chance to be readmitted to the school."

"That's odd, he told me he was thinking of joining the Army."

"That's part of my job. I'm to put feelers out amongst the students getting their thoughts on the war in Europe. I'll talk to Paddy about that. How about you Andy. What's your take on it?"

"I have a new family Ace. I want no part of it."

CHAPTER 18

I am writing my first article for the "Inquirer", and I start by interviewing a sampling of students in different grades about their thoughts on the war in Europe. Before submitting it to the home office I think again of the atrocities I witnessed at the Byberry Asylum, and so I also drafted an article about my visit there while seeing Roger. When the Sunday "Inquirer is printed I am amazed that my Byberry article is on the first page. It's on the bottom, but glory be it's on the first page. It looks like I started an inquest about the conditions at the establishment. I also reported that the higher percentage of students that I surveyed were against the U.S. entering into the war.

The addition of my duties at the "Inquirer" have added heavily to my responsibilities, and as a result of these time constraints, my relationship with Ginger is deteriorating.

My first official trip to the newspaper as a reporter has me again visiting Mr. Jacob's waiting room. As I enter, I smile, tip my hat, and give a wink to Irene. I ask her, "Is tonight a good night for an expensive dinner and my guide service?"

"Here is my address Ace. Pick me up at 7:00 pm. We are going to my favorite restaurant."

I say, "That's great news Irene!"

Mr. Jacobs opens his door and ushers me in. He says, "That article you wrote about Byberry was unexpected, but it was brilliant. There have been rumors about the horrors pertaining to that institution for some time now. Your writing on this subject has proven to be a catalyst for a full- blown investigation of their facilities. This is extremely good work Walker. This is the type of stuff your father was noted for. Do you want to re-visit the institution?"

"No sir I do not. I am still retaining nightmares of it."

"If you say it was as bad as you have written, then I don't blame you. I want you to know that the paper is giving you a bonus for your story. You deserve it Walker. I knew that I had found a gem in you. Keep up the good work son!"

And later that evening......

I hire a taxi to pick up Irene Jacobs at 7:00pm. She comes out wearing blue jeans and casual dress. I say to her, "I thought you would be in formal attire. Look at me. I'm wearing my best suit and my fedora is pure beaver. You said we were going to your favorite restaurant!"

"We are Ace. Will you just relax? Driver, take us to the park at 9th and "Passyunk Street" please."

We arrive at a food trailer parked on a curb, with a sign declaring itself to be "Rico's Cheesesteaks". I ask, "This is your favorite restaurant?"

"Absolutely it is, and after you take a bite, I think you'll agree that these sandwiches are the best you have ever tasted."

I order the cheesesteaks and drinks, and we sit at a table under an oak. After one bite I tell Irene, "These are incredible!"

"I knew you'd like them Ace. Philly is becoming famous for cheesesteaks. By the way, my father says you play for the U of D baseball team."

"I do. I'd like you to come to a game sometime."

We spend the rest of the evening walking and talking, with an occasional kiss in between. I tell her, "My dad used to say, "A kiss is saying I love you, in just one syllable." "Of course, he was always great with words."

"My father says that his son is also."

The worst part of the evening was taking her back home.

****The year marches on****

Baseball season is coming to an end, and we are tied with Delaware State for first place. We will play one game against them for the Division Championship on their turf in Wilmington. On my trips to Philly and Wilmington, Irene and I always meet. It seems our romance is growing stronger, and I invite her to the game.

The day of the game is all sunshine and not a cloud in the sky. It is a perfect Sunday and a perfect 75 degrees. A large contingent from the "Inquirer" is gathered together with the "Hen's Voice" staff. More importantly Irene is here. I glance up at her occasionally during infield practice, and that is when I spot Ginger sitting next to Andy and Becky. Oh no, they're both here! It looks like this day will require an extreme attempt at diplomacy. Love is the only game where two people can both win......but not three.

The game goes into the ninth inning, and the Hornets are winning one to nothing. Mike is pitching a one hitter, a homer to their third baseman. The Hornet's pitcher has given up only one hit to us. Our first two batters strike out. Jankowski singles and I come up to bat. I foul a few pitches off and work the count to 3 balls and 2 strikes. I'm confident that the next pitch will be a fastball, and if it is I'm going to crush it. There is no doubt in my mind that I'll win this game right now. I go into my crouch, I grit my teeth, and wait.

"And now the pitcher holds the ball, and now he lets it go,

And now the air is shattered by the force of Casey's bat.

Oh, somewhere in this favored land the sun is shining bright.

The band is playing somewhere, and somewhere hearts are light,

And somewhere men are laughing, and somewhere children shout.......

But there is no joy in Mudville—mighty Casey has struck out."[1]

Dejected, I walked back to the dugout. Mike gets his one hitter through nine innings, but we lose to the Hornets 1-0. As I walk out of the dugout, our first baseman Don Jankowski's little sister comes over to meet me. I always call her "little bit". She says, "I'm so sorry Ace, would you care to go and have a soda with me?"

[1]"Casey at the Bat" is a Poem by Ernest Thayer first published in 1888 in the San Francisco Examiner.

"No "little bit", you cute little thing, I have a prior commitment."

After the game I'm consoled by all, but it doesn't help. That's when I learned that success goes to your head, but failure always to your heart. Irene comes up to me, gives me a peck on the cheek, and says, "I'm sorry Ace." Then I see Ginger approaching. I wish I could crawl into a hole. I am a nervous wreck. What do I say to her about Irene? Then Don Jankowski cuts her off, takes her by the hand, and leads her away. She glances back at me and smiles, and I take a deep breath and sigh.

CHAPTER 19

Months later as the pain of our loss starts to fade away, as well as Ginger's affection for me, things start to get back to normal at our beloved university. Coach Jensen continues to teach Mathematics and Physical Education. Students still must endure Ms. Lockhart's never- ending study of "Chaucer". Professors Leonard and Simmons continue to enlighten students in the subjects of Chemistry and Biology. The "Hen's Voice continues to grow in circulation. My articles I write for the "Inquirer" are eagerly accepted by the paper's editors. My love for Ms. Irene Jacobs is blooming. And Paddy O'Brien is still slinging hash in our dining hall.

We of the senior class are looking forward to graduation.

And then it happens.

One day over the school's public address system it is announced that a very important message from the President of the United States will be broadcast. It suggests that all students, faculty members, and all other employees of the university tune in to the broadcast. This is what we hear on this fateful day of December 8th, 1941, from Franklin D. Roosevelt:

"Mr. Vice President. Mr. Speaker. Members of the Senate, and of the House of Representatives:

Yesterday, December 7th, 1941—a date which will live in infamy—The United States of America was suddenly and deliberately attacked by naval and air forces of the Empire of Japan.

The United States was at peace with that nation and, at the solicitation of Japan, was still in conversation with its government and its emperor looking toward the maintenance of peace in the Pacific.

Indeed, one hour after Japanese air squadrons had commenced bombing in the American island of Oahu, the Japanese ambassador to the United States and his colleague delivered to the secretary of state a formal reply to a recent American message. And while this reply stated that it seemed useless to continue the existing diplomatic negotiations, it contained no threat or hint of war or of armed attack.

It will be recorded that the distance of Hawaii from Japan makes it obvious that the attack was deliberately planned many days or even weeks ago. During the intervening time, the Japanese government has deliberately sought to deceive The United States by false statements and expressions of hope for continued peace.

The attack yesterday on the Hawaiian Islands has caused severe damage to the American naval and military forces. I regret to tell you that very many American lives have been lost. In addition, American ships have been reported torpedoed on the high seas between San Francisco and Honolulu.

Yesterday the Japanese government also launched an attack against Malaya.

Last night, Japanese forces attacked Hong Kong.

Last night, Japanese forces attacked Guam.

Last night, Japanese forces attacked the Philippine islands.

Last night, the Japanese attacked Wake Island.

And this morning, the Japanese attacked Midway Island.

Japan has, therefore, undertaken a surprise offensive extending throughout the Pacific area. The facts of yesterday and today speak for themselves. The people of the United States have already formed their opinions and well understand the implications to the very life and safety of our nation.

As commander in chief of the Army and Navy, I have directed that all measures be taken for our defense. But always will our whole nation remember the character of the onslaught against us.

No matter how long it may take us to overcome this premeditated invasion, the American people in their righteous might will win through to absolute victory.

I believe that I interpret the will of the Congress and of the people when I assert that we will not only defend ourselves to the utmost but will make it very certain that this form of treachery will never again endanger us.

Hostilities exist. There is no blinking at the fact that our people, our territory, and our interests are in grave danger.

With confidence, in our armed forces, with the unbounding determination of our people, we will gain the inevitable triumph --so help us God.

I ask that the Congress declare that since the unprovoked and dastardly attack by Japan on Sunday, December the 7th, 1941, a state of war has existed between the United States and the Japanese empire.[2]

We look at one another in disbelief. We are in a state of shock. We are angry. At that moment I believe that all of the students that I had interviewed about their feelings of war; those that said, "Let's not get involved," would have instantly changed their minds. Even only minutes after hearing the speech, men in our room start to leave to join our military forces. Again, I realize that when you start to plan a few things, that's when life happens. When life takes over, change will always occur; in fact, there really is only one constant in this life, and that is change.

We all scatter and leave the newsroom. Each of us have new destinations in mind.

I immediately go to my dorm. Upon my arrival I find Mike is typing. He stops and looks up at me, and we start to discuss what avenues we were going to pursue.

I say, "I think that graduation can wait. I've made up my mind to join the Army. What about you Mike?"

"Well Ace, my father isn't happy about it, but I've made the same decision."

"I have to say Mike that I'm somewhat surprised. I thought that your religious beliefs might stop you from doing so. "

"I have come to the same decision as Sergeant York did in WWI. Did you ever hear his story Ace?"

[2]"Infamy Speech" by FDR on Dec 8th, 1941

"Yes, I have. I saw the movie with Gary Cooper. He was the medal of honor recipient that captured a large number of Germans singlehandedly. At first, he was a conscientious objector. Then he decided that if he killed the enemy, he would save American lives."

"That's right Ace. He also read in the scriptures, "Render to Caesar the things that are Caesar's, and to God the things that are God's. I believe that Nazi Germany, and the Japanese Empire are the emissaries of pure evil, and I feel the need to be in self- defense of my country."

About that time Andy comes barging in, saying, "Are you two joining up?"

I laugh and say, "That didn't take you long. As a matter of fact, Mike and I both have decided to enlist. You have a wife and child Andy. Nobody would criticize you for not leaving them."

"I couldn't live with myself fellas. I'm signing up. What branch are you two joining?"

Mike answers, "We're both going into the Army."

Andy says, "That's what I've been thinking. Why don't we enlist at the same time. Maybe we can be stationed together in the same outfit."

"Andy, you meet Mike and me tomorrow morning at 10:00am and we'll go to the recruiting office together."

CHAPTER 20

On Tuesday December 9th, Andy drives Mike and me to the U.S. Army recruiting office in Wilmington. Andy tells us, "My parents say that I should wait, that maybe this conflict wouldn't last very long. I don't believe that. We'll be in this for the long haul. Becky is both sad and mad at me at the same time, but she tearfully said that she understands."

When we arrive at the recruiting office, I'm astonished at the long line of men waiting to join. They extend out in a line almost two blocks long. That's when we see Paddy O'Brien up ahead. He waves at us and shouts, "Over here! Over here! I've been a' savin' a place for ya!" We move up the line to join him and he says, "I be a itchin' for this fight laddies. I've always hated the Krauts."

Mike says, "Why do you think we'll be fighting the Germans Paddy? We might be sent to the Pacific."

"Oh no boyo, I've been told by Jensen where we'll be a headin'!" Large posters surround the area announcing that "Uncle Sam Wants You"! A record player is hooked up to an outside speaker playing patriotic songs. We hear the Andrew Sisters telling us about "The Boogie- Woogie Bugle Boy of Company B." Then the old George M. Cohan songs start to play. We hear, "It's a Grand Old Flag" and "Over There". A Corporal is walking down the line handing out brochures.

Then everyone starts laughing when we hear for the first time the "Spike Jones orchestra" play:

"When da Fuehrer says we is de master race

We seig heil (pffft) heil (pffft) right in der fuehrer's face!

When herr Goebbels says we own de world and space

We seig heil (pffft) heil (pffft) right in herr Goebbels face!"

The song continues on and on until the crowd becomes uproarious!

It takes about an hour for us to enter into the building where a Private First- Class hands us pen and paper saying, "Sign your name; last name first, first name, middle name last."

I say, "What?"

He repeats himself, "Last name first, first name, middle name last! You do understand English, don't you?"

We sign our intention of enlistments. And who is organizing this whole process? Paddy is correct. It is none other than Coach Jensen dressed in his Army uniform, and wearing his Master Sergeant stripes. He then tells us that we are to report in one week to "The United States Army Induction Center" in Philadelphia.

A few days later, I'm invited for a going away dinner at the Jacob's home in West Chester. Irene greets me at the door and leads me into the study, where Mr. and Mrs. Jacobs are discussing current events. They offer me a drink and I take a seat on the sofa next to Irene.

Mr. Jacobs says, "I wish you would have consulted me before signing a commitment to join the Army Ace. I might have had some other ideas."

I say, "My friends all wanted to join at the same time. The reasoning was that we could serve in the same outfit together."

"I understand that Ace, but you are certainly going to be missed at the Inquirer."

"I'm going to miss everyone also, especially this young lady sitting next to me."

Jacobs says, "We are not without power at the paper. If you have a preference among branches of the Army such as artillery, an armored division, or whatever, let me know. We do have some influence."

"I suppose I'll just let them decide on that sir."

"Do you have any idea where you'll be going Ace?"

"We hear that everyone from our region will be going to basic training at Fort Dix in New Jersey. I suppose we will also."

Jacobs asks, "In what theater of war do you believe they'll send you son?"

Irene says, "Oh daddy stop. Ace doesn't know yet, and by the way; why do they call the areas where men are fighting theaters? That is so stupid. It sounds like the men are just going to go and watch a movie."

I say, "What's horrible is what the Japanese have just done in Hawaii, and what the Germans are doing in Europe. They have invaded Poland and now have their sights on France."

Jacobs says, "Ace is right. This evil must be stopped. I believe that this Adolf Hitler is a madman. Anyway, it's time to eat. Let's go to the dining room before that roast gets cold."

After dinner Irene and I sit on the back- porch swing and attempt to make guesses and what-ifs about the future.

She says, "I've only known you for a short time Ace, but I think I'm falling in love with you."

"You better not be just thinking about an issue like that. You better be sure. I want you to know that I think of you constantly every day. If that's what love is, then I have it badly for you."

We kiss passionately, and as I look into her eyes my heart aches, knowing that I'll soon be leaving this wonderful woman. We kiss again as our tears mingle together.

"How long do you believe you'll be gone Ace?"

"I don't know. Like the song says. "And we won't come back til it's over, over there!"

"Promise me one thing."

"What's that?"

"Say you promise."

"Okay, I promise."

"Promise me that you'll come back to me. Promise me Ace. Promise me now!"

"Irene, I promise I'll come back to you. I promise!" And we kiss again......

Two days later I drive home to Rehoboth Beach to visit my mother and some other friends. It's time to say my goodbyes. I think of Irene and the promise I made to her. I ask myself how can I make a promise like that? How does a man facing combat in a war, make a promise to anyone that he is coming back. Am I being arrogant by saying I'm coming back, or just hopeful?

As I walk up my front steps my mom runs out and grabs me. She looks me up and down and cries. She just cries and cries. Then she cries some more. "Come in son. I've made the soft-shell crabs you like so much, and your Uncle Bob is here."

"Hi Uncle Bob. How you been?"

"I'm alright Ace. I heard you signed up."

"Yeah, I did. I'm headed to Philly next week for my physical, and the induction ceremony."

"Have any idea what they'll have you doing besides carrying a gun?"

"Nope. It's up to them."

"I just want to pass on one thing from my experiences. Do not. I say do not! Do not ever volunteer for anything! That's the best way to get yourself killed."

"I'll take that, under consideration Uncle Bob."

"Your father would have been proud of you. By the way did you finish school?"

"Nope, that will have to wait until later. But I only had a month to go. I heard that they might mail our diplomas out to us. At least to those of us who joined the military right away."

Mother interrupts us and says, "I will hear no more talk of war. Let's eat and have a few drinks. But I want you to know right now, that you will only be fed if we talk about pleasant things. Like about that new girl of yours. What's her name? Is it Irene?"

"Yes mom, it's Irene."

"Are you thinking of marrying her before you leave?"

"No mom I'm not. We have already said our goodbyes."

Bob says, "That's smart Ace. You should drink until they are beautiful and stop before you marry them."

Mom says, "Oh Robert that was terrible; but it's also probably wise in this case. I want you to promise me that you'll be careful and promise me, you promise me. Listen to me. You promise me that you'll come back home to me." "I promise mom." I spend two more days promising and relaxing at home.

PART TWO

CHAPTER 21

(To the tune of "You're in the army now.")

"You're in the Army now!

You're not behind the plow!

You'll never get rich

By digging a ditch!

You're in the Army now!

Uncle Sam does the best he can

Vacation in a foreign land!

You're in the Army now!

You're not behind the plow!

You'll never get rich by digging a ditch

You're in the Army now.

About fifty of us get off each of the Army buses and are ushered into the induction center. A Sergeant greets us with kindly shouts of "Just follow the yellow brick road you idiots!" We then are hurried into a large room to <u>wait</u>.

After the long <u>wait,</u> we are hurried into another room to <u>wait</u>. Finally, we start our physical examinations. Again, we are herded to a large room where we are told to strip naked, and then we are ordered to stand at attention in a single column to <u>wait</u>. I realized then that the Army is all about <u>hurry up and wait</u>. Eventually a doctor starts down the row, stethoscope in hand, and listens to heartbeats. One man is told to step forward and leave the room. Testicles are held as we are ordered to cough. He then proceeds down the row behind us, and we are ordered to "Bend over and spread your cheeks." The man next to me, while bent over, pulls his mouth cheeks apart, and the sergeant screams, "Your other cheeks you moron!"

We then enter another room called the "Green Monster" where we side- step in line and receive seven pairs of underwear and socks. We are issued our fatigue uniforms and caps next. Then we are given our class A dress uniforms and hats. The final uniform issued is our combat boots and low quarter shoes. We are issued a duffle bag, told to dress into fatigues, and to put everything else in the bag.

Next is the eye examination room. Two men are told that they have vision unfit for military service, and are mustered out. Audiology is next. After the guy ahead of me said, "What?" to the doctor three times, he also was rejected. We then line up again and proceed single file as we receive a number of injections. I don't know how many shots we received, but I didn't think that there were that many diseases. The four of us, Mike, Andy, Paddy, and myself all make it through to a large room with ceremonial flags staged on a platform. A captain is presiding over the ceremony to swear us into the U.S. Army. After we are aligned into formation the captain says, "Gentlemen raise your right hand and repeat after me....

"I (state your name) do solemnly swear that I will support and defend the Constitution of the United States against all enemies, foreign and domestic. That I will bear true faith and allegiance to the same: and that I will obey the orders of the President of the United States and the orders of those appointed over me, according to the regulations and the Uniform Code of Military Justice. So, help me God."

"Say I do."

In unison we say, "I do!"

The captain leaves the podium, and the sergeant replaces him. With a very loud and scowling face he shouts, "Now men you can give your heart to your sweetheart, but your ass belongs to the U.S. Army! Follow me to the buses for Fort Dix!"

An hour later we arrive near Trenton, New Jersey at Fort Dix. Other buses are arriving from other destinations. We are greeted again by loud and screaming Drill Instructors. One D.I. empties the men off our bus and introduces himself.

"I am Staff Sergeant Michael J. Jones! I am your Drill Instructor, and I am your worst nightmare! You will not like me. You will hate me. But because you will hate me, you will learn more. You will learn to respect me, because I will be hard, but I will be fair. You are lower than worms. You are the scum of the earth. My job is to take you maggots and turn you into killing machines. When you address me the first word and the last word out of your mouths, will be sir! Do you understand me?!"

We all answer in unison, "Sir, yes, sir."

"I can't hear YOUUU!!!! Do you understand MEEEE?!"

Again, in unison but louder, we yell, "Sir, yes sir!"

"Now you numbskulls line up as I direct you." The Sarge forms us into a marching platoon, and he marches us to our assigned barracks. We are an out-of-step sorry group as we stumble towards what will be our new home for eight weeks.

We enter our barracks and are each assigned a cot, clothes hanger, and a foot- locker. We are ordered to stand at attention in front of our foot lockers. Sergeant Jones then says, "You men have been assigned to my platoon. It is the 3rd platoon in Charlie Company, of the 1st Battalion, in the 2nd Regiment of the 2nd Armored Division. This Division is known as "Hell on Wheels". The commanding officer of this division is Major General Charles L. Scott, with old blood and guts himself, General George S, Patton in charge of training. You most likely will never meet them, but I assure you that you will be meeting the "Chief NCO" of our Charlie Company which is Master Sergeant John Jensen, and our company "Officer in Charge" Lt. Max Steiner. You will notice that there are cigarette butt cans filled with water and attached to the room's posts. They will be used when the smoking lamp is lit. It is not lit now. There will be no smoking in my barracks until I tell you that you may. You will have to earn that right by obeying, without question, my every command! The latrine is by the front door across from my room. It will be kept immaculate. It will be kept as though the Queen of England would be proud to take a dump there! I want every toilet seat there so clean that I can make a sandwich on it! One of you will be assign..... (a whisper is heard from one of the men) ......

3 Oath of enlistment into the Armed Forces

"Whooo said that?! Who is the #%@& dirty rat that said that?! I will personally choke you to death you rotten dirty #%@& s.o.b.!

The Sergeant has proven that he has command of a perfectly flowing group of curse words. He has in fact, elevated cussing into an art form, and he is the "Virtuoso of the Profane".

"If you don't confess, I will severely punish this entire platoon. You will be the most hated dog face in this outfit!"

A voice three men down from me says, "Sir, I did sir!" Jones runs towards him and puts his face inches in front of the recruit's face.

"What is your name soldier?"

"Sir, my name is Laskowski Sir."

"I want your full name you puke face!"

"Sir, my full name is Matthew Laskowski sir!"

"What did you say while you were ordered at attention you, dirt bag!"

"Sir, I was making a joke sir!"

"Are you a comedian Private Laskowski?"

"Sir, no sir!"

"Do you think that you're Groucho Marx?

"Sir, no sir!"

"Laskowski? What kind of a name is Laskowski?!"

"Sir it is a Polish name sir!"

"Are you saying you're a pollock Laskowski!?"

"Sir, yes sir!"

"Well, I don't like pollocks private. (Jones slaps him in the face) In fact, I hate pollocks! (He slaps him again) But then again, I am not prejudice, and I will treat all of you equally. I am hard but I am fair because I hate everyone equally. I hate all pollocks, wops, dirty Irish, limeys, negroes, and redskin savages the same. Do any of you @#%& low life's have a problem with that!?"

We all answer, "Sir, no sir!"

"I can't hear YOUUU!"

We answer louder, "Sir, no sir!"

"Your name is no longer Laskowski "Mr. Comedian"! You are now Private Alphabet, and you are now the platoon "Latrine Queen"! Drop to the floor and give me thirty pushups!

Sgt. Jones runs to a chubby recruit at the end of our line and sticks his face in his. "What is your name Private?!"

"Sir it is Vincent Andretti sir!"

"Andretti? What kind of name is Andretti?"

"Sir it is Italian sir!"

"Are you saying that you're a greaseball Andretti? Are you a guinea WOP Andretti?"

"Sir, yes sir!"

"Well, you greaser, you look like a can of biscuits that's just popped open. You are a very fat man greaseball. How much do you weigh?!"

"Sir, I weigh 275 pounds sir!"

"275 pounds? I didn't know that they piled cow dung that heavy! You are one fat man! Your name is no longer Andretti! Your name is now Private Fatso. Tell me your new name Fatso!"

"Sir, my name is Private Fatso sir!"

"Private Fatso you are on "Fire Watch" tonight. Take this helmet and baton, and station your fat greasy behind by the front doors of our barracks. You will protect us tonight against fire, or any intruder who desires to kill us!"

"Ladies all I do is eat gunpowder and run! I am warning you. You don't want to piss me off, or fire, hell, and brimstone will come down upon you!

It is now light's out! Goodnight, ladies....... I don't hear your answer."

We holler in unison, "Sir goodnight, sir!"

"I can't hear YOUUU!"

"Sir, goodnight, sir!"

The next morning at 0600 hours we hear the Reveille bugle call:

"You've got to get up

You've got to get up

You've got to get up this morning

You've got to get up.

You've got to get up

Get up to the bugles call.

The major told the captain

The captain told the sergeant

The sergeant told the bugler

The bugler told them all!

You've got to get up.

You've got to get up.

You've got to get up today!"

Staff Sergeant Jones screams, "Good morning ladies, out of your sacks! Atten…. tion! This is Corporal Richards! Corporal Richards is a genius! Corporal Richards is here to teach you how to make your bed! He will also teach you how to shine your boots! He will teach you how to roll your socks. He will show you how to arrange your footlocker! Corporal Richards will even show you how to brush your teeth and take a dump! You, lily livered excuses for human beings will learn from Corporal Richards. He is a genius!"

Throughout the day we are taught some basics of Army life by the corporal, and later Sgt. Jones makes his appearance again. "FALLOUT, he screams!! And the whole platoon of 60 men races through the doors, where the sergeant arranges us in the order of the formation in which we will always assemble. "On my command and starting with your left foot, FORWARD…...MARCH! He then starts to chant cadence. "Your left, your left, your left right left…... Your left, your left, your left right left. Hut two, hut four, hut two three four! Your left, your left, your left, right left! Platoon…. Halt." Some of us bump into each other as we attempt to stop. Jones screams, "You men look as stupid as a one- legged man in an but kicking contest! You are definitely retards!

We are taught the commands for left, right and about face, column left and right. We eventually are taught all the marching commands, and we drill the entire day, and into the night with breaks only to eat. We shower and climb into our bunks, as the mournful cry of "Taps" is bugled slowly and melodiously. All is quiet. Occasionally, in this quiet, you can hear a soldier crying. It is times like this; times of rest and quiet, that your mind starts to wander. You think of your parents, your friends, and the girlfriend or wife you left behind. You wonder if you'll make it through this ordeal of basic training, and you ponder how you'll perform in combat. But most of all, you attempt to remove from your mind, any possible thoughts of your death in this war.

The next morning after assembly and breakfast we are issued our weaponry. It includes one Model M1.30 caliber rifle, one M1 Bayonet, one Ka-Bar Fighting Knife, and one Model 1911 Colt .45 Caliber Pistol. We are also given a copy of the "Rifleman's Creed". We are to memorize it, and while holding our rifles in front of us, we recite it together as a platoon, while lying in our bunks each evening as follows:

"This is my rifle. There are many like it, but this one is mine.

My rifle is my best friend. It is my life.

I must master it as I must master my life.

My rifle, without me is useless.

Without my rifle I am useless.

I must fire my rifle true.

I must shoot straighter than my enemy who is trying to kill me.

I must shoot him before he shoots me.

I will keep my rifle clean and ready.

We will become part of each other.

Before God, I swear this creed.

My rifle and myself are the defenders of my country.

We are the masters of our enemy.

We are the saviors of my life.

So be it, until there is no more enemy, but peace.

Amen.

We are also given a copy of our "Eleven General Orders" to memorize.

At the end of our second week of training we are scheduled for our first general inspection. SSgt. Jones calls the barracks to attention as Lt. Steiner and MSgt. Jensen enter our building. We are ordered to "Present Arms", as Steiner and Jensen walk down the line inspecting each of us. My old coach stops in front of me and asks, "What is your 5th general order private?"

I answer, "Sir my 5th general order is "To quit my post only when properly relieved sir!"

He stops next by O'Brien and says, "You stink Private. You smell like failure and corn chips! Are you showering regularly private?"

"Sir, I am sir!"

"What is your 8th general order?"

"Sir my 8th general order is "To give the alarm in case of fire or disorder sir!"

The Lieutenant finds a few discrepancies. As they depart our barracks Lt. Steiner looks at SSgt. Jones and says, "If you have been training these men sergeant then you've got a lot more work to do!" Jones salutes and says, "Yes sir. Thank you, sir!"

After they leave Jones goes ballistic. I have never in my life heard as many; or such a variation of curse words strung together, as in a never- ending ode to nastiness! He says, "You ladies make me believe in reincarnation, because nobody can become this stupid in one lifetime!" He ends with, "Tomorrow at 0500 hours, you will fall out into formation with full backpacks and your rifles shouldered. We are going on a little twenty- mile hike. I refuse to let you idiots make me look bad in front of our C.O. You will either shape up or I will personally castrate the lot of you!"

We start our twenty -mile march exactly at 0500 hours, and it takes us fourteen hours to complete our marathon. We experience having our first meals of K-Rations during this time. Being exhausted we shower and climb into our bunks. I can't believe it when I look at Sgt. Jones as he does more personal exercises, and seems that he could do the whole twenty miles all over again.

Starting our third week we are put on a tight schedule of; reveille, breakfast, marching drills, calisthenics, lunch, obstacle course, Judo lessons, supper, and barracks duty. Although I am not religious, I am truly grateful for Sundays. The majority of men go to the chapel services of their choice. I however, thankfully, and leisurely, sleep in. I spend the rest of my day reading and stuffing myself in the mess hall, after which I gratefully take a long nap. This schedule continues for two weeks.

A change comes in our 5th week. We all are required to take written exams. Then we are scheduled for weapons training, and the live fire obstacle course. Bayonet and hand to hand knife combat start our mornings, followed by hand grenade training, and then trips to the rifle range.

Paddy is excelling in all forms of combat training, and he catches the eye of several NCO's and Officers. He's promoted to corporal this same week. Andy and Mike are progressing properly.

On Thursday of that week, I was called into the lieutenant's office.

I come into the lieutenant's office, snap to attention, salute, and say, "Private Walker reporting as ordered sir."

MSgt Jensen is present and says, "At ease Walker, and have a seat."

Lieutenant Steiner starts, "Private Walker your D.I. Sgt. Jones has given you a good report, and I understand that you know MSgt. Jensen here quite well. He also has given you excellent recommendations as to your character, integrity, and loyalty. He says you are extremely goal oriented, and by the way, one hell of a hitter! (The three of us laugh). The Battalion Commander Colonel Humphries has also caught wind of you and is recommending you for Officers Candidate School in Fort Drum, New York.

I ask, "Sir when I graduate do I return to this platoon sir?"

"No, you will not private. You will be reassigned elsewhere as needed."

"Sir, I would prefer to remain here as a private sir."

"I'm afraid that the decision has already been made Walker. You have no choice in the matter. The Army needs more officers, and they deem you qualified. You will report to Fort Drum in two days."

"Sir, yes sir."

As I leave, I am unhappy about serving in another outfit without my friends. I start to think about what Mr. Jacobs said about "The Inquirer" having some influence. When I arrive back at my barracks, Sgt. Jones calls me into his room.

He says, "Congratulations Walker. I believe that you'll make a good officer." I say, "Sir, thank you sir."

"You can cut out that sir stuff now Walker. That's for basic training only. Don't call me sir again. I actually work for a living, and my parents were not married. Soon it will be me calling you sir. I hope you understand why I was so tough on you men."

"Yes, I do Sarge, and I'll always remember you.

"I know you will,"

Will you be joining the men when they are deployed overseas?"

"No, I won't Walker. I would like to, but I'm assigned permanently here. Somebody has to train these new recruits, and I have a feeling that I'll be seeing a lot of them, because I believe this will be a long fight. I wish you good luck Walker."

That evening, I go to the Post Exchange to use the telephone. I call my old boss, Irene's father Mr. Jacobs.

He answers the phone:

"Hello, this is the Jacobs residence."

"Hello Mr. Jacobs sir, this is Hiram Walker calling."

"Well hello Ace. How's Army life son?"

"It's been an interesting experience Mr. Jacobs. But I have a dilemma now, and you told me to contact you if I had any requests or problems."

"What is it you need son?"

I explained my situation and said that I would happily take the promotion to 2nd Lieutenant if I could remain with my friends in our platoon.

Mr. Jacobs tells me, "I am friends with General George Marshall. He and I went to high school together. I understand that George is being groomed for "General of the Army", and I have an idea. Your father was the greatest war correspondent of WWI. How would you like the opportunity to become the greatest in WWII?"

"If it means staying with my current outfit and remaining with my platoon and company as a reporter, I will turn down OCS sir. Would I be employed by the "Inquirer" sir?"

Yes, technically. If I can arrange this, you would no longer be in the Army. You would be a civilian reporter for the "Philadelphia Inquirer." Of course, you would have to remain with your current platoon for the extent of the war. Is this something you'd be interested in son?"

"Yes sir, I believe I would be."

"Call me tomorrow night before you ship out to Fort Drum."

"Yes, sir and thank you sir!"

"By the way there is someone standing next to me that badly wants to speak to you."

Irene and I converse for the next few minutes......

The very next evening I receive a call from Company Headquarters to report once more to Lt. Steiner. Again, as I entered his office, I find MSgt. Jensen also present.

The Lt. says, "I don't know who it is you know Walker, but I just received a personal phone call from our Division Commander, Major

General Charles L. Scott himself. He has informed me that you are to nix your trip to Fort Drum, and Officer's Candidate School. He also has ordered me to give you an honorable discharge removing you from military service. But then you are required to sign an endorsement of a contract between the U.S. Army and "The Philadelphia Inquirer" newspaper company, to be an attaché to Charlie company, 3rd platoon of the 2nd Armored Division for the duration of this war. You are to serve as a war correspondent reporting all action that our Company will see in combat. Are you aware that this has transpired Walker?"

"Yes sir. My wishes are to remain with my platoon and my friends and to honor my father's legacy in WWI."

"Then here are your discharge papers, and the military civilian contract that require your signature."

After I sign, I ask, "What are my orders now lieutenant?"

You have no further orders from the U.S Army Mr. Walker. But you have been ordered by the "Philadelphia Inquirer", at the request of the Joint Chiefs of Staff of the U.S. Army, to travel to Hollywood, California, and report to Mr. William Fox, the head of The Fox Movietone news Studios. Let me give you this. This is a telegram from a Mr. John Jacobs of your newspaper. This will explain that you will receive two weeks training in Hollywood, and also receive the cameras and other equipment necessary for filming live combat action. You are scheduled to fly from this post tomorrow at 0900 hours. After training you will report back to me here at Fort Dix, as we prepare to deploy to our theater of war. Congratulations Mr. Walker."

"Thank you, sir."

Coach Jensen stands up (I know he's a sergeant now, but he'll always be "Coach" to me) and he says, "Congratulations Ace. Your father would have been proud."

"Thanks Coach, it looks like we'll be seeing a lot of each other."

I know that Jensen will see action again as he had in WWI, but I worry sometimes about his age.

Back at the barracks my friends all wish me well, and Sgt. Jones just shakes his head and says, "And now he thinks he's Cecil B. DeMille!"

CHAPTER 22

My plane lands in the land of sunshine and movie stars…. It's funny how you can't get a song out of your head………. Hooray for Hollywood!

That screwy ballyhooey Hollywood.

Where any office boy or any young mechanic can be a panic

With just a good- looking tan.

And any barmaid can be a star- maid

If she dances with or without a fan!

Hooray for Hollywood!

Where your terrific if your even good.

Where anyone at all from Shirley Temple to Aimee Semple

Is equally understood.

Go out and try your luck, you might be a Donald Duck

Hooray for Hollywood!

I hire a taxi to take me to "The Sunset Hills Hotel" in downtown Hollywood. I will be billeted here for my entire stay in glitter city. Tomorrow I'm scheduled to meet with Mr. William Fox at his Movietone news studios, but today and tonight are free time. After checking in I put on swimwear and go down to the pool area and stretch out on a lounge chair and watch the parade of women go by. Everything is beautiful in this town. Then I couldn't believe my eyes. Myrna Loy comes walking in with her "Thin Man" co-star William Powell. They take seats at the Tiki bar. I know that everyone poolside can see them, but nobody cares. Seeing movie stars in this town must be a common occurrence. I take a few laps in the pool, and when putting my watch back on I see that it is only noon. I decide that it must be 5:00 pm somewhere, and I saunter up to that poolside bar for a Bloody Mary.

The bartender comes over, takes my order, and I ask, "Is that really who I think it is?"

He answers, "Yeah, that's Bill and Myrna. They stop in occasionally."

I say, "You must get used to seeing celebrities in this town."

"Listen pal, in this place your apt to see Clark Gable, Jimmy Cagney, or Joan Crawford at any given time. Yeah, you do get used to it, and they usually don't want to be bothered by starstruck tourists seeking autographs."

"I understand, it's just novel for a kid from Rehoboth Beach Delaware."

I have my second drink and go up to my room. As I walk past the two stars Ms. Loy smiles at me.

That evening, I take a cab to the famed "Brown Derby" restaurant on Wilshire boulevard to eat, and then spent the rest of the day exploring the downtown.

****

The next morning, I meet with Mr. Fox at his studio......

"I'm Hiram Walker from the "Philadelphia Inquirer" Mr. Fox. Everybody calls me Ace. It's a pleasure to meet you sir."

"Welcome to Movietone news Ace. It's good to have you aboard. Let's go into my office and discuss what we expect from you and your newspaper."

We enter his spacious office and sit at a table with a large unopened box resting on it. "Your newspaper mailed this to our address here, for you to open Ace."

We open the box and find two Bell & Howell "EYEMO" video cameras for movie production. These are perfect for the task at hand because they are compact and operate on a wind- up mechanism instead of batteries. Also shipped are two KODAK "Medalist" cameras for still shots. This camera uses 620 size films. Telescoping lenses are provided for both types of instruments.

Mr. Fox says, "Well this equipment is up to date and perfect for what we are about to do Ace. I want you to know that you are solely employed by the "Inquirer", and not by us here at Movietone news. We will, however, be paying your paper for the rights to certain videos that you have produced. We will use them for release to theaters around the country. In turn, we will also allow Columbia Studios access to some of these films. Frank Capra and John Ford are planning to produce a major documentary on the war. Those of us in this business believe it is both our duty and responsibility to keep the public informed as to what will be transpiring in this terrible war. You will learn a large number of important things about film making while here with us. You must learn about lighting, film speed, and other related exposure issues. Of course, your newspaper will not only be wanting photographic still shots and movies, but also your written articles about the war. Tonight, we are invited To Mister Ford's home for dinner and drinks. You will be introduced to some very important people this evening, and they are anxious to meet you. You are a very brave man for undertaking this extremely dangerous job.

"To be honest with you Mr. Fox, this was really a selfish request on my part because it was the only way for me to remain with my friends as we endure this war."

"I just hope you'll keep your head down when it needs to be down. You'll be shooting a camera not a gun!"

Mr. Fords home is a mansion in Beverly Hills. Mr. Fox and I are greeted by servants offering us drinks and hors d'oeuvres as we enter the estate. We are ushered into a large parlor where a large number of people are mingling. I am thrilled when Mr. Fox introduces me to Mr. John Ford, the famous director. He says, "Good seeing you Bill, and nice meeting you Mr. Walker. Follow me. We'll go to my office."

We are seated in lush leather chairs in front of Ford's large desk. A number of exotic African taxidermy specimens hang on the walls. "This is quite an undertaking that you will be engaged in Mr. Walker," Ford says.

"Please sir, call me Ace, everyone else does. Really, I had already enlisted and was finishing basic training at Fort Dix when this situation arose. I was already going to see battle anyway. Now it'll be just in a different capacity."

There's a knock on the door.

Ford says, "Come in."

I am dumbfounded when Frank Capra and Jimmy Stewart walk into the room. I had just seen the Capra movie starring Jimmy Stewart entitled, "Mr. Smith goes to Washington." Introductions are made and the new arrivals actually greet me as Mr. Walker! I am trying not to look like a starstruck jerk, but I'm having trouble doing so.

Capra says, "John probably has already told you Mr. Walker that we are making a documentary film on the war. You are the last correspondent that we needed. We had the European and Pacific theaters covered but not the Desert Campaign. We understand that you will be serving in the Desert. Am I correct?"

"Please call me Ace Mr. Capra, Mr. Stewart; and If the 2nd Armored Division is going to the desert, then I'll be with them."

Stewart laughs his Jimmy Stewart laugh and says, "Good. Let's get rid of these formalities here. Ace just call us Frank and Jimmy!"

I can't believe that I'm in a meeting with William Fox, John Ford, Frank Capra, and Jimmy Stewart! I say, "I'm honored gentlemen."

Capra says, "We're extremely happy that your newspaper is allowing us to reap some of the benefits of you covering the war." And yes, I've been told by British General Bernard Montgomery that your General Charles L. Scott will be joining him somewhere around Libya.

"That's news to me Frank."

Capra says, "I believe that was divulged to me in order for you to better prepare your equipment against the conditions there. You must allow for extreme heat and damaging sands. I'm sure the rest of it is all hush- hush. I want you to know that you are to feel free to photograph any skirmishes your Charlie company gets into. No matter how terrible or gruesome it appears on your camera we want you to film it. We will determine if it is unsuitable for viewing by the general public. We will edit what we must.

Stewart says, "I'm starved. What's for chow John?"

"We're having pheasant under glass tonight and some excellent Chardonnay."

Again, Stewart says, "I'm ready. Shall we join the others?"

"Ford calls for his butler, "Watkins would you come in please."

"Yes sir Mr. Ford, how may I be of assistance?"

"Watkins please show my friends here into the dining hall, and bring in the others to join us please."

"Yes sir, thank you sir."

As we enter the large dining hall I am seated between Jimmy Stewart and another Columbia Picture's star, Van Johnson. Ms. Susan Heyward sits across from me.

I Introduce myself and Ms. Heyward asks, "Were you related to that incredible man William J. Walker from Delaware Mr. Walker?"

"Yes ma'am, he was my father.

"I met him once In New York. He was a dear, dear man.

"Thank you, Miss Heyward, we miss him."

Van Johnson says, "Frank has told me you are to be a war correspondent like you father was Ace."

"That's true Mr. Johnson."

"I'm disappointed that I won't be joining you or Jimmy. I had a bad car accident not long ago and the draft board certified me 4F. I understand you plan on doing some flying Jimmy?"

Stewart answers, "Yes, I've done some single engine piloting; and I'm training now in the Army Air Corps. I have been commissioned as a First Lieutenant and am flying the B-24 Liberator bomber. Looks like I've been elected to drop some bombs over a few enemy targets."

Ms. Heyward says, "God bless all you men!"

After dinner Jimmy Stewart pulls me aside and says, "I want you to know Ace, that both Frank Capra and John Ford are good honest folk. I know you'll have times when you will hesitate to shoot the action that you are witnessing because of the hideous happenings. Like they already have told you they'll edit what you film. I just want you to know that you can trust them both.

I answer, "Thanks Jimmy. Will do."

I spend the next two weeks at the Movietone news studios studying to be a professional photographer, and film maker. I was loaned out to Warner Brothers to practice my filming while their picture "They Died with their boots on" was being made. I shoot the film of their civil war and Indian war reenactments and meet Mr. Errol Flynn who was playing General George Custer. I think that he was drunk during most of the filming of that movie. Nobody said anything, but it was rumored that he was disqualified for military service because of his drinking and drug abuse. Mr. Fox and his staff later critiqued my filming of that picture's war scenes. They informed me that it was excellent.

It was at the end of these two weeks that I called Coach Jensen back at Fort Dix. He informed me that one-half of the 2nd Armored Division infantry would spend the next four weeks in advanced training at Fort Benning Georgia, while the other half of infantry, and the tank crews were being sent to Manchester, Tennessee. It seems that General George S. Patton, as well as our General Scott want to practice tank maneuvers there. Governor Prentice Cooper announced that nine counties would be used by the Army. This area was now being dubbed "The Tennessee Maneuver Area", and Mr. Jacobs orders me there. We both know that filming these maneuvers would be the perfect situation for me to hone my craft. I meet up with my friends in a large area filled with rows of tents of which are our barracks. We call this "Fort Tent City," and before it was declared off-limits, we go to a saloon in the small town of Manchester; and Mike Collins comes with us. We soon renew old friendships with whiskey and beer chasers, except for Mike of course, although he can put down cups of coffee like I have never seen before. He has certainly become a great friend, albeit a sober one.

We discuss our new assignment here, and I can't believe it when Andy explains that the maneuvers that will be conducted here, will actually mimic Confederate General Nathan Bedford Forest's calvary maneuvers during the Civil War. He had developed tactics so lethal to the enemy that they are still being studied at this site!

CHAPTER 23

During reveille the next morning I rise and shine with the rest of the troops. I simply stand aside since I no longer have to fall into formation. Sherman Tanks and infantrymen will conduct mock battles on this land belonging to the McFarland farm family. Infantrymen will dig foxholes from where they practice defensive positions. When on the offensive they follow behind tanks for the shielding protection they provide as they as they move forward towards the enemy. Luckily instead of becoming infantrymen, my friends Andy, Mike, and Paddy have been assigned a tank. I say luckily, although there are ways to die inside the Sherman tank. Its protective armor is to be desired during heavy combat fire. I hope this beast will also be my home as we travel. The tank commandeered by my friends is christened "Thumper" after the hard foot pounding rabbit in the Disney animated movie "Bambi". His caricature and name are stenciled on the tank's turret.

Andy has been promoted to Buck Sergeant and is assigned as the "Tank Commander". He is the "Boss", "The Man in Charge", "The Big Cheese".

Mike is the "Driver" taking "Left Stick", and "Right Stick" orders from the commander.

Paddy is in his glory. He is the "Top Gunner". With his foot he fires the huge 75 mm big turret gun. The coaxial mounted 30 cal. machine gun is fired by his hand.

The "Loader" is Private Matt Laskowski, who went through basic training with us. Nicknamed "Ski", he's from East St. Louis, Illinois, and it's his responsibility to keep all the weapons and the main gun fully loaded with ammunition.

The fifth member of the crew, the "Co-Driver and Bow Man Machine Gunner", is Private Joe Knight from Boston, Mass. I plan to sit in the tank next to the loader at times. But I'll spend the majority of time riding topside next to Paddy with his hatch open or walking along with the infantry grunts.

I ask Andy, "I understand Paddy's quick promotion to Corporal is because he is a fighting and killing machine, but how were you able to sew on those three Sergeant stripes so soon?"

Andy answers, "The Tank Commander position must be filled by a junior officer or at least by a non- commissioned officer. We had very few officers available in our Company, so they promoted a few men early. I have to prove myself by operating this tank or I'll lose these stripes. I can't afford to do that Ace. I need to send the extra pay back home to Becky."

"It's hard for me to believe that three former Blue Hens will operate this beast together. How are Matt and Joe working out so far?"

"They are both nice guys Ace. So far, we are starting to gel as a team. We are constantly practicing our drills every day. Right now, it's "Prepare to Mount –Mount," "Prepare to Dismount—Dismount". We must be able to quickly get in and get out of our tank. That could save our lives. Mike is becoming excellent at driving "Thumper" in the way I need it to go, and Paddy is a madman and already an expert in firing the weaponry. We'll be split up into two armies next week to practice maneuvering against one another."

That's great Andy. I promise to follow your orders and stay out of your way at all times. That is if you allow me to tag along with you."

"As long as Jensen allows it, I'm okay with it.

"Is there a space that I can stash my cameras?

"Yeah, next to Laskowski."

"Thanks Andy. I think I'm going to interview the owner of this property that we're playing war games on. I want to know how the people of these counties feel about their new uninvited guests."

That afternoon I take a Jeep from the motor pool and drive to the McFarland farmhouse. I meet the owner Mr. McFarland, and he grants me an interview. I can tell that this middle-aged suntanned man has mixed emotions about the Army's arrival.

He says, "It was a bit of a shock. There's not a day that goes by that my wife and I don't think about the young soldiers, and how they're preparing for WWII in our back yard. I know all of the farmers here feel the same way. It's winter so it's not costing us any cash crops but repairing all of these tank tracks and foxholes afterwards will be a monumental task. I believe the effort required in doing so is going to be miniscule compared to the danger that these men will have to face. God bless them all. Somebody has to protect our nation, or we wouldn't even have these farms for very long. That's my opinion. God bless them!"

CHAPTER 24

The next week becomes filled with the constant barrage of loud gunfire and explosions. Both blank ammo and sometimes actual live ammo is used during target practices in M3 105mm howitzer canons mounted on half- track vehicles, and in our Sherman tanks. In our tank Andy, the commander, now nicknamed "Boss", must control the revolving turret to the direction of intended target. Then it is the gunner, in our case Paddy, who using a periscope with a sight reticle and a six- power zoom scope, zeroes in on the object. It takes the average gunner five to six seconds for him to aim and fire the "Big Gun". Paddy can do it effectively in three! He is also best in both battalions in direct hits versus misses! It seems that Corporal Patrick Michael O'Brien was born to be a tank gunner.

Our once ace baseball pitcher Corporal Mike Collins has now received the nickname of "Preacher" and he has demonstrated his quick reflexes, and exceptional hand eye coordination, in positioning "Thumper" faster than all other drivers receiving their commander's orders. The driver needs to be able to drive the tank, often without knowing what he is driving into, while trusting the eyes of the commander to keep him out of trouble. He needs to know what his tank can drive over and climb, and what it can't. Allowing your tank to fall into an uncontrollable position is an embarrassing thing to do. If a tank were really disabled, it might require more than one tank to pull it out, and if the resources in your platoon couldn't do it, you had to call in for other help. Crews would get a lot of heat for doing that. It has never happened to "Thumpers" crew.

Our loader Laskowski, must service the big 75 mm gun. He would yell "up," and the gunner would know that it was ready to fire. The loader is also required to watch the ammo belts on the machine guns to make sure they don't run dry. If a lot of firing is taking place, the loader is a very busy guy. He has a fair amount of ease to get to the racks for the main gun, but since the turret basket is screened, he can only get to them with the turret at certain bearings. A good loader is paramount to rapidly firing the tank. "Ski" is remarkably fitting the bill!

The co-driver Knight nicknamed "Sox," is becoming highly efficient with the 30cal. machine gun mounted on the front. Every fifth round is not a bullet but a tracer thus indicating where you are hitting.

As tanks go our Sherman is reputed to be pretty easy to drive, our GAA powered model is the easiest. Learning to drive it is the easy part, where and how to drive it in combat and just over what terrain it could go, that will be the real challenge. Our tank's mechanical toughness makes it easier for Collins to worry about the important parts of his job. "Thumper's" five- man crew is responsible in keeping it running. This means keeping up on a long list of chores from checking track tension and adjusting it, to tightening the bolts on each end link on both sides of the track run, to checking the oil and radiator fluids, or the batteries. There are also numerous things to be hit with the grease gun, and others that have to be adjusted. The radios also require constant attention to keep them operating properly.

The first articles I write for the "Inquirer" is about the duties of the crew members on the Sherman. I also send film of target practices.

Daily life finds us living in our tents and eating in a large mess hall canvas structure. Everything is canvas, including the latrines and shower facilities.

All of the Sherman's are lined up in a tank park, with an area set aside for maintenance. Every day, we drill, clean, and maintain the tanks. We now participate with our other 3rd platoon basic training buddies, who have joined our infantrymen, in marching drills. Coach Jensen calls the regular cadence and sings it out:

Jensen: You get a line and I'll get a pole.

All: Honey, Honey.

Jensen: You get a line and I'll get a pole

All: Babe, Babe.

Jensen: You get a line and I'll get a pole

We'll go down to the fishin' hole.

All: Honey, oh baby, mine

Go to your left, your right, your left.

Go to your left, your right, your left.

Jensen: I had a girl who lived on a creek

All: Honey, Honey.

Jensen: I had a girl who lived on a creek

All: Babe, Babe

Jensen: I had a girl who lived on a creek

She was cute and she was sweet.

All: Honey oh baby mine

Go to your left, your right, your left.

Go to your left, your right, your left.

I did the filming as they did the marching, but I must confess, I wish I were marching and singing with them! I must remember I am not in the Army. And yet I find myself helping "Thumper's" crew and my best friends all that I can. I don't wear the uniform with insignias of rank or Division logos, but I do dress in U.S. Army fatigues. I have the word "PRESS" on my hat, my helmet and clothing. I will not carry a rifle into battle because I am not to take part in any offensive action, however, I have been issued a Colt 1911 model 45 cal. handgun and a K-bar knife for defensive purposes. I begin to realize more and more that I'm going to need an assistant to help carry my production equipment, and to film me with the action in the background.

After the fourth week of training, Charlie Company receives something that I believe they sorely need…. a three- day liberty pass! "Thumper's" crew decides it's too distant to journey to their homes, and the small hamlet of Manchester won't provide the fun they seek but, hold on to your hats; because Nashville is only 65 miles away! I don't include myself as a member of this outfit and my official title is "Contracted Observer," but I feel as much a part of this group as the next guy. Andy, Ski, Sox, Paddy, and I decide we'll go to Nashville to party hearty. Mike decides he needs to catch up on the scriptures and do some letter writing.

We hop on a Greyhound Bus Friday morning, not having to report back until Monday noon. My friends look sharp wearing their class "A" dress uniforms, and I'm pretty dapper in my tailored brown suit. We are all smiles, but as I look at Paddy talking to Ski, I already start to worry. He has that leprechaun's mischievous twinkle in his eyes. I've seen it before.

The "Boss" is sleeping, and in talking to Sox, I ask him, "I've been to Boston once, what part are you from?"

"I'm fum Chawlstown Ace. Home of the most bank wobbes in the nation. Hey, you eva' been to Fenway Pawk?"

"No, my dad and I were St. Louis fans and we used to see the Cardinals play the Phillies at Shibe Park in Philly."

"Say Ace you gotta talk to Ski he's fum that aea. He woots fau those boids also."

"I have to say Sox I love your Bostonian accent. It's funny how you never pronounce the letter "R" when it's there as in "Pawk the caw"; then you always pronounce it when it isn't there, as when in idea you say "idear.""

"The way we speak is wite, evybody else is wong!"

We arrive in "Music City" and check into the "Ryman Hotel." The "Boss" says, "I've been here with my dad once before, and I'm going to take you guys to the best place for lunch. We hire a cab and he says, "take us to "Smokey Joe's," driver"; and twenty minutes later we are stuffing ourselves with the absolute best, fall off the bone, melt in your mouth, smoked ribs known to man, while washing them down with pitchers of beer. As we continue our gluttonous indulgence, we watch the pedestrian traffic across the street strolling to a brick building, with a large overhead marquee stating that it is the "War Memorial Auditorium", home of the "Grand Ole' Opry". We walk over to investigate and see that Roy Acuff, Hank Williams, Ernest Tubb, and comedienne Ms. Minnie Pearl will be playing tonight.

We buy tickets for the 7 pm performance; and now having a few hours to kill, we fortunately discover the "Red Stag Saloon", which is right next door to the "Opry". However fortunately turns into regrettably, because after a full day of drinking we stumble fairly intoxicated into the show. Although I am no big country-western music fan, I enjoyed Hank Williams singing "Hey Good Lookin" and Minnie Pearl wearing her straw hat with the $1.98 price tag dangling from it. She cracked me up.

All of us were having a good time until a very tall man, wearing a large- brimmed cowboy hat scooted through the aisle in front of us and took a seat right in front of Paddy. Now Paddy, being only 5ft 4 inches tall, taps the man in front of him on the shoulder, and says, "Pardon me bloke, but I can't be a seein' the show. Could ye be movin' down a piece?"

The man turns to Paddy and says, "If you cannot see the stage, I suggest that you do the moving!"

Paddy says, "Again, I'll be askin' ye kindly, would ye take to leavin' a ways down apiece?"

The cowboy answers, "Look you little runt, you better be doing the moving!"

Well, that was all it took, and Paddy says, "By the saints, you be one ugly bloke. Ye were born at home and when your poor dear mother saw ye, she ran to the hospital! Take this ye bloody fool! Then Paddy punches him in the face, jumps up on his seat and throws himself on top of the man. They fall to the floor with Paddy on top, and our Irish friend starts beating the man mercilessly. Eventually an usher comes over to stop the altercation, but Paddy will not stop hitting the man. The usher starts blowing a whistle and a policeman runs over to us and starts grabbing Paddy by the hair. This makes Ski angry, and he throws a right cross into the cop's face. Meanwhile the manager upstairs in the balcony calls his security team and they race to the incident. They accidently knock Sox down while trying to get to Ski. This infuriates the Boston man, and he starts fighting two of the guards. Andy and I try to stop the fighting with no luck, and it continues until we hear whistles blowing and police making arrests.

I could take a long time explaining about what happens to us next, but I'm not. Simply, we all end up in the Nashville City jail. Andy calls MSgt Jensen at "Fort Tent City," and he in turn sends an Army bus with two M.P.'s to pick us up. The Nashville PD then releases us into the custody of the military. Our three days of liberty turns into one day of misery, and all five of us are taken to see the Regiment Commander Lt. Col. John J. Parker.

In his office Andy and I are seated while Paddy, Sox, and Ski stand at attention in front of the colonel. The 2nd Armored Division Provost Marshall a Major Frank Burns reads the City of Nashville's charges against us.

Lt. Col. Parker reads both documents. He asks me, "Mr. Walker I understand that you were a witness to these happenings. Do you have a written statement regarding them?"

I answer, "Yes sir, I do." I give him my report of the incident. He reads it as well.

He addresses Major Burns and asks, "What is your position on this incident Major?"

Burns says, "These men have been a disgrace to the United States Army sir. I wish to see Corporal O'Brien, PFC Matthew Laskowski, and PFC Joseph Knight stripped of their ranks, be issued Article Thirteens for misconduct, and serve a period of thirty days in the regimental brig.

The colonel stares at the major. He just stares. Then he turns to me and asks, "Your witness report suggests that this so-called cowboy instigated the altercation. Is that correct Mr. Walker?

I answer, "Yes sir, it did."

"Corporal O'Brien did you win the fight?"

Paddy answers, "Oh yes sir, colonel sir, we beat the bloody hell out of em!"

The Colonel looks at the Provost Marshall and says, "Frank we are about to embark on the most terrible war that our nation has ever known, and you are suggesting that we take these three men, who obviously have a tremendous fighting spirit, and happen to be the best tanker crew in the whole 2nd Armored Division and jail them? I don't say no, I say hell no! I want to give them commendation medals for their fighting spirit. In fact, I am issuing their five- man crew including one Corporal Collins "Achievement Medals" for being the top performing tank crew in the glorious 2nd! You soldiers keep that spirit and pummel to death those Nazi monsters! All of you are dismissed!"

The guys salute and leave, except for me. I figure that this is a good time to put in a request for an assistant. "Permission to speak Colonel."

"Go ahead Mr. Walker."

"Sir may I say that was a wise decision on your part sir."

"Thank you, Walker, but it was just common sense. We must win this war son."

"Yes sir. Sir it has come to my attention that I will need an assistant in order to fulfill my contract with the Army. Could you give me some assistance in this matter?"

"You are assigned to Charlie company of the First Battalion?"

"I am sir."

"I will contact your C.O. Lt. Steiner about this Walker. That is all. Dismissed."

As we go back to our quarters Paddy says, "I be lovin' this bloody Army, and that colonel is a mighty fine bloke. If he's a wantin' some Nazi killin', I'll be a givin' it ta him!"

I know that almost every man who has faced death before going into combat, from the Roman Legions through WWI, has feared for his life, and if given a choice would not go to war; and yet there are some, a small percentage of men, who actually love the idea of fighting. They not only relish the idea of killing, and the threat of being killed, but seem to thrive on it! Our friend Paddy is one of these men. He epitomizes a quote I once read from the author Ernest Hemmingway. He wrote, "There is no hunting like the hunting of man, and those who have hunted armed men long enough and liked it, never care for anything else thereafter."

CHAPTER 25

We have been in training for five months. I wake up one morning with an idea about a series featuring individual soldiers. After lunch in the chow- hall, I take my motion picture camera and walk up to a Private First Class and ask, "Hello soldier, would you like to say hello to the folks back home?"

"I sure would!"

"What is your name and where are you from?"

"My names Don Baylor and I'm from Athens, Georgia. How y'all doin' back there? Go you Bulldogs you!"

"Before the war what did you do in Athens?"

"I worked as a janitor at the University of Georgia. I loved it cause I got discounted tickets for football. My dad Billie Bob got me that job cause he worked there too ya know. Hiya mom! Hiya dad!"

"Do you plan on going back to Athens after the war?"

"Yes sir, as soon as we kick this Hitler fellas rear-end, I'll be headed back to Dixie!"

"Thank you, PFC Baylor!"

I continue shooting multiple sessions of these shorts and mail them to the Movietone news studios.

There are rumors of our deployment overseas daily now. Our tank crews are excelling in their maneuvers, and our infantry is well practiced in the use of their weaponry, and are skilled in close up combat. Our artillery units are ready. We have become a well-oiled fighting force. It has been said that Africa will be our destination.

Within a week we are shipped to the Brooklyn Navy yard for deployment overseas. We board four U.S. Navy troop -carriers, and the entire "Hell on Wheels" 2nd Armored Division is shipped out to Casablanca in French Morocco.

According to my contract, I have authored articles and filmed training exercises for my newspaper and Movietone news. One evening aboard ship the soldiers are treated to a movie called "The Philadelphia Story" starring Cary Grant, Katherine Hepburn, and my new buddy Jimmy Stewart! Before the film, a Movietone news flash is shown as their famous journalist Lowell Thomas narrates the film describing the action on different military training facilities. When our "Tennessee Maneuver" site comes on, I appear on film and explain some of the action that's being shot. Some of the guys recognize me and I get my first applause!

Right after the film I am approached by a young Private. He says, "I saw you in the film Mr. Walker. I am Private Jimmy Huston, and I have been told by your Company NCO Master Sergeant Jensen to report to you sir."

"What about Private Huston?"

"The sarge says I am ordered to be your assistant sir; that is if you accept me sir."

"Alright, let's go to my quarters and we'll discuss it. Follow me."

As I look at this soldier, I see a short, skinny, red-haired, and freckled face kid. He would be a smaller version of Andy when he was seventeen years old.

My quarters are actually a nook in a corner where my cot is.

"Do you mind if I film this private?"

"No sir, go ahead."

"I ask, "How old are you, Jimmy?"

"I'm seventeen sir, but I'll be eighteen in three months."

"Do you have any experience in photography?"

"Yes, sir I do. That was the question Sergeant Jensen asked all of us in Bravo Platoon. He said no one in Charlie Platoon had any experience. I raised my hand and told him I did. You see sir, my father owns a camera shop in Craig, Colorado. It's called "Huston's Photos" and I worked with him there. I was taught how to develop pictures in our darkroom. We did a lot of work for guides and their hunters by capturing on film the animals they harvested. I love the outdoors sir, and I became somewhat proficient as a wildlife photographer."

"Here are the cameras I will be using. Are you familiar with them?"

"I have used the Kodak Medalist before sir, but I have never done any motion picture filming. I want you to know sir that I am smart and I would quickly learn. Please sir, give me a try. Photography is the love of my life."

"You are an infantryman am I correct Huston?"

"Yes sir."

"I want you to know that if I agree to make you my assistant that you will be transferred to Charlie Company and be under my orders. You will be expected to carry your rifle and my equipment bag. I need to be able to free up my hands for filming combat action. Do you understand?"

"I do sir."

"Alright we might give this a try, and I stop the camera. I'm sure we'll have plenty of time in Morocco for practice, before the real action begins. Move your belongings over here by me. You may have the next cot. We'll be interviewing some of the soldiers in each Company.

125

You will do the filming and I'll ask the questions. Then you will take some portraits of them which will support the articles I'll write for my newspaper."

Days are spent talking and photographing. Each day Jimmy would follow me as I would approach a soldier and ask:

"Hello soldier I'm Ace Walker from "The Philly Inquirer", may I ask your name and where you're from?"

"My name's Eddie Sanchez and I'm from San Antonio Texas sir."

"You don't have to call me sir. I'm a civilian. Tell me a little about yourself."

"Well, my mother owns a restaurant in San Antonio called "Rosa's Hacienda." She serves the best tacos, burritos, tamales, and chili in the whole state of Texas. I work there as a waiter. I don't know about you two guys, but I think this Army chow is "muy malo por favor"! Oh, excuse me. I sometimes think in Spanish. I think this food is very bad senor! I miss my mother's cooking!"

"What Company are you in Eddie and what are your duties?"

"My buddy Ben and I are in Easy Company, and we are in Artillery. We fire a 60mm mortar. We plan on givin' em hell were we're going!" Jimmy films the sequence and also takes a snapshot of Eddie Sanchez and I draft the article.

All of our interviews use the movie camera, and film the soldiers as they look into it and tell their story.

We approach another soldier, Jimmy starts filming, and I ask, "What is your name soldier and where are you from?"

"My names Roy Williams and I'm from Casper, Wyoming. I'd like to say hello to my mom and dad. I miss everybody especially my dog Bailey. I want you all to know that I'll be coming home soon when this mess is over. I plan on starting up that gas station on Bridger Street."

We continue doing this daily as we head towards our destination. When I telegraph the Inquirer, Mr. Jacobs telegraphs me back, and tells me they want more of the same. He also says Mr. Fox at Movietone news wants the "Soldier of the Week" spots to become a regular part of the program for U.S. movie goers in American theaters. He claims that a large number of letters have flooded the studio in favor of them. Before the main feature film is shown in theaters an episode of the Movietone news will be shown, and Lowell Thomas will announce the "Soldier of the Week."

My new partner Jimmy is always ready, willing, and eager to learn new applications about our job. Sergeant Andy, "the Boss," Corporals Paddy and Mike "the Preacher," and Privates Sox, and Ski are all more than anxious to get to Morocco. I believe that the anticipation of the actual combat that is to come can become mentally draining on an individual.

Late one evening on the fifth day of our voyage I couldn't sleep and went outside to the bow of the ship to smoke a cigarette. I am all alone and enjoying the beautiful evening when a Navy commander comes over to join me.

He asks, "Got a light?" I light his smoke. "I'll never get tired of this view", he says. "It looks so peaceful"; as he exhales smoke from his cigar.

I say, "It is the calm before the storm Commander; the quiet before the hell. Older men and politicians declare war. But it is the youth that must fight and die. They called the last war "The War to End All Wars." They were sure wrong about that one, wasn't they sir!"

"Yes, they were. You're that reporter Ace Walker aren't you son?"

"I am."

"I saw you on that newsreel they showed on ship. You're becoming quite the celebrity young man. I understand that your films are being shown at theaters all over America."

"The real celebrities and hero's commander, are the young men that are going into battle ready to die for our country."

"War is hell Walker. The great General William Tecumseh Sherman once said. "I am sick and tired of war. Its glory is all moonshine. It is only those who have never fired a shot, nor heard the shrieks and groans of the wounded who cry aloud for blood, for vengeance, for desolation. War is hell."

"Amen to that sir! I might add the philosopher Herodotus said, "In peace, sons bury their fathers. In war, fathers bury their sons." It is not the natural order of things."

"No, it isn't Walker but right now it's what we have to live with. By the way, we'll be arriving in Africa tomorrow. I hope to see some of those "Soldier of the Week" shows you are producing. The American public needs to see them!"

"My newspaper and the movie studio have told me to continue to make them."

"That's good Walker. We need all of the diversions we can get right now. Keep up the good work."

He finally walks away, and I'm left alone with my thoughts. As I stare down at the waves slapping the bow of our ship, I become mesmerized by the monotony of its repetition, and I retreat deep within my mind. It doesn't take long for that empty feeling to consume me again. I know I am missing something in my life, but I have no idea what that something is.

CHAPTER 26

We arrive in North Africa. A city of Quonset huts and tents have been erected to house the thousands of troops. My friends in "Thumper's" tank, and Jimmy and I, are able to commandeer our own tent. I found a welder in Charlie company to construct an apparatus on the outside back of our tank to carry all of my equipment.

Jimmy and I have spent our days following "Thumper" and practicing with our filming equipment. At night Jimmy is sent to retrieve the beer for our tent. These are our daily rituals as we await orders to see combat. One evening a movie entitled "The Sea Wolf" is being shown at our newly constructed outdoor theater. It stars Edward G. Robinson, Ida Lupino, and John Garfield. Before the film we are treated to a Mickey Mouse cartoon, and then Jimmy and I see one of our "Soldier of the Week" spots on the "Movietone" episode. It starts with my smiling face as I ask the usual, "Hello soldier, what is your name and where are you from?"

"I'm Dan Rice from Punxsutawney, Pennsylvania."

"Isn't that where that famous weather- forecasting groundhog is from Dan?"

"Yes, sir it is, and I've been privileged to be a member of the "Inner Circle" that wear the big "stovepipe" hats during "Groundhog Day." When I get back home, I plan to open a museum in honor of

"Punxsutawney Phil." I want to say hello to my mom and dad and to my little sister Ruthie. Hey guys! Do you believe it? I'm in a desert!"

Then the serious and foreboding voice of Lowell Thomas announces, "And now for a look at the fighting in the Desert Theater of War! General Edwin Rommel head of the Nazi Afrika Korps takes the British 7th Armored Division by surprise near Benghazi. Rommel the so called "Desert Fox" and his Panzer tanks destroy over 110 tanks and other heavy equipment of the Allied forces, causing them to retreat to a defensive line near Tobruk. The Axis forces have made a great advance against the "Desert Rats." This is Lowell Thomas reporting for Movietone News!"

After the film we go to our hut for our evening poker game. Four of us Andy, Paddy, Ski, and I are playing. I deal after the ante. Andy opens with a dollar and the rest of us call.

Andy takes three cards, and says, "Things really are looking bad in Tobruk." Paddy takes one card; Ski and I both take three. Andy continues with, "I wouldn't be surprised if the Brits call for some of us Yanks to come to their aid.

I bet two dollars." Paddy folds and Ski calls. I'm holding three fives and raise two dollars. Andy calls, Paddy folds, and Ski calls. I lay my three of a kind down and find that I beat Andy's two Queens and Ski's Two tens. I win the pot and say, "Do you think that Division would lend some of us out?"

Andy says, "I do, and I believe that they will."

It turns out that Andy is prophetically correct, because in only two weeks the entire 1st Battalion, consisting of all of our six Companies, Bravo, Tango, Easy, Delta, Juliet, and our Charlie Company are ordered to join General Richard O'Connor's 7th Armored Division in the port city of Tobruk Libya. This will include 24 tanks, Anti- tank guns, heavy artillery, and about a thousand infantry and machine gunners that will be shipped across the Mediterranean Sea. We board our ship, two days after receiving our orders. Two U.S. Navy destroyers accompany our troop carrier during the crossing. They are guarding us against both air and submarine attack, and we safely arrive and join what seems to us as a beleaguered British 7th Armored Division.

When we arrive and set up our provisional tent. Lt. Steiner and Sergeant Jensen pay us a visit. Steiner says, "Sergeant Andrew Harrison You have been promoted to Staff Sergeant and now are the Charlie Company's Non-Commissioned Officer in charge. Your last NCOIC, and I don't even want to mention his name, has been detained in Casablanca with criminal charges." He hands Andy a set of stripes and tells him to sew them on and wishes him good luck. "We head into battle tomorrow gentlemen. Get a good night's rest!"

I take one look at Andy and say, "As quick as you're making rank, you'll be a Full Bird Colonel by winter!"

After they leave, "Preacher Mike" calls us together and says, "I know you're against this Ace, but please join us in prayer." We all kneel together, and Mike prays, "Lord we are in your hands as we are about to be baptized into the destruction and death of this war. We see this enemy as evil for they would destroy your holy word and your people. They would conquer our entire world with their filthy doctrine. We would say, as the prophet Isaiah said so many years ago in Isaiah: 6:8 "Also I heard the voice of the Lord saying, whom shall I send, and who will go for us? Then said I, here I am, send me!" Yes Lord, we say send us Lord. Help us dispatch this evil force, while keeping our crew safe Lord. We ask this in Jesus our Lord and Savior's name amen."

I don't believe that prayer can help our cause, but it made me feel better as our group voiced our desires together.

It's still dark as we advance towards the enemy, and our line of tanks are ordered to stop. The infantry starts to frantically dig foxholes in front of them. Mortars are positioned up front with the infantry and heavy artillery to the rear. The 37 mm anti-tanks guns are pulled next to our Shermans. I position Jimmy and myself on an incline about 100 yards behind our forces and quickly glance at my watch. It is 0500 hours. I start my verbal commentary as flares are shot upward by both sides. As

131

they slowly return to earth the dark becomes light and all hell breaks loose! Rifle fire is accented by machine guns rapidly discharging. The loud booms of the tank's big 75 mm guns, and the artillery, and mortar fire complete the ear deafening scene of death and chaos before us. I am screaming into my camera's microphone in an attempt to describe the madness that I'm witnessing and filming. Jimmy is my bodyguard at this time. He is not discharging his M1. We are to remain solely observers.

I look to find "Thumper" in my camera, and when I spot her, I zoom in on our tank and witness Paddy firing and hitting a German Panzer directly on its turret. The enemy tank bursts into flames. Andy immediately swings his turret at another target and Paddy swiftly shoots and cripples another Nazi tank by hitting its track drive. No infantry men are advancing toward each other. The battle is being waged by the large weaponry and foxhole fire. I tell Jimmy to continue to hold his position and film, as I make my way to the foxholes. I want to film the terror from their viewpoint. The firing continues for a long time, and as I look at my watch again, it informs me that a full six and a half hours of killing has transpired. The enemy is beginning to slowly withdraw...... Then they go into full retreat. We are ordered forward in pursuit as our tanks take the lead and the infantry vacates their foxholes and takes cover behind us. The thunderous consistent noise of heavy artillery fire slows, and now screams of agony can be heard. Cries of "Medic! Medic!" are shouted. Wounded men are crying and asking for their mothers. Severed limbs are scattered about. Jimmy and I follow behind all of the action while filming and taking photos of the devastation.

Eventually we catch up with our friends in "Thumper", and Andy and Paddy open their hatches and stick their heads out and greet us. Preacher Mike, Ski and Sox drop out in the bottom escape hatches. I put all my equipment on the tank, and except for Preacher we light cigarettes. Paddy is beside himself with joy and shouts, "We showed those bloody buggers boyos! I counted we killed 7 Panzer tanks. And you Sox emptied your 30 cal. into a great number of them filthy Krauts!

We are ordered to change our formation to a night- time defensive position. Afterwards we pull out our K-rations. As usual that is when the art of negotiations can be observed. Each package of rations contains various food items that are traded between the GIs, but the most desired items are the four cigarettes which can be bartered for sticks of gum or candy. At the same time Sergeant Jensen walks over to talk. He tells us, "That was a battle we won boys. The British reported they had 17 killed and 38 wounded. They also lost two tanks. Our Battalion lost 3 men 8 wounded but lost no tanks. We suffered no casualties in Charlie Company. Compared to the beating the German's took ours is minimal."

I think to myself why? What is so important, that old men somewhere, could possibly conceive that anything so horrendous as I have just witness could possibly be justified! I get out pen and pad and draft my article about the scene of depravity that happened right before my eyes!

The next day infantry and two British Commando troops move into the beleaguered town of Tobruk, Libya, to clear out any remaining enemy soldiers. They meet with little resistance. The 7th Armored and us, their attachment, moved into the city and set up a headquarters building. General O'Connor is in attendance himself and has scheduled a meeting for 1500 hours. All Officers and Company NCOs are ordered to come. I am also asked to attend.

British Lt. Colonel James Ashburn stands on a podium with a large map behind him. With pointer in hand he explains, "Rommel's Axis forces are progressing toward El Alamein, Egypt. As you can see, El Alamein is only 106 kilometers from Alexandria. By the way, that distance is 66 miles for you Yanks! At any rate it is imperative they be driven back. They are too bloody close to our shipping ports and supply lines. The 8th is to the west of them, and our strategy is to drop down and attack them from a southern position. We will call this Operation "Valley Forge" as a thank you to our American friends. By the way you Yanks, command has sent down a thank you for your fine effort at

Tobruk and is awarding your Charlie Company, of the 1st Battalion the "Africa Star" medal. It was recorded that your company destroyed 11 Nazi tanks. Good job gentlemen! You will be notified when we depart. That is all. Dismissed."

It is time for celebration in Charlie Company, because Lt. Steiner is promoted to Captain; and I can't believe it, but we actually find a restaurant in a Muslim country that sells alcoholic beverages. Let the party begin! We jam into the café and toasts are being made. One is made by our new Captain to Paddy, "Here's to our Irish bulldog Paddy O'Brien. He gets the deadeye dick award for blasting 7 of the 11 panzer tanks our Company destroyed. Nice shootin' "Thumper"! We slam our whiskeys. Then it seems like it comes out of nowhere; a beautiful tenor voice starts singing solo an old WW1 song:

"Johnnie get your gun, get your gun, get your gun,

Take it on the run, on the run, on the run,

Hear them calling you and me.......

Every son of liberty.

Hurry right away, no delay, go today,

Make your daddy glad, to have such a lad,

Tell your sweetheart not to pine,

To be proud her boy's in line.

(And then the whole Company sings the chorus!)

Over there, over there,

Send the word, send the word over there,

That the Yanks are coming, the Yanks are coming,

The drums rum-tumming everywhere.

So, prepare, say a prayer,

Send the word, send the word to beware.

We'll be over, we're coming over,

And we won't come back til it's over, over there!"[5]

Cheers! Laughter! Applause! We are showing our bravado, our toughness, and machoism. We are letting off some steam. And I believe that there is great joy and relief from the pressures and threats of dying a sudden death.

Two days later we leave for operation "Valley Forge" to engage the enemy at El Alamein. The fear of death remains in our throats but is lessened by becoming battle tested.

[5]**"Over there" song by George M. Cohan**

CHAPTER 27

The horrors of battle happen once again in "Operation Valley Forge". Our tanks and infantry are engaged in the destruction of the enemy. Again, SSGT Harrison and the crew of "Thumper" distinguish themselves. They actually break ranks and advance further towards the enemy while machine gunning German mortar nests, destroying anti-tank artillery, and decommissioning five Panzer tanks. I pride myself in capturing their heroism on camera! This fighting also has me looking and filming the battle in the skies, as our P40 Warhawks engage in aerial dogfights with German Messerschmitt fighters.

As I film men killing men, I am appalled again at the absurdity of it all. Hatred has ensued between the leaders of our countries, prompting these acts of killing and revenge. Confucius once said, "When one plans to take revenge against another, he should first dig two graves." I witness this truth as men are falling on both sides. These men are bitter enemies; and yet in some other place, in some other time, they could just as easily have been good friends, simply enjoying a beer together.

Jimmy is proving to be valuable to me. He has freed me to film sections of the action that otherwise would be impossible to obtain. He is also producing great close-up photos of the men.

The fighting in El-Alamein lasts for three days. We are victorious once again! The Nazi's are pushed back far away from our ports. We remain in our current position and relish the time we have without the battles.

There is one momentous occasion, that when it occurs, it trumps all others. It is mail call! A voice more beautiful than any heard at "Radio City Music Hall", is our postal man crying out MAIL CALL! All other activities cease, and we all run to the mail truck as our courier calls out Kassley! Mulroney! Donahue! Hursey! Walker! Upon grabbing the most precious gift a man could receive, he goes to a place as secluded and as quiet as he can find, and loses himself into the contents of the letter from home. This is actually a piece of home! It is more than read, it is consumed. It is studied at least three times.

I am fortunate to receive three letters.

One is from my mother informing me that she and Uncle Robert are growing closer. They just spent a week together on "Miss Minerva" cruising to the North Carolina Outer Banks, and Roanoke Island. She tells me how much she misses me.

Mr. Jacobs assures me that if I keep up the good work, that I will have a first- rate full time position with the "Inquirer", with a doubling of my current salary.

But the letter I treasure most, I open last. The envelope is saturated with Irene's perfume, and the letter reads,

"Dear Ace:

I hope this letter finds you somewhat safe. My thoughts and prayers are with you every day, and I worry so. You are becoming quite the celebrity, because it seems that everyone sees you and loves your segments at the theater during the Movietone episodes. I was thrilled when you wrote and told me that you met Van Johnson, Susan Heyward, and Jimmy Stewart! By the way, Ginger Gable and Don Jankowski, your old first baseman, got married and have an apartment near the college. Most importantly I want to let you know that because of your story, Pennsylvania state officials have closed the Byberry Asylum in Philadelphia for complete renovations. I understand that Roger Sutcliff is now incarcerated at a mental hospital in York Pa. It is said to have much better conditions. I love you darling. Always remember that you promised that you would come back home to me. The fragrance on this letter is from a Paris perfume I now wear called "Nostalgia." When you get home, you'll be smelling a lot more of it!"

XXXXX IRENE

Every day now becomes a boring, monotonous, but relaxing routine. Most of the time is spent on the cleaning and maintenance of "Thumper." We just await further orders from headquarters. Then one day I am called into the captain's quarters. I walk in and Sgt. Jensen greets me and asks me to sit.

He asks, "Coffee Ace?"

"Yes, please Coach. You don't mind me calling you Coach, do you? It brings back good memories of home."

"No go ahead. I wish I were back to being just Coach. I want you to know that the captain is going to ask you for a favor in going on an assignment. This assignment came down to him straight from headquarters. Personally, I don't think your newspaper will approve of it. I believe it could be quite dangerous. You do what you think is best."

"You have piqued my interest Coach. Oh, by the way, I had some news from home. Do you remember Ginger my old girlfriend? She ended up marrying our first baseman Don Jankowski."

"No kidding. I can't believe she'd marry that lunkhead! But after all he's a pretty nice guy. All our guys were except for one."

"The one you are thinking of was moved to a nicer facility."

Coach snaps to attention, as Capt. Steiner interrupts our conversation by walking in. I remain seated. "Good to see you captain. I understand that you wanted to see me?"

"Yes Mr. Walker thank you for coming."

"Please, just address me as Ace captain."

"Alright Ace. Although you are not officially a part of our 1st Battalion, we are thankful for what you do. Your films and photos help our "esprit décor" and encourages the folks back home to aid us with the things we need. Did you know that Jimmy Stewart mentioned your name as he was getting into his B-24 to pilot a bombing mission?"

"No sir I did not. I haven't seen that Movietone news flash as of yet."

"Well, he did. He said he met you in Hollywood at a Frank Capra dinner party. He said that you capture the spirit of our fighting men. ......Well anyway Ace, we need your help. The reason I called you in here, is because Division believes that a few different Companies of Nazi soldiers have parachuted into different sections of the Sinai Peninsula. We think if they really did, then they are planning to join together somewhere in an area there. We want to know if that's true, and if so, where they are. An Army Air Corps pilot has landed his P51 Mustang here yesterday. This is not a normal Mustang as it is equipped with two drop tanks allowing it a range of 1375 miles. It has a top speed of 437 mph. It is equipped with a "Fairchild K-17 camera" for high altitude reconnaissance. Its most unusual alteration has been to install a rear passenger seat to allow a co-pilot to operate that camera. I understand from the higher ups that you are familiar with this camera. Are we correct?"

"Yes Captain, I have had instruction with it, but I would be of no use as a co-pilot."

We wouldn't expect you to be Ace. All we want is a film of the entire Sinai area, you certainly won't be flying the aircraft. We need an expert cameraman. Would you accept such a mission?"

"I would have to get permission from my newspaper to do what you're asking. I understand our contract states that my duty is to film only on land, and specifically with Charlie Company."

"We will telegram your newspaper in code, and our translator who will be stationed at your paper, will decipher it for you. To whom should we address the telegram?"

"Send it to the assistant editor Mr. John Jacobs, and for his eyes only. His daughter is his secretary and my girlfriend, and I don't want her knowing about this." Captain Steiner and Coach laugh at this development.

Steiner concludes with, "Report back here at 0900 hours tomorrow, Ace."

Back in my tent, I lay on my cot, light a smoke, and think about the mission that Division HQ's wants me to undertake. If a force of Nazi's is building up south of us. Then they are planning to squeeze us from both sides. This is definitely intelligence we must obtain. It could prove to be vital as to which side will win in the desert campaign. Andy comes in, sits down next to me, and says, "Looks like your deep in thought Ace. What's up?"

"Division wants me to make a recon film over the Sinai."

"What would you fly in?"

"Some hotshot pilot just flew in with a Mustang."

"How do they expect you to do that? A P51 only has one seat for the pilot."

"Evidently this plane has been retro-fitted to carry a passenger and a high- altitude camera."

"Wow! I bet that's a tight fit. What did you tell them?"

"My answer depends upon what my newspaper decides. We're waiting for a telegram from Philly. If they give it their okay, then I'm all in."

Whiskey out of tin cups ends my night.

Time flies, and just when you think tomorrow will never come, it's already yesterday.

I'm back in the captain's quarters, and it looks like time isn't the only thing that's flying. The Regiment Commander Lt. Col. John

Parker is present, along with the captain and Coach. Steiner hands me the telegram. It reads: Go for it <u>STOP</u>. They have agreed to us give a copy of the film <u>STOP</u>. We have to wait one month to print it <u>STOP</u>. Just make sure you get it <u>STOP</u>. <u>Jacobs</u> STOP.

Captain Steiner says, "Ace this is Lieutenant Paul Mitchell. Lt. this is Mr. Ace Walker of the Philadelphia Inquirer newspaper. I understand that you both have previously met the colonel."

The LtCol. says, "Lt. Mitchell, we'll have you know that Mr. Walker here is a war correspondent that has seen combat action up front and personal. He's an expert cameraman. If you hot dog that P51 out there, Ace will get the filming done. I can't underestimate the importance of this mission we're sending you on. It is vital that we know of any enemy troop movement in the Sinai region. Your orders are to film the entire Sinai area at an elevation that would confirm any evidence of Wehrmacht or SS troops, as well as any artillery that they may possess. Your rules of engagement are not to fire upon the enemy under any conditions. This is strictly a reconnaissance mission. There is, however, one exception to these rules. If their Luftwaffe has aircraft in the air, I repeat in the air and not on the ground, you are to engage and destroy. The way your Mustang has been revamped it definitely will out- maneuver their Messerschmitt. Do you understand your mission fully Lieutenant?"

"Yes sir, I do Colonel."

"How about you Mr. Walker?"

"I do Colonel with one exception. At what elevation do you suggest that we film?"

"I don't have any suggestions. You're the expert. I don't care to see them eating sauerkraut and sausages. I just want to know if they're there, where they are at, and in what numbers. Is this understood?'

In unison we answer, "Yes sir."

Then you are ordered to depart in four days on the 20th of July at 0700 hours. I will personally see you off, in case I receive further instructions from the Division. Thank you, gentlemen. I'll see you then." Jensen and the two officers salute the colonel, and Mitchell and I leave together.

"Well lieutenant, it looks like you and I are going to spend some high times together; and yes, the pun was intended."

"Yeah, and the sooner the better Ace. I can't stand these periods of waiting before an assignment. The only thing that comes to him that waits is whiskers!"

"Why don't you join me in the chow hall, and we can get to know each other better."

"I'm in favor of that."

As we eat our meals I ask, "Where are you from LT?"

"Burlington Vermont. The land of green pristine mountains. It is breathtakingly beautiful Ace. What about you?"

"I'm from Rehoboth Beach Delaware. Land of the Atlantic Ocean and the Blue Crab!"

"Never heard of it."

"You never heard of which, the Atlantic Ocean, Delaware, Rehoboth Beach, or the Blue Crab?

"I'm just kidding. I know that Delaware is on the ocean, and to clarify my answer so is Rehoboth Beach and its famous culinary delight the Blue Crab."

"The crab might be famous to some, but not me. I'm strictly a meat and potatoes guy. By the way, I know you're in this miserable war, but I'm curious, how did you manage to stay out of a military uniform?"

"It's a long story LT, I was almost done with my studies at the University of Delaware when I enlisted in the Army and went through basic training as a lowly private. Then they were going to send me to OCS when my newspaper the "Philadelphia Inquirer" and the U.S. Army decided that they needed another war correspondent, and I was elected. I agreed when it was confirmed I could do my job alongside my original platoon I had in basic. Three of those guys are friends I went to school with. I now have a civilian contract with the Army.

"Are you married Ace?"

"Not yet LT, however I have a gal that I like, and she's pushing. Are you hitched?"

"No, I'm enjoying the bachelor life of being the "handsome, dashing and daring fighter pilot." That has definitely been working for me. I see marriage as a three- ring circus: engagement ring, wedding ring, and then suffering. .... and I have always been afraid, that if I put a ring on a gal's finger, that she'll put one in my nose."

"If you're finished eating, come with me and I'll introduce you to "Lulu.""

"Who is Lulu?"

"My plane. She is fast, hot, and beautiful. She has all the moves, and she has the curves in the right places. She really is a Lulu. We have only three days for us to get in some practice. You're not going to get sick, are you?"

"Whittaya mean? I just ate. We're not going up now, are we?"

"Absolutely we are! This is my ground ride. Hop in! Believe me this is not a Willy's; this is a Ford Motor Company Jeep. It has a much more powerful engine than the Willy's or the American Bantam Jeep models. All my rides must be fast whether I'm in the air or on the ground. I have a need for speed Ace!"

We drove the open- air Jeep to the airfield at a breakneck speed I never thought was even possible in one of these vehicles. Due to the ruts, we were airborne as much as touching the ground. We park next to a shining silver red-tailed P51 Mustang with the name "Lulu" painted on the cowl.

The Lieutenant asks, "Isn't she gorgeous Ace?" I admitted she was.

"When this war is over, I don't care what it costs, I'm buying her and taking her home!"

I ask, "Do those six small airplanes painted on her by the engine exhausts represent Messerschmitt kills?"

"Yes, they do. Lulu and I are most proud of those! It is her jewelry! She is one incredible aircraft Ace. Her heart is a Rolls Royce Merlin two-stage, intercooled, supercharged engine that takes her to speeds up to 440mph, and she's armed with two 6.5 caliber AN/M2 Browning machine guns, plus two 250lb bombs, one mounted on each wing. Come on let's take her up. You ride behind me. Put on the helmet and jacket that's sitting on your seat. Rolls of film are under your seat. Load it in and let's take a few practice shots. You asked the colonel a good question about what elevation we should film. You'll have to determine the best elevation for our needs. You'll also be advising me as to what speed you want to film at. But it will have to be over our 100-mph stall speed. Anything below that speed we will lose lift and plummet downward.

Have you ever experienced "G Forces" before?"

"No, I haven't, but I've read some of the science about them."

"Here's a piece of chewing gum. It may stop your ears from popping."

"Army Air Tower this is P51-Alpha niner -seven Tango requesting permission to taxi to runway."

"This is Army Air Tower. Taxi to runway 21 and hold P51-Alpha niner-seven Tango."

"Copy that tower."

We hold our position on runway 21 until the crackling sound of the tower comes back with, "P51 Alpha niner-seven Tango permission to takeoff and hold 280 degrees until clearing our perimeter."

"Copy that tower, this is P51 Alpha -niner-seven Tango taking off on a heading of 280 degrees. Roger and out tower....... Hang on to your hat Ace!" He fully depresses the throttle in and in mere seconds he rotates, and we gain lift! Evidently there was more throttle left, because my head jerks back and is glued to my headrest as Paul angles the plane steeply into the blue.

"I ask, "Where are we headed?""

"Let's head over and see King Farouk in Cairo. It's less than two hundred miles away and we'll try shooting film at different elevations. First, I'll show you some of the maneuvers "Lulu" can do. We'll do a loop, a roll, and then a spiral dive."

As LT is performing the maneuvers, I am doing everything I can to keep from vomiting.

"Now, I got to show you this Ace. I know of no other aircraft that can do a perfect 16-point roll. Watch this!"

I closed my eyes, gritted my teeth, and watched nothing.

"Isn't that amazing?! That was 16 stop and go while in a roll. That is a precise 22.5 degrees for every pause. My girl is a sweetheart!"

"LT, I have had enough of the air show theatrics, let's try filming at 1,000 feet."

"Roger that Ace. By the way, I want to ask you a question. You'll notice our friends the Brits use kilometers and meters instead of miles and feet. They use the metric system of measures. Why do we use the imperial system?" … …Because we Yanks believe if the good Lord wanted us to use the metric system there would have been only 10 apostles instead of 12." He laughs and I try to.

I ready my camera and tell LT to slow to 150 mph. The zoom lens on my camera allows me to focus in order to get the correct aspect ratio to the ground's clarity. After filming for a short time, I tell LT to drop to 800 feet, and I find that elevation perfect for what we need to accomplish. We also slow to 125 mph.

LT shouts into his headset, "We can't go any slower Ace, my controls are already getting mushy."

"Then take it back up to 150."

The aircraft responds, and LT says, "That's perfect Ace. Go ahead and take some more shots."

We continue to practice our aerial recons for about another hour when LT starts singing "We're off to see the wizard, the wonderful wizard of Oz! The wonderful, wonderful, wonderful, wonderful, wonderful wizard of OZ!"

Then in a fraction of a second my head's thrown backwards and is cemented to my head rest, as LT takes Lulu full throttle.

A half hour later we touched down at the Alamaza airport in Cairo. I ask LT, "Hey! The chewing gum didn't help the popping. Now how do I get it out of my ears?" LT gives me a stupid questioning look, then bursts out laughing."

When are we heading back?"

"Why are you in such a hurry Ace? We have two whole days to ourselves. Are you that antsy that you want to go back to that tent and cot? I want to show you how some of us flyboys live!"

He hails a taxi, and we go to a place called "The Private Villa" in the heart of Cairo. "I am under orders to keep "Lulu" hangered here in Cairo, so Uncle Sam has provided yours truly with an apartment. The taxi drops us off at an old but elegant hotel complex. I have no baggage, but upon seeing LT, a hotel valet immediately grabs his bag and follows us into the hotel lobby. As we walk past the desk clerk he says, "Welcome back Lieutenant sir."

"Thank you, Omar, we'll most probably be needing room service this evening."

"Yes sir, thank you sir."

As we walked through this elegant luxurious hotel I ask, "I thought that all aircraft were parked together at various bases. How did you manage to escape the fleet and become a singular entity?"

"There are four of us pilots positioned at various areas within the Desert Theater of War. We are what the Air Corps call SPB's or

Strategically Placed Bandits. When HQ needs somebody in a hurry, one of us is notified.

We climb some stairs, and the valet opens the door to room 201. "Wow, I exclaim! This place is fit for King Farouk! I walk through the four rooms admiring the elegance of LT's lodgings. I tell him, I don't think General Eisenhower himself has a place this nice."

CHAPTER 28

After the shock of seeing, (how did LT put it) how some flyboys live, I admit I'm jealous. I walk outside onto a balcony that overlooks a swimming pool that's nestled in amongst a number of palm trees, large leaf exotic shrubbery, and flora of all color. People are seated at a small outside bar; others are either sunbathing on lounge chairs or swimming. This entire scene exudes a setting of pure hedonism in the middle of a war. After the hell that I've been living in the 2nd Armored Division, this feels as though I have been magically transported to another planet, in an entirely different solar system. When I walk back inside LT is holding up a pair of swimming trunks. He says, "These should fit. Let's go down to that bar you were eyeing. I'm expecting some company. Oh, and Ace, would you please settle down and try to relax. Just consider yourself on two days of R&R (rest & recuperation). I have a full wardrobe of clothes here that will fit you. We also have carte blanche in this hotel courtesy of Uncle Sam. He wants his pilots to be happy. We live by that old Roman gladiator motto of "Eat, drink, and be merry, for tomorrow we die!"

All right LT I will. But before you get too cocky, let me remind you of another old adage that says, "Live fast, die young, and leave a good corpse. In your job that will be easy to do."

We take two stools at the bar and LT says, "Hello Nahab, how you been?"

The bartender answers in perfect English, "Very good lieutenant. What will it be sir?"

"Well now Nahab when I read about all the evils of drinking ......I gave up reading. So, give me a double scotch and soda; after a while I'll be too blitzed to read anyway."

"And you sir?"

"Canadian Club" on the rocks."

"Make it a double also Nahab because this man is always uptight. Please meet Mr. Ace Walker, whose only fault is that he thinks he has none."

It takes me a couple of drinks to mellow out. I light up a Lucky Strike, slowly exhale, and begin watching the two-piece swimsuit parade, as these exotic and beautiful women waltz around the pool. LT asks, "Pretty nice, huh Ace? Happiness is finding the owner of a lost swimsuit."

"Very admirable LT, you know statistics are like a two- piece bathing suit. What they reveal is suggestive, but what they conceal is vital."

Just a few minutes later two of these beauties come up from behind LT. One grabs him around the waist and the other starts kissing him passionately.

He laughs and says, "Girls, girls, slow down! There's enough of me for everyone! I want you to meet a friend of mine. This is Ace Walker. Ace these two gorgeous creatures are Shani and Aziza. They both are waitresses here at the villa. Shani is, what you might say taken; by me that is, but Aziza is in expectation! By you that is! We're going to have a great time Ace, let your hair down and enjoy!"

I say, "Well girls, I must admit it is a great pleasure to meet you both; and I believe Aziza that Cleopatra in all of her glory would be no match for your beauty. You truly must be the Queen of the Nile."

Aziza says, "Oh Mr. Ace, you are much kind to me. Will you take me boat?"

"What boat is she talking about LT?"

"I lease a 25 ft "Chris Craft" runabout here. It's kept in a marina on the Nile. Tell me Shani where would you want Ace and I to take you?"

Shani says, "We wish to go to Club Gezira! We wish to dance the "Rags Sharqui."

I say, "I'm sorry ladies but I'm afraid that I'm a very poor dancer." The three of them burst out laughing.

"And what did I say so funny?"

"The girls don't want you to dance stupid. They want to dance for you. They are belly dancers! The reason Shani mentioned the boat is because Gezira is an island in the Nile. You need a boat to get there. What do you think Ace, shall we go for it?"

Now, my judgement being somewhat numbed by four drinks, I say, "Absolutely!" Then the ladies laugh, and Aziza throws her arms around my neck and commences to kiss me.

LT says, "Ladies we will pick you up at Shani's place on Qesm Ambala Street at 7 pm this evening. Right now, I'm afraid we have some military business to attend to, and we must leave you." He kisses them both goodbye and we leave.

Buzzed and disappointed I say, "What military business? I want to stay and get to know the ladies better. What is wrong with you LT?"

"I guarantee that you will get to know Aziza very well Ace. But right now, we need to recharge. I have ordered kebobs for an early dinner in our room. Then we'll rest, because it is going to be a long evening my reporter friend."

After a delectable meal and a nap, we dress and leave. LT's wardrobe fits me perfectly. We are both dressed in light tan cotton suits and straw Panama hats, as we climb into a 1936 Rolls Royce Phantom convertible. As LT drives us in the open air on this beautiful warm Egyptian evening, everything seems surreal to me. My mind goes back to my dad, and I wonder if he experienced anything as delicious as this. Yes, I think, he undoubtedly did, and I am thinking of the right word…. delicious, not fantastic nor wonderful, but delicious, because I have never tasted anything so elegantly exciting as this. Then I get a pang of sorrow as I think of my friends back in the war zone. But this extraordinary evening…... in this unbelievable paradise…… quickly dissipates any thoughts I have…… except for those of the immediate future.

LT looks at me and smiles. He says, "You have no idea what you are in store for my friend. This will be the most sensuous evening of your life. But be careful and do not drink too much. They will be serving us Ouzo, which is a strong, but enchanting licorice drink. Pace yourself Ace, believe me you'll want to be sober for the last part of this evening. By the way, how much cash do you have on you?"

"Not much, remember you brought me here without any preparation."

"I thought as much. Here are five one-hundred-pound Egyptian notes. It's a loan. You can pay me back later."

"Why do you think I'll need so much?"

"The girls are usually a very expensive date."

"Thanks for the warning, because tonight, the hell with everything, and the devil can take tomorrow!"

We pick the girls up, and Aziza and I take the back seat. Palm trees pass overhead as we drive. We kiss and frolic all the way to the boat. I am now determined that nothing is going to spoil this evening for me, and I justify this premise because of the things that I have endured since the start of the war. I have had my own personal, private, pity party for too long now. It's time to let some festering frustrations out.

We arrive at the marina and trade the convertible for the boat. Again, Aziza and I take the rear seat, and we motor off. Never in my life would I have ventured to imagine myself cruising down a moonlit Nile, with a stunningly exotic woman in my arms. I look into her dark sloe eyes, fondle her copper-colored skin, caress her long black hair, and kiss her seductive lips.

I was almost disappointed when we tied up to the Gezira Club pier.

When we enter the club, I am taken by the colors of this ancient culture. The glitz and glamour of the reds and golds of these sultanic draperies and furnishings are beautiful. A concierge takes us to our seats, which happen to be cushions arranged on the floor looking toward a small dance area. Placed between the cushions is a large clear glass vessel with a long tube extending from it. I ask LT, "What is this?"

"That is a hookah Ace. It has water in it, and it is used for smoking hashish."

"You like?" Aziza asks.

I answer, "I don't know, I've never tried it before."

Shani says, "We fill hookah and get ouzo LT! Please LT!"

The waiter comes over and brings us our drinks, and then fills and lights the large pipe. "How do you work this thing?" I ask.

Aziza says, "Like this." She proceeds to inhale the smoke, then kisses me and exhales the vapors into my lungs. I attempt to smoke it myself and take in a big drag of the cannabis smoke. Then I had my first taste of ouzo. I think if you like licorice candy, this would be your drink.

LT warns, "Easy does it Ace!" Later they serve us finger foods, and kebobs with bowls of mouthwatering sauces for dipping. We smoke, drink, and eat for about an hour, then both girls leave us. I understand from LT that they are getting ready to perform.

When the curtain opens Shani comes on first. She is dressed in a traditional costume which has more skin and less costume. She is exposing a tremendous amount of cleavage and her belly button is winking at the world. She starts dancing to a musical instrument that I found out later is called a Zummara, a type of double reed clarinet. A single drum accompanies the dance. She uses her hips to punctuate the percussive beat of the drum. She moves in long flowing, sinuous movements in which her body is in continuous motion. Her abdomen modulates constantly while doing loops and tilts with her hips. Her ribcage shimmies, shivers, and vibrates sensually as her arms and legs are used to frame and accentuate the shape of her body. It is exotic. It is mesmerizing. When she ends the dance there is a tremendous applause.

Aziza dances next, but this time an instrument called a Ney replaces the Zummara. It produces a similar mournful sound as an oboe. She is dressed somewhat more scantily, and her movements seem to me to be more sensual, more fluid, and more passionate. I am filled with lustful cravings. I imagine myself entwined with her. I am lost within her visage and satiated with a lustful covetousness for her body. The night lingers on slowly as in a dreamful haze, aided by the drugs and alcohol. Hours pass by…………..

Later we arrive back at the Villa with the girls in tow. They will be sleeping over! My mind thinks of Irene. I do love her, but in my drunken haze I hum to myself, "Irene, goodnight Irene, Irene good night. Goodnight Irene, goodnight Irene. I'll see you in my dreams! But in the meantime, due to my inebriated estate, and while I'm yet conscious I will without remorse ravish Aziza.

****

It's the "next morning". The problem with "next mornings"; let me clarify; I mean when the "next morning" is the morning after.

I awaken with a nasty dry mouth, and what feels like a Nazi dagger piercing through my skull. My entire body is resentful with me. When I get the courage, I turn over and discover Aziza lying next to me, and I stare up at the ceiling and immediately think of Irene. I am full of regret that I cheated on her, but I did just experience the most incredible day of my life. Then in evaluating it, I wonder why I feel so empty inside, so hollow? I just experienced a night any man would have craved for. Why this morning, as I look at her, am I not overjoyed? Is it guilt? Everything seems to me to be meaningless. Everything is without merit. What is wrong with me?

I'm hungover, that's what's wrong with me. And I slowly drag my body out of bed and go to the shower. After dressing, I come out of the bathroom just in time to see LT handing the girls some money as they leave. Aziza looks back at me, smiles, and blows me a kiss. Then it hits me. They were hookers. I look at a still naked LT and he says, "What did you think Ace? Did you think she fell head over heels in love with you? I assure you Aziza liked you very much. However, it was her job to like you. That was one great, unforgettable evening Ace. Tonight, we will have another one but this time it's the casino and some gambling!"

The day starts out with a sumptuous breakfast of eggs, herring, and assorted melons. My hangover is starting to subside, and I believe that this whole experience with LT has been one amazing adventure, although I wonder what will happen as we canvass the Sinai for enemy troops. Now stop that, I tell myself. This war can wait for one more day, and I spend it recuperating by swimming in the pool, reading, and sleeping.

At 1900 hours we find ourselves in the "Lucien Barriere Casino" in the heart of Cairo. LT goes to play blackjack and I head to the craps table. Nine people are playing on this minimum ten-pound bet table. As I wait to throw the dice, I win three 20-pound side bets, and lose one on the pass line.

The croupier hands me the dice, I'm now the shooter. I lay down a 40-pound bet and toss the dice. I roll a 7, a winner. I leave the 40 pounds and throw an 11, another winner. I'm now up 80 pounds. I look at the croupier and say, "Let it ride." I shake the dice a little longer in my hand this time, and when I throw them a sweet 6 and a 1 stare up at me. Now up 160 pounds, and I'm feeling really lucky...... "Let it ride!" This time I throw the dice harder and they ricochet heavily against the back wall and after retreating they display a 5 and a 2, another seven. After four passes and being ahead 320 pounds, I'm starting to get the fever and I holler, "AGAIN!" As I start to roll a crowd begins to gather around to place side bets. This time I shake the dice with both cupped hands and toss them gently against the rear wall, and the result is another 11. Everyone surrounding the table breaks out in cheers! I can't believe it but I'm Up 640 pounds!

The croupier eyes me and says, "Please sir, use only one hand when throwing the dice."

"I look around at my fellow gamblers and say, "Last time, double or nothing!"

Right away a beautiful redhead snuggles up next to me and asks, "May I help?"

I nod affirmatively and she takes the dice and softly blows on them. "For luck" she says seductively."

I whisper back, "And eighty pounds are for you", and I throw the dice. No pass this time. I roll a 3 and a 2, and I realize that five is a tough point. I now must roll a five to win. If a seven shows it's face now, I'm dead. More onlookers gather around.

I hesitate for a minute, take a deep breath and I let 'em fly. After their tumbling a 4 and a 1 decide to reveal themselves! I JUST WON 1,280 POUNDS!!!

The crowd goes nuts!

The croupier scowls!

The redhead grabs me and drowns me with kisses!

I hand her eighty pounds in chips!

In a fit of joy, I throw the dice half- way across the casino floor (which is really the smartest way to throw the dice)!

More of the crowd draw closer to offer congratulatory praise, as I begin to gather up my chips…… I stop. I resume picking them up…… then stop. I think to myself, "Don't do this. Don't do this. Please don't be stupid and do this Ace! No-no-no don't!

And then I shout, "ONE MORE TIME!"

A hush comes over the crowd.

The croupier smiles, and flings me new dice.

I put them into my open hand and hesitate as I contemplate their glossy red hue. As I prepare to roll, the large, gathered group is totally silent. All is hushed. I feel a drop of sweat irritating my eye and I reach for my handkerchief that isn't there. The redhead smiles and gives me hers. I nod, turn, and throw the dice all in one motion.

Me and the entire mob rubberneck towards the dice as they land and settle on a 6 and a 6, BOXCARS. A LOSER. I just blew 1280 pounds.

No one in the crowd says anything, they simply walk away. Yeah, everybody loves a poor loser...... if they don't have any bets on him.

Red gives me a "I'm so sorry" love tap and leaves.

Oh well, so it comes to pass, as the gambler would say, and I tell myself to cheer up. It just proves that gambling is a way to get nothing from something. At least I had fun. There is a lot of people in this world that wouldn't even bet on a crap game, and yet they turn around and get married.

I need a drink and a smoke, so still somewhat dejected, I saunter over to the bar. The bartender, a tall, pale, mustachioed, and balding man asks, "And what will ye be a havin' tonight sir?"

I am really thirsty. How about a cold beer.

He asks, "is a "Sakarra" okay?"

I tell him yes, and I thought I detected a British accent. He brings it over and I ask, "English?"

He answers, "Yes sir, Liverpool. You American?"

"Yes", I answer, Delaware. I'm Ace Walker. Have you bartended here long?"

He says, "Bout two bloody years now. Good job. Great tips. My names George, and it's nice to be meetin' you. And can you believe it? We have one bloody Kraut with us in hiding tonight."

"Where?" I ask.

"Take a look at that bloke with the blonde hair, white dinner jacket, and black bowtie standin' over by the roulette table. I 've been a watchin' him tonight. I can smell 'em. He's a bloody "Heinie" alright! Probably a spy."

"George has grabbed my interest, and I ask, "How can you tell just by watching?"

"Look at the way he holds his cigarette. He holds it between his thumb and index finger with the lit end pointing to the ceiling. Germans do that. Everyone else cradles their cigarette between their first and second fingers, pointing the lit end away."

I study the man's movements, and think that he may be correct. I add, "Have you noticed anything else peculiar about him?"

"He and another bloke were sittin' in here at the bar last night. The joker we're eyeing speaks English perfectly, but the other chap spoke with a definite German accent. I think they're up to somethin'."

"I believe I might investigate more closely George."

I light a smoke, carry my drink over to the roulette table, and take a seat next to the blonde- haired man. When the wheel stops, I place a 20 -pound bet on 21 black. He is talking to a woman sitting next to him. When the wheel stops the ball lands on red 32. The man says to the croupier, "I think we must throw der ball out and get a new one." The players around the table start to laugh. I mock laugh, but I have caught an error in his speech. He used the German word "der" instead of "the." I place another bet on 21 black and lose again as red 6 comes up. I listen carefully and hear no other mistakes in his speech and put another bet down on 21 black. Third time is charm, and my number comes up. A winning bet on a single number pays 35 to 1, and the croupier pays me seven-hundred pounds. Everyone at the table applauds my good fortune. The suspected spy says, "Very lucky sir!" I nod my head in thanks, and say, "Luck is when preparation meets opportunity kind sir."

Learning my lesson from the craps table I picked up my chips and went back to the bar. George comes over with another Egyptian beer. I ask him, "Is he booked into the casino hotel George?"

"Yes, he is. In fact, he always runs up a bloody tab and has me charge it to his room. It is number 515. He's a big tipper too, usually thirty percent."

"What time does he usually quit playing?"

"He usually quits roulette at 12:00 and then plays some blackjack until 2:00 am."

I thank George, leave a 10-pound note on the bar, and go over to the blackjack tables to see LT."

Take a break LT. There's something I want to discuss with you."

"Hit me dealer...... Damn another bust! Okay Ace I'm out of here."

"Let's go to the Lobby. We need to find someplace private to talk."

"What a night Ace. I'm down 600 pounds! How are you doing?"

"Better than you I'm up 700 pounds, in fact here's the 500 you loaned me. But listen closely LT we may be bigger winners tonight!"

"What do you mean?"

"I think I've spotted a German spy in the casino."

"How?"

I explain everything to LT and he says, "We need to make sure we're not wrong. We have to check out his room. When we came in tonight and passed by the front check-in desk, I think I saw the spare room keys hanging on a board behind the clerk."

I look at my watch and say, "It's 11:00 p.m. now. The bartender said he doesn't stop gambling until 2:00 a.m. You go to the front desk and buy a newspaper, then take it to the far end of the long check-in desk and engage in a conversation with the clerk. Keep him occupied until I can sneak around and take the spare key to room 515."

LT does just that, and gets into a conversation with the clerk. I get on my hands and knees and crawl around to the keyboard. I stand and search down through the columns of keys and notice that there is only one hook empty. It is the key for room 515. This, at least in my mind, confirms to me that blondie is being cautiously secretive by keeping the spare key to his room. Then I sneak back around the desk, and see that LT is still conversing with the night clerk. I tap the bell on the countertop and the clerk looks around to me.

"I'll be right with you sir."

I say, "Thank you, I'm rather in a hurry."

LT takes his newspaper and goes and sits down on a lobby sofa. I tell the clerk, "I know it's rather late, but I gambled longer than normal. I would like a room for the night." I peruse the keyboard and see that two sets of keys are hanging for room 513. "If you please clerk, I have stayed in room 513 before and would prefer it."

"Yes sir, quite right sir, please fill this out." I pay by chips and go to the elevator. LT, newspaper in hand, follows me. On the fifth floor we walk past room 515 and open the door to the adjoining room 513. LT and I immediately investigate how to gain access to blondie's room. There is no adjoining room door. We walk outside onto the balcony. It is a good fifty feet from us to the suspect's balcony. A narrow ledge extends between them. I stare horrified at the prospect of traversing that tiny protrusion to the other window. I am an admitted acrophobic. Heights scare me to death. I look at LT and say, "You or me?"

"You look white as a ghost Ace. Are you afraid of heights?"

"Yes," I admit.

"Then get out of the way, I can do it."

I watch as LT steps over our balcony and then starts inching his way across the six- inch ledge to the other one. It takes him but five minutes to negotiate the crossing. He tries opening the sliding balcony door, but it is locked. Then I see him slide up the adjacent window. He looks at me, gives me the thumbs up, and climbs inside. I run out of the room and stand in front of Room 515, when it opens, I enter.

We each start searching for evidence, confirming that our accusing minds are correct, that he is indeed a Nazi spy. We find nothing until I open a closet door and discover an elaborate short wave radio system installed. "LT come here! Look what I found!" I slowly turn the radio on, and we hear crackle and static.... then, "Lesen sie, lessen sie, das ist deis isteagle! Das is deis isteagle! Lesen sie, Lesen sie!" I shut the thing off. LT opens some shelves and hands me a passport. I look and see the German's face with the name Gregory Andersen, age 39, Swedish citizen. LT then finds an official looking document with the Nazi Swastika printed at the top. Then we discover a picture of a beautiful woman with words written on the bottom saying, "Zu Helmut wth liebe! Katerina." I find a gold ring engraved with the Gestapo skull, pocket it, and tell LT, "My souvenir!"

We look at each other and smile. We have just found the operation of "Helmut the Nazi spy!" "What do we do now Ace?" I make the sound of the stuttering "Porky the Pig" and say, "Th-th-th the, th-th-th-the.... That's all Folks!"

"I think we have two choices LT. One, we turn him over to the local authorities, or two, we kill him."

"I don't trust any of these corrupt politicians or police here Ace. Let's off him!"

"How?"

"Let's not make any noise. We'll sit here in the dark and wait for him. See those cords on the draperies?" LT walks over and cuts a length of it off. "This will make a great garrote! When he comes in you tackle him to the ground and I'll strangle the dirty Nazi to death!"

"Yeah, what about his buddy?"

Hey there Hercules! One at a time Ace! One at a time!

"I'm with you LT!

I sit in a chair against the wall on the side of the door, and LT sits on the bed looking toward the door. Minutes go by seeming like hours. Finally, the door latch starts to click and our quarry steps in, flips on the light switch, sees LT, and screams, "Wer bist du?"

I tackle him to the floor, and he lands on his stomach with me on top of him! LT straps the garrote around his neck. Everything is going to plan until I hear a scream from behind me, and another man jumps on top of me!

I roll over and off of him reversing our positions. He is noticeably stronger than me and pushes me off. We both get to our feet, and I punch him hard in the face. He flies backward through the open sliding door onto the balcony's floor.

Meanwhile LT remains strangling blondie.

My opponent gets to his feet, and I hit him hard again. This time he falls backward over the balcony railing and screams the entire five floors down to the pavement below!

LT makes sure his Nazi has drawn his last breath before releasing the garrote. I quickly pick up the heavy brass base of a table lamp and run to the closet to smash the radio a few times. I holler, "Let's get out of here LT! As we run to the door, I hit blondie in the head twice, just to make sure that he won't be saying any more "Seig Heils." We exit the room and I say, "Let's use the stairs! We scurry down the five flights of stairs and exit the casino hotel. We then slowly and nonchalantly go to our car and proceed back to the villa.

Once in our room, LT grabs a bottle of Jack Daniels and pours us both tall stiff drinks. LT starts laughing and I start shaking. It has always amazed me that the "adrenaline shakes" occur after the action is over and not during it.

"That was incredible Ace!

"You were amazing buddy! Who would have expected that second Kraut. But you took him and went slam, bam, and thank you ma'am, and once again it was "That's all folks!"

I start to regain my composure, quit shaking, and say, "You weren't so bad yourself "Batman"! We laugh again at our exploits and fill our glasses to the brim. "Let's get some shut eye LT. Tomorrow we get out of town."

As I lay on my bed, my mind retraces the events that had just occurred here in Cairo, and I am my own judge and jury. What I did was eat like a pig, stayed drunk, used drugs, had sex with a prostitute, and murdered a man. This was not a Horatio Alger story.

CHAPTER 29

We touch down in El Alamein, and LT goes to headquarters, and I go to my tent. Andy comes over and says, "Where did you fly off to for two days?"

"I was on a secret mission Andy; LT and I killed two German spies in Cairo."

I laugh and he says, "Yeah right! I don't care if you don't want to confess what kind of fun you two had; but it's been boring here Ace. I guess that's better than the opposite though. HQ says our tank crew is up for a commendation."

"That's great Andy, you guys deserve it. I'll talk to you later, right now I need to get some letter writing done." I sit at my make-shift desk and address a letter to Ms. Irene Jacobs, Philadelphia, Pa. I start to write, Dear Irene:

"I hope this letter finds you......" I stop, crumple the paper, and throw it away. Guilt keeps me from writing to her. I start another letter to my mother, finish, and seal it. I realize that I have started to evaluate things I have done in my life that I am not particularly proud of, about certain things that I have never ever scrutinized before. I don't know why I do now .... Is this guilt? Or is this simply a sort of progressing maturity? Life's decisions have always been easy for me; just go for it. If it feels good, do it. I have always been my own man, and I'll do it my way.

Morning comes quickly and Colonel Parker, LT and I are chauffeured to "Lulu". The plane has been fueled, armed, and readied for takeoff. No permission is needed from the tower, because we are priority. The Colonel says, "I have no further orders for you gentlemen. Bring us back some good photography. Good luck!"

We roar off in our Mustang and proceed straight to the Gulf of Suez, then we continue to fly the western shore, then east and cross over into the Sinai at Ra's Gharib. LT says, "Alright Ace, we'll drop down to our agreed upon 800 ft and slow to 150 mph. Then we'll continue along this line until we hit the eastern border and the Gulf of Oman. We'll then turn 90 degrees north for 50 miles and then another 90 degrees west. This heading will take us back across the Sinai to the Gulf of Suez. At our current air speed each crossing will take about three hours. We'll continue crisscrossing this grid until dark"

"Roger that LT. Just keep your eyes out for any troop movement below." I search the landscape with my binoculars. After three crossings we see nothing but sand.

On our fourth crossing back, we are approaching the higher mountain elevations. Mount St. Katherina is the highest elevation at 8,200 feet. LT is faced with the difficult task of flying low in the valleys between the mountain peaks. LT announces, "Look over the to the south Ace. That's Mount Sinai where Moses received the Ten Commandments."

I say, "That's just a story LT. Don't tell me you actually believe that?"

"That is actual history Ace. You know you atheists are all alike. Did you know that there is now an atheist's telephone line? They call it dial -a- prayer when the phone rings on the other end nobody answers!"

"Go ahead and laugh LT. I just don't believe in fairy tales."

We continue our reconnaissance for about another hour until LT exclaims, "We've got company Ace. There's a bogey at 11 o'clock!" I look up and spot the aircraft. It is just a dot above us. I am overtaken by two strong emotions at once. I am elated, because if there is an enemy plane here it must be guarding something, and secondly and more powerfully I feel scared to death!

LT screams, "Yahoo Ace! Let's get him!" ……Then he hits full throttle, pulls back on the yoke and we shoot straight up like a rocket. We then do an inverted loop and attempt to get behind the Messerschmitt but fail. Instead, he is on our tail targeting us with his guns. LT says, "Watch this Ace. I'm going to bank sharply to my right. He'll try to follow but he can't turn as sharply." Sure enough, after our turn the Nazi is on our right wing. Immediately LT shoots straight up an does another inverted loop this time positioning us behind the enemy aircraft. LT has him in his sights and fires both wing's guns! Black smoke comes gushing out of the German plane and it goes into a spiral downward to earth! We fly after it and watch it explode into the ground! "That's right Lulu you wonderful girl! Add another pearl to your jewelry box you sweet thing you! Whittaya think of my girl now Ace!"

"She's quite an aircraft LT, and look down at 5 o'clock!

"We'll I'll be damned if we didn't find them Ace. Look at those Krauts! How many do you think are down there Ace?

"Looks like a full regiment. My guess is about 2,000 troops. Let's head northeast. I want to see if any more are wanting to join them." We head in that direction and approximately 75 miles away we spot another group that appears to be a battalion of 1,000 troops joining the others. I get some great film of their movements and we head back to base.

When we land at El Alamein and immediately report to Colonel Parker, we are surprised that the Division Commander General Scott is present. A meeting is called to order to review our film of the enemy in the Sinai. The General starts by saying, "I have received a letter sent to us from Hollywood, California by Mr. Frank Capra. It reads and I quote:

"Keep up the good work Ace!

You have become quite the celebrity here at home, and

A hero to all of us! It appears that we may just have to offer you

A movie contract in the future!"

General Scott then announces his plan....... "We will meet the enemy in the Sinai where they have gathered and destroy them! I want the entire 2nd Regiment to confront them as quickly as possible. There are two ships already here in this port to transport you to the lower Sinai. It is crucial that the enemy will not be allowed to move further north! We will call this "Operation Clearinghouse." Five tanks will accompany this mission. Lt. Steiner I especially want the 3rd Platoon and especially Charlie Company involved in this action. You depart tomorrow at 0500 hours!"

The remainder of the day is spent moving our regiment aboard the two transport ships.

In the hold of the ship Andy, Paddy, Mike, Sox, Ski, Jimmy, and I sit next to "Thumper" and the seven of us discuss going into battle again.

Andy starts with, "We just need to concentrate on our jobs boys, then we will be fine."

Paddy says, "I canna' wait to be in action again laddies. I love the smell of it! Mother McRae I love firin' the big gun don't ya know!"

Ski adds, "Let's just hurry up, kill 'em all, and go home!"

Sox says, "You got that right Ski. I just wish I were back at "Fenway Pawk" watchin' Ted Williams clubbin' the Yanks."

I look at Jimmy and say, "Jimmy and I agree on one thing and that's simply staying alive!"

Preacher Mike prays, "Lord bless us all. Give us the strength and wisdom to do our jobs properly, and with honor. Bring us safely home."

We spend the evening upon the gulf's eastern shore before commencing into the Sinai.

CHAPTER 30

That morning when we awaken the temperature was already 90 degrees. There are no clouds in the sky, and not a breeze is blowing. Everything is perfectly still. We hear the temperature will reach close to 110 degrees. The interior of the tanks will become like ovens. As we march towards the coordinates of where LT and I mapped the enemy, all tank crews are outside and walking. Only the commanders and drivers have their heads outside their open hatches while driving. We proceed towards the enemy for five hours, then make camp. As the sun slowly recedes into the west we get some relief from the sweltering heat. I say to Mike, "What do you think preacher? Do you think hell is a lot hotter than this?"

Mike says, "I don't know Ace, but I know that I'm not going to find out. What amazes me, is that some men want to gamble their lives away in ignorance of hell's existence."

We continue for another two days before our advanced scouts inform us of the enemy's proximity. We ready ourselves for combat. Jimmy and I take our normal elevated positions behind our lines. We find ourselves on a long, narrow, and rocky outcropping with drop-offs of 30 feet or more on each side. Our front lines are dug in with expectations of the Nazi advance......and it happens quickly. I start to tape the loud explosions of the battle beginning. The large 75mm guns of the tanks start their deadly competition with each other. Then I hear Jimmy firing his rifle behind me. When I turn, I see him shot and falling to the ground. Evidently a group of German snipers circled around our position from behind. I drop to the ground, throw the camera down, and pull my sidearm from its holster. Three Nazi soldiers are to my left and I start firing upon them.

Then, everything turns black!

PART THREE

CHAPTER 31

The first thing I feel is that my tongue is swollen and stuck to the inside of my cheek. I try to unstick it and can't. Then I feel the agony of an acute headache. My helmet is lying next to me, and when I pick it up, I see where a bullet hole has penetrated completely through. I go to touch the left side of my face and discover it is burnt and blistered. I reach further up above my ear and feel a large gash. I look at my withdrawn hand and notice scabs of dried blood. I try to get up but can't. I just lay there and attempt to recall what had happened.

I remember Jimmy falling from enemy fire, then seeing the German soldiers shooting at me. Everything after that is a blank. In a panic I look for my pistol and find it lying right next to me! I'm able to roll over onto my back expecting to see Nazis, and when I scan for them, I see only the outcroppings of the rocks above that I fell from. I know that I fell about 30 feet from that precipice. I attempt to get up and find my right arm useless, and I surmise that it is broken, so I roll on to my left side and am able to get up onto my left knee…… Thirsty! I'm terribly thirsty and grab my canteen off my left hip. The water is hot, but I delight in it. I gather my thoughts, then make an effort to stand, but am not able to do so. Then I look in horror at my right ankle and foot. My right foot is at a 90 -degree angle to my leg with its toes pointing at the heel of my left boot. It is badly broken. I realize I need help and I start screaming, "Medic!…… Medic!"

Nothing but silence greets me. I listen carefully for a long period of time and hear no gunfire, no voices, no movement of men or tanks. Being crowded between these rocks makes me feel as though I'm in a painful cocoon; and the war has left me. I have been deserted! Then I decide that I can either lay here and die or start crawling. I glance at my watch and start inching my way forward on my left elbow and knee along the bottom of the narrow crevice I had fallen into. After an hour I can see outside of my walled prison. A sandy hill comes into view, and I elect to wriggle my way to the top of it in order to get a better view of my surroundings. And then I can see the foothills of the mountains. Thirsty again, I drain my canteen. I realize I need shelter from the sun and heat, so I continue crawling my way towards an outcropping of boulders about a hundred yards away.

Another hour passes before I'm able to reach it, and when I do, to my amazement, I see a cave entrance. After another hour I'm eventually able to drag myself into the darkness, and I notice that the temperature has cooled significantly. I manage to squirm my way further into the cavern and stop against a wall. I hear a dripping sound and move my head, with an open mouth around, until I feel a drop of water enter it. I lap some of it up, and then exhausted, I fall asleep.

My sleep is disturbed by the sound of voices that are echoing inside the cavern. At first, I believe that my mind is playing tricks on me, but when I open my eyes there is a lantern shedding its light, and it is being held by a man. Next to the man stands another man. I think, "Am I still dreaming? The two of them are bald and they are dressed in white robes cinched by blue ropes around their waists. They are wearing sandals on their feet. I believe that I am hallucinating, and I shake my head and rub my eyes. When I open them again their visage remains. Their appearance has frightened me, and I yell loudly, "Who are you!?" The one holding the lantern says, "Do not fear Mr. Walker. I am Brother Isaac, and my companion is Brother Mordecai. You have been injured and we are here to help you. We will carry you to our medical facility." He points to a stretcher lying on the floor.

I am immediately both surprised and confused at the same time. I am surprised that here in the middle of nowhere are two people ready to offer me their assistance. Where did they come from? How did they know I was here. How in the hell did they know my name? Most of all I am puzzled by their speech. I ask again, "But who are you? How did you know I was here?

The man who introduced himself as Brother Isaac says, "Everything will be explained to you Mr. Walker. Please, we must go now!" I deliberately watched his mouth move when he spoke, and his lip movements did not match the sounds that came out. I ask, "Where will you take me?"

He answers, "Lartz hugant!" This time the words lartz hugant matched his lip movements. I realized he was speaking in Hebrew. Lartz Hugant are the words for, "To the fair land" in Yiddish. He is speaking in Hebrew, and I am hearing in English. It is like watching a foreign film with the English language dubbed in.

They slide the stretcher next to me and roll me onto it. I wonder where they are carrying me because they proceed in the opposite direction of the cave entrance. We turn a corner to the left and another to the right and I see light protruding from the end of the tunnel that we're in. We eventually exit the cave into the light of day. The men set me down, and Brother Mordecai lifts up the end of the stretcher my head is at, in order for me to see where we ended up.

What I see is surreal. No, a better word would be imaginary! It doesn't look real. It appears to be a portrait that some romantic artist had painted sometime in the 17th century! We are at a high elevation gazing down upon a narrow strip of land completely surrounded by tall mountain peaks. I estimate that it is about four miles long and only a couple of miles wide. Nestled at its far end I can see a waterfall draining down from one mountain into a blue lake with a stream coming out from it and running completely through the center of the entire area. White viaducts sprout from it in places. A thick forest is scattered near the water. Nearer to us fields of land are checkered in squares of greens, yellows, purples, and various hues of earth tones. I see the figures of people on them. To the right, built up upon the mountainside is an enormous castle-like structure sitting upon a flat top earthen mound. The stone architecture appears to be out of the middle-ages with its fortified walls and tall towering keeps on both sides. Small white cottages dot both sides of the castle, and a larger structure that appears to be a barn or stable is at the end of the cottages on the side closest to me. I see animals, which because of the distance, I can only identify as quadrupeds grazing inside a fenced enclosure. Then I am astonished by the atmosphere! The entire area is cloud covered. There is not even a patch of blue sky peeking anywhere through this dense cover; and yet the whole scene is illuminated brightly with no evidence of the sun's rays breaking through anywhere. The temperature feels like 75 degrees with no apparent humidity. The vista before me is a panorama of breathtaking beauty! It is an exhibition of peace and tranquility! As I survey the wonder of it all, I am reminded of the movie I had once seen with Andy, Becky, and Ginger entitled "Lost Horizon" by Mr. James Hilton. It was about a plane crashing in a snowy high mountain range in Pakistan. They are rescued by Sherpas and taken over the icy mountains to a beautiful warm paradise called Shangri-la, where its citizens lived long lives.

They resume carrying me down a narrow pathway towards the valley.[6]

[6]"Lost Horizon", a novel by James Hilton first published in 1933 by William Morrow & Co.

CHAPTER 32

Arriving at the bottom I continue to be dumbfounded at the beauty of my surroundings. Flowers of endless varieties and colors spew enticing fragrances into the air. The grass is dark green and appears to be mowed like a golf course. A large flora of yellow eight feet tall Pampas grass, and huge red Hibiscus bushes line the sides of the stone walkway my rescuers are carrying me on. There are trees everywhere, and I can see apples, oranges, peaches, and a plethora of other fruits dangling from their branches. I am in a paradise. Other than the pain I feel, the war and the vast wilderness I had just left seems as though it was an illusion; or am I now in an incredible fantasy? Do these surroundings really exist? I notice a red rose bush and tell the men to, "Stop please. May I have one of those roses?" They stop, lower the stretcher, and Mordecai smiles at me. He walks over, plucks one off, and hands it to me. I examine it closely. Its texture and smell are divine. It is real! This is real! This place is real! I am not dead, I am real! I ask them, "Is this Shangri-la?"

Isaac answers and says, "No Mr. Walker, this is Shashani!"

I answer, "I know what Shashani means, it means "the second." This place is the second what?"

We ultimately arrive at the large castle gate. Isaac yells, "Petash at hasher!" This time I hear it in the Hebrew language and know it's meaning as "open the gate." Thank you, my dear Hebrew teacher

Professor Abramowitz. But I wonder why this time, I heard Isaac's words in Hebrew and not in English. The gate opens and I'm carried inside. The entire stone construction of everything is a pure glistening white. The floor is a black ebony-like shining slate.

We enter into an open doorway and three women greet us. They are wearing long white robe-like dresses, white nurses' hats, and have thin veils draped over their faces. Each one has long black flowing shoulder-length hair. I think that they might be sisters, and each are incredibly beautiful! Now I'm convinced that this really might be paradise! The five of them carry me down a corridor opened to the outside and lined with the same white stone columns. One of the ladies opens a wooden door and we enter inside. It's a fairly large room with a bed in the center and with cabinets and medical paraphernalia nearby. They transfer me to the bed. Isaac and Mordecai, in unison, say, "Goodbye Mr. Walker. We will be seeing you soon."

"So long fellas, thanks for the help."

One of the women looks down upon me, smiles, and says, "We wish to welcome you here Mr. Walker. I am Sister Esther, and these are my two assistants, Sister Rebecca, and Sister Sarah. I am the "Chief Healer" here in Shashani. It appears that you have suffered some terrible injuries, therefore we will begin your healing process now."

I ask, "You say that you are a healer, does that imply that you are a medical doctor?"

"I would prefer to be thought of as a healer sir."

"Well, I would prefer that a common ordinary M.D. work on me."

"Your preference is noted Mr. Walker, however there are no, what you call medical doctors, here in our facilities. If you would please just relax I will attend to your wounds. You are very fortunate to be alive sir. Had you not fallen into that gulley those soldiers would have killed you."

"Now that's just it! How in the hell could you have possibly known that!? Also, I'm not wearing a nametag. What about that! How could you know my name!?"

"Well, Mordecai and Isaac just said your name; and please sir, there is no cursing in Shashani. We find foul language to be rude and very nasty. It is not permitted here......now please just relax and look me in the eyes." I watch her extend her right hand to my forehead. She touches me there and I remember nothing else.

I awaken after a much- needed sleep, and when I do I feel no pain whatsoever. In fact, I feel exhilarated, and refreshed. Better yet I feel alive. I am dying for a cigarette, and I am hungry. No, I am ravished. I look around and discover that I am in a small room with an open window to my left. I can only see mountains through it. My healer Esther comes in, walks over to me, and places her hand on my forehead. She says, "That's good Mr. Walker, your fever is gone, how are you feeling?"

"I need a cigarette."

She laughs and says, "I can assure you sir that there are no cigarettes in Shashani."

And that's when I noticed it for the first time. She is speaking in Hebrew, but I can actually hear her speak in either English or Hebrew. I only have to think in either language, and that is the dialect I will hear!

I say, "I am also very hungry."

"Your food will be coming shortly, and by the way what do you think of our handiwork?" She pulls my covers back to the side and shows me the cast on my ankle and foot. Then I notice the one on my right arm. "Thank you," I say.

"You are most welcome. You will be here in this room for two more days then assigned a cottage. Your casts will remain on for five weeks. Do you have any questions?"

"Yes, I do. I need a telephone or radio to contact my army unit to advise them of my location."

"You will have to discuss that with Brother Jacob."

As if on cue we are interrupted by a tall slender middle -aged man. He is bald and wearing the same white robe. He walks into the room carrying a tray of food, looks at me, smiles, and says, "It is a joy to meet you Mr. Walker. I am Brother Jacob. It will be my honor to indoctrinate you into the ways of Shashani. I also will be your ancient history teacher. I hope you like fish."

The meal looks delicious. It's comprised of baked fish, potatoes, green beans, sliced apples, a roll, and a large glass of milk.

Jacob says, "You enjoy the food sir. I'll be right back." They both leave me my food, and I hastily devour my scrumptious feast, fall asleep, and dream of Irene.

CHAPTER 33

When I awake again, I notice that Jacob is sitting in a chair next to me. I tell him I need to go to the toilet, and he hands me a bedpan.

I finish and ask, "What is the date, Jacob?"

He answers, "It is the 30th day of Cheshvan Mr. Walker. You would call that date November 30th. It is our year 5,704. Did you enjoy your food sir?"

"Thank you. I did. And by the way, would you please stop addressing me as Mr. Walker. My name is Hiram, and my friends call me Ace."

"Oh, it would never be proper to call you by a nickname in Shashani. Nicknames are considered somewhat vulgar here. Therefore, I shall address you as Hiram."

"That will be fine Jacob. I must say I believe it to be somewhat entertaining hearing you speak in Hebrew and then choosing which dialect that I want to hear in."

"That is an age- old gift we call "tongues" Hiram. It was first used on the 50th day from Passover in the year you call 33 A.D. That day we call "Pentecost. When we speak others hear in their own languages.

"I have many questions to ask of you Jacob; but first I need to contact my army unit to give them a report on what has happened to me."

"That will be impossible Hiram. We utilize no electricity here, and the mountains prevent any radio signals to be sent or received."

"Well, that's absurd! How do you stay in contact with the outside world?"

"We have no desire to contact the outside world. What we need to know is provided to us by messengers."

"And just who are these messengers?"

I am not sure if I am allowed to tell you this Hiram, but I shall. They are "Malakis."

My mind translates "Malakis" to the English word for angels. You're telling me that angels tell you of everything that you need to know?"

"That is the truth, Hiram."

"Yeah……right!"

"Well then, how do you obtain food, clothing, or other items that you require for daily life?"

"You must believe me when I say this, Hiram. We are completely self- sufficient. We have large farms and orchards, the necessary tools, and animals to tend them, a large lake filled with an abundance of fish, a dairy, a bakery, a carpenter, and a blacksmiths shop. We are most of all proud of the services we offer such as our medical facility and our schools. Physical activities abound such as horseback riding, archery, canoe racing, a game similar to what you call soccer, and general Olympic type activities like foot racing and swimming. I Tim 4:8 states "Bodily exercise profits little." Which suggests it profits some. Therefore, we know the Lord encourages us to keep our bodies healthy."

"Did you just quote a bible verse?"

"Yes."

"It's interesting to me that you just quoted a verse from the bible, is your community a religious organization?"

"We do not consider ourselves to be an organization but rather a community."

"Do you have a name?"

"We are a very ancient order, Hiram. Since we have written much about men, others such as Pliny the Elder, Philo of Alexandria, and Josephus have written much about us. WE ARE "THE ESSENES"! I have been told that you have not heard of us."

"There you go again! You've been told I didn't know certain things! This is not only puzzling to me but also aggravating! How do you people know so much about me?"

That will not be explained to you until you begin taking classes."

"What do you mean class? I have to get healed and get out of this place! I must complete the contract that I have been assigned!"

"I must ask you to be patient Hiram. You will be given a great gift....... the greatest gift known to man."

"And what is that?"

"You are to be given the gift of life Hiram! You will be given life, and life more abundantly! But you must accept this free gift! I have conceived a letter for our new arrivals. Please take it. It will explain some things pertaining to us."

Before I can say anything else he leaves, and I sit there alone with the letter he gave me. It is entitled "D"QX", meaning in the ancient Hebrew ESSENES.

The first thing that comes to my mind is anger. Although, I am eternally thankful that these people have rescued me, treated my injuries, and indubitably saved my life; I am angered by their desire now to proselytize me. I am firmly convinced that they wish to brainwash me into believing their edition of some kind of religious fanaticism. I, however, have nothing else to do but lie here, and so I begin to read the letter.

Our order has been in existence for thousands of years. We are the copiers of Jehovah's word. We have handwritten copies of the Talmud and the Torah from generations to generations. We have studied and have transcribed copies of the law of Moses. Our community had at one time 4,000 members. Today in Shashani we number only 400. During the time of the Roman occupation of Israel we congregated in the wilderness. We dwelt in the solitude of this desert to write and to pray. We did so because Isaiah 40:3 says, "The voice of him that crieth in the wilderness. Prepare ye the way of the Lord, make straight in the desert a highway for our God." We have done so and today we live in the place God has provided for us. We also see in this scripture the prophecy of John the Baptist.

We possess no money, and all that we own is shared amongst each other. We desire a type of communal living. One class of our men, called the "Contemplatives," take a vow of celibacy. The others marry that we may replenish the community. We have devoted ourselves to charity and benevolence to those whom the Lord sends to us. The great historian Flavius Josephus wrote about us in chapter 8 of his book "Jewish Wars" saying, "There are three sects among the Jews. The followers of the first of which are the Pharisees; of the second, the Sadducees; and the third sect, which pretends to be a severer discipline are called the Essenes. These last are Jews by birth, and seem to have a greater affection for each other than the other sects. They avoid the other sects and prefer a hermit-like life of monasticism. They very rarely visit the temple."

Today, we follow our ancient customs by immersing ourselves in water each morning, and then assemble for prayer together. Our meals are usually taken as a group. We study the Holy Scriptures daily.

It is our admission of faith that although we are Jews and have once rejected the man Jesus as the Messiah, we now through the study of prophecy in Old Testament scriptures and the teachings of the Holy Spirit, we realize that He is the Christ the Son of the Living God. He is the only messiah. Since we are Jewish, we assemble to break bread on the Sabbath, however we honor other Christians that do so on the first day of the week. Although our order has changed dramatically over the millennia our love of God remains the same.

After reading his letter of introduction I once again start rationalizing my predicament. I believe Jacob is correct in telling me to relax and be patient. After all, in my current physical condition I can do little else. Even after the five weeks when my casts come off, I will still need weeks of physical therapy. I recognize the benefits I may accrue by being a good medical patient, as well as the perceived eager student of their religion and culture. It is easier to catch flies with honey than with lemons. There is, however, another emotion that is haunting me. I am above all things a reporter first. This place that I've blundered into is an amazing, incredible world. It is a story all unto itself! I feel the need to know everything about it and its people. Initially my thoughts were to hurry back to the war. I now feel that the war can wait. Here in this valley is an untold tale that must come out, and I'm prepared to remain here until I have absorbed all knowledge of Shashani. This now is my new goal, to remain here for however long it takes to draft this story. I also realize that, once strong again, I can climb back up the mountain, enter the cave, and exit again into the Sinai wilderness.

CHAPTER 34

Today I'm being moved from my hospital room to my cottage. As Jacob pushes me in my new wheelchair, we progress down the stone pathway, and occasionally a passerby would smile and say, "Good morning Mr. Walker." It seems that the knowledge of my presence, as well as my name, is already common information in the entirety of Shashani. When we arrive, I see that I'm in cottage number 127, and it is a simple white limestone structure. Jacob pushes me inside past the green painted wooden door. Once inside I notice that there are no locks on the door. I say to Jacob, "Where are the door locks?" He laughs and answers, "You will require no door locks Hiram. No one locks their doors here because there is no crime."

The building is a small four room structure. It has one bedroom, a kitchen, a bathroom, and what Jacob describes as a reading room. There is a large bookcase in this room that contains numerous volumes of literature. Both the kitchen and bath are furnished with small handpumps to provide the flow of water. The toilet is actually inside! No outhouse for me! The ceilings and walls of all the rooms have lighting fixtures. I ask, "What fuel do the lanterns use?"

Jacob says, "All the buildings in Shashani have natural gas piped in. Its source is our large gas well hidden inside the mountain we call "Triumph."

The thing I am most curious about is the temperature. I see no evidence of any kind of a furnace or cooling device. "How do I control the temperature, Jacob?"

"You do not Hiram. The temperature of all Shashani remains consistently at 75 degrees both day and night. It never fluctuates. Should you get chilled there are extra blankets in that closet. In that corner is your icebox. You will have ice and milk delivered to your door daily. We make ice using our gas operated compressor. You will also find your complete wardrobe in this closet. I need to consult with you about clothing. We, the Jewish people are an extremely modest people. We consider nudity shameful, and in our minds a man dressed only in his underwear is naked. It is said that the apostle Peter and other first century fishermen went naked. In the gospel account of Peter's nakedness, after fishing he would have donned his tunic by tucking it up between his legs and used a belt to hold it in place. This action was called "girding your loins." It allowed Peter to swim ashore clothed, yet unencumbered. We wear what you would call a modest one- piece swimsuit for swimming. We wear three basic items of clothing. The undergarment is a linen sleeved tunic cinched into place by this cloth sash. Over that we drape this cloak. We use this square piece of cloth as a topcoat, blanket, bedroll, and in ancient times as collateral for a loan repayable by sunset. Also, although we do not keep all of the Mosaic Laws any longer, we still tie a blue sash to the four corners for a belt. We then wear our outer garment of this robe. Finally, we shod our feet in leather sandals. Ours are made here in Shashani. The women you may have noticed dress similar. We wish you to dress as we dress. White clothing displays our purity and is worn daily. Our community provides a laundry service. Bag your soiled exterior clothing and also your underwear and place it outside. It will be picked up on Tuesdays. The most important thing I must tell you Hiram is that there is a strict timetable to which you must adhere. I will give you this pamphlet which will outline your scheduled responsibilities. Your ancient history class will start in two days in the Castle's Elijah Room. Here are two crutches to assist you to stand. Please feel free to enjoy your personal library. I will pick you up tomorrow at 6:00 a.m. for immersion. I wish you a good day Hiram.

After Jacob departs, I study my schedule.

DAILY SCHEDULE

<u>Monday thru Friday</u> (Sabbath at 6:00 P.M. on Friday until Dusk on Saturday)

(1) 6:00 a.m. Carriage pick-up to Lake Shashani.

(2) 6:30 to 7:00 Immersion.

(3) 7:00 to 7:30 Songs of praise.

(4) 7:30 to 8:00 Breakfast in Dining Hall.

(5) 8:00 to 9:00 Free time.

(6) 9:00 to 12:00 Work time.

(7) 12:00 to 1:00 lunch at your cottage.

(8) 1:00 to 3:00 Work time.

(9) 3: 00 to 4:00 Home prayer.

(10) 4:00 to 6:00 Group Bible Study at assigned classrooms (unless already scheduled for another class)

(11) 6:00 to 7:00 Dinner in the Dining Hall

(12) 8:00 to 10:00 curfew (Mon-Thurs. free time)

Sabbath Schedule

(1) 9:00 to 10:00 Bible study

(2) 11:00 to 12:00 Worship Service and Communion at Christ's Chapel.

(3) 1:00 Lunch in one's own cottage.

(4) Free time to 5:00 for Ministry Meeting.

(5) Sunday Meal 6:30 to 7:30 Supper in Dining Hall

(6) Free time

<u>Sunday Schedule</u>

<u>Sports and Entertainment</u>

<u>Recreational Activities</u>

<u>Special Events</u> As <u>Listed On Bulletin Board</u>

CHAPTER 35

My appointed caretaker, consultant, and teacher Jacob picks me up promptly at 6:00 am. He comes in and inspects my clothing to ensure that I am dressed properly. He says, "Very good Hiram! Let's go outside and wait for the carriage." When it arrives, it is as large as a "Greyhound" bus. It has no top. It is completely open and is being pulled by four large draft horses. As we board, I ask Jacob, "How many people does this hold?" "This carriage holds 50 people Hiram. It sometimes makes two trips. Some people, as you see, have their own small carriages, and others who reside near the lake, simply walk."

When we arrive not one person is talking. They take to the water, bathe, and swim. Everything is in total silence, except for the splashing of water. I wish I could join them, but my casts prevent that. A bell rings and everyone comes out onto the shore. In one of the carriages a choir and a small band start playing a soulful Jewish melody. When it's over, they play a tune that is even familiar to me. They play:

"Shall we gather at the river,

The beautiful, the beautiful, river.

Let's all gather at the river that flows by the throne of God.

Yes, we'll gather at the river,

The beautiful, the beautiful river.

Gather with the saints at the river, which flows by the throne of God."

Four hundred people are singing in perfect harmony. It is a breathtaking scene. It is a picture of pure worship that I have never witnessed before. It is evident that this entire community has real faith towards their God. I feel a peace come over me, and then it is displaced by guilt. I feel this guilt because I'm here in the safety of this paradise, and my friends are in sweltering heat, and fighting for their lives while killing others.

I then notice that Jacob had his hand on my shoulder. He says, "We have done this every morning for centuries. Can you see why Hiram?"

I answer, "Yes I can."

"Let's walk back Hiram, and as I push you in the chair, I may be able to show you a few things on the way. Have you noticed the above ground viaducts?"

"Yes, I have."

"The principle that they operate on dates back to the ancient Romans. It is impossible to tell by their appearance, but they are slanted down only about a half centimeter, and yet they convey to us all of our pure drinking water."

I hear the sound of hoof-beats and a few horse- drawn surreys pass us by. They are all painted black and are similar to those I have past seen in Amish communities.

"You will notice a variety of agricultural fields as we walk Hiram. Corn, wheat. potatoes, sugar beets, lettuce, cabbage, and all other types of vegetables are grown here throughout the entire year."

"I certainly am no farmer Jacob, but how do you have any success growing any type of plants without sunlight? I have yet to see the sun shining since I have been here."

"I am not allowed to explain that to you yet Hiram. You will learn many things in class."

"Here we go again! Who's on first. What's on second, I don't know is on third!"

"I'm sorry Hiram, I do not know what you mean?"

"That's alright. I'm sure you have never heard of Abbott & Costello; but when you avoid my questions it frustrates me."

"You must be patient Hiram."

"I've heard you tell me that before Jacob; but Confucius say, "Only man who desires pretty nurse must be patient.""

"I don't understand."

"Never mind, it was a joke."

"I am sorry, should I laugh now?"

"If you laugh now, I will hit you with the cast on my arm!"

"Please do not do so Hiram, for that would demonstrate anger! Anger is frowned upon here in Shashani."

Everywhere I look I see plenty. This place is a cornucopia of abundance! There are dairy cattle, beef cattle, herds of sheep, and a hatchery for their chickens.

Then the guilt starts to creep in again, but this time I realize I had no control over what has happened. Nothing that has happened has been my fault. Everything is decided by fate. Therefore, I plan to continue my job at this location for the "Inquirer." I want to write a story about these people. I want to learn everything about them.

We pass my cottage and end up at the castle dining hall. "I must admit Jacob, I'm curious about the food I'll be served here. Honey and locusts won't be the main course for breakfast, will it?"

"Jacob laughs and says, "It will not. I think you will enjoy your meal."

In surprise I gaze up at him and say, "Jacob, did you laugh Jacob? Did you actually just laugh? Really! In point of fact, I was beginning to believe that laughter was not allowed in Shashani."

When we walked into the Great Dining Hall I was impressed by its size. It is massive! We both enter one of several chow lines. We will be served cafeteria style. The food looks wonderful! There are scrambled eggs, loaves of bread and jam, salted and smoked fish, fried potatoes, and fruits of all kinds. When we get to our table, I notice that no one was sitting down. About 390 people are standing at their tables waiting for the last ten to arrive. A bell rings and one man prays and asks the Lord to bless the food. Then everyone sits and starts enjoying their breakfast. It seems like each is having the wonderful experiences of fellowship with one another. The thing that strikes me the most about these people are their smiles. All of them seem to be smiling all of the time. You can see through their faces and into their souls that they have not been brainwashed, but that they are genuinely happy. But one thing puzzles me. As I study the hundreds of men and women around me, I see only three children. I plan to ask why there are so few.

Weeks later my casts are removed, and my physical therapy has concluded. I feel fit, mobile, and whole again. I still plan to climb up the mountain and exit back into the world again, but not until I have thoroughly scrutinized these remarkable people. To do this I must agree to their teaching programs.

CHAPTER 36

Today is my first day in school! As I meander to my class my mind drifts back to the 3rd platoon and all of my friends. Every time I think of Jimmy dying tears come to my eyes. I know that I should have joined him in death. What twist of fate has saved me. and brought me to this paradise? My resolve to learn all I can about these Essenes has increased. I now accept what has happened to me, however it is still my fervent desire to leave this place and resume my life in the real world.

The castle gatekeeper guides me into a room adjacent to a large hallway. Two desks are arranged opposite each other. Sitting behind one is Brother Jacob, now my newly appointed teacher. Jacob says, "Welcome to class Hiram. Set yourself up behind the desk and we'll begin. First, I should ask about how much religious instruction did you receive during your formative years as a youngster?"

"Not much. My father was a confirmed atheist. My mother was an agnostic. I did have an Aunt Annie who would come to visit with us after church on Sundays. She would tell me Sunday school stories. I remember as a child I enjoyed the one about a man being swallowed by a whale. Also, I remember a story about a man named Noah, and a flood. I do remember my father telling me, after Aunt Annie left, that they were all just fairy tales. He told me not to believe them. Of course, when I got older, I saw movies and stories on Easter and Christmas.

That's about it Jacob." To tell you the truth, I thought those tales were just for entertainment purposes only.

By the way, "Where are my other classmates?"

"You will be the only student in this your first course entitled "Truths of the Past." You will find notebooks and pens in the drawer."

"Where are my textbooks?"

"There is only one. It is in the top drawer of your desk."

"There is only a bible here."

"Hiram you should know that the bible says in 2nd Timothy 3:16 &17 "All scripture is given by inspiration of God, and is profitable for doctrine, for reproof, for correction, for instruction in righteousness. That the man of God maybe complete, thoroughly equipped for every good work.""

"Therefore, it is the only textbook that we need for this course."

"That's all well and good Jacob but I am not a man of God, and I also believe that the bible is a fairy tale and total rubbish."

"May I ask you Hiram how long you studied the bible before you came to that conclusion?"

"You're asking me how long I have studied the bible? That's simple. I have never ever studied it. I have never even opened the book to any page. Does that answer your question?"

"Yes, Hiram it answers my question, but I am confused. If you have never studied the bible, how can you come to any conclusion at all about its veracity? In fact, how can you have any opinion about it at all? Pliny the Elder" once wrote, "No opinion may be offered by one, lest the subject matter be well versed and studied." So, I am asking you to at least have an open mind as we start our studies. If you do, I am prepared to answer some, but maybe not all, of the questions that you have regarding Shashani."

"Now we're getting somewhere. I have a lot of questions. If you promise to answer them, I'll reciprocate and go along with your program. Fair enough?"

"Fair enough Hiram. I just want you to understand that some of your questions I will not be able to address. They will have to be answered by your instructors in either your "Current Events" or "Future Prophecies" classes. Do you understand?"

"Alright brother, but I get the first question. I have counted the number of children since arriving here and have seen only three. Why so few?"

"That would be very observant of you Hiram. There are actually four. One was just recently born and remains in infant care. We have been instructed to maintain a population of 400 souls. This number allows us to remain in harmony with the environmental conditions that we enjoy in Shashani. Therefore, a new birth is not allowed here until a death happens, and deaths are very infrequent. I can best explain this phenomenon if we both turn to the first book of the bible called Genesis. Please turn to Gen 5:25-27 and read these verses aloud please Hiram."

I begin to read the verses. "Methusaleh lived 187 years and begot Lamech. After he begot Lamech, Methusaleh lived 782 years, and had sons and daughters. So, all the days of Methusaleh were 969 years; and he died."

"Now do you see Jacob why I believe that this book is hogwash. No one can live that long. This whole thing is ridiculous!"

Jacob says, "If you read other verses in these chapters, you will discover that many people lived hundreds of years during that time. A number of things contributed to their longevity, such as a thick cloud cover over the earth that filtered out the sun's harmful rays. But mainly it was God's desire that man should have an extended life. These conditions exist here in Shashani today. If you continue to read, you'll discover that man's life expectancy was shortened after the Noahic flood. Also in the book of Psalms 90:10 it says, "The days of our lives are seventy years; and if by reason of strength they are eighty years." This is the life expectancy of humans in your world today, Hiram."

I laughingly say, "This is nonsensical. I suppose that you are 900 years old Jacob!" "Not quite Hiram. I am only 376 years old."

CHAPTER 37

((December 1, 1943)

(Mr. Jacob's office. Philadelphia Inquirer.)

"Irene come in here. I have just received a telegram from the U.S. Army. It's about Hiram."

Irene stops typing and enters her father's office. She sees him standing at the window, staring out, and with both hands clasped behind his back. He says, "Sit down dear." He then turns to face her, and while still standing picks up a telegram off his desk. He reads, WE REGRET TO INFORM YOU [STOP] THAT YOUR EMPLOYEE HIRAM WALKER [STOP] HAS BEEN REPORTED MISSING IN ACTION WHILE ON AN EXERCISE IN THE SINAI PENINSULA [STOP] WE WILL CONTACT YOU UPON RECEIVING ADDITIONAL INFORMATION] [STOP]

Jacob's looks at his daughter and says, "I'm so sorry sweetheart."

Irene glares at her father in disbelief. Soon tears start to stream from her eyes and she cries, "Oh daddy! It can't be true. Can it?'

Jacobs answers, "I'm afraid it is dear."

CHAPTER 38

(Back to Jacob's classroom in Shashani)

"That's just great Brother Jacob, you're 376 years old and I'm Napoleon Bonaparte! And here you are right in front of me; and I swear you don't look a day over forty. This is all a bunch of gibberish, and I'm leaving." I get up, look at my demented tutor with a dour face, and walk out the door.

I return to my cottage and plop down on my bed. My mind starts racing and analyzing my current situation. Here I am in what I now consider to be "Fantasy Land". I miss Irene and my friends fighting the war. I feel guilty that I have become derelict in my duties to my employer, the war effort, and again to my unfaithfulness to Irene. My resolve to further study these people has soured. I now believe I have enough information about them in order to write a newsworthy article for the "Inquirer." I simply conclude that they are a misguided, self-serving bunch of fanatical religious zealots. They are just another misinformed ignorant cult contaminating the world. I am thankful for their efforts in rescuing, and nurturing me back to health, but I've had enough of them. I get up from the bed and walk over to the desk in the corner of the room. I need to think, and my best thinking comes to me with paper and pen in hand. I start planning my escape from "Lalla Land". On paper I have decided to leave two weeks from now. I'll leave at midnight when all of the (376-year-old) Essenes are asleep. I'll also need time for reconnaissance. I will need to discover my way back to the path leading up the mountain. I start to compile a list of things for my journey. I can don my military clothing and boots. I'll pack my canteen, lantern, compass, and what I calculate will be enough food and water. I hope that I can locate my pistol when I get into the cavern. It should still be there; I reason, because these pacifists would have no need of it. I've been in their paradise for two months now, and although I'm anxious to leave, when I consider the trek across a vast dry desert wilderness with threats of not only a few Nazi stragglers, but native tribes as well, it alerts and readies me to be extremely cautious. Although what I fear the most is not death but rather becoming a prisoner of war.

I decide what's in my best interest, in order not to cast any suspicion on my escape plans, is to apologize to Brother Jacob and resume my normal activities, including my scheduled lessons.

I leave my cottage and walk to the dining hall for lunch. I enter the large room and take my assigned seat next to Jacob. Sheepishly I sit down, glance at Jacob, and say, "I'm sorry. Sometimes my temper and impatience get the best of me." He says, "No need to apologize. I realize you have been under extreme duress Hiram. You will of course continue your studies?" I smile and answer, "Yes."

CHAPTER 39

After my final medical examination, I have been cleared for mandatory work duties. Evidently there are no free rides in Shashani, and I have been given several choices of jobs. With my plans for escaping, I realize that whatever I select will be short lived. I choose the stables. My reasoning being that the use of a horse will allow me to travel faster and cover more ground during my search for the mountain path to my freedom. I report to the stablemaster, a woman named Sister Ruth, on Monday morning.

As I walk into the main barn I see two people. Instead of the white robe regalia normally worn in Shashani, they are dressed in western wear. It includes blue denim pants, grey cotton shirts and cowboy hats and boots. The woman greets me with, "Hello, you must be Mr. Walker. I am Sister Ruth. Welcome to the Shashani stables."

"I'm not sure, but I think I'm glad to be here."

I am immediately taken by her appearance. Although not beautiful, she is cute, the girl next door kind of cute. In fact, she reminds me of Judy Garland. She is short, slender, with haunting gray eyes, and her hair is long, coal black, and tied back in a ponytail. She has the most contagious smile. I would guess her age as about thirty, but you never know in this place.

"I have compiled a list of the duties that you will be expected to perform. I am afraid that some of your tasks may not be very pleasant.

Since we board two dozen horses here your chores should keep you quite busy. You will be Brother Luke's assistant and I am positive that he will appreciate your help. You should know that our Arabians are maintained for the pleasure of those in our community who enjoy horse-back riding, and the Clydesdale draft horses are used by our farmers who groom and feed them themselves."

She hands me a handwritten chore list, and says, "I am certain you will adjust suitably to this everyday routine."

(1) Feed and water the horses twice daily (5:00 am and 3:00 pm)

(2) Clean dung from bays daily.

(3) Brush each animal before they are to be ridden.

(4) Distribute saddles and all tack to potential riders.

(5) Care for the returned animals (see Brother Luke about this.)

I smile at her and say, "Looks like I've got a few dirty jobs ahead of me."

She laughs and says, "It will be good for your soul Mr. Walker. Let me ask, have you ever ridden before?"

"I have but it's been a long time ago. I'm afraid I might be a little rusty."

"Then I believe that we should saddle up a couple of horses and I will demonstrate how to adorn our animals with their proper tack; after which we shall take them for a little trot. You will find suitable clothing of your size in a storage room next to the last stable."

As I walk back to change clothes, I pass the man named Luke. He says, "Nice to meet you Mr. Walker. I am Luke. I sure am glad you will be helping us."

"Hi Luke. I'm glad to be here."

I return to Ruth looking like I star in the movie "Stagecoach". I swagger up to my new boss like John Wayne and say, "Howdy pilgrim. Just call me Tex!"

Ruth says, "And why Mr. Walker should I call you Tex? Is not Hiram your given name?"

"Yes, it is. I was just fantasizing."

"What is this fantasizi......?

"Fantasizing. It means being stupid. Forget it."

"I have selected for you a very gentle animal. This is Lizzy, and she should suit your needs."

As I size up Lizzy, an Arabian beauty that is pure white with black highlights around her ears and tail, Sister Ruth demonstrates the proper way to saddle and bit the horse. She does the same with her horse, and we lead them outside. We mount the horses, and she instructs me to take it slow at first. She says, "We shall ride south to the lake and then enter a trailhead that leads through the forest. It is a very pleasant ride Mr. Walker."

"Could we please drop the formalities. Just call me Hiram."

"Then you should address me as Ruth."

Lizzy is responding to any gentle nudge of a command that I give her, and we ride side by side toward the lake. I am enthralled and almost hypnotized by this activity. I am also quite taken with my new acquaintance and boss. I ask her, "Are you happy here in Shashani Ruth?"

She answers, "Why would one not be pleased to live in a paradise such as Shashani Hiram? Although different, in some ways Shashani is similar to a second garden of Eden."

"If you say so, but for me I have always sinned, and have had a wanderlust and a curiosity about places that I've never seen. Allow me to ask you Ruth; for I'm curious, have you done any traveling outside of Shashani?"

Ruth laughs and says, "No Hiram. I was born and have lived here my entire life, and although I am content to live here forever, I must admit I have a curiosity about the outside world. But your world scares me. It seems so cruel and barbaric."

"Cruel and barbaric is a good way to currently describe my world. Today it is infused with death and horror. I assure you however, that most of my life before this terrible war, was rather idyllic. May I ask you another question?"

"Of course, you may Hiram."

"How old are you?"

I believe that it is not only customary in your world, but in ours as well Hiram, that a girl never discloses her age."

"Please excuse me. I understand. May I ask what your thoughts are about my new teacher Brother Jacob? He said something to me yesterday that I thought was beyond incredible."

"I believe him to be a wonderful God-fearing man. And by all accounts a gifted teacher. It is imperative for you to learn of the Holy Scriptures before leaving us Hiram."

"Why."

"So, you will be prepared for your future destiny."

"And what would you know of my future destiny?"

"I am afraid that I am not authorized to answer that question; but allow me to ask you one question."

"What would you like to know?"

"All of the people of Shashani have heard how you were injured in your war, and that you were near death. Is it your belief that finding our cave was an accident, and that your rescue was purely coincidental?"

"What else would it be? I don't believe in providence or fate."

"I think that you will come to realize that God has a plan for you."

"I'm just a plain newspaper man. What plans could He have for me?

"I believe that your teachers will inform you of His plans."

I sarcastically say, "I can hardly wait!"

We persist riding in silence for a period of time, until I twist around to face her, and she suddenly turns to me. We smile at each other and then she raises an eyebrow inquisitively and asks, "Penny for your thoughts?"

I gaze into those beautiful eyes and declare, "I'm afraid you wouldn't get your money's worth dear Ruth."

The temperature cools as we enter the forest. The pathway is narrow and well worn, and I begin to wish our jaunt would never end.

But in only two weeks I plan to escape from these people, and although I've only known Ruth for a few hours, I may just miss her more than the others. In our "Miss America" beauty pageant, she would be "Miss Congeniality."

We remain mostly silent during the rest of our excursion.

CHAPTER 40

Since my first feeding of the horses is at 5:00 a.m. I'm up earlier than usual, and I meet brother Luke at the main barn. He is a red bearded, rotund, and jolly young man. He greets me with, "Good morning Mr. Walker. I am happy that you will be sharing duties with me. Now I may even get to the lake for immersion on time."

I reiterate that I'm happy to work with him.

Mr. Walker, may I address you as Hiram?

"Of course, Luke."

"Well then Hiram the shovel, rakes, ropes, and all such other tools are in the building we named the "tool shed". There is an actual sign on it saying so."

Chuckling I say, "Now that's a mighty inventive name for that shed Luke!"

"Anyway, Hiram we shovel out the manure and hose the stalls in the morning and brush and feed in the afternoon. Say! I saw you and Ruth saddle up the other day Where did you ride to?"

"We took a nice jaunt on a trailhead by the lake."

"Is not our Sister Ruth wonderful Hiram. I love her very much. If I had never taken a vow of celibacy I would have wished to marry her."

"Well, I must say if you took that oath, you're either a smarter or dumber man than I am. I'm not sure which. You never know Luke; some

couples marry and they're as compatible as a cat and a goldfish.......
Anyway, as soon as were done here I have to hurry to school."

****Back in class****

"Welcome back Hiram. I hope our session today lasts much longer than our previous one."

"As do I Brother Jacob."

Let us start with the book of Genesis, chapter one, verse one. In bible annotation it would be written, Gen 1:1. Please read this verse aloud Hiram."

I read, "In the beginning God created the heavens and the earth." Sarcastically I say, "Yeah, right."

Jacob says, "You sound as if you do not believe that."

"Of course, I don't believe that."

"Then how else would you account for the creation of our world?"

I explain, "Intelligent scientists today refute that there is a God. They theorize that gases had formed and there was a huge explosion. They refer to it as the "Big Bang Theory." I mean in your story where does God come from?"

"Well in your theory Hiram, where do the gasses come from?" I believe you have witnessed many explosions during your current war. Have you not?"

"Yes, I have."

"What were the results of those explosions? Did they cause destruction and chaos, or were they creative, resulting in something beautiful?"

"They caused nothing but death and destruction."

"Of course, they did. Therefore, I ask you how a chaotic explosion could create the beauty of this world. Chaos is not a creative force, and it certainly could not result in any form of intelligent design. Observe the anatomy of a man. The heart alone is an amazing example of what the scriptures say that "We are fearfully and wonderfully made". The human heart for instance can pump blood sixty beats a minute, sixty minutes an hour, twenty-four hours a day, three-hundred-sixty- five, days a year, for a hundred years! Show me any mechanical pump that man has created that can equal God's creation! Oh Hiram, when you were born God breathed into you the knowledge of His existence. You, on the other hand have been spending your entire life trying to forget that knowledge. But I believe that a smidgen of Him still remains within you Hiram. Now I want you to read Gen 1:1 in Hebrew."

I read the verse in Hebrew to myself.

"Did you find anything interesting in that same verse?"

"I believe I did, but I'm not sure. I thought that the Jewish religion believed in monotheism; that there is only one God."

"We do."

"But the Hebrew word for God in this verse is Elohim. That is the plural word for God. Eloha would be God singular."

"The plural word (Elohim) for God is used to indicate that there are three persons in one God. That is called the trinity. God consists of the Father, the Son, and the Holy Spirit. The Gospel of John tells of the work of the Son. Please turn to the New Testament and read aloud John 1: 1-3."

I read, "In the beginning was the Word, and the Word was with God, and the Word was God. All things were made by Him; and without Him was not anything made that was made."

"These passages indicate two things. One is that the "Word" is the Son of God, and He was not created but always existed with the Father and the Holy Spirit. Secondly is that He spoke the world into existence.

Let's go back to Gen 1: 3, 6, 9, 11, 14, 20,24, and 26, Read out loud the first three words of each verse."

I read aloud from each verse, and they all say the same three words, "And God said…."

"When you open your mouth to speak, what comes out Hiram?"

"Words."

"That is correct, words spue forth. The Son of God is the creator. He is the Word of God. I am showing you these scriptures to demonstrate to you how the different scriptures from both the Old and New Testaments weave together. This book Hiram, this word of God, was written by many different authors, from different walks of life, from not only different centuries but from entirely different millenniums and yet they all meld perfectly together. That is because God inspired his writers to pen what they wrote.

You spoke of science earlier Hiram. The science of men. Do you remember in elementary school when you were required to remember this poem? "Columbus sailed the ocean blue in fourteen-hundred-and-ninety-two."

"Yes, I do."

"Do you recall that the prevailing scientific theorem of that time was that the earth was flat. In fact, most of the crew that shipped on with Columbus thought that they might fall off the edge of the world. And yet the Bible in the book of Isaiah 40: 22 reads. "It is He that sitteth upon the CIRCLE of the earth." "Scripture recorded that the earth was round long before Columbus' time.

If you want accurate science, and a picture of this earth that we dwell on then you must read the scriptures. Please turn Hiram to Job 26:7 and read."

"Where is that book at?"

"It is right before the book of Psalms. In fact, it is the oldest written book in the bible."

"I found it Jacob." I read, "He stretcheth out the north over the empty place and hangeth the earth upon nothing."

"That is a pretty good description of what your science believes today is it not? Do you see Hiram, that your so-called science has been in error many times during the centuries; but this book, this bible has never been in error. As hard as you may, you will find no incongruities in it."

Our study session ended, and I had to admit to myself, although grudgingly, that I somewhat enjoyed it.

CHAPTER 41

(December 23, 1943)

Ace's old contingency of the 2nd armored Division has pushed the Nazi group that they had discovered in the southern Sinai northeast into the Gulf of Aqabah. The Germans make a stand near Eilat and start an encounter with the Americans.

The tank "Thumper," with its crew of Ace's friends, head into battle. Two other tanks join them. As the three armored vehicles push towards the enemy they start to receive mortar from the German line. A group of Nazi Wehrmacht also move towards "Thumper" from the opposite direction, and start shooting. Paddy, in control of the top canon, starts firing towards them as Mike drops down out of the tank from its lower escape hatch. He has his M2 fully automatic rifle in hand and he belly crawls to the side of the tank. Joe Sox joins him with his M1. They lay down and begin returning fire. Bullets start whizzing by their heads, as they continue returning fire. Two German soldiers suddenly appear on their right flank. They are close; maybe only ten yards away. Joe fires his weapon and kills the enemy soldier on their left. The other German throws a grenade (a potato masher) at Joe and Mike. Immediately Mike races towards the device and throws his body over it.......and it detonates beneath him. Joe stands and kills that soldier. He runs to Mike and lays down next to him calling Mike's name. "Mike!" "Mike!"

"Mike!" Meanwhile Andy leaps off the tank and joins the two men. He turns Mike over and sees that the explosive has eviscerated him. Mike is dead. Joe jumps back up and starts running towards the enemy. He is screaming, "No!....... No!.......No! You bastards killed my friend! He continues screaming, while rapidly discharging his weapon at the enemy. Andy sprints after Joe and tackles him. He shouts, "He's dead Sox! He's dead! There's nothing you can do about it! Stop it before you get yourself killed! He's dead." Then they both commence shooting at the Nazis while remaining in prone positions.

The battle ends a short time later. The allies are victorious. The Germans have been totally decimated. There are even no prisoners to contend with.

Helicopters fly in to remove the dead, and to evacuate the wounded. The Quartermaster orders an encampment to be established at a level area near the battlefield.

Four hours later the men of Thumper's crew recuperate inside their newly erected tent. They start a conversation, but Joe won't speak. He just lays on his cot with his face to the tent's wall.

Andy says, "If we truly believe that there is a heaven, then why are we so sad when a friend or relative dies? I know where Mike is right now."

"Paddy says, "It's been a' said, "Only the good die young. Ah, so be it. Ye should ner'regret bein' of old age, for there be many that'll ne'r have known it. "Aye, and he'll be a recievin' a medal for what's been done."

Ski adds, "Poor Mike. He was a great guy. It should have been me. It really should have been me."

Andy adds, "You know guys, not long before Mike's death today, he said to me, "I've heard that there are no atheists in foxholes, and I believe that's true. He said I feel so sorry for the men that fear death. I believe it isn't death that they fear, but not knowing what happens after death. The unknown is the root of all fear; and then he added, but I know without a doubt what occurs next after death, and I have no fear of it. I'm ready to meet my Savior. Like the apostle Paul said, 'Oh, death where is thy sting? Oh, grave where is thy victory?"

Ski says. "I remember he told me that he hated those jokes and Hollywood movies that suggest a man can get to heaven by being good. You know, by doing good deeds. He said that makes a mockery of the Gospel. The only way to eternal life is by faith; by believing that Christ died for you."

Night falls upon their encampment, as the bugler wails "Taps".

CHAPTER 42

(In Shashani)

As I walk to my scheduled class with brother Jacob, my mind is actually at the mountain top looking for the cave entrance to my freedom. I have decided that I can wait no longer. I'll leave in two days.

When I arrive for class, the forever smiling Jacob says, "Good to see you again Hiram. Are you ready for today's study? Because the teacher will arrive when the student is ready to learn."

"I'm as ready as I'll ever be Jacob."

"We need to start discussing the issue of blood in the scriptures. The bible gives very early examples of the importance of blood. You have heard the account of Adam and Eve in the Garden of Eden. Have you not?"

I giggle and say, "Yes I have."

"After man's first sin he felt naked. God then took animal skins and clothed them. This was the first shedding of blood. I also would like you to remember your Aunt Annie's story of Noah. He built a large ship called an ark to save him and his family from the impending flood. What do you think kept the waters out?"

"I don't know."

"The ark Hiram was covered in pitch. What we would call tar and oil. Pitch is the blood of the earth. Sap is the blood of the tree. Yes, Hiram the blood saved Noah and his family.

You said you saw a film about the ten commandments. Do you remember the ten plagues that God put upon the land of Egypt? The last plague was the angel of death that would kill all the first-born male children in Egypt. God told the Hebrews to kill a lamb and wipe blood above the doors of their dwellings. The angel seeing the blood would Passover them. Their children were saved by the blood." There are many other accounts of life saving blood. For instance, did you know that the Hebrews practiced animal sacrifice?"

"My old Hebrew language professor Mr. Abramowitz had me translate a few Hebrew texts into English that pertained to that subject, but I don't believe that the "Humane Society of the United States" would have approved of it.........That was meant to be a joke, Jacob."

"I am sorry, I failed to understand the humor. But did he explain to you why they killed the beasts?"

"No, he did not. My course was only for learning the Hebrew tongue, not for any theological reasons."

"Turn with me to the book of Leviticus to Chapter 1:3. Do you see that this is called a "Burnt offering," and that the animal was to be from the herd, guaranteeing a healthy animal. Then it indicates that the beast was to be male animal, a bull. It had to be free from blemish, in other words free from any type of sore or discoloration. Meaning it had to be sin free. The person who brought this offering would then lay his hands upon it. He was identifying with the bull, and in essence was saying to the Lord that he was a sinner and was deserving of this death, but instead accept this animal's death for the forgiveness of my sins. This sacrifice is similar to another offering called the "Sin offering" in Leviticus 4. Both of these sacrifices were for the forgiveness of sins. More importantly they pointed toward another offering to be made in the future. Can you surmise Hiram, who that is pointing to?"

"I would guess Jacob, that you are going to tell me that it points to Jesus."

"I am, and I will. Now turn for me to Hebrews 10:12. Please read that verse aloud."

I read, "But this man, after He had offered one sacrifice for sins forever, sat down at the right hand of God."

"Now read verse 14 please Hiram."

I read again, "For by one offering He hath perfected forever them that are sanctified."

"Now allow me Hiram to read the last part of Hebrews 9:22, "Without the shedding of blood there is no remission of sins." All of the Old Testament burnt sacrifices were only pointing to the one perfect sacrifice made on the cross by Christ. You see all animals were created by God, they belonged to Him, and therefore He could accept them as an offering unto Himself. What the Godhead wanted was the perfect sacrifice; Himself through the Son. There is a verse Hiram that says, greater love hath no man then he lay his life down for a friend. Praise God for His love towards us. Turn with me to John 3: 16 and read about the perfect sacrifice for sins."

I read aloud, "For God so loved the world, that He gave His only begotten Son, that whosoever believeth in Him, should not perish but have everlasting life."

Do you see the importance of the blood Hiram?"

"Yes, I see that it is significant in your bible, but there are many other religions in the world Jacob."

"Yes, and we will discuss that issue at another time. By the way, I understand you have been seeing Sister Ruth. Not only at the stables but elsewhere. If this is correct listen to her carefully. She will have much to teach you."

"That concludes our session for today, Hiram. I would leave you with but one thought. God indeed has a blueprint for your life."

CHAPTER 43

(Meanwhile in Philadelphia Pa.)

(March 28th, 1944)

On a cold, rainy, and dismal day, Irene Jacobs, and her mother Rosemary walk down a street towards their usual Friday luncheon engagement. With umbrellas they hide their faces from the rain and blustery wind until they enter the "Le Canard Noir", their regular restaurant of choice; an expensive, but popular bistro in downtown Philly. After checking their coats and hats, the maître de happily seats them at their favorite table with a window view. It overlooks a number of high-end department stores, but due to the weather there is little movement of pedestrians outside, and the normally crowded eatery is sparse of customers.

Mrs. Jacobs starts the conversation with, "Irene have you heard any further news about Hiram?" The situation does look rather bleak."

"No mother, not since we received that horrid telegram. And by the way, why do you insist referring to my fiancé as Hiram?"

"Well, that is his name is it not?"

"You know perfectly well that it is, but since his childhood he's been called Ace, and he prefers that name."

(The waiter comes to their table to take their drink order.)

"A Vodka Collins please Raymond; and I just think you must prepare for the worst dear."

"The same as mothers, please Raymond."

A period of uneasy silence ensues. Then Irene asks, oh mother, why do you persist in burying him before we know what is going on? He was declared MIA, missing in action, not KIA, killed in action."

"Irene dear, we must always plan for the future."

"Yes, mother I am, and I'm planning for a long and happy life with the man I love. For me, there will be no other man but Ace. I love him deeply."

The waiter approaches their table and asks, "Are you ladies ready to order?"

Mrs. Jacobs says, "Yes Raymond, I'll have the "Chateaubriand.""

"Excellent choice Mrs. Jacobs. And for you ma'am?"

"I think I'll have the "Pasta Primavera," if I may."

"Thank you, ladies. Would there be anything else?"

"No," they answer in unison.

The conversation continues. "I am not trying to upset you dear. It is just that I have always attempted to keep disappointments from your life. I want to see you happy."

"And I will be happy mother, when Ace returns home."

"But what if something terrible has happened. What if something dreadful has occurred?"

"Oh mother, what if we get struck by lightning, what if we get sick, what if we die in an awful accident? Mother would you please keep your what-ifs to yourself."

(Their food comes)

Mrs. Jacobs adds, "You know that handsome young attorney of your father's, I believe his name is Xander Bascombe, has been asking about you. I hear that he has been visiting the newspaper quite frequently, and I do not believe he goes there just to see your father."

"Oh really.......and what other gossip have you heard about the newspaper mother?"

"Oh, you know that your father rarely confers with me about his business."

"Well, I have some news for you mommy dearest. Your daughter has been promoted to "Editor of the Society Page" starting next week."

"Congratulations dear. I know that this isn't a case of nepotism, but that you were truly deserving."

"Thank you. I just wish I could be happy and excited about it, but I can't. I will never be the same until Ace comes marching home. And please don't ever mention to me the name of Xander whoever again."

CHAPTER 44

(Back in Shashani)

(May 9th, 1944)

Tonight's the night. I am outta here! I have hoarded food from the dining hall to munch on, and today I'm skipping my stable duties and the classroom. I'm sorry Jacob, no school for Acey boy today! It's funny, but I've always thought that in school there were three kinds of people. Yeah three. Those who can count and those who can't....... Yeah Jacob, you wouldn't have understood that joke either.

When the witching hour of midnight comes, and with backpack on, I head to the stable to fetch Lizzy. As I approach her, she whinnies. I say to her, "Yeah I love you too girl, and tonight we go for a midnight ride just like Paul Revere; except this time, you come back lonesome." I pet her nose, and I whisper sweet nothings in her ear. Then I saddle her.

We head slowly to the northern mountains. Everything is silent except for the clippity-clop of my horse's hooves. I should be there in less than an hour, but after reaching the piedmont, I am having trouble finding the trail that leads up the mountain. I dismount and search for the trail with my lantern. It takes me another hour to find it, and I tie a yellow ribbon around a small tree branch. I then return to Lizzy, slap her on the behind, and watch her saunter off back to the stables.

While ascending the elevation to the peak I start to tire quickly. I realize I am out of shape, and it takes me a while to catch my breath. When I resume my hike, a critter scurries across the pathway and gives me a scare. I didn't see what it was, but I stopped again. It's stupid, but I wish I had a cigarette. I'm actually exhausted and sweating profusely when I finally reach the level plateau that leads to the cave entrance. I take my pack off and sit on a flat stone to rest a while. My spirits are high in anticipation of seeing my friends again. As I contemplate a reunion with Irene, I'm a little puzzled. I really have missed her, but do I really love her? If I did, would I have cheated, and spent that night in Cairo with a whore? Am I ready for marriage? Has meeting Ruth muddled my mind? I shake my head to rid myself of these thoughts, in order to resume the task of finding my freedom.

With my lantern I scan the stone precipice, and I move the beam up and down and left and right. Finally, I see a large boulder. The opening should be here. Then to my amazement, I discern writing on the boulder. Painted on the stone in red paint is the Hebrew word "HASHAR." My mind translates it into English. It means "The Gate." It is closed. I ask myself, "Why is it closed"? I approach it and place my hands on gaps attempting to pry it open. It doesn't budge. I try again with all my strength and it still does not move. Thinking there may be some device, such as a lever or a latch, I scour the surface with my hands looking for it, but it is void of any such apparatus. Then finally, to my horror, I realize that the boulder is sealed shut and I am a prisoner in this land. My mind races madly! Why!? Why!? Why!? Why did they lock me in? Then my curiosity turns to anger! I scream, "YOU MADMEN YOU! YOU MADE ME YOUR PRISONER! THIS IS NO PARADISE! THIS IS A MADHOUSE! A MADHOUSE!

I feel drained and I surrender all hopes of leaving, I just lay down on the ground in anguished disgust!

All kinds of thoughts invade my mind.

After a long time, I regain my composure, stand back up, and commence going back down the mountain.

I eventually reach the bottom and walk back to my cottage. When I enter, I remove my clothing and flop onto my cot.

CHAPTER 45

I wake up late the next day and decide that I would see none of these people. I'm afraid of what I might say or do, and instead I spend my time reading and sleeping. Time goes by slowly, when your mind is filled with anxious uncertainties.

Finally, after three days of tempering my anger, I resolve to leave and see Ruth. Maybe she could explain why they locked me in. Then for the first time I wondered if I needed permission to leave, but that thought makes me even madder. I need to see Ruth.

When I get to the stable's barn, I see Luke haying an animal. He greets me with, "Hello Hiram long time no see. Where have you been?"

"You might say I've been sick Luke......yeah, you might <u>say</u> that."

"Well, I sure hope you are better now Hiram."

"Thanks, I am. Where's Ruth?"

"Oh, she went to get some oats. She should be back shortly."

As soon as Luke's words leave his mouth Ruth comes into the stable carrying a large bag of oats over her shoulder. I say, "Speak of the devil and here she is."

"What devils are you referring to? There are no devils here in Shashani, Hiram."

"There are certainly devils in my world Ruth."

She says, "Well stranger, and just where have you been?"

"Let's go into your office and I'll tell you about it Ruth."

"If you help me carry these bags in, we will do just that Hiram. I want to hear about this mysterious story."

"And I want to share it with you."

After I bring in and stack about two dozen bags, she ushers me into the office, and I take a seat at her desk.

She asks, "Coffee?"

"I suppose so."

"Black right?"

"That's right."

"What is on your mind Hiram? Although I should ask you first why you have been hiding in your cottage for three days?"

"Word gets around here quickly, doesn't it?"

"Hiram, you know that Shashani is a very small place. You seem troubled. Why?"

"I'm not sure how to begin, but a few nights ago I attempted to leave Shashani and return to my platoon."

"Why would you do that?"

"I felt that I had been derelict in my duties to my country."

"Your duties are to remain here and prepare for when it is your time to leave. You still do not comprehend that duties to God, take priority over duties to country. And by the way, why would you depart without saying goodbye? That would have been quite rude, don't you agree? I know that would have hurt me and disappointed many others. I care for you Hiram."

"Ruth, I'm sorry, but to say that I'm angry about being denied the privilege to depart from here would be an understatement. I am not angry, I am furious. I feel like Shashani has imprisoned me. To me this place is no longer a paradise, for me it has become a penitentiary. I am now a captive. Would you know why the gate was closed Ruth? Was it blocked to prevent me from leaving?"

"I have no knowledge as to when, or to why the gate was either closed or opened Hiram. I am not privileged to have that information. It is possible that Brother Jacob would know. I do know that Romans 8:28 says, "That all things work together for good to them that love God, to them who are the called according to His purpose." I also know that He has called you. Right now, you can do nothing about it except share this day with me. Would you do that for me Hiram?"

As I take in her beauty, especially her inner beauty and innocence, my heart melts. I say, "Oh Ruth, even though I am as mad as a hornet's nest I could never say no to you. What do you have in mind?"

"Right now, I believe a place of rest and solitude would do us both some good. Although I have rarely experienced any stress in my life, at this moment I am feeling yours. I know of such a place Hiram. It is only a short ride from here. I will pack us a picnic lunch. Will you go with me?"

"Of course, I will."

"Wonderful! I still have some questions for you Hiram."

In about an hour, we saddle our horses and head south. I ask her, "Is there a name for this place we are going?"

"Yes, it is called "Joshua's Grove". My parents and I would go there often when I was a child. Please Hiram, relax and enjoy the day.

I think that this woman could soothe the savage beast. I tell her, "I'll do just that Ruth", but what I'm really thinking is that I can't wait to give Jacob the third degree.

My horse Lizzy underneath me, seems to be content as we slowly ride towards the grove. Ruth has suggested that everything that happens to me is for the good, and although my mind doesn't agree, my frayed nerves and anger are starting to subside.

Within the hour we enter into a clearing that is surrounded by tall cedars. Three rustic log cabins are arranged in a triangle each equidistant from the others. All three have covered porches. In the middle of the three is a large fire pit. Wooden benches surround the pit. A small brook runs gently through the clearing. This place is the epitome of peace and solitude.

We dismount from the horses and go to one of the cabins. Ruth places our picnic basket on a table under the porch roof, and we take seats in Adirondack style chairs. She asks, "Are you thirsty Hiram?"

"I am, what do we have?"

"Cold apple cider and a few sweet biscuits."

"I would prefer a cold beer and a cigarette."

Ruth laughs and says, "You are forever incorrigible Hiram. It seems that your world has addicted you to some nasty habits."

She pours the cider into two glass jars and hands me one. I raise mine and clink it against hers. She gives me a puzzled expression and says, "What was that?"

"That was a toast."

"What is a toast?"

"A toast is a gesture made to wish the other person good health. In ancient times it was understood that the clinking sound of the glasses being tapped together would ward off evil spirits."

"There are no evil spirits in Shashani Hiram."

"There are in mine dear."

She pouts at me and says, "You just called me dear. Was that simply one of your expressions......one of your colloquialisms, or do you really hold me dear?"

"I think that you are truly wonderful Ruth, and if I was able to leave Shashani when I tried, I would have missed you above all."

"Thank you, Hiram. Sometimes beneath your course exterior you are really sweet. I said that I wished to question you. Please tell me some things about your world."

"What would you like to know?"

"I have read about the world from the Bible, and books in our library. Some indicate that many are very bad, and others have very good manners. Is this true?"

"Manners? This Irishman once told me that the only substitute for good manners are quick reflexes."

"Do you mean that they fight?"

"Yes, they do."

"What do they fight about?"

"They fight about all sorts of things Ruth. They fight over money, politics, women, and a myriad of other subjects."

"Why would one fight over money? Money is not necessary. The good book says that "The love of money is the root of all evil." Here in Shashani we use no monetary system. We are self-sufficient and are all friends."

"In our world Ruth money can't buy you friends, but it can get you a better class of enemy. Greed is prevalent in our society.

We call a greedy person a miser. Now misers may not be good friends, but they make great ancestors....... But money is needed in the world, even churches need money. I heard a story once about a pastor who asked God, "How long is a million years to you? God answered and said, "About one second." Then the pastor asks, "How much is a million dollars worth to you?" And God answered, "About one penny." Then the pastor asked, "Would you give me one of those pennies God?" God answered, "Yes, but give me a second."

"Oh Hiram, I never know when you are joking or telling the truth!"

"I am jokingly telling you the truth."

"Well, what about women? Why would there be fights about women?"

"Because some men when they want to take a woman, they don't know which man's wife they want to take. Listen Ruth when men fight with women it's usually pertains to their marriage. I actually have never seen a perfect marriage in our world. I truly believe that there has only been one good marriage, and that would have been the marriage of Adam and Eve."

"Why Adam and Eve?"

"Because Adam never had to hear from Eve about all the other men she could have married, and Eve never had to put up with her mother-in-law."

"Oh Hiram, you make me laugh. But I am glad that you are in a better mood now. Please get serious. What is politics?"

"Politicians are a group of men belonging to a club they call an organized party. My father, a Republican, once said it best when he claimed that Democrats did not belong to any organized party.

In essence it is one man fighting with another about what is best for the country, and it's too bad that the men who could do that best, are instead driving cabs and cutting hair."

"I don't understand this politics."

"Neither do I Ruth. Neither do I. But let me sum this up for you. In our world there are consequences. For instance, there are oceans that people drown in. There are bears that attack people. There are addictive drugs that companies make.

But the ocean doesn't care if a person doesn't know how to swim, the bear doesn't care, if you're on a family camping trip, and he decides he's hungry enough to eat your child, the drug manufacturers don't care if you take to many of their pills and never wake up. In my world there are consequences Ruth. In Shashani there are few consequences if any. You live in a perfect and idyllic environment, ours can be a living hell."

"That is because sin has entered into the world Hiram. Whatever tragedy befalls mankind it is because of the first man's sin; although God is often blamed, He shouldn't be."

We eat our picnic lunch and Ruth tells me, "I think that I am beginning to like you too much Hiram."

"That is highly possible Ruth, because I'm really a likeable guy."

"You must promise me something Hiram. Please promise me you will not hurry to leave Shashani. I would enjoy knowing you better. Also promise me you will continue your studies with brother Jacob. Will you promise me this?"

"Yes, I will. In fact, Ruth, I believe I would do anything that you asked of me. But I want you to know that I still am upset at what happened up on that mountain, and I have many more questions about that."

We talk until dusk, and ride back together.

CHAPTER 46

After my time with Ruth, I feel somewhat better, although I'm still planning on sinking my fangs into Jacob.

When I reach my cottage, I find there is a note tacked on my door. It reads:

Dear Mr. Walker,

You have been scheduled an appointment with Brother Samuel this Friday for 10:00 am In the castle library. Please be punctual.

Thank you, Brother Elijah

After reading this message I speculate whether this is good or bad news, and by the time I enter the castle's library, I decide that either one would be fine. At least I'll be getting some questions answered. I see a man sitting in a far corner of the room, smiling at me with acknowledgement. It's crazy how the mind works at times, but as I walk over to meet him, I think of Stanley meeting Dr. Livingstone in Africa. I greet him with, "Brother Samuel...... I presume?" (I laugh to myself knowing that he wouldn't grasp the humor.)

"Yes Mr. Walker. I am. Please be seated. I believe that you may have some conceptions pertaining to this meeting's purpose?"

"Yes, I have a few, and I also I have many questions for you. For starters did you actually close that damn gate to hold me hostage?"

"Not me Mr. Walker, we......and please refrain from using foul language."

"Why was it closed?"

"Allow me to answer that question, with a question I propose to ask you."

"Be my guest."

"Please think back to that dreadful day Mr. Walker when you were brutally gunshot while photographing your war. When you first became conscious, what did you comprehend your condition to be?"

I answer, "I knew I was badly hurt. My leg and arm were broken, and I thought my ribs were also. I thought I could possibly die. My first instinct was to find my platoon. When I realized that was hopeless, I went into survival mode. I knew that I needed food, water, and some type of shelter from the sun's heat."

"Did you actually believe your condition would have allowed you to obtain those things?"

"What else was I to do? I wasn't going to give up and "kick the bucket."

"Kick what?"

"The bucket. That was slang for die. "Give up the ghost." "Croak." Pass away." "Meet my maker."

"In your condition at that time, it was of a great certainty that you would have met your maker. However, I am confident that He would not have been particularly pleased to meet you Mr. Walker."

"What are you implying?"

"I am implying that you would never have been capable of doing those things. You were already dying Mr. Walker. Neither would you have seen the cavern entrance, nor would you have had the stamina to crawl a distance of three-hundred meters to attain it. Do you not understand that you had assistance?"

"Assistance? Assistance from whom?"

"The Lord God sanctioned your rescue. Messengers assisted you."

"You're saying malakis saved me; angels came to my rescue?"

"That is correct. Without their help your body would be decomposing in the desert as we speak."

I frown and say, "B. S."

Samuel asks, "What is "B. S."

"Never mind. You wouldn't understand."

"I apologize for not being familiar with your slang."

"Listen brother Samuel you still haven't answered my question. Why was I prohibited from leaving Shashani?"

"Because Mr. Walker you would have died in exactly eight hours and sixteen minutes after your departure. Simply put, to prevent your perishing, God saved your earthly body."

"That is a hard thing for me to swallow brother Samuel. If this is true, I must be truly blessed."

"Nevertheless, it is the gospel truth; however, Mr. Walker you should understand that many more people, of all millennia, have been blessed much more than you."

"What do you mean?"

"I mean that you have witnessed with your own eyes the marvel that is Shashani, and deep down in your heart, you must know that you would have never survived your ordeal in the desert. I am saying that you are cognizant that your earthly salvation was a miracle. The Lord said, and I paraphrase, "Those who have not seen with their eyes these miracles I perform, but believe by faith alone, are more blessed. You have seen God's miracles, those who have not seen and believe are therefore more blessed. "For faith is the substance of things hoped for; the evidence of things not seen." I believe, taking an expression from your own world would be, "Wake up and smell the roses." Wake up Mr. Walker and recognize that God has brought you here for His purpose! Not until you accept that, will you satisfy that hunger...... that blackness, that emptiness, that you feel within you. Think about your past life. Think about the times when you thought something was missing within yourself."

I feel as though I have been scolded as a schoolboy; that the teacher has just ordered me to write on the blackboard "I have been naughty" one-hundred times. Brother Samuel has just admonished me, and for the first time I realize that I'm deserving of it. I tell him, "Please brother, understand that this experience has educated me, and I seek your indulgence in allowing me a measure of time to fully digest what you have told me, but I must know when I'll be permitted to leave Shashani."

"We will open the gate for you only when you have completed all, one hundred percent; I say the entirety of all your scheduled curriculum in your assigned classes. I shall assume Mr. Walker that you that you will resume your studies with Brother Jacob, and continue with your future curriculum. You have much to contemplate Mr. Walker. I will pray for you."

"I will do just that sir." "Thank you."

As I leave my mind is reeling, and I ask myself, "Can all this be true?" But if I honestly assess the events of that episode in the desert, I'm starting to believe that Samuel may be correct.

CHAPTER 47

(Returning to the war, May 29ᵗʰ, 1944)

The crew of thumper is sleeping in their tent. They are frightened awake by a soldier running in and shouting. "Liberty!" "Liberty!" "Liberty!" We have been awarded liberty guys! Wake up and get dressed fellas. A plane's comin' to take us to Cairo!"

An hour later the four arrived in Cairo. They hail a taxi, and the driver says, "How be you soldiers? I am Abdullah. Where you go?" Since they have already decided to forego any military barracks Andy speaks up and says, "Take us to a nice hotel Abdullah."

"I take you to "Private Villa." Is nice place, no?"

"Paddy says, "Aye me good man you'll be takin' us there and may ye slide down the banister of life with the splinters pointing in the right direction!" They all laugh except Abdullah. "What is funny," he asks.

Andy says, "Never mind Abdullah, just drive. Just drive!"

Upon arrival at the hotel the four men check in, and Joe gawks at his surroundings and says, "Get a load of this place guys. This is betta' then the Pawka House in Boston. Let's go to the baa." Good idea Joe," says Ski.

Andy says, "In memory of Ace I'm having "Canadian Club" over rocks. Ski, Joe, and Paddy look at each other and smile.

Ski says, "All for one and one for all." Then they lift their glasses in a toast loudly announcing, "Here's to Ace!"

Paddy chimes in with, "Aye, and may ye be in heaven an hour before the devil knows yer dead!"

A man in an Army Air Corps uniform takes a stool next to them. Andy asks, "Hi lieutenant, are you enjoying Cairo?"

A somewhat drunken LT stammers, "I usually do. Hello yourself, I'm Paul Mitchell. Just call me LT. And yes, I enjoy Cairo because I spend most of my time here. I fly a P51 Mustang that's hangered here."

Andy makes the introductions. "We're with the 1st Division of the 2nd Armored. I'm Andy, this is Joe Sox, that's Ski, and that's Paddy. Nice to meet you. Wow, sure is nice duty you've got yourself here LT."

LT answers, "Yeah, I guess it beats pounding the ground. Say, I met a guy from your outfit. He's a photographer named Ace Walker. You don't" know him, do you?"

Astounded, Andy says, "What? You met Ace Walker? Yeah, we know him. The four of us where in the same company together, in fact we crewed the same tank. Ace was assigned to us as a war correspondent. Really, I can't believe you met Ace. Did you meet him here?"

LT says, "Yep, right here in this resort. We had some good times together. How's old Ace doin'?"

Andy relates, "I'm afraid he's listed as MIA. We lost him in a skirmish with some Krauts in the Sinai."

"Oh no! I'm sorry to hear that. That's really hard to believe." LT leans forward and whispers in Andy's ear, "I have to be careful who I tell this to, because there are always ears listening in Cairo; but Ace and I whacked two Nazi spies while he was here with me."

Andy laughs, and then whispers back, "You know, Ace mentioned that to me. I thought he was kidding."

LT then stands and loudly announces, I'm also the one that piloted us on that reconnaissance mission that we flew over the Sinai."

Paddy chimes in, "Well shor an be gora, ye are, are ye? Well then here's to be drinkin' doubles and be seein' triples! Set em up barkeep the drinks be on me!"

Just then two women join them and say, "Hello G.I.'s. I am Shani, and this is Aziza. We love soldier boys. We have girlfriends. You want good time?"

IT'S PARTY TIME IN CAIRO!

After one week of debauchery, in which Andy partakes in the partying while abstaining from the girls, he decides it's time to do something a little more constructive; maybe a little more educational. With a morning hangover, he says, "You know fellas, I think we should maybe take a break from all this madness and do something different."

"What do you have in mind Andy?" asks Ski.

"I'm thinking I'd like to see the pyramids."

Ski answers, "Good idea. I'm all in."

Paddy says, "Not I laddies. I like me women like I like me whiskey!"

Joe says, "I'm with Paddy."

Andy tells Paddy and Joe, "Alright Ski and I'll go. You two can stay here and finish getting your cases of the clap."

CHAPTER 48

(In Cairo)

The next morning in the hotel lobby Andy and Ski spy a poster offering a tour of the Giza pyramid. They walk up to the counter and the man behind it says, "The tour, she be ten American dollar. Fifteen dollar if you want horse."

"Andy exclaims? "Why horses?"

The man explains. "Is simple, no? No horses. You walk."

"Then we'll take the horses bud," says Ski. "I'm just glad they're not camels."

"My name no Bud. My name Haji I take thirty dollar. Go outside. Leave fifteen minutes."

Andy says, "Really Ski, we're going to ride horses to the great pyramid of Giza?"

"Why not Andy? Have you ever ridden before?"

"Never. But if Tom Mix can do it so can I."

"We are both absolutely crazy Andy!"

They mount up and could be heard laughing, as Ski starts singing "I'm back in the saddle again! Oh, the horse this old horse is my friend, Whoopi-ty-aye-yay I go my way, I'm back in the saddle again!"

****

The next day in Andy and Ski's room they hear a knock on the door. Upon opening it Andy finds a porter standing with a letter in hand. "Message for Sergeant Harrison", he announces.

Andy reads the letter out loud to Ski, "Attention all personnel. All liberty has been cancelled. Report today at 1600 hours to the Cairo Phoenix Hotel for briefing and orders. Signed, MSgt. Jensen."

"Wow! What do you think that's all about Andy?"

"I don't know Ski, but better go and tell Paddy and Joe. We'll grab some late lunch and then head over there,"

At 1600 hours sharp all the Officers and NCOs of the 2nd Armored Division were assembled within the large ballroom of the hotel. The Division commander General Charles L. Scott was standing alongside an aide on a platform with microphone in hand. He announces,

"Today June the 6th 1944 marks the greatest invasion in the history of the world. It has been dubbed "Operation Overlord," and as we speak gentlemen, we and our allies are invading the beaches of Normandy on the French coast. 160,000 of our troops are assaulting Omaha, Utah, Gold, Juno, and Sword beaches. 24,000 paratroopers have dropped into the fight, and 6,000 planes are leading the battle. 1,213 American, and 892 British warships are positioned in the area for support. We intend to push Nazi Germany out of France and ultimately and utterly destroy their war machine. To do that, we have been ordered to deploy to England in readiness to cross the channel into France. We will join with the French 2nd Armored Division to liberate the country of France!"

CHAPTER 49

(In Shashani)

This time as I head to Brother Jacob's classroom, I'm actually excited about the lesson I'll be studying. I now accept without any doubt, that I would have died in that desert unless a miracle was performed on my behalf. Moreover, these people, this valley, are miracles unto themselves.

Brother Jacob welcomes me with, "Good afternoon, Hiram! May I say that you are looking extremely well today!"

"Ah Jacob, I just took a deep breath, inhaled peace, and exhaled happiness! And how are you today my fine man?"

"I am well Hiram. I am well. Are you ready to go to work?"

"Jacob, nothing is really work, unless you'd rather be doing something else, and right now, this is what I would prefer to be doing dear brother!"

Jacob smiles and says, "I appreciate your enthusiasm. May I inquire as to how your meeting was with Brother Samuel?"

"You may Jacob, but I have a sneaky suspicion that you already know what that meeting was about, and also how it went. Am I Right?"

"You have surmised correctly, and I wish to no longer discuss those matters. Today let us look at something the Lord said to our brethren the Pharisees and the Sadducees. Turn with me to Matthew 16 and read aloud verses 2 and 3."

"I read, "He answered and said unto them, "When it is evening, ye say, it will be fair weather: for the sky is red. And in the morning, it will be foul weather today: for the sky is red and lowring. O' ye hypocrites, you can discern the face of the sky; but can ye not discern the signs of the times?"

"That's interesting Jacob, sailors still use that phenomenon today in predicting the weather."

"That is true Hiram, however what I wish you to notice is that the Lord called them hypocrites. Why did he do that?"

"I believe because they could forecast the weather but not believe who He was, am I right?"

"Yes, you are, and they, being knowledgeable in the scriptures, should have known both when the Messiah would come and where He would be born. Here is why. Turn now to Daniel 9:25. This scripture occurred in the year you would call 500 B.C. What has transpired here, because of the Jews unfaithfulness to God, He allowed them to be conquered by the Babylonians under a king named Nebuchadnezzar. This king destroyed Jerusalem and took many of its people captive into Babylon, but the Babylonians are soon conquered by the Persians. In this verse that you will read a God-fearing man named Daniel is given a prophecy from the angel Gabriel in Dan 25a. Please read the verses aloud."

I read, "Know therefore and understand, that from the going forth of the commandment to restore and build Jerusalem unto the Messiah the Prince shall be seven weeks, and threescore and two weeks: the street shall be built again, and the wall even in troublous times."

"This is an amazing prophecy, Hiram. It is called the seventy weeks of years, or the 490-year prophecy. It is an example of the absolute accuracy of the holy scriptures. Let me break it down in simple terms for you. Threescore and seven plus two weeks total 69 weeks. These if you read above are weeks of years, thus 7 days in a week times 69 equals

483 years. What this prophecy is saying is that the exact day the Persian king tells his Jewish servant to go to Jerusalem to rebuild the city until the coming of Jesus Christ the Messiah will be exactly 483 years! And we have the starting date of this prophecy In Nehamiah 2:1.

"And it came to pass in the month Nissan in the twentieth year of Artaxerxes......And we can stop right there because now we have the date; for historians have discovered through their irrefutable archeological findings that Artaxerxes reigned from 465 BC to December of 424 BC. Therefore, the twentieth year of his reign would be 445 BC, and 483 years from that date (by using their method of calculating the calendar) Jesus the Messiah will be born unto man. That is why Jesus told the Pharisees and Sadducees they were hypocrites. They should have known! For goodness sakes even Daniel's predecessor's the magicians (the wise men) who were ordered by the king to serve under Daniel, were told by him of the date, which is why they came to worship Him. Also, these pompous, self-righteous religious rulers should have known where Jesus was born. But do you know Hiram?"

"Was He born in Philadelphia?"

"What!? No!"

"Was it in Pittsburgh?"

"Of course, not Hiram. The book of Micha 5:2 says Jesus was born in Bethlehem."

"I knew it was someplace in Pennsylvania!"

"Oh, Hiram you are always joking!"

"I'm sorry Jacob.......no, really, I'm sorry. This wasn't the proper time for me to be clowning around. Please forgive me."

"No need to forgive Hiram, Sometimes I think that we could use a little more levity in Shashani."

"What an amazing study this was Jacob. Thank you. If you keep this up, I'll be almost persuaded to become a Christian,"

"That is exactly what a king named Agrippa said once to the apostle Paul in Acts 26:28 "Then Agrippa said to Paul. "Almost thou persuadest me to be a Christian." But let me say to you Hiram. "Almost" is not good enough."

"There's a few things that I still need to ask about."

"Well then you have come to the right person Hiram. Because I may not have all the answers, but I surely have all the questions. I will try to help you ask them."

CHAPTER 50

(Philadelphia Pa.)

(July 11th, 1944)

Irene Jacobs hears a knock on her newly appointed office door. She looks up and while peering above her reading glasses says, "Come in please."

A tall, slender, and handsome man, wearing a finely tailored three-piece suit walks in. He smiles, removes his fedora, walks over to her desk, and hands her a bouquet of flowers. "Please understand dear Irene, that these are a bribe. They are to encourage you to say yes to my offering of a dinner invitation."

"Hello Xander. They are lovely. She puts her fingers on her head in thought and says, "I suppose the answer is yes." She pauses for a long time, and with a sad face announces, "It's been months now that we haven't heard from Ace. Both mother and father are encouraging me to move on. But I must ask you Xander to be patient with me."

"I just left your father's office. I had to drop off some papers for his signature, and he suggested that I should do the same. I will treat you with kid's gloves Irene. Where would you like to go?"

"I would enjoy going to that French restaurant "Le Canard Noir." I have never been there without my mother. I think that without her constant nagging presence I would enjoy it even more."

"Nous irons a' la "Le Canard le Noir, Mon Cher!" I shall pick you up at 7:30 sil vous plait?" "That time will be fine Xander. I'll see you then."

CHAPTER 51

(In Shashani)

There is a fight within me. A struggle within myself. A part of me perceives that there is truth in what the brothers have taught me. However, that old man inside of me, that old Ace Walker is resisting these new dogmas. There is one question that still plagues me, and I hope that Jacob can answer it to my satisfaction. I'll find out now as our next session begins.

"Brother I'm confused about one issue."

"That would be a great achievement for us Hiram; if there is but only one issue you need resolved. What would you wish to know?"

"There are so many religions in the world. Are they all wrong? Is Christianity the only true religion. I find that difficult to understand. How could so many people be wrong?"

"The scriptures say in Prov 14:12, "There is a way which seemeth right unto man, but the end thereof are the ways of death."

There was a very famous countryman of yours Hiram, in fact a true believer in the Lord, named Benjamin Franklin. He created a system that he employed whenever he had a need to make a decision or solve a problem. He called it his "Pro and Con Method." Simply put, he drew two columns on paper and wrote the heading on top. Therefore, if we

242

used his system our heading would be "Religions of the world." In the left column we could write "the names of religions that require what a person must accomplish in order to gain salvation." In that left column we would have to include Islam, Buddhism, Shintoism, Sikhism, Judaism, Mormonism, Sun worship, and all of the entire religions of the ancient world. But you could not include Christianity within that group. You would have to write it in the right column with a heading that states, "The religion that states, "There is nothing that a man can do to gain salvation". It has been done for him." Do you see? It is just one way that Christianity is unique.

The bible is very clear Hiram. Jesus said it Himself in John 14:6 "I am the way, the truth, and the life: <u>no man cometh unto the Father but by me</u>." And Paul is inspired to write in the book of Acts 4:12, "Neither is there salvation in any other: <u>for there is none other name under heaven, given among men, whereby we must be saved</u>."

The scriptures say, "Seek and ye shall find." And indeed, you have been seeking Hiram; but be not confused. You must understand Hiram that religion in itself has been the bane of mankind. It has caused many problems and even wars in this world. You are not seeking the correct religion, Hiram. Allow me to repeat myself. You are not seeking a religion. You are seeking a person. You are seeking Hiram, a close and personal relationship with our Lord and Savior Jesus Christ. Our good deeds are all awash Hiram. Isaiah 64:6 states, "But we are all as an unclean thing, and all our righteousness are as filthy rags." Salvation is a gift we receive from a loving God. Ephesians 2:8 & 9 says, "For by grace are ye saved through faith; and that not of yourselves: it is the gift of God: Not of works lest any man should boast". "We are only saved through the shed blood of Christ on Calvary's cross. You only have to accept His gift."

What you must now do Hiram is to acknowledge to God that you are a sinner. You must pray and repent of your past transgressions against Him. Then you must ask Him for forgiveness. The 1st Epistle of John 1:9 says, "If we confess our sins, He is faithful and just to forgive us our sins and cleanse us from all unrighteousness." Now listen to me Hiram. For Romans 10:9 says, "That if thou shalt confess with thy mouth the Lord Jesus, and shalt believe in thy heart that God hath raise Him from the dead, thou shalt be saved."

But Jacob, you don't really know me. I have been a drunkard, a fornicator, I have cursed God, I have even killed men. I'm the most horrible person!"

"You may have some competition there Hiram, because the Apostle Paul once declared that he was the "Chief of sinners."

"Listen to me Hiram and listen to what Jesus says in Matthew 12:31 "Wherefore I say unto you, all manner of sin and blasphemy shall be forgiven unto men: but the blasphemy against the Holy Ghost shall not be forgiven unto men." Every sin you have committed past, present, and future will be forgiven you and forgotten by the father except one."

"What sin is that, Jacob? What sin is blasphemy of the Holy Ghost?"

"When the Holy Ghost convicts a person of their sins and asks that person to accept Christ's sacrifice for forgiveness, if that person denies Christs forgiveness they are forever lost."

I stare at Jacob. I just stare at him. I believe that this may be the first time in my life that I am truly speechless. Finally, after a long pause, I say, "Thank you."

"The Lord is thanking me, Hiram. I will pray for you."

I get up from my chair and head to the door, but I hesitate, and turn to face him. I start to speak, but I don't. I turn again and walk out the door.

CHAPTER 52

The next morning at the stables Ruth strolls up to me and says, "Is that a smile I see on your face, and so early in the morning?"

"It is, and it is a pleasant day, isn't it?"

"When have you ever awakened in Shashani, when the day was not pleasant Hiram?"

"I wasn't referring to the weather Ruth. It is your appearance this morning that is so pleasant to me."

"I am not accustomed to such flattery Hiram. I think I am blushing."

"That would only enhance your already beautiful face, Ruth."

"Would you please refrain from embarrassing me. Today being Sunday, I have had an idea for us to share."

"And that would be?"

"I propose, that is after our duties here in the stables, that we entertain ourselves with a long hike."

"You say a hike; meaning we exclude the horses?"

"Yes. I wish to show you the most grandeur scene in all of Shashani. However, you must put on your climbing legs."

"Climbing. This sounds like severe exercise. I must warn you that whenever I get the desire to exercise, I lie down and rest until the urge passes."

"Very funny. I shall meet you here an hour after immersion."

This time during my bathing in the lake during "immersion", I realize that something is different. When the group begins singing their beautiful Christian melodies, I feel my inhibitions, my unbelief, and my resistance to the Gospel starting to fade away.

We begin our hike heading northwest. In my mind, as we walk, a recording seems to be replaying my last session with Brother Jacob. It is interrupted when Ruth says, "Look up high towards where we are heading Hiram. Do you see a white stone structure? Do you see it? It is about halfway up the mountain."

"Yes, I do. It must be at an elevation of at least five -thousand feet. Is that a house?"

Ruth answers, "Yes, it is Rabbi Micha's residence. He is a Levite."

I remember from my studies that the Levites were the tribe of Israel that made up their priesthood. It made me wonder what tribes my other acquaintances where from. I ask, "What tribe are you from?"

"I am from Judah."

I recall that Jesus was called "The Lion from the tribe of Judah", and I say, "Oh, then you must be the lioness from the tribe of Judah."

Ruth laughs again and says, "Hardly my dear Hiram, hardly."

"Is that where we are going Ruth?"

"No not today, although you will be going to meet with the Rabbi at his home the day that you will leave Shashani. Today we will climb higher up to a small plateau called "Gen Aden."

I translate Gen Aden in my mind as the Hebrew word for paradise.

Ruth laughs and announces, "Today Hiram, I take you to paradise!" She laughs some more. We reach the wooden gate of a very long stone wall. Ruth pushes it open and says, "Now we test your physical prowess. Follow me."

I followed her up a well-worn trail for a very long time. The more we climb, the steeper the incline becomes.

We come to a fork in the trail, and Ruth says, "To the right it leads to Rabbi Micha. We will hike to the left on the Gen Aden trail."

I am worn out, and don't want to admit it, so I comment, "This is a good place to take a break Ruth!" I am astonished at her endurance. She isn't even breaking a sweat. I take a seat on a large rock, and she joins me. Then she gazes into my eyes, deep in thought, and says, "Do you really want to leave Shashani?"

For the first time since arriving here, I know truthfully my answer is no. But instead, I answer, "I have duties to perform Ruth."

She says, "Now you sound like one of those politicians in your world that you do not understand. I would have thought that a simple yes or no answer would have sufficed."

"Unfortunately, the simple answer isn't that simple," I add.

We renew our assault on the mountain. Eventually after reaching a small plateau, we rest once again. As I peer upwards, I can tell it would be impossible to attain higher altitudes without professional climbing gear.

"What now Ruth?"

"There is a small pavilion and a campfire just around this bend Hiram."

We skirt around a ledge that is only a foot wide. Sheer rockface is against my shoulders, and as I sidestep along the tiny ledge, I can peer straight down thousands of feet. I must look terrified because Ruth looks at me and says, "I am sorry Hiram, I did not know you were afraid of heights."

"I am not afraid of heights Ruth, and I'm not afraid of falling off this ledge. I am afraid of what it will feel like when I hit the ground below!"

I finally navigate the sparse pathway, and I fall onto the ground. Ruth chuckles and says, "You can be happy and relax now Hiram. We made it."

"No, I can't"

"Why not?"

"Because we'll have to go back!"

"Come Hiram, let us go and sit under the lean-to. I wish for you to take in the panoramic grandeur of paradise!"

We sit together in total silence beholding the splendor, the majesty, the brilliant spectacle that is before us. All of the glory that is Shashani is being presented to us in all its magnificence, and at this elevation it is even more breathtaking...... Immediately I know I'm wrong. It is not the higher elevation that has magnified the beauty of this frozen-in- time -valley. It is the light of God's glory, shining above a sunless Shashani.

Ruth smiles at me and asks, "What do you think Hiram?"

"There are no words that can describe it Ruth. It's the essence of indescribable."

We sit together and say nothing. Finally, after a long period of time Ruth says, "The scripture says, "Be still and know that I am God."

A long time passes. I'm not aware of how much. Time has become inconsequential. It has vanished. It has vaporized into nothingness. Then I feel a warmth, a glow.

I look at her and ask, "Will you listen closely with what I have to say?"

"Yes of course Hiram."

"Will you pray with me?"

"Yes. Oh yes."

"I have never prayed before Ruth, but I believe that now is the time that I should be starting. And I begin.

"Lord, I know what I am. I know that all sorts of evils have been within me. I have been a drunkard. I have been a fornicator and have killed men. Most of all, I have been self-pleasing, caring only for the pleasures of this life.

This day I repent of my sins. This day I ask you to forgive me for my sins. I accept your blood bought sacrifice on the cross. THIS DAY I CONFESS WITH MY MOUTH, AND BELIEVE IN MY HEART THAT YOU ARE THE LORD AND SAVIOR OF MY LIFE!"

Ruth starts crying and exclaims, "Praise be to God! Praise be to God! I can now call you my brother Hiram! I shall give you a holy kiss!"

She then embraces me and kisses me on the cheek. I have cried many times in my life. I cried at my father's funeral, I cried when Irene and I last departed, and I cried at the horrors I've seen at the Byberry Asylum. But now I'm experiencing something new. I am now shedding tears of joy! A happiness and a peace have overcome me. I stand up and stretch both arms into the air and with palms outward I cry out, "Thank you Lord for saving an idiot such as me! Praise be to the Lord!"

As I sit back down and continue to sob, my thoughts go back to all the times in my life that I had so foolishly denied Him. I do not deserve this love He has given me. Now I realize more than ever that I have been singled out for a purpose and am eager to resume my studies. But more than anything I recall a scripture from 2nd Corinthians 5:17, "Therefore if any man be in Christ, he is a new creature: old things are passed away; behold, all things are become new." The reality of this my newfound salvation is just now settling in. The old Ace is gone! The new Brother Hiram is born. I have been born again!

CHAPTER 53

(Dover England October 15th, 1944)

Sgt Andrew Harrison walks into MSgt Jensen's office at 1000 hours on a rainy Monday morning. "Mornin' Coach."

"I truly wish that's all I was right now, just Coach. How are you doing Andy?"

"None the worse for wear, I guess. I just got a letter from Becky. She sends her love, and says little Brian is just a growin' like a weed."

"It's hard to imagine we'll be seeing him in a Hen's uniform, and in not too many more years. How can I help you son?"

"Well off the record Coach. I mean to say; I know it's probably classified and all, but the boys are getting kind of nervous just sitting around here in merry old England. When do you think we might be crossing over the channel into France and joining the fighting over there? There's been hints that we'll be joining the French 2nd Armored Division."

"Now you know Sergeant Harrison that I couldn't possibly divulge, that half of our division, including Charlie company, are scheduled to ship out and join that French Division in exactly seven days. To do so I would be derelict in my duties. However, if I did somehow accidentally let that information slip out, it would have to be kept within your tank crew, and for your ears only. Do you understand?"

"Yes sir!" I understand completely. And thank you sir!"

"Good. Oh, and by the way, you have been assigned a new driver. He's Private Douglas Fowler from Ashtabula, Ohio. He has never seen action before, but I've been told he received excellent marks at the Tennessee training school. He is to receive no knowledge of what I have just told you."

"Understood. Again, thanks Coach. See you at supper."

CHAPTER 54

(In Shashani)

When I finally get back to my cottage late that evening, I am too excited to sleep. I shower, pray, and find myself hungering for only one thing: the word of God. I crawl into bed, turn to the Gospel of Mark, and devour God's holy words until my eyes eventually close.

I awake early in time for my Monday morning stable duties, and I remember that old saying of "Today is the first day of the rest of your life". And today truly does have a new and significant meaning for me. Ruth sees me enter the barn and shouts to Luke who's in a stall, "Luke there is someone new coming to see us today."

"And who would that be Ruth?"

"He is here now. Why not come out and see for yourself?"

Luke comes out with pitchfork in hand and says, "Hello Hiram....... I see no one but Hiram Ruth."

Ruth announces, "Oh, but Luke, he is no longer just Hiram. Praise God! He is now our brother in the Lord Hiram!"

Luke drops his pitchfork, runs, and grabs me, picks me up off my feet, grins, and shouts praise be to God Brother Hiram! I am so pleased for you! Praise be to God!

I laugh and say, "Put me down you big gorilla! I love you too!"

He says, "You must be baptized now!"

I hadn't even thought of that. "Yes", I say. "Yes, I shall! I will tell Brother Jacob. Perhaps he will schedule my baptism!"

After our chores, the three of us go to "immersion," and I enjoy the spirituality of the experience like never before. I'm like a child on Christmas eve, filled with the excitement and anticipation of revealing my conversion experience to my beloved mentor and teacher Brother Jacob. I decide I'll share my decision for Christ with him at breakfast.

Ruth and Luke join me across from Jacob at the morning table. I'll wait until breakfast is almost over.

Jacob taking his last bites of food, looks up at me and says, "Well what did you do on Sunday Hiram?"

"Ruth and I went for a long hike."

"Oh, and where did the two of you hike?"

"Ruth was anxious to show me Gen Aden."

Jacob says, "That certainly was an ambitious albeit an arduous journey. I have always enjoyed meditations there, but I am afraid I have not been there in years. Did you enjoy the view of Shashani?"

"I did brother. But I enjoyed more than that. IT WAS THERE AND THEN, THAT I ACCEPTED JESUS CHRIST AS THE LORD AND SAVIOR OF MY LIFE!"

Jacob hesitates for a long time then stands. Then with a loud voice, and with tears trickling down from his eyes, he says, "Will everyone in the dining hall please rise. I have an announcement to make. Today...... I wish you all to welcome a new member of the church, the body of Christ; a new son of God and an heir of salvation....... Please stand Hiram....... Brothers and sisters in the Lord, I introduce you to your new brother, "Brother Hiram Walker!"

Then song breaks out among all the Essenes.

"Amazing grace how sweet the sound

that saved a wretch like me

I once was lost but now am found

Was blind but now I see.

Twas grace that taught me how to fear

And grace my fears relieved

How precious did that grace appear

The hour I first believed

Thru many dangers toils and snares

I have already come

Tis grace that brought me safe thus far

And grace will lead me home."

I am in tears, joyful happy tears. I remain standing as each one of the four hundred Essenes align themselves to personally shake my hand and welcome me to the kingdom of God.

After the flock leave, I sit alone with Ruth, Luke, and Jacob.

Jacob says, "I will now schedule your "Present Days course with Brother Joseph. Also, may I ask is it your wish to be baptized?"

"Yes, it is Jacob"

"Then I shall schedule that as well Brother Hiram. You must understand your future studies will be intense. Luke asks, "Why will they be so intense Brother Jacob?"

Jacob answers, "Because Luke, Brother Hiram was sent to us for a "Divine Purpose", a special mission from our God. Brother Hiram must be about His Father's business."

CHAPTER 55

Brother Joseph's classroom was adjacent to Jacob's. I was intrigued about what curriculum I would be exploring. Since the course was entitled "Present Day" I assumed that current events would be the main topic.

When I entered the room, I noticed it was sparsely furnished similar to Jacob's classroom; decorated in what I would call "early attic". Brother Joseph stood up and greeted me with, "Hello Brother Hiram. It is my honor to be meeting someone so highly venerated by God."

"Thank you, Brother Joseph, but I'm not sure if I'm worthy of your comments of how much God values me."

"That is simply because you do not, as of yet, understand what your mission will be brother. However, I do, and I am amazed at what is in store for you, and what you must accomplish. Nevertheless, it is not my place to discuss these matters with you. These issues will be conveyed to you by Rabbi Micha. I do believe, however, that you will be interested in the events that are occurring now, both in the war and at home."

As I look at Joseph, I perceive him to be a jovial old man with a mischievous twinkle in his eye. He is clean shaven, and like most others in this community, he is bald. He is short in stature and forever smiling. I could easily imagine him to be on stage as a stand-up comedian at a New York city comedy club. I tell him, "Yes brother, I'm anxious to hear about what's going on in the world."

"Very well. Please have a seat. I want you to understand that this is a one session lecture and is for you ears only. You are neither to discuss these matters with anyone here in Shashani, nor with others when reentering the world. Do you understand?"

"I do."

"We feel it is imperative for you to be knowledgeable not only in current events, but also somewhat able to peer slightly ahead into the future."

You will be glad to hear, that on the home front, things are well in America. War Bonds are selling well. A phenomenon called "Rosey the Riveter" has overtaken the women of your country, and your GI friends are painting a cartoon like character called "Kilroy" on the walls across Europe.

It is important for you to know Brother Hiram that God dictates, or if you will, arranges all of history. He either sits back and just simply allows an individual to come into power, or He actually decides to orchestrate, and selects the leaders of various countries to ascend to their positions.

For instance, if we read in Isaiah 44:28 "That saith of Cyrus, He is my shepherd, and shall perform all my pleasure: even saying to Jerusalem, thou shalt be built; and to the temple, thy foundation shall be laid."

Here the Lord God prophesies that a man named Cyrus shall be born, and He and calls him by name over two hundred years before his birth. He says that he will be the king of the Persians that conquered the Babylonians. This prophecy then says that Cyrus will order that Jerusalem and the temple to be rebuilt. The book of Ezra then finishes the story of the temple articles to be sent back to Jerusalem, and the men who will carry them back.

Also, if you will recall in the Gospel of John 19:10&11 there is a discussion between Jesus and Pontius Pilate. It reads, "Then saith Pilate unto Him. Speakest thou not unto me? Knowest thou not that I have the power to crucify thee, and have power to release thee?"

Jesus answered. "Thou couldest have no power at all against me, except it were given thee from above: therefore, he that delivered me unto thee hath the greater sin."

Jesus was saying that all officials' power was God given.

Now in a secular sense.

The Allied forces are winning the war in Europe. On June the 6th of this year the Allies staged the largest invasion in the history of the world in Normandy France. They were successful there and also are now pushing north into France and will have liberated Paris by August of this year. Your friends in Charlie company have battled bravely against the evil Nazi enemy. Understand when I say evil Brother Hiram, I am not able to find in my vocabulary any words to describe the depravity of their evilness. It seems that Adolf Hitler, in his madness, has instigated a plan he has called "the final solution." This plan simply stated is the mass genocide of the Jewish race. Your Supreme Commander General Dwight D. Eisenhower has witnessed this holocaust in person himself at a Nazi concentration camp in Auschwitz, Poland after it was liberated. Jews and other prisoners were gassed to death and cremated there. The conditions of the living were horrendous, they were starved and endured freezing conditions. The odor and stench of feces and death permeated the entire area. Open mass graves were filled to the top with naked skeleton- like corpses. The inhumanity of this has never been seen before Brother Hiram. Other camps such as this one are still being discovered. The results of this genocide will prove to show that Nazi Germany will have in the end murdered six-million Jews."

I am speechless. "Could his have really happened?"

"It has indeed. In fact, I have been told that your Charlie company will discover a satellite concentration camp in Germany.

I am afraid I do have some bad news to share with you brother."

"And what would that be Joseph?"

"Your good friend Michael Collins was killed in action and is now with the Lord."

"Oh no! Poor Mike. His family will be devastated, but I know that Mike was saved by the blood of Christ."

"Yes Hiram. Be consoled. He rests in the third heaven as we speak.

Furthermore, since the duration of your absence from your Charlie company your status has been changed from MIA to KIA. Your death has been reported by your Division Headquarters to your family, your employer, and since your fiancé has received the news, she now accepts your death; and although I am positive that initially you will receive this information as detrimental to your goals, I believe that when God's purpose and mission is revealed to you, you will understand that this is for the better. Lastly, and maybe of the most importance to you, this terrible war will cease in Europe on the 8th of May 1945. That day your Allies will call VE Day.

"I wish you well Brother Hiram. You will be scheduled to meet with the head of our order Brother Elijah sometime after your baptism. You will visit with him in his quarters in the highest of the castle towers. This is an honor to have an audience with Brother Elijah. There have been twenty-five visitors sent to us in Shashani over the millennia. Only three of them have met with Brother Elijah. Although I am not allowed to mention their names, they became very famous; two were Englishmen, and one was Scottish. One of the English gentlemen excelled in the world of science. He was also knighted by the queen of England. You would have heard of them. I will pray for you. God speed Brother Hiram."

I'm shocked. I am dead to the world at age twenty-four. At the same time, I'm intrigued. There is a great mysterious adventure on which I'm about to embark.

CHAPTER 56

(July 22nd France)

Two brigades of the 2nd Armored Division roll off troop carriers onto the shores of Calais, France. They receive no resistance from enemy gunfire, and immediately proceed to establish a base camp. General Scott, in a meeting with his officers, is talking on a secured line with Headquarters Command. "Yes sir. Understood sir." He hangs up the phone and looks at his men and announces, "We have our orders gentlemen. It is called "Operation Garter Belt." We are to advance and destroy the enemy until we have liberated Paris!"

A week pushing south goes by and the boys of Charlie company have yet to see any action. They pass by a sign that says Paris 274 km. SSgt Andy yells down at his new driver Private Doug Fowler and says, "This thing is not a pinball machine Fowler. You need to smooth out the controls some. You're being too herkie jerky."

"Okay Sarge. I guess I'm just a little jittery."

Paddy says, "I'll give ya the jitters ya bloomin' banshee! I'll be a comin' down there and a beatin' it out a' ya boyo!"

Sox joins in "Come on guys, give the kid a bwake. He hasn't even seen any action yet."

Ski adds, "Yeah and I hope he doesn't see any until we all hear "Parlez vous Francais!"

Andy turns around to look at the troops marching in the rear of Thumper. He hollers, "Hey guys how y'all doin' back there?"

One infantryman answers, "Very funny sarge, very funny. You get to ride in the limo, and we get to tread on with our poor old, tired doggies. How ya' think we're doin' sarge? But ya know? We kind of like this mud don't we boys?" A few of the grunts holler in unison, "Yeah, we love this mud!" Then packing mud balls into their hands, they start pitching them at a ducking Andy.

Andy laughs and turns back. He then receives orders through his headphones to halt for lunch. "Hey fellas we're stoppin.'" It's chow time!" The entire brigade comes to a stop.

The crew exits "Thumper" and leans up against her half-tracks. The K rations are pulled out and the normal negotiations begin. Some of the other soldiers join in, and kibitz back and forth,

"Hey, I'll trade some Chesterfields for some Lucky Strikes."

"I've got Spam. I'm lookin' for some beef!"

"Cheese for caramels!"

"I'm tradin' this here Juicy Fruit Gum for a biscuit."

This is an everyday occurrence at every meal. Ski says, "Man I can't wait until we get to some village somewhere and get some real food!"

Andy answers, "Quit your belly aching Ski. This stuff isn't so bad."

Ski adds, "Yeah Andy, well with this stuff I'd rather not eat it on an empty stomach."

Traveling resumes single file on the long dirt road towards Paris. They pass another sign reading Compie'gne 2 km. As the Brigades 2,500 men 22 tanks, and towed artillery, accompanied by a small French contingent enter the city they start to receive the rat-a-tat-tat of enemy machine gun fire. This fire along with single shot sniper rifle shots are coming from windows high up in the city's buildings. The Nazi's have taken to high ground in order to defend the town. Infantrymen start to race in front of their tanks towards the buildings. Some start to fall from wounds and it doesn't take long before screams of MEDIC! MEDIC! are heard throughout the battlefield, and soldiers are dragging their wounded from harm's way.

The enemy's tanks and artillery have been positioned strategically between buildings and they commence firing at the Allies.

Paddy starts laughing while firing his canon towards windows of the buildings that enemy gunfire has been dispensed from. He's blowing large holes through brick and mortar. He is shouting, "I love this!" Andy is firing his machine gun, and Doug Fowler below is weeping.

The Allied troops are entering buildings, in order to clear them of the German soldiers.

Andy receives orders to forward advance. But before doing so he drops down below. He commands, "Get the hell out of that seat Fowler! Sox you've been the Bow machine gunner and co-driver, now you're our driver! Quit your crying Fowler before I knock you silly. You take Sox's position with that gun! I want you to start killing a few Jerrys. Maybe it will make you wake up and realize you're in a war, and not home playing with little Susie cutie pie!"

Ski you're doin' a great job. How's our ammo holding up?"

"We're good to go Sarge. Let's give em' hell!"

All the tanks move forward and continue to fire towards selected targets. Upon clearing buildings of the enemy, our soldiers' wave red flags through openings to avoid friendly fire. The battle rages into the night, until finally victory belongs to the Allies.

"Thumper's" crew happens to be in what's left of a restaurant, watching LtCol Parker and Capt. Steiner tally up the casualty list. The captain says," We have accounted for 63 deaths and 118 wounded of our men. We have lost 5 tanks and two artillery units. We have killed

631 German soldiers and sent 187 more as prisoners to the back lines. We destroyed 8 of their tanks and decommissioned the remaining 5. All in all, this certainly has been a decisive victory colonel."

The LtCol says, "Send a runner around. There will be no K rations this evening. I'm sure we'll be able to find some grateful citizens here for us getting rid of this Nazi vermin, and would love to provide us all with some good French food and wine for dinner tonight. That warehouse over there captain looks as though it's still intact. Let's set up a mess over there."

"Yes, sir Colonel. Yes sir!"

That evening after a fine dining on French cuisine Andy calls on Private Fowler, "Step outside with me Doug."

"Alright Sarge."

They walk away from all the other personnel, and Andy looks at the private and says, "You know Doug in that tank we are a team, and it's vitally important that we function as a team together. That is how we accomplish our mission, and more importantly that is how we all stay alive. You have been losing control of yourself and I can't allow that to happen. I want you to know that the man you're replacing was a good God-fearing man that performed his duties without error. That is what I expect from you."

"I'm sorry sarge. I was just so scared. My whole body had the shakes, and I couldn't control myself."

"Listen Doug we're all scared, except for maybe that crazy Irishman shooting our cannon on top. Being scared is nothing to be ashamed of, but you must be able to function properly. Do you understand me?"

"I do sarge."

"I saw you kill a least two Krauts with your machine gun. Great job. That's what we're here for. In the meantime, I'm keeping Sox as our driver and you as co-driver with the Bow gun. If you get the shakes, you just start firing that darn thing. Got it?"

"Got it. And thanks, sarge."

The Brigades continue to engage the enemy when entering other towns, as they continue to march toward Paris. They sustain more casualties but annihilate the enemy in each encounter. They have become a weary rag-tag bunch of men just hoping and praying for the war to end.

Then on August 25th They pass a road sign that reads "PARIS 2 km", and their hearts starts to fill with anticipation at the arrival of their destination. Although the French under General LeClerc may have beaten them there, as they close the gap and start to enter the city proper, they begin to hear the sound of crowd noises.

Andy yells below, "Hey guys, come up on top!" Thumper" is near the front of the line moving into the city and the roar of the crowd is getting louder. A band can be heard playing "America the Beautiful," and throngs of people are lining the streets welcoming the conquering heroes. The Nazis have vacated Paris. The music and crowd become louder as they start to pass through. Thousands, no, tens of thousands of Parisiennes' are waving small American flags and shouting "LA VICTORIE! LA VICTORIE!" Men are jumping onto the tanks and handing out bottles of wine. Women are grabbing and kissing the marching soldiers. Some are jumping on the tanks. Four hop onto Thumper, and start kissing Andy, Paddy Ski, and Doug. Sox driving down below hollers, "Hey, how about a driver replacement down here? I want up there for a while!" Paddy starts handing out chocolate bars to kids; and we with our faces all covered in lipstick, swill wine from bottles. The band starts with an old WWI song,

"How ya gonna keep em down on the farm after they've seen Paree'

How ya gonna keep em away from Broadway

Jazzin around, paintin the town

How ya gonna keep em away from harm

That's a mystery

They'll never want to see a rake or plow

And who the deuce can parley vous a cow

How ya gonna keep em down on the farm after they've seen Paree'?"

The celebration continues as the Allies continue down the Champs-E'lyees and through the Arc de Triomphe where Hitler once stood.

Ski says, "Isn't this is the greatest thing ever guys?"

Andy says, "I just wish both Ace and Mike could be with us for this,"

Sox adds "I think this wahs just about ovah now boys."

Paddy says, "Now don't ye be countin' yer chickens before they be a hatchin' boyo."

The celebration continues for the remainder of the day.

All the hotels in Paris have been emptied for the soldiers to be housed.

CHAPTER 57

(In Shashani)

After our stable duties, Ruth, Luke, and I change into our robes. We plan on riding to the lake for "immersion" and my baptism. As we approach, we hear "What a friend we have in Jesus" being sung by those already in attendance. We dismount and the singing ends. Brother Jacob leads me by the hand into the water, and he announces, "Brothers and sisters, today our brother Hiram has decided to make a public confession that he has accepted Christ as the Lord and Savior of his life. In doing so he desires to be baptized. Which is the sign of going under the water unto death, and the rising up again unto a new life unto Christ. I ask you Brother Hiram, have you accepted Jesus Christ as Savior for the forgiveness of your sins?"

"I have Brother Jacob."

"Then I baptize thee my brother, in the name of the Father, and of the Son, and of the Holy Ghost." I am then dunked and raised again. Immediately the crowd starts singing,

"Blessed assurance Jesus is mine.

Oh, what a foretaste of glory divine!

I'm heir of salvation purchased by blood.

Born of His Spirit, washed in His blood."

After my baptism, a great feast was set up on the picnic grounds near the lake. It seems the fatted calf was killed in my honor. I sit at a table with Jacob, Ruth, and Luke but when the three of them leave to procure our food and drinks, a man walks over to me and asks, "May I sit Brother Hiram?"

"By all means, yes you may," I answer.

"I am Brother Aaron, and I have been wanting to talk to you about another man who was called here to Shashani as you have been."

"I thought those names were never to be mentioned."

"You are correct, and although I will not mention his name, I will tell you that he and I became very good friends while he remained here with us. I know that you are now aware that we in Shashani live to very long ages. I am 198 years old. This man was sent to us in what you would call the 1800's. He was from Scotland. Since we became so very dear to one another, he told me once, although he should not have done so, that his assigned mission from God was to journey to Africa to set up missions. I have often wondered how he fared there. Do you perhaps have any idea of whom I speak of?"

I emit a slight chuckle and admit, "Yes, I believe I do Brother Aaron, and if it's who I'm thinking of, he did great work for God on that continent, bringing thousands of people to Christ in darkest Africa. He became honored throughout the world, and many books were written about him upon his death."

"That is surely good to know. I am most satisfied. Thank you, brother. I wish you well on your mission for God." With that he bows his head towards me and leaves.

I am astonished that I have shared my experience here in Shashani, with so revered a man as our African traveler was. It also makes me ponder who the other two Englishmen were that met here with brother Elijah. This makes me even more excited and more inquisitive of what

God has in store for me. I am in anticipation of my meeting, and in only one week, with Brother Elijah.

CHAPTER 58

I head to the castle today to meet with Brother Elijah the head of this ancient order of Essenes. When the gatekeeper allows me entry, I'm immediately met by two castle guards. They smile, bow their heads at me, and say, "Follow us please brother." We climb an innumerable number of stairs to the highest peak of the castle's eastern tower and arrive at an ancient wooden door with lit candles perched on both sides. One guard knocks and announces, "Brother Hiram Walker has arrived sire." "Have him enter," a coarse voice says from inside. I enter into the circular room with open portals on all sides and see the brother standing to greet me behind a desk. His hand is extended to shake mine. I walk towards him and greet him by saying, "It is my honor sir."

"The honor should most certainly belong to me Brother Hiram. Please be seated."

I sit. In turn, when he attempts to sit, he does so very slowly and gently into a throne like chair behind his desk. He takes his seat as though his bones are very brittle. As I perceive the chief of this Essene order, I can describe him as being very old. His dark eyes are sunken into the hollows of his head. He wears a black yarmulke on top of his long white hair, and his white beard flows down to his chest. His face is wrinkled like a sun-dried prune, and it is stern, like it has witnessed the history of centuries past, and peered into the panoramas of the future.

After settling in he speaks to me with his gravelly voice, "Yes Brother Hiram it is now your time to obey Romans 12:2, "And be not conformed to this world: but be ye transformed by the renewing of your mind, that you may prove what is that good, and acceptable and perfect, will of God." "For this is the oath you swore unto Him at your recent baptism. Is it not?"

"Yes, I did sir."

"This will be your "Futures Course" my son. But in order to peer into the future, perhaps we must first look into the past. Please, if you will, turn with me to the book of Daniel 2:31-36, and allow me to capture the events leading up to these scriptures. The scene that we are reading takes place in what your calendar would call 500 BC. It is in ancient Babylon where King Nebuchadnezzar of Babylon has recently conquered Judea and brought away unto its land many Hebrew hostages. One of which is a young man of God named Daniel. I have been told that you studied some of the book of Daniel in a previous course.

"I have sir."

"Well, it seems the king has had troubling nightmares regarding the vision of a giant statue of a man. He has attempted to have his magicians and soothsayers interpret the dream without disclosing what his dream was about. They insist on having the king describe the dream to them before they can interpret it. However, the king cogitates that they might simply make a story up in reference to his dream, and he insists on interpretation before description. He then threatens to put them all to death unless they can comply with his request.

God then gives Daniel the king's vision in a dream and the interpretation thereof. The king hears of this and summons Daniel before his throne. We may now read in our verses what Daniel tells the king.

"Thou O king, sawest and behold a great image. This great image, whose brightness was excellent, stood before thee; and the form thereof was terrible.

269

This image's head was of fine gold, his breast and his arms of silver, his belly, and his thighs of brass.

His legs of iron, his feet part of iron and part of clay.

Thou sawest until that a stone was cut out without hands, which smote the image upon his feet that were of iron and clay, and brake them to pieces.

Then was the iron, the clay, the brass, the silver, and the gold, broken to pieces together, and became like the chaff of the summer thrashing-floors; and the wind carried them away, that no place was found for them: and the stone that smote the image became a great mountain, and filled the whole earth."

This is the dream: and we will tell the interpretation thereof before the king."

"Now Brother Hiram let us read from the last part of verse 38 through verse 45."

"Thou art this head of gold.

And after thee, shall arise another kingdom inferior to thee, and another third kingdom of brass, which shall bear rule over the earth.

And the fourth kingdom shall be as iron: forasmuch as iron breaketh in pieces and subdueth all things; and as iron breaketh all these, shall it break into pieces and bruise.

And whereas thou sawest the feet and the toes. Part of potters' clay, and part of iron, the kingdom shall be divided; but there shall be in it of the strength of the iron, forasmuch as thou sawest the iron mixed with miry clay.

And as the toes of the feet were part of iron, and part of clay, so shall the kingdom be partly strong, and partly broken.

And whereas thou sawest iron mixed with miry clay, they shall mingle themselves with the seed of men: but they shall not cleave one to another, even as iron is not mixed with clay.

And in the days of these kings shall the God of heaven set up a kingdom, which shall never be destroyed: and the kingdom shall not be left to other people, but it shall break to pieces and consume all these kingdoms and it shall stand forever." "This part of the prophecy points to Jesus's millennial kingdom on earth.

"Then in verse 46 Hiram it reads:

"Then the king Nebuchadnezzar fell on his face and worshipped Daniel and commanded that they should offer an oblation and sweet odors unto him."

"This is history in a nutshell Brother Hiram. It traces the history of nations through the Romans. First the gold is the Babylonians, second the silver is the Medes and Persians, third the brass is Alexander the Great and Greece, and fourth the iron is the Romans. But then the history continues past this your twentieth century unto the future, to a time when ten countries form a league into a ten-nation confederation. This is the statue's ten toes. This is the revived Roman empire. This is the future kingdom in which is led by that "Son of perdition, that evil one called "The Antichrist", and it is he in whom God will ultimately destroy. But before his destruction he will play havoc with the world for a period of seven years. This is the seventieth week of the prophecy in the book of Daniel. The completion of the 490 years you studied with Brother Jacob. This is the "Great Tribulation." Our Lord speaks of it when asked by his apostles in Matthew 24: 3.

"Tell us when shall these things be? And what shall be the sign of thy coming, and of the end of this age?"

(Verse 4) And Jesus answered and said, unto them, "Take heed that no man deceives you.

(Verse 5) For many shall come in my name, saying. I am Christ; and shall deceive many.

(Verse 6) And ye shall hear of wars and rumors of wars: see that ye not be troubled: for all these things must come to pass, but the end is not yet.

(Verse 7) For nation shall rise against nation, and kingdom against kingdom: and there shall be famines and pestilences, and earthquakes in divers' places.

(Verse 8) All these are the beginning of sorrows.

(Verse 11) And many false prophets shall rise and shall deceive many.

(Verse 12) And because iniquity shall abound, the love of many shall wax cold.

(Verse 21) For then shall there be great tribulation, such as was not since the beginning of the world to this time, no nor ever shall be.

(Verse 22) And except those days be shortened, there should be no flesh be saved: but for the elect's sake those days shall be shortened."

"Oh yes dear brother, the Lord will then destroy all the warring nations at a battle called "Armageddon."

(Verse 29)" Immediately after the tribulation of those days shall the sun be darkened, and the moon shall not give her light, and the stars shall fall from heaven, and the powers of the heavens shall be shaken."

(Verse 30) "And then shall appear the sign of the Son of man in heaven: and then shall all the tribes of the earth mourn, and they shall see the Son of man coming in the clouds of heaven, with power and great glory."

"Brother Hiram read the book of Revelation when you depart from me today. When you read of the opening of the seven seals, you will be given a further description of the horrors to befall mankind during that awful time. In fact, in Revelation 9:18, and I paraphrase, it says that a third of mankind will be killed.

Even the fish of the sea will die. These famines, these diseases will be horrifying. Mankind will in your twenty-first century, endure what they will term the coronavirus, which the nation of China will spread upon them, and it will kill hundreds of thousands, but it will be meek compared to what is to come thereafter. And yes, Brother Hiram the Lord Jesus is coming again, but your world will forget this. Instead, they will in that day scoff, and I quote II Peter 3:4 For they will say, "Where is the promise of His coming? For since the fathers fell asleep, all things continue as they were from the beginning of creation."

"They will believe that our bible is nonsense. As it is said in II Timothy 3:5, "They will have a form of godliness but denying the power thereof: from such turn away". But it is true of all unbelievers in I Corinthians 1:18 that says, "The preaching of the cross is to them that perish foolishness; but unto us which are saved it is the power of God."

But thank God for it has been written in I Thessalonians 1:10, "And to wait for His Son from heaven, whom he raised from the dead, even Jesus which delivered us from the wrath to come."

Yes, Jesus will save His believers, His bride, the "Bride of Christ", from that wrath to come.

In fact, one of the three men I met from your world, wrote much about Jesus saving all believers from the Tribulation period. This man was from Plymouth, England and he formed a great assembly of Christians. He taught the truth of this blessed event we refer to as the "Rapture." Let us read of it in I Thessalonians 4:13-18, "But I would not have you to be ignorant brethren, concerning them which are asleep, that ye sorrow not, even as others which have no hope. For if we believe that Jesus died and rose again, even to them also which sleep in Jesus will God bring with Him. For this we say unto you by the word of the Lord, that we which are alive and remain unto the coming of the Lord shall not prevent them which are asleep. For the Lord Himself shall descend from heaven with a shout, with the voice of the archangel, and with the trump of God: and the dead in Christ shall rise first: Then we which are alive and remain shall be caught up together with them in the clouds, to meet the Lord in the air: and so, shall we ever be with the Lord. Wherefore comfort one another with these words."

"And of assurance this rapturous event will be prior to that terrible "Day of the Lord".

This rapture of the saints, both dead and alive into heaven is a blessed event and the hope of all believers. The world will marvel at the instant vanishing of an unmeasurable number of people."

I ask, "How will they account for this happening? After all, the governments of the world must somehow explain the disappearance of millions human beings. What will they say?"

The bible says that they will "Receive strong delusion that they should believe a lie". There will be great signs in the heavens. At tribulations end the sun and the moon will be darkened. But even before the "Rapture" other signs will appear. In Ezekiel chapter ten the prophet sees a number of wheels in the sky. Have not your military and people around the earth seen wheels in the sky?"

I answer, "Yes, and we call them UFO'S or unidentified flying objects. Sometimes they're referred to as flying saucers....... Oh, I see! You're suggesting that they will say the vanishing of so many people was due to an alien abduction?"

Elijah answers, "Although the scriptures are hush here, logic could prevail. Remember this is a delusion, a falsehood, or a trick they will receive. In fact, the occurrence of these sightings of your so called UFO'S will increase dramatically in the 21st century. They will increase to the extent that the U.S. government will finally admit to their citizens that they exist and have no idea of what they are. What other plausible explanation could they give?

After the "Rapture" of the saints into heaven, the believers, the "Bride of Christ", will then attend a great feast at the "Marriage Supper of The Lamb." Then the first judgement, called "The Judgement Seat of Christ" will award members of His body "Crowns" for their works on earth. You must search and read of these "crowns" Brother Hiram. They are for your edification.

By the way brother, I Corinthians 15:51-54 also speaks of the rapture saying, "Behold I show you a mystery; we shall not all sleep, but we shall all be changed, in a moment, in the twinkling of an eye, at the last trump: for the trumpet shall sound, and the dead shall be raised incorruptible, and we shall be changed. For this corruptible must put on incorruption, and this mortal must put on immortality. So, when this corruptible shall have put on incorruption, and this mortal shall have put on immortality, then shall be brought to pass the saying that is written, death is swallowed up in victory."

"Yes brother, we shall receive new bodies of flesh and bone that cannot die. And why so? Because when Christ returns to earth at His second coming the scriptures clearly state that all of His own shall return with Him. Christ then will set up His kingdom on His throne in Jerusalem, and with our new bodies we will reign with Him. This is the seventh dispensation called the "Millennium" for it will endure for a thousand years.

It is somewhat sad, that a great number of Christians today believe that after death they will go to the spiritual heaven and remain there for eternity. This is not true! We will have new physical bodies to reign and to serve Him on this earth for those one-thousand years! Then Revelation 21:1 states, "And I saw a new heaven and a new earth: for the first heaven and the first earth were passed away; and there was no more sea. It is on that new earth where we shall spend eternity!"

"I have been somewhat brief because I tire easily, and I am sure you may have questions"

"Yes, I do brother, and if I may ask, where is my country America in the scriptures?"

"I have much to tell you of your country, but alas, I am not bodily able to do so today. I must rest now. We will continue this "Futures Course" during our next session. I will ask you to take your leave now, and God bless you."

The guards meet me outside the room's door and escort me out of the castle.

CHAPTER 59

The next day after work and immersion, I invited Ruth to my cottage for lunch. I know that she will be anxious to hear about my meeting with Brother Elijah. As she sits at my dining table, I prepare a lunch of sauteed chicken breasts and collard greens. As I take my seat with her, she smiles at me. Silence ensues for a long time...... until I say grace. We do not speak but begin to enjoy our meal....... Finally, she can't withhold her curiosity any longer and she says, "Well?"

"Well, what?" I ask.

"You know very what well Hiram Walker! What is what you ask? Here I sit with a man, one of the only men that has ever had an audience with Brother Elijah, and you ask what!"

I laugh inside at her inquisitiveness and impatience and say, "Well, what do you want to know sweet Ruth?"

"What I want to know is everything! Everything he said to you Hiram! That is what I want to know! I mean what did he tell you? What did he look like?!"

"Patience dear Ruth......patience. Don't you know that patience is a fruit of the spirit?"

"Oh, please tell me all Hiram, or I will surely burst!"

"He is extremely old Ruth. In fact, he is almost decrepit. But through his aged feebleness, his mind is very acute. He led me through the course of history in the book of Daniel and then into the future pertaining to the ten-nation configuration of the Antichrist. He then spoke of the rapture, the great tribulation, the second coming of Jesus and His saints, the millennial kingdom of Christ, and the new heavens and earth."

"That sounds wonderful Hiram. Did he give you any indication as to when you will be departing Shashani?"

"No, he didn't mention that, although I have another meeting with him.

"Then we have more time together Hiram. I am happy about that. Did he mention anything of what your mission in the outside world will involve?"

"No, he didn't, and of course even if he had, you know that I couldn't share that with you."

"Of course not. I am sorry I forgot."

"How's the chicken?"

"The what?.......... Oh, the chicken is delicious. Thank you." She pauses and then says, "I must share something with you Hiram."

"And what is that, Ruth?"

"I am afraid that I do not have the proper words to express what I need to say to you."

"Why don't you just shoot straight from the hip."

"Shoot what from the hip?"

"That was American slang for just tell me what's on your mind."

"Well, the Apostle Paul in First Corinthians, chapter seven, discusses the subject of marriage. He is inspired by God to write that it is good for some to marry and for others it is not. I have never been betrothed to another man through my parents. Of course, most men in Shashani already have wives, or they are celibate, therefore I have always thought of living my life as a spinster. I have always been content with my situation, because I thought that remaining single would be pleasing to the Lord. However, now It seems that I cannot continue to deny what my heart desires, and yet I am saddened because it is something that never can be satisfied."

"And what is that, Ruth?"

"It is that I have grown to love you deeply Hiram."

I take her hand in mine, and we gaze intently into each other's eyes. Soft tears start flowing down onto our cheeks as we gaze at one another. The minutes we continue staring at one another seems like hours. I finally break the silence and admit, "And I love you also Ruth!"

We kiss passionately, and when we part, we begin to cry, knowing that our love could never be truly consummated. She asks, "What do we do now Hiram?"

"What else can we do Ruth? We share each other's love until I must leave. But we will trust in the Lord and not sin. We will always have our memories of Shashani."

Our hearts ache with the knowledge that we could have nothing more.

CHAPTER 60

(In the social section of)

(The Philadelphia Inquirer)

(D)ated October 28th, 1944) Mr. and Mrs. John and Rosemary Jacobs of West Chester Pa., proudly announce the wedding of their daughter Miss Irene Jacobs to Mr. Xander Bascombe, son of Mr. and Mrs. Marshall and Francis Bascombe of Bristol Pa.

Ceremonies to be held at St. Paul's Episcopal Church

1544 Thurmond Avenue, Philadelphia Pa.

Saturday September 22.

Reception to follow at the Knights of St. Andrews, 1233 east 22nd St. Philadelphia, Pa.

All invitees are requested to attend.

CHAPTER 61

{Paris France, October 29th, 1944)

After General Eisenhower's arrival into Paris, and another great speech by the leader of the High Command, the men of Charlie company awaken one morning to something quite opposite to the previous festivities. After leaving the hotel for breakfast, "Thumper's" five men stop and stare at men hanging by their necks from light poles.

Andy says, "Those guys must have been traitors to their country; part of the Nazi Vichy government that was installed during the occupation."

Ski says, "Looks to me like they got some sweet revenge."

Sox says, "Wonda' what's up with that bunch by that buildin'."

Paddy says, "Those blokes, they be a shavin' those lassies hair dontcha' know!"

Andy adds, "I think I know what's going on. Their shaving their heads to shame them."

Ski asks, "What do you mean Andy? Why shame them?"

Andy answers, "Evidently, they collaborated with German soldiers. Since they probably didn't want to hang women, they're doing that to mark them so everyone will know they became Nazi whores."

Doug asks, "What do you think will become of them?"

Ski answers, "They'll become shunned for the rest of their lives."

****

After breakfast, the brigades moved northwest on their continued mission to search and destroy.

For two days they meet with no resistance. On the third day they encounter a large group of the enemy. The allied infantry move towards the Germans and rifle fire breaks out within the large forested area. The French and American group receive neither tank nor mortar fire. The fighting is between both Allied and German infantry only.

Paddy is unhappy and says, "Come on boyos, let's be jumpin' out of this tank and be killin' us some Jerrys."

All five of "Thumper's" crew desert her and begin following their infantry into the fight.

Doug says, "I'll stay here and guard "Thumper."

Andy orders, "The hell you will Fowler, you're coming with us."

After a short time, they redeploy to the east of their infantry buddies and immediately receive rifle fire.

As they take cover behind trees they return fire, killing four of the enemy.

Andy looks at Doug who is also engaging with the enemy, and out of nowhere a Nazi soldier runs at him and fires with his Luger sidearm. He misses Doug, and when firing again he's out of bullets. Then he charges Doug with a knife. Doug fires his rifle and misses. The German then throws his body onto Fowler. Doug's rifle is knocked away from him and they both end up in a life and death struggle. As they roll on the ground Doug's arm is holding back his attacker's knife, until he pulls out his own blade and thrusts it into the German's stomach. He pushes the man off of himself and retrieves his weapon.

Andy rushes over and asks, "You okay Fowler?"

Doug answers, "Yeah, I'm alright."

Andy says, "Nice job soldier!"

Doug then starts shaking uncontrollably, and Andy stays with him until he settles him down. The crew then continues its push forward terminating several enemy soldiers.

After the victorious fighting the remainder of the Germans flee into the woods. A lieutenant takes the casualty count. He tells MSgt. Jensen, "We lost 8 men and have 7 wounded, but we tallied 32 dead krauts and have 7 prisoners."

MSgt. Jensen does a tour of Charlie company and comes upon Andy and his men and gives him the tally. He also says, "You, Paddy, Joe, and Ski are to report to the colonel A.S.A.P. I think he has some good news for your crew Andy."

"Right this minute coach?'

"I said right now, didn't I?"

"Yes sir, MSgt. Jensen sir!!"

"Good I'll follow you boys in."

We report immediately, stand at attention, and salute the LtCol.

He says, "At ease."

"SSgt Harrison your tank crew has demonstrated exemplary behavior and bravery during all of our combat situations. Our brigade is in need of more officers, and as of this moment I am giving you the field commission of second lieutenant. You will resume your current duties as your tank commander."

Andy answers, "Yes sir. Thank you, sir." He salutes.

He then calls out Paddy, "Patrick O'Brien you have been promoted to TSgt. Get those five stripes on your arms immediately."

Paddy answers, "Yes sir, and I'll be a thankin' ye sir!" He salutes.

"Privates Laskowski, and Knight you both have been promoted to corporals. Lt. Harrison what is the name of your tank?"

"Sir we call her "Thumper" sir."

"Well, that's a hell of a good name for your tank. We've watched her in battle, and she certainly is a thumper. Your crew has more kills and has outperformed every other tank crew in this outfit, and now she is being operated by the highest-ranking men. Congratulations soldiers. You are dismissed."

As they leave MSgt Jensen says, "Halt! I want to do this right now!" And he salutes Lt Andrew Harrison for the first time while saying, "Congratulations sir!" The other three men do as well.

Andy returns their salute and orders, "At ease gentlemen! I'll be in the area all day!" They all laugh, and Jensen says, "This calls for a celebration, and I happen to have some very good brandy in my tent! Why don't you call Private Fowler over to join us!"

CHAPTER 62

(In Shashani)

When I arrived at the stables early one morning both Ruth and Luke were in the office laughing. Walking in I ask, "What's so funny?"

Luke answers, "Come with us and we shall show you Hiram."

When we reach the last stall I exclaim, "What in the world? That is one ugly beast! What is it doing here Ruth?"

Ruth giggles and says, "That camel Hiram, was brought over to us last evening, and it seems it has been given to you."

"To me? Why? Who gave this hideous creature to me?"

Luke answers, "It was sent over to us, believe it or not, by Rabbi Micah."

"What am I supposed to do with a camel?"

Ruth says, "Maybe this book and letter will explain it all."

She hands me a hard bound book entitled in English, "Camel Training and Voice Commands" by Ahmed Bey. I open an envelope addressed to me, and find a letter folded inside.

It reads: *Dear Brother Hiram:*

I am most anxious to meet with you to discuss your future. Until then this camel, if trained properly, will be instrumental in the successful accomplishment of your imminent missions. Please also be advised that it is essential for you to grow a beard. God be with you.

Yours In Christ,

RABBI MICAH

"Looks like I have some work ahead of me," I utter.

Luke says, "You best be careful with that animal Hiram, it has attempted to bite and spit at me. It is a nasty beast!"

Ruth starts laughing again and says, "I shall surely enjoy watching you train this brute!"

"Did they tell you its name?"

Luke answers, "As of yet he has no name. The man who brought us the animal said it is for you to name this camel."

Ruth says, "Oh Hiram, please allow me to name him. I have a perfect name for this camel."

"Fine with me Ruth. What should we name him?"

"Hiram please let me to introduce you to your new friend "Nabob.""

I move over closer to Nabob and utter, "Well hello there my new pet." And when I extend my hand to pet him, he bites it, while at the same time expectorating a large glob of spittle right into my face. Luke and Ruth both go into hysterics. I look at them and ask, "Would you both quit laughing and please fetch me a towel? I believe you were correct Luke. He is a nasty beast! It looks like I would be best advised to study Rabbi Micah's book before doing anything further with this critter."

Days and weeks pass by, and Nabob has become another daily routine that I must feed, clean, and train; however, Rabbi Micha has said that this animal will be an important part of the mission God has planned for me. The guide- book I was given pronounced camels to be fearless, friendly, and very intelligent animals. It was handwritten in the guide that Nabob is three years old, which is the supposed perfect age to begin training.

I am to start with a head rope and lead him around. During this exercise I must establish a mutual relationship with him, by stroking his flanks and shoulders, and calling him by name. I do this with great caution to avoid further indignities of spitting and biting. Then I proceed to use voice commands. I decide to utilize English for this purpose. I hobble one of his front legs with a rope, and with a stick tap his other front leg as I say, "couch" for him to sit. Later I must introduce the commands of "stand", "walk", "halt", "right", "left", and "rest down". The book recommends I train for four hours a day, and I do just that. After four weeks I feel we have made good progress and are becoming buddies. He seems to enjoy the exercises and starts to nestle his head against me.

During the fifth week I introduce the harness to him. This arrangement will be used to attach the paniers and other bags for the carrying of food, water, and other required necessities that I'll possibly need. The last element of training will be actually riding Nabob. The voice command will be "mount". Then from the lying down position I will board him and order, "stand". I have not done this yet, and I must admit I am extremely tentative about doing so. One thing I'm happy about is that he has refrained from spitting and biting.

One day Ruth interrupts our training and asks, "When will you allow me to ride Nabob Hiram? This is the first camel ever seen in Shashani for hundreds of years, and I would enjoy doing so."

"When his training is complete, and only if I get a kiss before each ride Ruth." She stands on her tiptoes and kisses me on the lips.

Our love is growing stronger every day, and although I have had Irene, Ginger, and other girlfriends who I have kissed, I have never felt true heartfelt love before. I have only experienced passion and lust. However, I believe now that it was simply superficial. In fact, I'm not altogether sure I was truly able to love another person until Jesus came into my heart; for He is love.

CHAPTER 63

(November 1944)

O n my way to my second meeting with Brother Elijah my mind drifts towards the war and how my friends are faring, and I realize now that I may never see them again. This makes me even more anxious to learn the future fate of America.

Again, the two guards escort me to the presence of Brother Elijah, and he greets me with a stern look upon his face. "Be seated Brother Hiram. But before we begin to discuss more of the future, especially the future relating to the country of your birth; I wish to remind you that as a Christian your home is no longer of this world. Your place on this earth is one of a pilgrim. You now have a heavenly home. Truly the book of Ephesians already sees you as being "in the heavenlies" Brother Hiram. If you understand these matters, we can start our study."

"I understand completely sir."

Brother Elijah begins, "The Lord has deemed that the Allies will defeat Nazi Germany and your war in Europe will cease on May of 1945. The current president of America will not see this ending. Franklin D. Roosevelt will die in the month of April 1945. World War II will continue in the Pacific. As we speak Brother Hiram, a group of scientists in your country are engaged in what they call "The Manhattan Project". They will succeed in producing a weapon of mass destruction, and this weapon will change the entire course of man's history. As a result of their efforts mankind will be able totally self-annihilate. A man from the U.S. state of Missouri named Harry S. Truman will succeed Roosevelt as your president. This man and his friend named Eddie Jacobson will become very significant for you. I am prohibited from speaking more of them. That will be Rabbi Micah's responsibility. However, I may say that it is this Truman who will have to make a decision to save hundred-thousands of lives by using the weapon manufactured by "The Manhattan Project". It will be a terrible decision for him to make, but it's use will end the war against the Japanese immediately, thus saving countless lives. This weapon will be called an atomic bomb, and it will be first detonated on the city of Hiroshima, Japan. The detonation will kill 80,000 people instantly, and its effects of something called radiation shall kill another 100,000 Japanese afterwards. It will totally destroy the city. Three days later another device will be detonated on the city of Nagasaki, Japan with similar results. Due to these two bombings Japan will surrender unconditionally on August 15th, 1945. Your World War II will be ended Brother Hiram."

"I can't begin to imagine a bomb that would be that destructive. It's a horrible thing to even comprehend, although I must say that I'm relieved that we will win this war."

As terrible as these weapons are, they will not even come close to the unimaginable destructive power of the bombs they will produce and use during the "Great Tribulation".

You must understand Brother Hiram that the Lord God is now blessing and will continue to bless your country for decades to come. He will do so because He has promised the seed of Abraham in Genesis 12:3 "And I will bless them that bless thee, and curseth him that curseth thee: and in thee all families of the earth shall be blessed."

"Indeed, all the families and nations of the earth have been blessed by the coming of "The Lion of the tribe of Judah"; Our Savior Jesus."

Now listen Brother Hiram, America has been blessed by God since her inception.

Let us think back in history together to the time of the 15th century. Spain was a powerful nation in the world. Then their leaders used lies and blasphemies against the Jewish people that resided there. They accused them of the horrendous crime of the human sacrificing of children. This was done to rob the Jewish people of their wealth and to confiscate their properties. In fact, it was the stolen wealth of the Jewish people that financed the costly expedition of Christopher Columbus in 1492. Without Jewish money the incredible expense of financing the voyage of those three ships would have been improbable. And remember, Columbus set out to find a new route to India. Do you think it an accident that he arrived on the shores of North America instead? No, it was not. It was God's providential hand that directed him to your shores. He did so in order to prepare a great haven for His people, the Jewish race. Now look at the nation of Spain today. It has lost its holdings and is somewhat inconsequential in today's world. It is no longer a great power, because the Lord has promised to curse those who curse the Jewish race and bless them that befriend them."

Consider Great Britain. In the early 20th century, they signed a document called "The Balfour Declaration". This document agreed to aid the dispersed Jewish people scattered throughout the nations, and give to them a homeland in Palestine. As we speak today Brother Hiram they are reneging on that promise and even attempting to prohibit Jewish refugees from returning to Palestine.

In 1884 Britain claimed that its Army had conquered one-quarter of the earth's surface. The once proud nation of England has boasted that "The sun never sets on the British Empire." It will eventually lose all of its conquests and be left with only with its own small island nation because it has cursed God's people. Britain will be left dependent upon the United States for its very existence.

The anti-Semitic holocaust perpetrated by Germany has destroyed their nation, and it will soon split into two separate states.

Your nation of America is indeed blessed. Understand brother that the Lord has raised up the United States of America for two main purposes. One which is to conquer the evil which has sought to commit genocide against the Jews, and then to provide a secure place for His people to dwell safely. Secondly, He has anointed America to be the leader in the world for spreading the Gospel of Jesus Christ. Your country has in the past, provided more missionaries, evangelists, and financial support for Christ's Gospel than any other nation, and it will remain doing so in the future. Yes, indeed Brother Hiram, God has surely blessed America. God is not slack concerning His promises and He will continue to "Curse them that curse the Jewish people and bless those who bless them.

Before we talk further about America, we must again look at the Jewish race. One might ask that if God loves the Jews so fervently, then why has he allowed His people so much suffering throughout the centuries? The Jewish nation has been conquered by, and suffered under the Babylonians, the Persians, the Greeks, the Romans, and now the Germans. They have lost their homeland, and its people have been disseminated throughout the world. Why has God allowed this? The answer to that question can be found in the scriptures. Although Jehovah gave His people an unconditional covenant in that He would give them the land of Israel, its boundaries from the Mediterranean Sea on the west unto the Euphrates River on the east, in what will be modern day Iraq. They have as of yet never occupied that much of their promised land. But God has unconditionally promised them that they will possess all of this land forever. No matter what they did, no matter how much they have sinned, this land will belong to them for eternity. It is unconditional.

But God did also give them a conditional covenant. He gave them laws to obey. Some of which may be read in the book of Leviticus. The conditions were if they obeyed His laws then Leviticus 20:6 would apply: "And I will give you peace in the land, and ye shall lie down, and none shall make ye afraid: and I will rid evil beasts out of the land, neither shall the sword go through your land." Verse 9: "For I will have respect unto you, and make you fruitful, and multiply you. And establish my covenant with you."

However, if they broke God's laws then verses 14-17 would apply: "But if you will not hearken to me, and will not do all these commandments; And if ye shall despise my statutes, or if your soul abhor my judgements, so that ye will not do all my commandments, but that ye break my covenant: I also will do this unto you; I will even appoint over you terror, consumption, and the burning ague, that shall consume the eyes, and cause sorrow of heart: and ye shall sow your seed in vain, for your enemies shall eat it. And I will set my face against you, and ye shall be slain before your enemies: they that hate you shall reign over you; and ye shall flee when none pursueth you."

"Many other verses in scripture Brother Hiram speak of these covenants. Israel was to be the light of the world, instead they worshipped false gods and disobeyed God's laws. Oh yes, my ancestors have been punished for millennia, however the unconditional covenant that God has promised to us remains in effect. Israel will become a nation again, and in the future, it shall inherit all of the land that they have been promised by God. Israel will one day find its eastern border stretching all the way to the Euphrates River in Iraq!

There is a false doctrine being purveyed by some churches today entitled "Replacement Theology". This error states that since The Jewish people crucified Our Lord and Savior Jesus Christ, therefore God has nothing more to do with Israel. Nothing could be further from the truth, for no one killed Jesus. He laid down His own life for mankind. His was the perfect sacrifice for the forgiveness of sins. One only has to accept and believe this."

I ask, "When Brother Elijah will Israel become a nation again? For never in the history of the world has a sovereign nation been destroyed, its extinction complete, and then rise again into existence."

"Again, Hiram the bible predicts this occurrence in Ezekiel chapter 4 starting at the end of verse 3 to and excerpts from verses 4,5, and 6. They read: Verse 3 "This shall be a sign to the house of Israel. Verse 4 and 5, "Lie thou also upon thy left side, and lay the iniquity of the house of Israel upon it: according to the number of the days that thou shalt lie upon it thou shalt bear their iniquity. For I have laid upon thee the years of their iniquity, according to the number of days, three-hundred, and ninety days: so shalt thou bear the iniquity of the house of Israel." Verse 6, "And when thou hast accomplished them, lie again on thy right side, and thou shalt bear the iniquity of the house of Judah forty days: I have appointed thee each day for a year.""

Elijah continues, "Therefore Brother Hiram, the prophet Ezekiel was commanded to lie on his side for a total of 430 days, a day for each year. Now many bible scholars have searched what events took place 430 years after Ezekiel was told to do this and nothing of significance occurred. This was simply because in 536 B.C. after serving their 70-year captivity in Babylon they did not repent of their sins. Instead, the majority desired to remain in Babylon because they became colonists doing well. That meant that they continued to worship Babylon's gods, breaking God's laws. Therefore, Lev 26: 18 must be used in this equation. It reads, "And if ye will not yet for all this hearken to me, then I will punish you seven times more for your sins,"

Simple multiplication of 430 yrs-70 yrs. served=360 yrs. x 7 = 2520 years -minus start date of 536 B.C. = 1984 - the Jewish 360-day year lunar calendar when then adjusted to our 365-day year solar calendar is 36 years, which when deducted will point exactly at the year of 1948.

Four years from now Brother Hiram, in the year 1948 Israel will once again become their own sovereign nation. And this is the greatest sign to mankind that The Lord Jesus will soon be coming back to earth with all of his saints. His resurrected saints, with their new perfect bodies, will then reign and govern the earth with Christ for one-thousand years, during His "Millennial Kingdom"!

I say, "Praise God Brother Elijah, and I say even so come Lord Jesus!"

Elijah continues, "In 1917 what is called the "Bolshevik Revolution" happened. Its two leaders were Karl Marx and Vladimir Lenin. They introduced to Russia and the world their doctrines of Communist Socialism. These governmental philosophies are tremendously evil. They are atheistic in belief and their quest is to bring powers to themselves while enslaving the minds of the masses. Their intent, along with the world's secret societies is world domination. They wish to control all of the wealth and laws of mankind. They and the nation of China, which are referred to in scriptures as the "Kings of the North", will cause wars of insurrection upon the earth. Although America will enjoy a level of prosperity for a number of decades, it will be involved in regional wars combating this evil and defending democracy. Fanatical and terroristic Islam will again wage war with America and her allies. A day will come when Islamic terrorists attack and destroy two great buildings in your New York city. But as Karl Marx predicted in his manifesto "Das Kapital" your country will eventually start to decay from within. There will be political leaders elected by the people of America that are godless and corrupt seeking only power and money. They and certain "secret societies" will be proponents of "The New World Order". They desire a one world government. They will slowly but just as surely attempt to crumble fragments of your Constitution. They will introduce a form of American Marxism into the U.S. under the guise of a terminology they call "Progressivism". America will continue her moral decay by "Progressive" politicians actually attempting to negate what God deems as sin. They will actually pass laws making infanticide legal. These political leaders, along with the news media, and your film industry, will attempt to legitimize what God says is abhorrent and deviate sexual behavior.

The American government will pursue mindless myths for financial gain, such as a false science called "Global Warming". They will say the earth is warming dangerously and pronounce the world's destruction. But in saying this they will ignore the bible when it says in Gen 8:22, "While the earth remaineth, seedtime and harvest, and cold and heat, and summer and winter, and day and night shall not cease." Jesus has told us Brother Hiram that Christians will be hated for His namesake. This hatred will abound during this time.

Your country will split into two factions; those of your leaders who are globalists, and desire a one world government, and those who are nationalists defending the sovereignty of America. This is the mortal battle America will fight; that a house divided cannot stand.

I am afraid to tell you Brother Hiram that in the future, after decades of prosperity, your country will see chaos begin to reign. Murders and crime will increase in your major cities. The threats of war will begin to surround you as Russia and China begin their military aggressions against other nations. Your monetary system will be disheveled, and inflation will be rampant to the extent that living is nearly impossible. The scriptures say there will be a day when a loaf of bread costs a day's wages.

That is when he will appear. He will be a great charismatic orator. The western world will receive him as their savior. Although he will have no desire for women, women will love him. Men will want to be him. This is the "Antichrist", Satan's son, the man of perdition, the evil one. He will announce that he can solve all of the world's problems. He will promise to restore prosperity and end all wars; and he will be believed.

He will form a ten-nation confederation with its boundaries encompassing the revived Roman empire. This would include the British Isles, Italy, Poland, Germany, and the other countries of Europe. In fact, your country America is comprised of a high percentage of immigrants coming from those nations, and is thus connected.

It is when the masses will finally shout, "Safety and security!" Then sudden destruction shall be upon them. In Matthew 24: 37-39 the Lord says, "But as the days of Noah were, so shall also the coming of the son of man be. For in the days that were before the flood they were eating and drinking, marrying, and giving in marriage, until the day that Noah entered into the ark. And knew not until the flood came, and took them all away; so, shall also the coming of the Son of man be."

These prophecies of the end of this age are terrifying to the unbeliever, but a joy to those belonging to Christ.

Internalize these things Brother Hiram. Study to show yourself approved unto God!"

He strokes his beard as in thought, then leans forward, and while smiling says, "I should make you aware, that since I have been the head of this order of Jewish Christians for the past 485 years, I receive all news pertaining to this organization. Rabbi Micah and I have discussed the mission that you are about to undertake and although I shall not disclose any details pertinent to it, I must inform you that it is of the upmost importance. Your pursuit of these assignments the Lord has charged you with, will at times be imbued with danger and espionage. I will pray for your safety and success. And above all I wish you Godspeed. I will see you no more until we meet again in glory. Farewell my brother, and God bless!"

"Thank you and God bless you Brother Elijah."

As I leave his presence and the castle, I am in awe of what I've been told. However, my feelings are mixed. Although I'm happy this war will end, I am equally saddened about the future news of America. However, I feel enthused and excited about what may become my greatest adventure. That feeling must be coming from the reporter that remains ingrained within me. Most of all I wish to serve the Lord in any way he leads me.

CHAPTER 64

As the days and weeks go by, I am content with my daily schedule in Shashani. My chores at the stable, Nabob's training, the study of scriptures, morning immersions, and the exercise routine that I began a month ago, have all become an enjoyable and acceptable routine for me. My and Ruth's love for one another has increased to a level that will exponentially cause greater heartbreak when I must depart. I have developed other friendships amongst the inhabitants of this God-filled valley, including a young boy, no older than 13 named Ishmael. Our first meeting transpires at the stables in the afternoon. He walks into the barn and approaches me while staring, and smiling and says, "Call me Ishmael!" I respond saying, "Aye matey, and be you the lad wishing to sign on to the "Pequod" to chase the great white whale?" He laughs and says, "I see you have read "Moby Dick" Brother Hiram."

I answer and admit, "That I have Ishmael; and I see that you know my name."

"Oh, everyone in Shashani knows your name sir."

"What brings you to our stables today, Ishmael?"

"I am most curious sir."

"About what?"

"I am keen on seeing your camel close up. I have seen him only once, and that was at a distance. Is one permitted to pet him?"

"Yes, if that one happens to be a young lad as yourself. Follow me."

We go to Nabob's stall where my camel sees me and starts grunting and braying excitedly.

"What is wrong with him? Why does he make those sounds with his mouth?"

"He's just happy to see us. Although I must warn you that though camels are very friendly, they also can be shy and wary of strangers. Let me hold his head rope and you may pet his shoulder. While you do this you must continue to softly say his name. He's called Nabob. Go ahead son."

As Ishmael pets him, Nabob starts purring contentedly, and Ishmael giggles.

"The way he gets to know you is by your smell and voice. Put your hand by his nose and say hello Nabob."

Ishmael extends his hand and says, "Hello Nabob. Good boy!"

"Have you ever ridden him sir?"

"Not yet," and then Ruth comes over to join us.

She says, "Well hello Ishmael."

"Hello Sister Ruth."

"Do your parents know you're here?"

"Yes ma'am. They know I wanted to see the camel."

I say, "Well I'm glad you came Ishmael. By the way do you know how a camel hides?"

"No sir."

"He gets camelflaged!"

Ruth and Ishmael laugh.

"Do you know how a camel knows it's lost?"

"No sir."

"He gets frozen!"

They laugh loudly again.

Then as I look at the boy, I get an idea, and I say to him, "Do you think that your parents would allow you to help me with Nabob's training; that is of course if you would like to."

"Oh yes I would surely like to sir, and my parents would have no objections!"

"Well, yes you would have to ask your parents for permission, and Sister Ruth's also."

Ishmael looks at Ruth and she shakes her head in the affirmative.

"Now I shall go sir and ask them. When would I start?"

"Same time tomorrow afternoon."

Ishmael runs out of the barn.

Ruth asks, "Why Hiram, would you want a thirteen old boy hanging around you all the time? I did not realize you were so fond of children."

"I believe for three reasons Ruth. One, I do like kids. Two, I'm still somewhat afraid to ride Nabob, and I believe that the boy's lower weight may be just the ticket for him to accept a heavier rider as myself later. And three, I no longer trust myself around you when we're alone together. Ishmael will make us a great chaperone....... if you know what I mean."

Ruth blushes, gives me a peck on the cheek, and says, "I believe this is good, because God forbid, I would find it difficult to say no."

CHAPTER 65

(February 18th, 1945)

(Northeastern Germany)

The Allies move to the German border at Strasbourg France. Heavy snowfall is upon them, and the temperatures are in the teens. "Thumper's" crew is in the lead position of the tanks as they begin to enter the city, and they are greeted with heavy artillery fire. Eight other Sherman's move to the front flanking them on both sides. They commence returning fire as they move forward while infantry soldiers move with them. The buildings in the city are hit hard and a few are demolished, as they continue their forward progress the soldiers begin engaging with the enemy while clearing the Nazi's from damaged structures. Overhead P40 Warhawk fighters are in arial combat with German Messerschmitt's. The battle continues into the night and persists through the morning. A great tally of casualties is being sustained by both combatants. After thirty- eight hours the constant barrage of explosions finally begins to diminish, but victory hasn't been achieved by either side.

At 0:700 hours on the 23rd MSgt Jensen rounds up a few men from Charlie Company with orders he received from H.Q. He gazes at a bunch of cold, tired, and disheveled men. They regard him with sad bedraggled eyes, as he says, "Men I know we are all tired, but this just came down from the top. I need four volunteers, but before I get any takers, I want you to know that this mission that we'll be sending you on is an extremely dangerous one. One where none of you may survive. There seems to be a bridge over a tributary of the Rhine River called the Neckar River. It flows through the village of Villingen- Schwenningen, and it happens to be the main artery of the supply chain for the Germans. Command has decided that we cannot push forward to Berlin unless that bridge is destroyed. We seem to be at a stalemate with the Krauts here at this juncture. I need four men willing to infiltrate enemy lines and blow that damn thing up. Who among you has experience with high explosives?"

MSgt Jensen is answered with total silence. A few of the men stare at one another, and the others put their heads down to look at their boots. Jensen says, "Take your time gentlemen." An infantryman in the rear says, "Count me in sergeant. I'm Private Ben Shields, and I worked in my father's granite quarry in Elberton Georgia detonating large boulders. I'm in."

"Thank you, son," Jensen says. He adds we'll also need an NCO."

TSgt Paddy O'Brien jumps up and hollers, "Now ye won't be a leavin' me out of this melee' sarge! I was a blowin' things up back in me country of Ireland, with me boyos of the Irish Republican Army a long while back dontcha' know! I enjoy doin' that more than kissin Mary Alice O'Shea."

"Jensen says, "Thank you O'Brien, but aren't you Lt. Harrison's top man on your tank?"

"That I am sarge."

Jensen looks at Andy and says, "Only with your permission Lt. Harrison sir."

Andy answers, "I can have Corporal Laskowski to take over on the top for a while and recruit another man from a downed tank to replace him. Let this insane Irishman go sergeant."

"Thank you, sir," Jensen says, "and we still need two more volunteers."

More silence ensues. Then Jensen sees two men talking to each other. One stands up and says, "I'm Private Tom Redfeather and my friend here is Private Sam Standing Bear. We are both from the Cherokee Indian Reservation in Tahlequah, Oklahoma. We wish to go sergeant."

Jensen says, "Thank you men. You four remain with me and the rest of you are dismissed."

"Come over to this table soldiers. We have some things to map out. First, you'll take the ordinance you'll need. You'll detonate both "Composite B" and TNT simultaneously. After wiring you'll have type 578B detonators. Are you familiar with these items?"

Shields answers, "I am sergeant. We used them in our quarry back home."

"Good," says Jensen. "How about you Sergeant O'Brien?"

Paddy answers, "Afraid not sarge. We blokes had only the do-it-yerself bombs, but I'll be a learnin'."

"How about you two men?"

Tom Redfeather answers, "Sam and me just used rifles for huntin'."

Jensen orders, "Private Shields you're going to have to instruct them on the use of these explosives. Also take all of your regular weapons and gear, plus this compass. We believe your escape will be better served using two small inflatable, black rubber rafts. They'll take you quickly downstream until you feel it's time to ditch them."

Jensen spreads out a map, and instructs, "The source of the Neckar River is in the Black Forest itself. When you depart you go in this direction completely around our encampment and proceed northeast at 48 degrees until you reach the forest. You'll be travelling by night and since this forest is dense it will provide you with excellent cover. You shouldn't run into any major Nazi resistance, but you could encounter a patrol. Do not, and I repeat do not engage in a firefight with the enemy. Yours is strictly a secretive mission. Avoid the enemy by hiding, and continue moving at a heading of 71 degrees. In eighteen miles you will arrive at the Neckar's head waters. Follow the river downstream another eight miles and you will arrive at the bridge. Then it is your call O'Brien. From then on it is all impromptu on your part. Obviously attaching the explosives must be done under the cover of darkness. Expect at least four soldiers guarding the bridge. They must be killed silently. I have written a list of everything you shall muster with. You are hereby ordered to leave in three days and ignite the charges in the early morning hours. That will be a great present to give our Nazi friends.

Are there any questions men?"

Paddy answers, "No Sergeant Jensen, but us boyos will study the plans a wee bit more."

"Jensen ends with, "God bless you men. Check with me at 1000 hours by Lt. Harrison's tank the night you leave."

CHAPTER 66

(In Shashani)

The boy Ishmael has proven to be a help to me in the care of Nabob. He enthusiastically grooms and feeds him, and anxiously awaits the day he will be allowed to ride the camel. Ruth and I continue our platonic love affair, as we occasionally hold hands and kiss. Things persist to remain as usual in Shashani. But that is much to my delight.

Then one day, I deem it is time to train Nabob to a rider on his back. On a Sunday after the Sabbath, Ishmael comes to the stables early one morning, and I announce, "Today is the day Ishmael!"

"I will ride him today?"

"Yes, you will young man. Today you become a cowboy.........well, at least an Arab cowboy."

I harness and lead Nabob out of the barn and command him to "Rest down Nabob. Rest down!"

The camel obeys, and I say, "Mount", and then, get upon him Ishmael."

Ishmael looks at me rather tentatively, hesitates, and then climbs upon the animals back. I command "Stand Nabob, stand!"

He obeys in the way that camels awkwardly attempt to stand from a lying position but feeling the extra weight on his back he starts complaining with grunts and brays. Ishmael tells him, "Good boy Nabob, good boy." Then I slowly begin leading the camel by his head rope. I look up at Ishmael and he is smiling and chuckling. He says, "This is wonderful Brother Hiram! It is simply wonderful!"

I command, "Walk Nabob, walk!" And then I lead the camel around the barn's fenced enclosures.

Ruth comes running out to join us. She laughs and shouts, "I was wishing to be the first!" Then she challenges me with, "And yes when will it be your turn to mount him, you being the big, brave, strong man that you are?"

"My turn is next, you "Doubting Thomas.""

After a half hour, and with excellent results, we ride back, and I command, "Rest down Nabob, rest down!" Then, "Dismount." Ishmael climbs off the camel, and I command "Mount", as I board the animal. "Stand Nabob, stand!" Again, he has more difficulty standing because of the extra weight, but manages. I pause. "Walk Nabob, walk!"

I find the experience somewhat unwieldly and my riding position too elevated. This is much different than riding a horse, however I manage to ride him as I sway back and forth. I realize this swaying motion could lead one towards sea sickness. Nabob takes another dozen steps, then his front legs kick up high while leaping on his rear legs, and with great power he bucks me off his back! I do a 180-degree backwards somersault and hit the ground chest and face first.

Ruth screams and yells, "Ishmael, run quickly to Brother Luke and have him summons Sister Esther at the medical clinic. Tell Luke that Hiram may be badly injured!

Ishmael hurries off, and Ruth runs to me asking, "Are you hurt badly Hiram?"

The wind is knocked out of me and I'm gasping for breath. When I'm finally able to speak I utter, "I think I broke some ribs Ruth, and maybe my nose." I sputter and spit dirt out of my mouth. Ruth puts her arm around me and says, "Help is on the way Hiram. You just lie there and rest."

It doesn't take long before Shashini's healer Sister Esther is by my side and Luke with her. She asks, "Where are you hurt Brother Walker?"

Again, I'm not able to speak and Ruth tells her, "He said it is his nose and ribs."

"Alright brother just relax. Help me turn him over Luke."

As I look at her, she instructs me to, "Just close your eyes Brother Walker."

I feel her touching my closed eyes and that is all I remember. I'm out like a light. When I awaken, I realize that somehow, she put me to sleep, and I ask, "How long was I out?"

Esther says, "Only ten or fifteen minutes. How do you feel?"

"Actually, I feel pretty good now."

"Try standing up," she says.

I do, and it's true. I feel great; more than great, I feel refreshed and enthused!

"Thank you so very much sister! What did you do?"

"I am a healer Brother Hiram. The Lord has given me the gift of healing. You are perfectly fine now."

"Praise God. That was amazing," I say.

Esther says, "Please Luke, take me back to my clinic I have two patients to see soon."

Yes sister, we'll take the carriage back," Luke answers.

As Ruth, Ishmael, and I watch them leave Ruth says, "Let us go to my cottage for you to rest awhile."

I think about it and say, "Absolutely not! What would a cowboy do after he's thrown from his horse Ishmael?"

"I have read a book from our cultural library by Mr. Louis Lamour, that says when a cowboy is thrown from his horse, then he must immediately get back on sir."

"And I believe that should apply to camels as well! "Rest down Nabob, rest down."

"Mount Nabob", I mount!" "Stand Nabob, stand!" "Walk Nabob, walk!"

We take a stroll around the entire stables and barn area before I dismount and lead him back to his stall. Ruth joins me and says, "Oh Hiram, I shall miss you terribly."

"We still have a couple of months left Ruth."

She says, "Give me a kiss."

I do and she giggles. I say what's wrong?"

"Nothing is wrong. Your beard is much longer....... it tickles. Oh Hiram, Sometimes I think you are very stupid. Why did you get back up on that camel again?"

I laugh and say, "Because we've got a healer over at the Medical clinic."

She scowls at me and says, "Do not tempt the Lord thy God, Brother Hiram."

CHAPTER 67

(The German French Border)

The four soldiers on their mission to destroy a bridge on the Neckar River, eventually reached the Black Forest at 22:00 hours. It is pitch black in this thick arboreal landscape. TSgt Paddy O'Brien leads the small group while studying his compass. He orders, "No lights laddies and no fire for a cookin'. We'll be a eatin' our rations cold now. I have me compass bead on where we'll be a goin', and we'll be a stayin' together now!"

Night goes by, and dawn breaks before the squad stops. Private Ben Shield's whispers, "So far so good Sarge. We need a place to hunker down for the day."

Private Redfeather says, "Let me scout ahead sarge. Maybe I can find a cave, or someplace good to hide?"

Paddy says, "You'll be a doin' just 'a that private. But be a movin' slow and sneaky like."

A half hour passes before Redfeather returns, and he advises, "I found a small cavern 'bout a quarter mile from here. Should be a good place."

When the four attain its entrance, they find it surrounded by a wild tangle of bushes and young saplings. Although bare in the winter months, it manages to hide the cave's entrance.

Shields says, "This place is great! How in the world did you find it through all this brush Tom?"

Tom Redfeather answers, "How? Me Indian...... How!"

Paddy says," We may not 'ave found the pot-o-gold, but we still got lucky boyos. Let's be gettin' some shut eye till she be a gettin' dark agin'."

The suicide squad settles into the small cavern and lights candles. Paddy says, "Listen up. It'll be Shields and me self that'll set the explosives. Red feather and Standing Bear you'll be a killin' the guards."

The two Cherokee's hold up their K-bar knives. Standing Bear says, "Watch sarge", and he tosses an apple into the air. As it comes down upon the blade it splits in half. "We are ready sarge!"

Some time and a long silence go by, then Paddy asks, "What'll ye lads be doin' after this war?"

Private Shields says, "I'll be going back to our quarry in Georgia. There's a gal in Elberton named Cathy Cozart. We've been sweethearts since the seventh grade. I'm going to marry her boys. Here's a picture of her." He hands Paddy the picture and they pass it around.

"She's a beauty Shields. In me country, we'd be a callin' her an Irish Rose", says Paddy. "How about ye injun' boyos?"

Tom Redfeather says, "I was going to law school before this mess started, and I plan to finish and be an adjutant for my tribe. Someone needs to stop you white men from taking further advantage of us." Then he laughs.

Sam Standing bear adds, "I've been a huntin' and fishin' my whole life. I don't know how to do anything else. When I get back home, I'd like to start a guide service for you palefaces. I've watched some of you hunt, and you all stink at it. How about you sarge?"

Paddy answers, "I be a lovin' this man's Army. I think I'll stay in 'til they be a throwin' me out."

After a breakfast on K-rations they bed down for the day in their own little nest.

PART FOUR

CHAPTER 68

(In Shashani)

I have received notification that I will meet with Rabbi Micha in three days. My emotions are racing, and although it is my fervent desire to serve my Lord and to do his will, leaving Ruth and this paradise is breaking my heart. I'm truly thankful for what God has done for me in preparing me for whatever mission He has appointed me, and I am cognizant that if He hadn't directed me to the Essenes, that my bones would be baking in the Sinai sun right now. I believe I will put a sign on my desk at church proclaiming, "The day I gave my life over to Jesus, I took it out of the hands of an idiot."

On Sunday morning Ruth and I decide to take one last trip to Joshua's Grove, and we invite our youthful chaperone Ishmael to join us. Ruth mounts her horse, Ishmael takes Lizzy, and as his trainings complete, I ride Nabob. As we jockey to the grove, I see Ruth on my left side crying. Ishmael notices it also, and asks, "What is wrong Sister Ruth?"

"Do you know Ishmael, that Brother Hiram will be leaving Shashani?"

"Yes sister, he told me so, and I shall miss him."

"Well, I may miss him more. That is all." She sheds more tears.

I interject, "Let's stop this right now. I for one am looking forward to a wonderful day and that fried chicken you brought for us Ruth."

"I shall try Hiram. I shall try."

After we arrive at the grove and dismount the animals, I look at Nabob and tell him, "Good boy Nabob. Good boy!" I pet him on the head and recognize that he is ready for our journey; to wherever that may be. I am pleased with him.

Ishmael takes a bucket to the creek for water, and Ruth and I walk into the woods for firewood. After gathering a few fallen branches, we start carrying them back until she drops hers and grabs me. We embrace and kiss. She says, "I do not like this saying goodbye Hiram."

I answer, "Then don't try."

"Will I see you tomorrow?"

"No, I have to pack and meet with Brother Jacob for meetings at my cottage. We'll have to part today. It may be best if you and Ishmael stay here a while longer. I'll ride Nabob back alone."

"Oh, Hiram, I love you so!"

"And I you Ruth, and we will always have had Shashani."

After we eat, I said goodbye to Ishmael.

Ruth walks s over to Nabob, again, we embrace, kiss, and I leave.

CHAPTER 69

That evening while I pack, I take the list given to me to check off the articles needed for my retreat. I stop when I hear a knock on my door. When I answer the knock Brother Jacob greets me.

"Good evening, Brother Hiram."

"Hello Jacob. Did you come to say goodbye?"

"Yes, and to give you this for your perusal."

"What is it?"

"This briefcase contains the documents you will need after leaving Shashani. Rabbi Micha wants you to review its contents now. If you feel the need for any changes, I am to inform him so corrections may be made."

He hands me a brown leather briefcase with lockable clasps. I open it and find the following:

"PASSPORT"

American Citizen

Pastor David H. Greene

1159 Bent Ave, Asheville. North Carolina

Occupation: Christian Minister and Missionary

British Driver's License 8887350US

Expires January 14th, 1948.

First National Bank of New York Checkbook

Account # AE22739996114

Diploma from

Fruitland Theological Seminary

Hendersonville, North Carolina.

An ordination Certificate from "Grace Christian Church"

Bristol, Pennsylvania

I also found: (1) Three copies of a book in hardcover entitled "God's Witnesses" authored and copyrighted by David H. Greene.

(2) Various photographs of myself at different ages.

(3) Pictures of a man and a woman with the words Mom & Dad Penciled in at the bottom in my handwriting.

(4) 3,000 pounds in British currency.

(5) A sheet of paper with an address of 881 Mesilat Yesharim street, Jerusalem, Palestine.

I ask Jacob, "What is all of this?"

"I have no idea, Hiram. All will be explained to you by Rabbi Micah."

"Well, it certainly is mysterious, and it definitely has my curiosity piqued!"

"I am certain that it does. I must say goodbye to you now my good friend, but before I leave, I wish to pray with you."

We both get on our knees and offer our prayers unto the Lord.

CHAPTER 70

(Two months before Hiram Walker's)

(Departure from Shashani)

(Somewhere in the Black Forest)

(February 1945)

As night falls on TSgt Patrick Michael O'Brien's squad of four, they make their way towards their objective of the Neckar River's headwaters. They encounter no enemy for miles. Then upon climbing a large rise in the landscape they hear voices near the hill's top.

"Paddy whispers, "Krauts! Lie low!"

The voices become louder as the squad unsheathes their knives. "Ready now," orders Paddy. They remain silent in the hopes that the German patrol will pass them by. Private Shield's foot accidentally slips against some loose stones and deflects them downward making a loud audible noise. They hear………..

"Was war das fur ein gerausch?" (What was that noise?")

Another German soldier says, "Ich werde gehen, umzu sehen!" (I'll go look!)

Immediately Privates Standing Bear and Redfeather start making raspy and loud imitation crow calls. "Caw…. Caw…. Caw…. Caw!" And again, "Caw…. Caw…., Caw!"

They hear, "Es ist nichts als Krahen!" (It's nothing but crows!) "Komm schon Heinrich!" (let's go on Heinrich!)

Paddy lets out a sigh of relief, and they stay motionless until the Germans pass them by into the night. The four Americans wait a good half hour before their leader says, "Now it looks like I be a havin' two injun lads who've been a kissin' the blackbird's blarney stone!"

Private Shields says, "Wow, that was lucky!"

Their sergeant says, "There be no luck in the things we be a facin' laddies. We be all meant to go through hell and come back a smilin'…… Let's be a movin' out!"

After two more days of striding through the dense forest they come to a small lake. Redfeather says, "This is it sarge. This has to be the headwaters. Why don't Sam and me scout further down south and find the river's beginning. You wait here and watch for Krauts. Do you know the sound of a wolf howling?'

"I never heard one in me life," says Paddy.

"It sounds like this." Then Redfeather cries out a loud hideous howl of a wolf calling for its mate.

"I'll be a knowin' what it'll be soundin' like for now."

"When you hear that howl, we've found the stream. We'll wait for you there."

Paddy says, "Be a soundin' like a plan. Go for it!" Paddy and Ben Shields lie down in a thicket and wait.

In about an hour the blood curling scream of a wolf can be heard.

The sarge and private hike to meet them there.

"Say hello to the Neckar sarge," laughs Tom.

"Daybreak be upon us boyos. There be a bunch of St Patrick's big stones a waitin' for us over in the gloamin'. We'll be a hidin' there."

CHAPTER 71

(To Rabbi Micha's)

All my gear is packed onto Nabob as I ride to the north mountains and Rabbi Micha's cottage near Gen Aden. My thoughts are still only on Ruth, and I must get her out of my mind.

I gaze up and see his building against the mountainside, and continue commanding Nabob onward. My heart is pounding rapidly in anticipation of what God has in store for me, and I'm also somewhat tentative about reentering into a world full of death.

We arrive and I have Nabob lie as I dismount. I snicker to myself that I'm becoming an excellent camel jockey. I take my briefcase with me, and two men greet me on the porch of the Rabbi's dwelling to usher me in. I recognize them as Brothers Isaac and Mordecai. The same men who rescued me in the cavern and first brought me into Shashani. I say, "Long time no see brothers. Do you spend all your time up here on the mountain?"

Isaac answers, "Yes Brother Hiram. We are permanently stationed up here. We provide Rabbi Micha with support for whatever he requires."

"I see."

"Follow us."

We entered the house and into a spacious room with a large picture window overlooking the Shashani valley. "Please be seated the Rabbi will be with you shortly."

I take a seat on a sofa by other furniture arranged in a circular fashion around a large coffee table. After only a few minutes the Rabbi walks in to greet me. He says, "Hashalom Brother Hiram. It is my honor to meet you."

I answer, "And I you sir." As I study the rabbi, he is anything but what I expected him to be. He wears no Shashani robes, sandals, or other garb indicative of the Essene people, but rather a well-tailored European business suit, tie, and wing tip shoes. He is clean shaven, wears glasses and has a yarmulke on his head. But the most surprising thing to me is what appears to be his young age. He looks to be in his thirties; although in Shashani, one's age can never be judged by outward appearance. We shake hands and he takes a seat opposite me and lays a pamphlet on the table. He then says, "Are you ready to reenter your world brother?"

I answer, "Yes, but not without reservations. I am, however, ready, and eager to be about the Lord's work."

"Praise God brother! Praise God! I wish to inform you that the mission you are about to undertake is for your ears only. I believe that the terminology in your world would be that this is a "Top Secret Mission".

"I will accept anything that the Lord requires of me."

"That is good brother, because at times you may find what you must accomplish to be most difficult."

"I must admit Rabbi Micha that your personage is certainly not what I expected. May I ask you what your age is? Also, I must admit your choice of apparel puzzles me.

"Yes, I am actually only thirty-seven years old, but Sister Esther after my last physical informed me that bodily, I am actually 55 years of age.

All of my organs, bones, and my entire anatomy has advanced beyond my true age. You see, on rare occasions, am required to enter your world for God's purposes. That is the reason for my, what you would call my modern-day apparel. Unfortunately, when duty requires me to remain in your world for extended periods of time I age rapidly.

By the way, would you like a coffee or other drink?"

"No, I'm fine."

"Have you studied the material that I enclosed in your briefcase?"

"I have, and I found it most confusing."

"Then I shall explain the issues within. I suggest that you take notes for there is much that I shall relate to you."

"When you depart Shashani it is imperative that your status as being "Killed in Action" by your Army remains in effect. Hiram (Ace) Walker is dead, and must continue to be dead. Your mortal remains never to be found. It seems the Lord loves to change a person's name. He changed Abram to Abraham, Saul to Paul, and He has changed yours Hiram Walker. The passport you are given declares your new name. You are now, and forever to be Pastor David H. Greene, an ordained pastor from America. You have a twofold mission, Pastor Greene. I shall address you by your new name now. You will be a missionary in Jerusalem of Palestine preaching the Gospel of Jesus Christ. You will be fulfilling your duty of "Matthew 28 by witnessing and baptizing in the name of Jesus. It is important that you understand that on the day that you leave Shashani, the Holy Spirit will endow you with two spiritual gifts. They will be the gifts of "Evangelism", and the "Gift of Tongues". Understand that this is not of unknown tongues, but of the languages of all the worlds dialects. It is the gift that you have already received here in Shashani; and you will be allowed to keep it. As In the Day of Pentecost when you preach, every person hearing your words will comprehend your speech in their own native language. In turn when spoken to by anyone you will understand their speech in their tongue. Arrangements for a church building in Jerusalem and your residence within, have already been established. You are expected there as we speak. Your duties there will be conducted as a pastor from any other non-denominational Christian church. As the note in your briefcase suggests you have already established yourself in the clergy by graduating from a theological seminary and have also pastored a small church in Bristol Pennsylvania. You have also established yourself as a scholar and a noted author by writing a book pertaining to Christian witness. This is the first assignment you have been given by God. Do you have any questions regarding this position?"

"I have. Will I have other personnel assisting me there?"

"Yes. There are three employees presently there, and you will appoint others at your discretion."

"How strong will my new credentials hold up if someone desires to examine them?"

"That will not occur Pastor Greene. The Lord will prevent that from happening. But by the way there is nothing false about your God-given gifts that will enable you to perform your functions. It is the Lord's desire that none should perish but all come to salvation. God bless you. Your efforts will be fruitful in that many will come to be saved. Also, there will be no confusion about your gift of tongues. No one will understand that others have heard your message in a different language."

"What is my second mission rabbi?"

Micah raises an eyebrow, smiles, and says, "This becomes one of espionage. You are to be a determined Zionist. You are to be a most important cog in Israel becoming a sovereign nation once again Pastor Greene! Do you remember Brother Elijah telling you that Israel will become a nation again in the year 1948?"

"Yes, I do."

"Then let me ask you, and be profound in your thoughts, what would a people need to develop once again to become a new nation after centuries of extinction?"

I am silent for a long time as I gather my thoughts, and then I expound, "They will need a massive arsenal of weaponry to defend themselves against those wishing their failure. They will need infrastructure as in bridges, roads, schools, hospitals, buildings for its inhabitants, and a myriad of other necessities."

"You are correct. And what will be needed to create that infrastructure?"

"Vast amounts of capital would be needed."

"Yes, much money will be required, and that is where you come in."

"Me? How in the world will I bring that about?"

"You must listen to me carefully now pastor. I am about to give you an ancient history lesson that only Brother Elijah and myself have knowledge. It is a secret that only our ancestors have retained through the centuries. Do you recall what happened to the Hebrew people in about 500 B.C.?"

"Yes, king Nebuchadnezzar of Babylon attacked the Hebrew kingdom of Judah and took its people away captive. He also plumaged Solomon's temple of its treasures and put them into the house of his gods."

"That is correct. What happened next to those temple treasures?"

"The Persians later conquered Babylon and I believe we can read about that in the books of Daniel and Ezra."

"Correct again. Turn with me Pastor Greene to Ezra 1:2, and I shall read, "Thus saith Cyrus king of Persia. The Lord God of heaven hath given me all the kingdoms of the earth; and he hath charged me to build Him a house at Jerusalem which is in Judah."

Now let us read verse seven. "Also, Cyrus the king brought forth the vessels of the house of the Lord which Nebuchadnezzar had brought forth out of Jerusalem and had put them in the house of his gods."

Let us pause there and read verses 9, 10, and 11 for this is an inventory of the treasure. "And this is the number of them: thirty chargers of gold, a thousand chargers of silver, nine and twenty knives. Thirty basons of gold, silver basons of a second sort four-hundred and ten, and other vessels a thousand. All the vessels of gold and silver were five thousand and four hundred."

Then we read in 5:15 king Cyrus' decree given to a prince of Judah named, Sheshbazzar, "And said unto him, take these, go, carry them to the temple that is in Jerusalem, and let the house of God be built in His place." It is also interesting to note that verse 2:64 gives a list of the number of those who are to return to Judah as 42,360.

"Quite a fabulous treasure is it not?"

"Yes, an incredible wealth," I answer.

"What happened next to this treasure Pastor Greene?"

"You know every time you address me as Pastor Greene I want to look back over my shoulder and see who you're talking to."

We both laugh. Then the Rabbi rings a loud bell. In a minute Mordecai comes into the room.

"Brother Mordecai would you be so kind as to bring our guest and myself a pot of tea please?" Mordecai nods and leaves the room.

"Again, what happened next to this treasure?"

I answer, "It remains in Herod's temple in Jerusalem until 70 A.D. when the Romans destroy Jerusalem and the temple."

"Again, you are right. But allow me to ask this. What happened then to this treasure? Did the Romans and the newly elected Caesar Vespasian confiscate it?"

"I don't know. If I were guessing, I would say they did."

"Then you would be wrong."

Mordecai returns with the tea and pours us each a cup. The rabbi waits for him to leave, takes a sip of his tea, looks sternly at me, and says, "Of what value would you assess this treasure by today's standards?"

"I think that its historical and monetary value would make it incalculable to assess. It would be worth greater than billions of American dollars."

We both take another taste of tea.

Again, he stares at me for a long time, sets his cup on the table, and says, "What if I told you, I know how we can find this treasure today?"

"You're joking," I utter. Then......I pause......and say, "You're actually serious aren't you."

"I am most serious. Allow me to explain how I know. Let's go back to the year 69 A.D. A prophet of the Essenes named Zussya, was the first of our sect to believe that Jesus was indeed truly the promised messiah, the Son of God crucified for the forgiveness of our sins. In a dream he was told by The Lord the date on which Caesar Vespasian would command his centurions to destroy Jerusalem and the temple. With this knowledge a year before the obliteration of Jerusalem, and while obeying God's instructions, a plan was formulated by my ancestors to steal the temple's holy valuables and hide them initially in caves to the east of the Mount of Olives, near the village of Bethany where Jesus often went to visit Lazarus and Mary. From that location they were transferred over time to caves in the Qumran area of the Dead Sea. I shall not go into detail as to how they managed to successfully accomplish this feat, except by saying that God's miraculous hand was involved! That is their location today.

Today in Khirbet Qumran Pastor Greene, there are eleven caves containing 981 ancient manuscripts of the holy scriptures penned by the Essenes. Most importantly for you, there is one cave that contains scrolls made of copper. These copper scrolls are maps, and give directions to the locations of 63 of the 64 places where the treasures have been buried. Your appointed mission is to go to the cave of the copper scrolls and acquire the directions to 63 of these treasures. The directions are written in Aramaic and Hebrew. You will then copy all of these directive routes from the scrolls in Hebrew on the notebook that is in your briefcase, and number them from 1 to 63. You will then travel to the first location indicated by the scroll. I will repeat, you will go to location number one. Please understand you will only go to just that one treasure, and upon finding the cache, you will take only three items from it and leave the balance undisturbed. You will then proceed with those three items to Jerusalem and hide them in a lockable strongbox in the basement of the church you are to pastor. You will not have to fear for their safety because two new and additional malakis will be waiting there to receive the articles, and will remain there to guard them day and night. The two angels who accompanied you on your journey upon leaving Shashani will continue to follow you. May I ask what questions you have regarding this?"

I laugh and admit, "Yes you may. But I am flabbergasted, and don't know where to start! Let me reiterate what you just said. I go to a cave in Qumran and find these copper scrolls. I write down in Hebrew the locations of 63 hidden treasures. I then go to find the treasure I listed as number one. I just find that one only. Upon finding it I take three pieces of treasure while leaving the rest. I take them and go to my new church in Jerusalem and hide them in its basement. Am I correct?"

"Yes."

"What do I do next?"

The Rabbi continues, "You will start your evangelical outreach at the church. Then you will occasionally receive sealed envelopes that will instruct you further. I cannot emphasize how important it is for you to successfully complete this mission. Later, arrangements will be made to unearth and retrieve all of the caches by those men whom you are told to contact. You will only guide them there."

"May I ask for what purpose the treasures will be used?"

"Yes, you may.

The gold and silver buried amount to one and a half tons in today's measure. Now hear this Pastor Greene, THE WEALTH OF THIS TREASURE WILL BE USED TO FUND THE NEW AND

SOVERIGN STATE OF ISRAEL. It will be used to finance all of what is needed for the things you just said would be required to birth a new nation."

For the second time in my life, I am speechless. I just sit there and smile.

CHAPTER 72

Paddy and his men follow the river south. At 0600 hours Private Sam Standing Bear, while scouting ahead, spots the bridge at Villingen-Schwenningen. He watches Nazi movements and waits for the other three men of his squad to arrive at his position.

Private Sam says, "There it is sarge, in all its glory. Won't it be lovely to see it crumble down?"

Paddy answers, "And aye it will be laddie. Aye, it will be! "He takes the binoculars from Standing Bear and glasses the bridge. "Look at all those slimy grey uniforms!"

"Shields, you should be a takin' a good look at that bridge," says Paddy. Shields takes the glasses and eyeballs the bridge.

Paddy asks, "Are ye seein' the I-beams underneath leadin' up from each end to the center?"

"Yeah sarge. Are you thinking that we'll crawl on them and attach the bombs towards the center?"

"Aye, I am."

Shields says, "I'm with you sarge. Then later I'll detonate them both from your side."

"That'll be the plan."

Private Ben Shields says, "Redfeather and I will take our explosives, inflate our raft, and cross over by that bend down river apiece."

Paddy says, "Aye, and Standing Bear and I'll be a goin' on this here side. Ben you 'll be a takin' our raft with ye and leavin' it where ye be puttin' in."

Ben says, "Alright sarge, and I think we should move elsewhere to spend the day. We're too close to the bridge at this point, and we're more likely to encounter an enemy patrol here."

"Righto," answers Paddy. "Let's be a movin' west for a bit."

They come across a rocky overcropping that will provide some shelter, and wait for dark.

Paddy says, "May our pockets be heavy and our hearts light. May good luck pursue us each morning and night." Standing Bear laughs and says, "You must have an Irish saying about everything sarge!"

CHAPTER 73

(Rabbi Micha's residence)

"Are things beginning to clear for you Pastor Greene?"

"I believe so, but what is the distance I'll be traversing from here to Qumran?"

"It is a distance of approximately 275 miles. By traveling about ten hours a day you should reach Qumran in four to five days. You will travel northeast until you reach the strait of Aqaba. Then follow the strait to the north.

"You will leave Shashani tomorrow morning. Brothers Isaac and Mordecai will be waiting for you at the caves gate. They will have another camel there to carry the items you will recover, as well as any other incidentals you wish to put upon it. We have already put sufficient food and water for you on the beast. Unfortunately, your only repast will be K-rations that we have procured. This camel is to carry loads, and not to ride. It has not been broken or trained for that purpose. Furthermore, you must be aware of dangers at all times."

"And what do you perceive those dangers to be rabbi?"

"We have been informed that that there is no presence of German troops anywhere along the route to Qumran. There are, however, Bedouin tribes within your itinerary that could pose a threat to you.

Groups of both the Qasis and Muzziena tribes are scattered throughout the region. Most are shy and peaceful citizens of the desert, but there are some who are murderous thieves who would steal your animals, rob you of your goods, and cut your throat."

"Sounds like fun," I sarcastically say. Will you provide me with a weapon?"

"There are no weapons allowed within the borders of Shashani, however your army pistol and some ammunition remain in the cave if you wish to recover it. This is strictly at your discretion pastor. It seems that it would be improbable for you to have need of it."

"Why is that?"

"Although you will have no perception of them, two malakis will accompany you on your journey, and will intervene if you face any threats." "

You say two angels will be guarding me?"

"Yes, but of course you will not see them." "Now I need to give you more directions with this map. He spreads it onto the table and narrates, "You will find three oases on your trip. Each will be at distances of about 75 miles from each other. These oases will provide water for your animals, and shelter for you. At the last oasis you will be in the Qumran area near the Dead Sea. At that point you will align your compass at 295 degrees and travel approximately two miles until you find an ancient ruin. It will appear to be only a circular stone wall. Come to it and then then look upwards towards the westward mountain at exactly 259 degrees. You will see an overhanging cliff with an opening below it. This will be the cave you are seeking. It is the one containing the copper scrolls. You will find them at the extreme end of the cavern.

Most importantly, although you will be copying from the copper scroll all of the clues to each of the other 62 locations into your notebook, the only one treasure that you will need to discover will be found by following its instructions to yet another ruin. The scroll will point to a ruin which is in the valley of Acor. That is all of the information that the Lord has given to us. It is because the clues written there on the scroll are for the eyes of the finder only. None of us here in Shashani, not even Brother Elijah, knows the clues to that treasure. You will be that finder Pastor Greene. After recording the clues to all 63 of the 64 hidden treasures, you must exit the cave and proceed again westward over the same mountain's ridge and down into the next wadi. You will then be in the Valley of Acor searching for that particular ruin that holds the treasure you require."

I ask, "What does the ruin look like?"

"A small stone hovel."

He then hands me a sheet of paper with three objects written on it: a knife with a bejeweled handle, a golden basin engraved with the depictions of bulls, and a golden candlestick.

"I assume these are the three items I am to pilfer?"

"Yes, they are. Please be advised that at this juncture you will be only 28 miles from the city of Jerusalem. Continue due north and you will arrive at a road that will lead you to a roadblock which has been established by the British Army. As you are aware, the Government of Britain continues to control the region of Palestine. Although the British soldiers there will be surprised by your Bedouin appearance, since your passport claims you are an American, they will allow your entry."

"You say I will look like a Bedouin?"

"Certainly, pastor we cannot have you traversing all over this wilderness region looking like a lost American. If you did you would be begging for misfortune and conflict."

"I guess I would be sticking out like a sore thumb."

"I am sorry, you say that you have injured your thumb?"

I laugh and say, "No rabbi I haven't hurt my thumb. That was just an analogy as to what I would appear to look like in the desert without costume."

"I am sorry, I do not seem to understand; however, when Mordecai ushers you to your room tonight, he will present you with some Bedouin clothing. There will be a white cloth dress called a "thoab", Bedouin boots, and a turban style of headdress called a "keffiyeh". He will show you how to wear this garb and also give you a can of salve for your face. This salve will darken your face. That and along with your beard should make an adequate disguise."

I laugh again and say, "I think I'll make a very good impression of Rudolph Valentino when he played in the movie "The Sheik!"

The rabbi looks at me with a dour expression. He says very slowly, "Why.... are.... you.... laughing.... pastor? This is very serious business."

"I apologize. I was simply trying to relieve some stress."

His face tells me he doesn't accept my apology. Instead, he says, "Have you been able to write all of this down so far?"

"Yes, I have."

"Fine, let me resume please."

"Then you shall continue until you arrive at a road sign advertising the "Muhammed edh-Dhib Stables and Auction"."

I interrupt, "How do you spell that rabbi?"

He spells it for me and says, "It is on the outskirts of the city. There you will be met by a Mr. Joseph Ben- Hur. He will be driving an older green truck with the name of "Grace Christian Church" stenciled on its sides. This is the name of your church. He will assist you in transferring all of your cargo from the animals to his vehicle. The next requirement is for you to board your camel. What is his name?"

"His name is Nabob."

"Yes Nabob. You are to board Nabob for future use and sell the other camel. Your new acquaintance will be very helpful for you. He is the custodian of your church, and what you would call "A jack of all trades". He is a devout Christian, and will be elated to meet you.

Then you will both go to; and write this address down, to 881 Mesilat Yesharim St. This is the address of your church."

"Rabbi, you said I will be receiving messages in sealed envelopes for new orders and instructions. Where and how will they come to me?"

"They won't, you must go to them. "You will go on the Sabbath day only, to the "Ahmed Hussein Market Place".

"Spell that again please."

He does and continues, "Behind this market is an alleyway lined with a wall of bricks. One brick near the top is marked with a small star. Remove that brick, take the envelope behind it, and replace the brick. This area of Jerusalem is usually bustling with many people, however on Saturday, the Sabbath, it is very quiet."

"Please take your notes and read back to me a synopsis of your written text. I wish to inspect it to ascertain if we have affected proper communications."

I read aloud, in a nutshell, all that was explained to me. Then I question, "I'm curious as to why I am recording the clues to locations of only 63 of the 64 hidden treasures. Why not the 64th?"

He lifts his cup, finishes his tea, and then says, "Because Pastor Greene even you with your gift of tongues will not be able to read the 64th and last set of clues that lead to that treasure."

Why?"

"Because it is written in the tongues of angels. That treasure is reserved for the new third temple which will stand at the time of the SECOND COMING of Our Lord and Savior Jesus Christ. It also contains His anointing oil."

I exclaim, "Even so come Lord Jesus!"

I believe that the rabbi is finally satisfied that I have internalized my mission's plans, when he says, "My brother, let us pray for your safety and success."

We get down on our knees and ask the Lord's blessing for our venture. Then he says, "Again I am honored to have met you my dear brother. And then as an afterthought he pauses and says, "By the way, you would be interested in knowing that in 1946, just about a year from now, a Bedouin boy will throw a stone into a cave and hear the crashing sound of pottery breaking. He will get his father and they will have found what will be called the greatest archeological find in history. This find will be called "The Dead Sea Scrolls". No one will ever know that you discovered it first! We both laugh. "The Lord will be with you Pastor Greene."

"Yes, and don't forget two angels will also!"

"But I have one question to ask you rabbi."

"And that is?"

"Has anyone from the outside world that has entered into Shashani, and then exited it again like me......... has anyone ever returned?"

He answers, "Never!"

CHAPTER 74

(The Bridge on the Neckar)

(Germany)

At dusk, TSgt. O'Brien's squad moves to a position about a mile south of their intended target. Upon reaching the river they inflate both rafts. Privates Shields and Redfeather deposit their explosives into the boat in readiness to cross. Paddy and Standing Bear cut some vegetation to camouflage their raft.

Paddy says, "Here we go boyos, let the shenanigans begin!" Shields and Redfeather push off the bank to cross, and Paddy and Standing Bear move north towards the west end of the bridge. Upon reaching their objective they move under the overpass and wait for Shields and Redfeather to show themselves on the other side. They must synchronize the killing of the four guards. Eventually the two privates show up on the other side. Redfeather waves his hand at his friend and they both sneak up to opposite ends of the overpass.

Redfeather sees the soldier guarding the east end of the bridge. He waits. On the west end Standing Bear does the same. As both guards loiter towards their ends, both privates simultaneously rush them, gag their mouths with their hands, and finish them with their knives. They then drag their dead prey downwards out of the visibility of any other enemy. Two down, two to go. In the center of the bridge the two guards are stationed in makeshift guard shacks designed to operate a swinging gate that allows or prevents entry across the span of the bridge. The two Cherokees sneak quietly to the shacks. They both kneel and wait against the small structures that are aligned opposite one another. A few minutes go by until they hear,

"Hey Hans du hast einen rauch?" (Hey Hans, do you have a smoke?) Then from the other booth they hear, "Ja Ollie, komm hier ruber." (Yeah Ollie, come over here.) The privates wait until one guard is lighting the others cigarette, then they rush them both knocking them to the ground, and again, while muzzling their mouths, they use their knives to dismiss them. They rid the two bodies by tossing them into the river. After the killings they race below the bridge to their respective sides.

Paddy waves at them and when Standing Bear gets to him, he says, "Shor an' begora' that was a fine, fine job laddie! Now you two boyo's head to the rafts and Shields and I'll do the nasty." Both Indians take off south, and Paddy and Shields start climbing the support beams to the bridge's center.

One half hour elapses before the composite B and TNT are attached properly to the columns. They shimmy down the bridge's supports and Shields proceeds south, safely away from the coming blast, before kneeling and readying the detonator. Paddy stops the same distance on the other side of the river, and they glance at each other across the murky water and give thumbs up. Shields looks at his watch it is 0:48 hours. At 01:00 hours he'll pushes the detonating plunger in. They both wait while seconds turn into minutes.......until......!

"KABOOM!!! The deafening explosion demolishes both ends of the bridge and its center collapses into the river below!

The four stand and watch with admiration as their handiwork obliterates what once was a bridge, being turned into flying splinters and rubble! They seemed mesmerized by the spectacle until Paddy cries,

"Bless me little Irish heart and every other Irish part, for we surely kissed the shamrock that a time! To the rafts boyos!"

Upon reaching their rubber crafts they begin paddling away. All four men start laughing. Shields proclaims, "Happy New Year Adolf!" They continue downstream about a mile when suddenly German troops appear on both sides of the river. They start to receive gunfire. Redfeather and Standing Bear in the front of their boats, persist on rowing rapidly. Shields and Paddy turn towards the banks and begin returning fire. Bullets crossfire and a few Germans are felled.

Then Paddy feels a red-hot sting to his right shoulder causing him to drop his weapon and fall flat into the raft. Shields, on his knees, continues firing until he's hit in the chest by a 9mm round. He falls overboard into the Neckar River. The two Cherokees paddle for their lives. Eventually they outdistance the German soldiers and maintain rowing steadily for another hour until they both veer their rafts onto the western bank. Paddy moans as the two privates carry him out of the boat and onto the shore.

Redfeather asks, "How ya doin' sarge?"

The sergeant answers, "I am feelin' worse than bein' hit by me pappy's Shaleigh Ly!"

"Get the first aid kit Sam!"

Redfeather says, "You're lucky sarge. The bullet went clean through. Looks like it may have caught a bit of a bone though."

Paddy says, "That'll be the luck of the Irish boyos, but where's Ben?"

"He didn't make it sarge," answers Tom.

After Paddy receives his field dressing, they knife the rafts to flatten them. They pile on stones to sink them into the river. They want no trace as to where they portaged.

They then begin their long hike back to the Battalion's encampment. Two days later they reach it. Paddy is taken to the MASH unit (Mobile

Army Surgical Hospital) to be treated for his wounds. After his surgical procedures, his tank crew arrive to see him and gather around his bed.

"That was an incredible thing you did up on that river Paddy," says Andy. "You are one brave but nutty Irishman."

"Ah, twas nothin' but a bit of tomfoolery. But when that bridge went KABLOOIE, those heinies were a runnin' like a bunch o' screamin' banshees", laughs Paddy!

LtCol. Parker and MSgt Jensen arrive at the field hospital to see Paddy.

"Hello Sergeant O'Brien. How are you feeling?"

"Oh, I'm a feelin' fine sir. Just had me a wee bit of a nick dontcha know. Can't be sayin' the same for Private Ben Shields though. We lost him colonel."

LtCol Parker asks. "Tell us about the operation sergeant. Were you successful?"

Paddy answers, "No, and we weren't colonel. I just been a tellin' ya Private Shields is dead and be dammed with ya!"

Jensen interjects, "Come on now Paddy. Take it easy. This is the colonel you're talking to. We're sorry about Shields. But you all knew how dangerous this mission was before you went on it. Is the bridge still standing?"

Paddy answers, "No it isn't, we done blew it to smithereens!"

The LtCol. says, "God bless you men! This will allow us to push further into Germany! I'm awarding you O'Brien, and both Privates Redfeather and Standing Bear "The Silver Star" for bravery. Private Shields will receive his posthumously."

"I'll be a thankin' ye sir," Paddy says.

The colonel adds, "I'm also promoting you to Master Sergeant, and the two privates who accompanied you to corporals. Looks like you also received the "Purple Heart" with that wound Master Sergeant O'Brien."

The bridge being eliminated halted the German's ability to receive additional ammunition and supplies and allowed the Americans to win the battle and push further onto German soil.

CHAPTER 75

(Leaving Shashani)

That morning, I dress in the Bedouin garb provided for me. The salve I smeared onto my face has darkened it considerably. When I look into the bathroom mirror, I laugh at my apparition. My own mother would not have recognized me.

Mordecai comes in to take me to Rabbi Micah for farewells and last-minute instructions.

"Good morning, Pastor Greene. How are you feeling today?"

I smile and say, "The way that I'm dressed I feel like a native to this Sinai wilderness. Most of all I have mixed feelings about my departure. Although I am very excited about completing my mission."

"Let us pray," he says, and we do on bended knees. He gives me a holy kiss and a key. He says, "This is the key to the basement strongbox." We hug and I depart with Mordecai.

We lead Nabob up the mountain trail to Shahani's gate and Mordecai says, "Brother Isaac is waiting for us in the cave with the other beast. It has already been laden with all of your required essentials. We enter the cave and I'm filled with an unpleasant "de je vous". Brother Isaac says, this camel has no name. She is just called Camel." I inspect to assure all of the items that I need are actually on the camel's paniers, and say, "Nice job brothers," and I shed a tear. "I'll be missing everyone here."

Isaac says, "And we you, the one who will now be called Pastor Greene. We say goodbye as well." Then they leave the cave, and as I watch them depart the boulder gate slowly closes shut. Then the realization sets in, that after a year, I am now back in the world. I have reentered into this world of misery.

I go to the corner of the cave where I had once laid near death, and discover my Army issued 1911 Colt government pistol and a box of ammunition. I retrieve them while laughing and thinking of the slogan written on all American currency, I yell out loud, "In God we trust". This is just for back up!"

I lead both camels into the sunlight. At 11:00 am it is already hot. My pocket thermometer is recording 90 degrees. I've been told to expect temperatures up to 110 degrees in the day and then cooling to the forties at night. I order "Walk Nabob," and he takes the first step of our 275-mile journey. I start to enjoy the rocking motion that camel riding generates, and I start laughing and tell Nabob, "Do you know who we look like Nabob?" Nabob grunts. "We look like that British soldier and archeologist T.E Lawrence and his camel trekking through the desert back in 1916. They dubbed him "Lawrence of Arabia". I guess I am David of the Sinai"! Nabob brays, and I ask, "Are you two angels listening?" I received no answer. "I know you're there. You just aren't talking are you."

I need to calculate how far I'll travel in a day. Since Nabob can sustain an average walking speed of about six miles an hour, I simply can tally each hour I've ridden. My watch becomes my pedometer.

After three hours of steady and ceaseless riding, I halt my small caravan near a group of Acacia trees, and halter Nabob and Camel. I eat a late lunch. Then I take out a copy of the book "Christian Witness" to read. Since I supposedly have written it, I need to know its contents. We rest for an hour and continue on.

Eventually Nabob starts to act excited, and brays, grunts, and spits excessively. I interpret his behavior as smelling water, and true to his nose I see an oasis in the distance. We come to the first of the three watering holes on my map. It is a small pool of water surrounded by date palms and acacia trees. After leading the animals to drink and graze, I secure them to one of the palm trees. It is 7:30 in the evening and I make a camp. The rabbi warned me not to make a fire because it could be seen for miles, and possibly attract visitors with bad intentions. I don't however relish the thought of a cold supper, so I heat my canned rations over a candle's flame. My sleeping bag, "Made in Shashani (sans tag of origin), will keep me warm at night. As I lay and gaze up at the stars I think of Ruth. Just saying her name seems to warm my heart. Will my love for her ever diminish? But then again, our love for one another was doomed, even before it first blossomed. Then my mind starts to recall various chapters in my life. I think of my father, my mother, past loves, and good friendships that I have known in my life…… until I fall asleep.

The second- and third-day's excursions were similar to the first with the exception of not encountering another oasis. I'm concerned that I may have veered off course and missed it. Then on the morning of the fourth day as we climb over a high sand dune, I see water a long way ahead. I have discovered it only a short distance from where I had bivouacked the night before, and I reason it to be the Strait of Aqaba, so I turn due north.

In another couple of hours, I spot the second oasis. Although it is only noon, I decide to give the animals and myself a day of rest. This oasis has no open pool of water, but rather a dug well, with a circular mud brick wall enclosing it. Knowing that my camels can go without water for weeks, I forgo watering them. After my campground is organized to my satisfaction, I lie under a group of acacias and relish the shade they provide from the heat of the sun. I pray and then grab my bible. The rest of the day I spend napping and reading the book of "Isaiah".

In late afternoon I am awakened by the sound of hooves hitting the sand and rocky terrain of the desert ground. When I open my eyes, I see a caravan of Arabs on camel back entering into the oasis. I sit up against my tree and count nine of them approaching. As a new child of God, I am loathe to kill any man, but I will defend myself if necessary, and I put my pistol on my lap and conceal it under a fold of my thoab. They stop at a distance of thirty yards from the well, dismount and hobble their animals. They then remove a little cargo from their camels and place them together in a pile. They sit down. I'm now about fifty yards from them, and the entire group gawks at me. I acknowledge their presence by nodding my head towards them.

Some time passes before one man stands and says, "al-Salam alikam seddick." I am amazed that me new gift of tongues is allowing me to understand their language as, "Peace be to you friend."

I answer "Peace also to you to friends. It is good to meet you." As I think in English the words that are proceed from my mouth come out in the strange dialect of their Badawi Arabic.

He says, "elly ayn tedheba", meaning, "Where are you going?"

(The following conversation is translated to English)

"I am going to Aqaba."

He says, "Are you going for trade?"

I answer, "No friend, I go to visit relatives."

He asks, "I know of some in Aqaba. What are their names?"

"My father is Ahmed Hussein."

A bold and nasty look appears on his face, and he says, "Hussein? Hussein? There are no Hussein's in Aqaba! I don't know no stinking Husseins! I think you lie to me friend! You are going for trade!"

I answer, "I have nothing of value in my possession."

All nine men reach for rifles in their bundles and raise them towards me. Their leader says, "We shall come and look for ourselves!"

They stand, and their leader with three others start to approach me. I grab for my pistol, but before I can remove it from my dress, a powerful strong wind starts to blow towards them. It begins kicking up sand and dust and hurling it into their faces while blinding them. It is accompanied by a loud high pitched screeching sound. The sound gets louder to the point where it is piercing to the ears. They have to drop their weapons to cover their ears. They panic and scream as they run to their camels, mount them, and race away, leaving their weapons behind.

My camels are frightened and pulling at their reins, so I go to calm them. I am shocked. I get on my knees and proclaim, "Oh gracious Lord, I thank you. I praise you for delivering me from these men. You are my hope and my strength. I will serve thee all the days of my life!"

It takes me a while to calm my nerves, and to regain my senses. Then I stand and look around me. I smile and say," I don't know where you guys are at, but you sure gave a powerful demonstration that you're hanging around! Thanks a lot." Then I take my gun and toss it away. I say out loud, "I won't need this anymore." And I silently apologize to the Lord and think again of Proverbs three, "Trust in the Lord with all your heart and lean not unto thine own understanding".

CHAPTER 76

The next day my journey continues. I estimate that I should reach the third and last oasis in about five hours. I start to recall the book of Exodus, and Moses leading about two million people through this wilderness. I am honored to be going along this same route they took millennia ago.

As Nabob, Camel and I proceed through the desert, I wonder why me? Why me Lord? Of all the born- again Christians in the world why did you single me out for this duty? Then I recall what Mike Collins said once before we went into battle. He quoted the book of Isaiah in chapter six, "Also I heard the voice of the Lord saying, whom shall I send, and who will go for us? Then said I, "Here am I. Send me."

I say a short prayer and then as loud as I'm able to I cry out, I shout, "Here am I Lord send **me!**"

It startles Nabob and he makes a sound of discontent that only camels can make. It's sort of a crying growl. I say, "Yeah Nabob, but you want to know why that has to include you." He gripes his complaints again.

The solitude of the desert wilderness may cause strange ideas to be released into your mind. With no one to converse with, except two animals, I decide to name my two angels who are following me. Afterall, they've already saved me once; or maybe they're the same ones who rescued me when I was dying in the desert a year ago. If so, they have salvaged my carcass twice. I ask, "What are your names boys?" I know the names of only two angels, Michael, and Gabriel; therefore, I can't use those. "What shall I name you?" I ponder my ludicrous question and decide on "Tweedle Dee" and, "Tweedle Dum, from the Lewis Carroll children's novel "Alice in Wonderland". I'll call them "Dee" and "Dumm" for short. The more I think about it, maybe I'm being irreverent....... No, I tell myself, that's their names.........

What am I doing in this desert? Only yesterday I was hitting a baseball. Wasn't I? Just yesterday, wasn't I fishing on Miss Minerva? It seems that time has a way of either slowing or accelerating dramatically, according to its own peculiar whims.

We journey another three hours before Nabob's nose starts acting up again, and another oasis comes into view. I AM HERE!!!

I water and give the camels a treat of some grains, rest for a while, eat a K-ration chocolate bar, and drink a few gulps of water from my canteen. After our break I check my notebook, and I'm to align my compass at 295 degrees and proceed two miles further in order to find the ruin. I take the heading and resume for the required two miles to the north. As I ride, I glass with my binoculars and eventually see a cairn about a quarter mile ahead. I dismount, secure the camels, and proceed on foot. When I come upon the cairn its stones are stacked about four foot tall, and it is in the middle of an old stone enclosure. I'm a little confused, because the rabbi never mentioned the cairn, but I reassure myself that this is the correct marker. When I align my compass to 259 degrees and glass in that direction, I spot the overhang at the mountain's top and there definitely is an opening below it. I have spotted the cave. "Thank you, Lord," I pray. I make camp and decide to wait until the morning to resume my scavenger hunt. I'll be needing lots of daylight tomorrow.

CHAPTER 77

(The Search for the Copper Scroll)

I'm up early in the morning and I'm packed. We go in the 259-degree direction to the cave. Knowing when I find the copper scroll, and the clues to the treasures, I will eventually have to navigate my way back over the mountain with the animals into the next valley; so, I glass the ridge line in an attempt to find a pass. About a mile to the northwest, I see a low saddle that will allow me to traverse over it on the way back. It's always good to plan ahead because of the six P's. which states, "Poor Planning Promotes Pee Poor Performance".

It takes only forty minutes to reach the foot of the elevation. I tie the camels to a small date palm, shoulder my backpack, and head upwards on foot. I tell Nabob to behave himself, and I say a little prayer asking the Lord for success. I gauge it to be about a steep forty-degree ascent and a fifteen-hundred-foot climb. It's hot when I start my assault of the peak, and it doesn't take long for me to work up a profuse sweat. I stumble frequently on the loose rocks underfoot, and fall once sliding downwards. Ace Walker would have shouted out some expletive, but David Greene said, "Thank you Lord. Keep me humble."

I eventually reach the mouth of the cave, and as I amble in, I find the temperature much cooler, so I remove my pack and rest my back up against a boulder. I wipe my brow, take a swill of water, remove my lantern from the knapsack, and recline on the ground. I continue to rest, as my mind speculates on how far into the cave I'll have to tread. I glance at my watch and decide to give it another fifteen minutes before I resume my efforts. When time expires, I walk into the depths of the fissure. Then I see them! A great number of large brownish- orange containers of pottery. When I approach one to inspect its contents, I perceive that they are filled with rolled up paper, not ordinary paper, but a different texture. It is papyrus. I have a great desire to remove one and unroll it, but I hesitate. That is not my assignment! I must find scrolls made of copper sheeting. When I check my notes, they indicate they'll be at the rear of the cavern, so I push further in. They're they are! That must be them in that dark blue urn!

I look inside one and see two metallic copper sheets partly discolored to a greenish hue! I must find the name <u>ACOR</u> written somewhere on one of them! I need more light, and assemble a candle lantern the rabbi supplied. It illuminates the entire rear of the grotto. I realize that these ancient artifacts must be fragile, so carefully and slowly, I start removing them from the vase. Now I start the tedious task of rolling each out the ground. I kneel down and use my oil-lantern to view the ancient writings. The inscriptions are not in the normal Hebrew vernacular. My gift of tongues tells me that the writings are in "Mishna", an older form of the language. I read a list of clues to directions of treasure caches. FINALLY, I SEE THE WORD ACOR! My heart is racing as I copy those particular clues first. They read:

In the ruin that is in the valley of Acor,

Under the steps,

With the entrance at the east,

a distance of forty cubits,

a stronghold of silver and its vessels,

with a weight of seventeen talents

I think of the gold prospectors of old, upon striking it rich, and I scream, "EUREKA"!! I write the clues down, tear them from my notepad, and place them in an envelope that I place in my pocket. I then write all of the remaining 62 down and put them into a small lockbox provided by the rabbi for that intended purpose. This requires five full hours of my time. Then I stare in wonder at the 64th location. It is illegible. Even with the Holy Spirit's gift of tongues I could not fathom its meaning. I laugh to myself and think even Hitler's "Enigma Machine" couldn't decipher this. This one is reserved for the second coming of the Lord Jesus!

I have got what I came for and as much as would like to explore everything here, it's time to get out and leave everything as it was. I head out of the cave and clamber down the mountainside. When I finally reach bottom, Nabob greets me with his cordial brays, growls, and grunts. I am exhausted and assure myself that I'm finished for the day. I unleash the camels and search for a suitable camping spot for the evening. I decide to reward myself by doing the one thing I was advised not to do. I say to my camel, "Let's build us a fire Nabob. Afterall Dee and Dumm are around here somewhere. They're watching over us." Then I remembered what Ruth once said to me. "Hiram do not tempt the Lord thy God." But I reason that this camp is not out in the open desert, but close to the mountain side. It won't be seen from afar, so I gather some dry kindling, a couple of larger pieces of wood and light a fire. I'll have a hot dinner and a warm sleep tonight.

CHAPTER 78

The next morning, I find the animals cranky. They both complain vocally when I attempt to get them to stand. Finally, when they do, I wonder why they're so difficult to control at times. These are creatures I'll never be able to understand.

Eventually we get underway, and I focus on finding the low saddle in the mountain I had previously seen. After riding an hour north, it comes into view, and I then head west through my discovered overpass, and jockey until the ascent becomes too steep. I then dismount and lead the animals upwards. It doesn't take long before we reach the downhill slope. I continue to walk and lead the camels. Upon reaching the flat terrain at the valley's bottom I mount Nabob again. When I review my notes, I am reminded to look for a stone hovel; some sort of a stone structure. I proceed north for at least a mile and have sighted nothing but sand, rocks, and an occasional buzzard overhead. Then I say to myself, "Hey stupid, the ruin should be about due west of the Copper Scroll cave!" I do an about face and head south. I rest the animals and myself for a time, and then continue my search.

It finally comes into view. It appears to be a small blockhouse in the middle of the valley, resting in its own solitude. I reach it, dismount, hobble the camels, and take out my pick and shovel. This small structure is only an eight-by-eight square with an open doorway on its east side.

The clues said I should find steps at the east; therefore, I start digging at the portal's entrance. The temperature is heating up, and I'm virtually baking in the sun; while finding myself frequently resting and toweling my head. Although the sand is soft and easily shoveled aside, there are large stones that stop my spade's progress and must be lifted out. My efforts resume until I again hit something hard, but it didn't clank like a rock when I struck it. It seems softer. I drop down on hands and knees and start sweeping all the impediment off it with my hands. Minutes later a wooden cellar door reveals itself. I try opening it, but it doesn't budge, so I take my pick and attempt to pry it open. It creaks and parts slightly, and when I use greater force, it finally swings open noisily and falls to the left. I lean in to eyeball this cellar, and it appears that the floor is...... moving? I jump back in horror! Both the cellar floor and its door are covered with creepy crawlers! I despise spiders! I especially despise large furry spiders. I stand back and watch a large number of them scatter off the door and abscond into the desert, and I take my lantern and peer down into the hole again. There are steps leading down into it, and arachnids are everywhere. They are not only on the steps, but on the walls and floor of the entire underground area. I look at Nabob and say, "Well don't look at me that way! I'm not about to go down there until I can eradicate those things!" I ponder how I can do that. I have an idea. I need fire! The next half hour finds me gathering a large amount of dead wood and flinging into this subterranean room. Then I remove a can of lantern oil off the panier that's attached to "Camel" and empty it in, light a match, and toss it in. The stairs won't damage because they're stone. The fire starts and it doesn't take long before the entire area is in flames. More spiders scurry out in order to escape. Most are being cremated. I continue hurling wood in to maintain the flames. Then I stop. I decided it's time to sit down, relax, and eat my dinner. Night will be falling soon, and tomorrow's another day. But I know that what I'm really doing is procrastinating, for I really don't want to go down that hole.

I get chilled during night, because I camp far away from the ruin and its slinking insects, without starting a campfire.

The next day it's time to resume my desert adventure, as I walk slowly towards the ruin's east side while watching for any insect survivors. I peer into the cellar of the hovel. I flash my light into it and see no movement. As I study the steps again, I analyze that they are not solid but stacked as rungs with spaces between each one. "Lord be with me," I pray, and I descend down the stairs. At the bottom I survey the area with both oil and candle lanterns. The scroll's clue said to go under the steps and continue for forty cubits. But when I duck under the stairs there is nothing but a solid wall. I'm puzzled until I think I should attack this barrier with my pick. I retrieve it and return. Without wasting any time, I forcefully swing the pick against the wall, and it starts to crumble. Again......and again...... I hack away, until about the twelfth blow it gives -way revealing a tunnel. "Well, that was easy enough," I say aloud. The aperture remains too small to squeeze my body through, so I hammer away again. More stone and mortar break apart until it is large enough for my passage. Again, I recall the clue saying to go forty cubits. That would in today's measure be only about forty yards. With lantern in hand, I bend down, and I move through the tunnel until it ends into another room where I can stand.

What lies before me can only be described as magnificent! No! Better words would describe it as resplendent in its glorious beauty! An entire cache of gold and silver objects is piled together at the room's end. It sparkles in my light! I kneel to pray, "Blessed Lord, I thank thee for allowing me to discover these riches which are thine! For all riches are thine Lord. "You own the cattle on a thousand hills and the wealth in every mine!"

This is unbelievable, I say to myself, and I start looking for the three objects that I'm required to confiscate. I immediately see gold basins on top of the cache, and quickly find a smaller one with the depictions of bulls engraved near its rim. I think "Kismet" and take it and put it into my cloth bag. One down, two to go. My next search takes longer. I must move some objects around, and then I discovered a knife with a gold handle. Three red jewels are imbedded in its handle. I take it. I need one more item, a gold candlestick, and I find it buried under an array of silver plates. I put it in my bag with the other two objects. Mission accomplished. I take a few moments to gaze at this horde of fortune and turn to sneak back through the tunnel. Now I must reconstruct the wall that was hiding the low walkway.

Upon completing that task, I exit the cellar, take my prizes to Camel, load the bag of opulence into a panier, and lay down under the tree my animals were secured to.

My leisure time will have to be brief, for I must close the door to the cellar and cover it back up. I work for an hour doing just that, and then take a branch off a small tree with foliage to brush my footprints away. I end my cover up by scattering some rocks and pebbles over it all.

I feel that I must vacate this area in a hurry. I don't know why those sentiments are so strong, but they are. It is almost as if I suspect someone was watching me, although I know they're not. Maybe it's just some misplaced guilt because I stole three items from this treasure that were possibly three thousand years old.

CHAPTER 79

(On to Jerusalem)

I head due north through the valley. I do not have to cross back over the mountain because fifteen miles straight from here I should encounter the road leading to Jerusalem. I'm thrilled at the prospect of leaving this heat, this wilderness, and I'm looking forward to civilization again. I smell like my camels and require a good hot shower. I guess there is good in everything. If men never reeked of filth like I do now, nobody would have invented perfume. I laugh to myself at my thoughts and think maybe, just maybe, a little bit of "Ace Walker" still remains in me. Most of all I crave a warm soft bed.

We saunter through the Acor valley until we come to what appears to be a road. It is hard- packed gravel instead of sand; and I steer Nabob on to it. To my delight I ultimately come to a small sign that reads, "Jerusalem 8 km". "Hallelujah"! "Hallelujah"! I am almost there!"

Then I can make out two small buildings in the distance. It is the blockade installed by the "British mandate". Four soldiers are guarding the gate that denies entry. When I stop Nabob at the blockade, two of them walk out to receive me with hands up, and one commands, "Halt"!

One man says to the other, "Looks like we have us a bloody "Haji" wantin' to pass Alfred."

The other laughs and says to me, "Hello bloke, and just why ya want ta come to Jerusalem may I ask of ye?"

I answer, "I am the new pastor of the Grace Christian Church."

They both burst out laughing, and the other two soldiers come out of their shacks to join them. The man called Alfred says, "You? You be a bloody Christian pastor? Then I must be Sir Winston Churchill. What do you be thinkin' Sir Neville Chamberlain?"

"I be thinkin' he's a stinkin' Arab Bedouin. That's what I be thinkin'. You come to blow up our barracks Haji?"

I answer, "Here is my passport gentlemen. You'll see that I'm an American." I hand them my passport, and after they study it, they look at one another and laugh again.

Alfred says, "These can be bloody falsified. No way bloke! You're not a comin' through this gate! Turn your sorry arse around and go back where ye came from!"

All four of them stare at me. One soldier unshoulders his rifle and readies it up. Then the wind suddenly starts to blow slowly, and the expression on their faces turn from forbidding to being dumbstruck. They become frozen as statues and the gate swings open by itself! I command, "Walk Nabob", and we casually pass through their blockade. When I look back at them a hundred yards down the road, they remain petrified. I look up at the sky and say, "Thank you boys," and continue my trek towards the city.

As I enter the outskirts of Jerusalem, I see a sign advertising the "Muhammed edh-Dhib Stables". I stop there and dismount, and although I see a green truck, no one is standing near it, so I tie my camels to a hitching post and enter into the office building. An Arabic man is standing behind a counter and I approach him, and explain, "I have two camels. I wish to board one and sell the other. He says, "I Ahmed no speak the English." I guessed that he would speak Arabic and he says, "Anna athadth al-arabia." Which in my mind, by the gift of the Holy Spirit, recognizes as Arabic Fus-ha, the language that the Qur'an is written in. We therefore converse in that tongue. I repeat my request in Fus-ha and he answers, (*conversation translated to English*).

"How long do you wish to board the animal?"

I answer by the month. What are your rates?"

"We shall charge ten British pounds each month sir. That will include both food and water for the beast."

"Fine," I answer, and hand him a twenty-pound note. "This is for two months my friend. He is a very good animal. I wish him to be taken care of properly. Now what are your terms for selling the other……. I get interrupted by a man who approaches us mid conversation and asks, "Pardon me, but I am seeking an American that I was sent to meet here. Have you seen such an American man?"

Ahmed is aggravated and says, "You interrupt our business fool! Step aside, or I shall whip you with this stick!"

"Please Ahmed stop! Please stop! I think I am to encounter this man here; and I ask him, "Are you Mr. Joseph Ben-Hur?"

"I am he sir, but I am confused, I am to join with the new American pastor of our church."

"I may not look like him Mr. Ben-Hur, but I am him."

"Praise God!" "But almost surely sir, you look to be nothing like a Christian minister!"

"I am most happy to meet with you Mr. Ben-Hur, and I assure you that in the near future you shall recognize me as one. Now please, allow me to finish my dealings with Mr. Ahmed.

Before we were interrupted sir, we were discussing the terms of the sale of my other camel."

"That is correct sir. Upon the animal's sale at auction, we shall withhold thirty percent of the proceeds as our commission."

Ben-Hur chimes in, "That is highway robbery sir! Their normal commission is only twenty percent!"

I perceive that everything in Jerusalem is going to be a negotiation, so as a rebuttal I say, "Twenty percent seems more satisfactory sir."

Ahmed looks at me and says, "twenty-five percent then."

"Agreed," I say.

Ben-Hur and I walk outside to my camels. He says, "I shall load your belongings into our truck sir."

I reciprocate and say, "Thank you Joe but I'll take this bag. He stacks the balance of my cargo into the truck's bed, and as I board, I place the treasure items at my feet. Then I watch, and as a man leads Nabob away, he turns his head towards me, and grunts, growls, and snarls in protest.

I look at Ben -Hur. He is a smiling, slender, middle-aged man, with black hair, a coffee complexion, and dark brown eyes. He is wearing a Brooklyn Dodger baseball cap, and has a long scar on his forehead. I say, "So you are the custodian of the church. You are Mr. Joseph Ben- Hur."

He reaches over, grabs my hand and admits, "Oh yes, my pastor, I am your humble servant. God bless you for meeting me here in this war weary place; and please, I wish you to address me as Joe."

I say, "Well then Joe lets go to the church. I am in need to shed these awful clothes, and I wish to wash this desert off my body."

As we drive into Jerusalem proper, I am amazed at the dichotomy of old structures mingling with the new. It seems that this ancient city has accepted the old and the new simultaneously as one. We finally arrive at my new church. It is a small structure finished in a smooth pure white stucco, with a steeple containing a belfry. A gold-colored cross tops the steeple.

Joe says, "Our church, she is beautiful, no?"

"She most certainly is Joe."

The parsonage is behind the church Pastor Greene. We will go there to unload your things."

I say, "First I must go to the basement of the church Joe. I have one package I wish to store there."

"Whatever you say pastor."

I grab the bag containing the three assets and tell Joe to lead the way. We go through the front mahogany doors and into the sanctuary, then proceed down a flight of stairs to the basement. When we come to another door Joe says, "I have the key," and he unlocks it.

I tell him, "Please wait outside Joe. I have something I must do." As I enter I spot the strongbox in the left rear corner of the room. I take the key that the rabbi gave me at our departure and open the box. It is empty. Then I place the bag of treasure into it and lock the lid. I look around and say, "Alright Dumm and Dee it's all yours now!"

Outside the door Joe says, "What did you say pastor?"

"Oh, nothing Joe. I was just talking to myself."

He says, "I shall take you to the parsonage now sir."

"I'm ready. Let's go."

CHAPTER 80

As Joe and I walk to the parsonage, I admire its beauty. It is a ranch style structure with the outside finished in a white stucco similar to the church. When we enter Joe says, "Allow me to show you around. There are two bedrooms. This larger one is for you."

My bedroom is painted white. There are a few landscape paintings hanging on the walls. My bed is queen size with a wrought iron headboard. There is a bedside table with a reading lamp upon it. As we continue my tour, I notice that every room is also painted white. The small kitchen has every appliance needed, and what would be called the living room has an array of cushioned chairs and a sofa surrounding a coffee table. Joe then showed me a small bathroom with a shower stall. I point to another door and ask, "What is this room?"

Joe smiles and answers, "This is your office pastor, and has also a small library of books that you will require for your work." We enter and I see shelves of different Christian commentary from various authors. There is also a concordance and all the volumes of John Nelson Darby's collected works.

Joe places my bags in a walk-in closet and says, "Breakfast, lunch, and dinner will be brought here for you pastor, unless you wish to dine out. You only need to use this intercom on the wall to give instructions."

I ask, "How many people are currently in our congregation Joe?"

"At the present sir there are fifteen congregants."

"Only fifteen? Let me ask, because I have never been informed Joe, as to whom I am replacing."

"Pastor Davies, God rest his soul, he went to be with the Lord eight weeks ago sir."

"I see. I'm so sorry Joe. He must have been a good man."

"He certainly was a man of God Pastor Greene."

"You should know sir, that in the congregation there are three married couples. Doctor Archibald McLeish of Liverpool, England is on the medical staff at Bikur Cholim Hospital. His wife Annette is a nurse there as well. They have a young daughter named Patricia. Mr. and Mrs. Stephen Clemens are from New York city. He is a jeweler here in Jerusalem. Four British soldiers attend our services. They are Captain Charles Benson, Lieutenant Morgan Adams, Privates Richard Smith, and Reginald Allister. There are also three Jewish citizens who have converted to Christianity. Mr. and Mrs. Benjamin Goldstein. Mr. Goldstein is the main partner in his firm of "Goldstein & Levin Attorneys at Law". Then there is a single Jewish attendee. He is Mr. Reuben Cohen, who teaches at the "Ben-Harran School for Children". Also, our three staff members attend, which are Naomi, a servant girl, Eve the cook who doubles as our church organist, and me of course. Although it is a small congregation its members have been very faithful sir."

"Thank you for that information Joe. May I ask if you'd write those names down for me please?"

"Yes pastor. I will most certainly do so."

"Now Joe, I will let you take your leave. I am going to shower, shave, remove these awful Bedouin clothes, and get some rest from my journey."

"Yes sir, but I am most curious."

"About what?"

"Where were you coming from when I met you riding into those stables? You must know pastor that I found your dress and appearance to be highly unusual. Most of all your arrival from the Sinai wilderness was incredibly bizarre."

"Let's just wait and discuss that at another time Joe. Right now, I am very tired."

"Yes sir, as you wish sir." Then Joe takes his leave.

I shower for a long time, relishing the hot luxurious water, then shave off my beard and flop onto my new soft bed. I fall asleep immediately and dream of Ruth.

CHAPTER 81

When I awaken, I have no idea where I'm at or what time it is. I rise from my bed totally confused.

When I check my watch, it indicates that it is 11:00 a.m. Then consciousness slowly emanates to my brain, and I realize where I am.

I hear a knock on the door, and covering myself with a bed sheet, I answer the call. When I open the door, a young woman exuberantly says, "Good morning pastor, I hope you have slept well! I am Naomi and I have your breakfast! I must say it is a pleasure to meet you sir!"

I look at this young lady and smile. She is very short. My guess would be about only five feet tall. Her black hair is in braids and she has a pretty smile. We meet at the kitchen table, and she serves me a breakfast of kippers and eggs with sliced mangoes and coffee. I say, "Thank you Naomi. This is very kind of you."

I almost laugh when she curtsies, nods her head, and goes to leave. I stop her by saying, "Naomi do you know where I may find a barber?"

She says, "Oh yes sir, my cousin Ephraim has a barbershop on King David Street. It is only two blocks from here. I could take you there."

"Thanks again, but I think I can find it."

Again, she starts to leave and stops, then turns to me, and says, "Pastor Greene?"

"Yes Naomi?"

"Well......I am......I am so very happy that you have come to our church. I wish you to stay and be happy here. Please......please know sir, that if you have need of anything; just call me on the intercom. I will come promptly. I assure you sir. Just remember if you want anything, (and with a sly seductive smile) she says, and I mean anything at all sir, just call." She turns and leaves.

I think to myself; did I just get that wrong? I sure hope I did. No...... did she? Did Naomi just suggest she would provide me with things other than food and normal house chores? No, you are being silly Pastor Greene. You have absorbed too many of the sun's rays in the desert.

After finishing my meal, I notice a calendar on the wall. I realize I don't even know what day it is. I ascertain that it is Saturday, which means I must check if an instruction envelope came for me, so I'll go to the rabbi's brick wall. I don't remember the name of the marketplace so I get my notes. Now I remember. It's an alleyway behind the "Ahmed Hussein Market", and a brick marked with a star.

I am glad that I can put on clothing indicative of a citizen in today's world. The only break I've had from Essene, and Bedouin robes for over a year was the western wear at Shahani's stables. After I put on tan slacks, a white polo shirt, and penny loafers, someone knocked on my door. It's Joe. We greet each other good morning, and he says, "Pastor It looks as if you wish to go out."

"Yes, I have a few places I must visit."

"Please pastor, before you leave, there are some things I must discuss with you."

"Alright Joe. Would you like some coffee?"

"No pastor."

I tell him, "Let's sit in the living room Joe. What's so important that you're in a such hurry to discuss?"

"I should ask first sir, when you wish to resume our regular worship services?"

"Well Joe, I believe three weeks from now would be good. I need some time to prepare a few sermons. The first Sunday will be more my introduction. In fact Joe, now that you mentioned it, I think it would be a good idea if we planned for a luncheon after that first service in the fellowship hall. That would be an excellent way for me to meet and talk to everyone. Don't you agree?"

"Yes sir, I would."

"Is there anything else you wish to discuss?"

"Yes Pastor Greene, you are new to Jerusalem and the Palestine. My I ask how much you know about our current situation here?"

I laugh and say, "I believe that the violence here proves that the residents generally have the opinion, that in order to avoid having enemies you must outlive them. I know there have been bombings, shootings, and a lot of killings going on. And I'm aware that both the Jews and the Arabs hate the British, as they hate each other even more."

"Very well said pastor. There are Jewish groups within Palestine who wish to see the birth of the new sovereign state of Israel. If that happens, I am positive the Arab population will start a war for the purpose of defeating that new state. The British on the other hand, are attempting to maintain some semblance of order, while reneging on their promise to support the birth of Israel. The British are also involved in prohibiting Jewish refugees from returning to their true home. I am afraid sir that Jerusalem has a fuse on it and is ready to detonate, therefore I must warn you that when you are amongst the general population, you will be constantly in danger."

"I appreciate your concern about my safety Joe, but I want you to know that the Lord will protect me."

"I pray so sir, but may I inquire as to your political persuasions in these matters?"

I would have liked to tell Joe that my main mission in Jerusalem was to aid in the propagation of a new state. Instead, I say, "I have neither political opinions nor aspirations Joe. I simply wish to spread the Gospel of Christ and allow the Lord to grow this assembly of believers." (Which is true also.)

"Praise the Lord pastor! I also wish to know how you will travel within the city?"

"I have saved some English pounds for the purpose of buying an automobile. That will allow you the full use of the church's truck."

"Please allow me to aid you in that regard. I wish to accompany you when you go to purchase the car."

"Let's do better than that. I'll give you the required cash to make the purchase. Then I'll have you go alone to procure my auto."

"Thank you, sir, for trusting me with such an important decision pastor."

"I'm sure you'll do fine Joe. Today I'll take a taxi to my desired destinations. By the way, I noticed a belfry in the church's steeple. Is there a bell up there, and if so, who rings it?"

"Oh yes Pastor Greene, there is a bell, and it is I who rings it. I am tasked to ring it once each day except on the Jewish Sabbath and never at times the Muslim Muezzin sings the Adhan, which is their call to prayer. He sings it five times a day from his minaret, or in the English, his tower. To do so at those times would draw the ire of the local Arabic population. On Sundays, I ring it at 9:50 a.m. It is the call for worship."

"I understand Joe. Now are there any other issues you'd like to chat about?"

"No sir."

"Then call me a taxi please."

"Yes sir, most certainly sir. But I would have you know that since it is the Sabbath most of the stores are closed for the day."

"I realize that."

"As you wish sir."

I grab a small empty box tie a red ribbon around it, place it in my pocket, and walk out to the front of my church.

The cab arrives and I tell the driver to take me to the "Ahmed Hussein Market Place". He informs me, "It is closed today sir." I tell him, "No matter, take me there." When we arrive, I instruct him to wait for me, and I then exit the taxi and proceed to amble through a walkway that divides the two buildings of the market. When I reach the end of the walkway, I come to the brick wall that Rabbi Micah told me of. I turn to the right, and in only ten paces I see the star painted on a lone brick. It is higher than my reach, so I pick up a cement block that was lying on the ground and use it to stand on. I look around to see if anyone is watching me. When I discern that no one else is around I remove the brick. There indeed is an envelope inside. I remove it, replace the brick, and without opening it, I place it into my pants pocket. I return to the cab with the ribbon tied box visibly in my hands and the cabbie asks, "Did you find what you were looking for sir?"

I lift up the box, showing it to the cabbie and explain, "Yes, I met an acquaintance at a back door, and he gave me this birthday present. He nods his head in the affirmative and drives me back to the church.

Back in my quarters I open the envelope. It reads:

Dear Pastor:

It is most imperative for you to

Meet with Mr. Reuben Cohen

Privately at your church.

I recognize the name as the single Jewish man who attends our services. My thoughts are; THE ESPIONAGE BEGINS!

CHAPTER 82

(Somewhere in Northern Germany)

(May the 10th 1945)

Now a Master Sergeant, Paddy O'Brien, having fully recovered from his injuries at the Neckar bridge in February, leads another patrol into a forested area. His two Cherokee corporals, Corporal Laskowski, as well as a contingent of eight other infantrymen are with him. They are searching for enemy stragglers. The Nazi war machine has been in retreat, moving closer to Berlin for its defense. Paddy's patrol doesn't expect to encounter any of the enemy. As they saunter through the woods Corporal Redfeather smells a bad odor coming from over a rise. It stinks of death, and he goes to investigate. Shortly he comes to a chain link fenced area with barbed wire stretched across the top. Standing and gazing outward are people, naked people. They are emaciated. They are only skeletons of what they once were. Three of them raise their arms and hands up for the corporal's acknowledgement. They are weeping. Redfeather says, "Oh Lord no!" He looks at them and says, "I'll be right back!" He then hurries and finds MSgt O'Brien.

"Sarge, get the other men and come with me. I found something horrible."

Paddy says, "What is it Tom?"

It looks like the kind of concentration camp that they found at Auschwitz."

Paddy assembles his troops, and they follow Redfeather. When they arrive at the prisons gate they enter in, and those prisoners who were able to walk, run towards them crying, "Wolnosc! Wolnosc! Oni sa Ameryicanami! Chwala Bogu! Chwala Bogu!"

Paddy asks, "What is that they be a sayin' Redfeather"?

Redfeather answers, "I don't know sarge."

"I know sarge they're speaking Polish, answers Ski. They are saying praise God, we have been liberated. These are Americans."

Paddy calls a private over ordering, "Siemens you'll be a goin' back to the detachment and tell em what we've been a findin'. Let em know we'll be a needin' an ambulance some medics, and food and water! Hurry yourself along now!"

"Ski, ask em if there be Germans here."

In Polish, Ski asks, "sae kazdy niemieckizoierze tuta."

One of the prisoners' answers, "Nie. Vciekli!"

"He says no sarge. They ran away."

It doesn't take long before the camp is overrun with American soldiers. The Colonel walks over to Paddy and says, "Well sergeant this is an abomination! It paints a picture of just how inhumane man can act towards his fellow man." MSgt. Jensen joins the two men, and they start to explore the camp. Soldiers are covering their noses and mouths with handkerchiefs because of the stench of the decaying bodies lying everywhere. Bodies are also hanging from ropes in gallows designed to execute eight men at once. They come across open mass graves piled with naked Jewish bodies. Then Paddy and Jensen leave the colonel and go into what appears to be a barracks for the housing of the imprisoned. The stink is unbearable. There are the dead lying next to some captives barely living. The living raise their arms for help, but the soldiers notice they are too weak to stand.

372

Jensen says, "I'll get some men with stretchers to evacuate them from here.

He leaves, and a Private Heinz joins Paddy. He says, "This is disgusting sarge."

"Aye soldier it tis."

Then the private sees a fast movement in the building's rear. He asks, "Did you see that sarge? Somebody was running back there!" They go to investigate and find a German soldier crouching against the corner wall and screaming, "Nein! Nein! Nein! Ich kapituliere. Bitte, tote mich nicht. Ich bin nur ein soldat der befeher befolgt! Bitte! Bitte!"

Paddy asks, "Do you know any German Private Heinz?"

"I know some sarge, my grandparents spoke it."

"What's the bloke a sayin'?"

"He said, "No, no, don't kill me. I surrender. I was just a soldier doing my duty."

Paddy draws his pistol and walks toward the German. He says, "So ye just be a doin' yer duty?" He aims the firearm at the man's head.

The private says, "Oh no sarge, don't shoot him, he's our prisoner."

Paddy says, "Prisoner be damned" .... He shoots the man directly into his forehead. He looks at the private and says, "Now ye be a helpin' the others with the live ones."

A -M.A.S.H. style hospital is set up outside the perimeter of the camp, away from the stench and squalor. Tents are arranged for the living prisoners, and a Rabbi and Catholic priest are ministering to the survivors. Arrangements are underway to return the living to their own towns and villages. LtCol. Parker orders photos to be taken to document the horror. He plans to use them in a war crimes tribunal. He then orders the entire concentration camp to be burned, and all bodies cremated within it. After the blazing fire subsides, tanks are employed to flatten and bury all remaining debris. The crew of "Thumper" participates in the exercise. When all has been completed Lt. Andy Harrison and his men exit their tank and glower at their handiwork. Andy says, "Guys, of all the horrors we've witnessed in this war I think this will be the one that I'll continue to have nightmares about for the rest of my life."

CHAPTER 83

(Jerusalem May 7th, 1945)

Although I know that the business of helping finance the new state of Israel is vital to my work and the Lord's mission, I feel that saving lives for Christ is my immediate assignment. I am determined through prayer, and the Lord's will to exercise my duties as pastor here with all of my heart and soul. My mind has truly accepted that Ace Walker is dead, and that Pastor David Greene is his spiritual re-incarnation. Thank God I am born-again; and I pledge to the Lord I will fulfill my mission in order to help bring the prophecy of a new Israel to fruition.

Joe has been instrumental in our functions here at Grace Christian church. Not only does he perform the menial tasks such as cutting the grass and all of the general maintenance, but he has become my prayer partner. We spend many an hour on our knees before the Lord.

Tomorrow will be the start of conducting my services at the church. I have prepared my introduction and a short sermon. I have some built-up stage fright within me. Although I've penned the written word often and have had some experience with "Movietone News", I am somewhat of a novice at public speaking.

Then, the morning comes. Joe is in the belfry ringing the bell, I'm at the front door welcoming my flock. I count them as they arrive.

All fifteen are in attendance. Eve, who is an older, rather plump, and very tall Jewish woman with grey hair, plays two hymns on the church organ, as the attendee's settle in. I smile at my congregants as I walk to the podium.

Then I begin:

"Let us pray......Dear Lord with all the turmoil that surrounds us, we give you thanks that we are able to peacefully assemble here today. We give you praise for your perfect work on calvary's cross, and I ask a blessing for all who have come to worship you today. In Jesus, our Lord and Savior's name we pray.......

Amen."

"God bless you all for coming today. Allow me to introduce myself. I am David H. Greene your new pastor. Originally, I hail from the United States of America. I have studied the holy scriptures, and with the Holy Spirit's guidance, I wish to aid you in your Christian goal of becoming transformed into the image of the Father's son. Brother Joseph Ben-Hur has provided me with all of your names and a short synopsis of your positions here in Jerusalem. I feel that I know you already. However immediately following today's service we have scheduled a luncheon in the fellowship hall for the purpose of getting better acquainted.

Today's message is from the book of Matthew chapter 28, and it pertains to the Lord's command for His followers to spread the Gospel. Let us stand please for the reading of God's word."

After my sermon, Eve plays, "To God be the Glory", and we all vacate the sanctuary for the fellowship hall. Our food is spread upon a long table, and we will be served cafeteria style, as Eve pours drinks of iced tea and lemonade. I ask the blessing for our food, get in line last, and then deliberate at which table I should sit. I see that Reuben Cohen, a tall handsome young man, wearing black horn-rimmed glasses, is at a table with Patricia and her parents. Mr. and Mrs. Stephen Clemens, the American Jeweler, and I decide to join them. I wish to comply with the message that I retrieved from the brick wall. It ordered me to talk with

Mr. Cohen, and I'm thinking I may have an opportunity to schedule a meeting with him privately in my quarters.

I sit and say, "It is a pleasure to have other Americans here at our small church Mr. Clemens. I understand you are a jeweler. How has your business fared here in Jerusalem?"

"I would say pastor, that regardless of the war, the Lord has indeed blessed our family business. Our retail sales have been average at best, but we also deal in antiquities, and our export transactions with them are better than excellent."

"How long has your family been in Jerusalem?"

Mrs. Clemens speaks up, "Ten years pastor, but I miss New York terribly. However, Patricia seems to love it here. Don't you dear."

"Oh yes mother I do," the girl responds. I love my school, especially Mr. Cohen's class."

I look at Cohen, smile, and say, "Well, put a feather in your cap Mr. Cohen! That was a nice compliment."

Cohen says, "Thank you Patricia, and please pastor call me Reuben."

An hour later, our conversation is interrupted by the four British soldiers. Captain Benson addresses our table with, "We enjoyed your sermon Pastor Greene, and the food that Eve prepared as well. Our detachment here in Jerusalem is happy to have you. We will see if we can enlist more of our men for your services. They are such lazy blokes on Sunday."

I reply, "Thank you captain, and yes, please be assured, I would welcome more of your men to attend."

"The captain says, "Be careful in your travels here sir. Unfortunately, there are a few active terrorist groups that wish Britain would take her leave of Palestine. If you have any trouble, call me. Here is my card. Until next Sunday then......." And they take their leave. The wives of McLeish and Goldstein stand at their table, smile, nod at me, then exit the church. Their husbands come to our table. Mr. Archibald McLeish laughs and says, "That was a fine sermon, if I should say so myself Reverend. Our families enjoyed it. I can assure you."

I stand, shake their hands, and say, "Thank you Mr. McLeish, I hope you were satisfied also Mr. Goldstein?"

"Indeed, I was Reverend! But I also prefer on occasion, a little of our Jewish history. Maybe from the book of Judges or the like."

"I'll keep that under consideration. Thank you both gentlemen. I hope we can meet together soon to get to know each other better. But by the way there is no need to call me "Reverend". I believe that title insinuates reverence, and there has only been one man that has deserved to be called reverent; Our Lord Jesus. It would suffice if you would address me as pastor, or just plain David if you prefer."

Goldstein says, "Of course pastor. As you wish." And they depart.

Clemens looks at his daughter and says, "I'm afraid we must leave also now pastor. Tomorrow is a school day, and Patricia has procrastinated in doing her homework. Haven't you dear?"

Patricia, feeling ashamed, looks down at her feet, and answers. "Yes papa."

I shake Clemen's hand and thank them again for coming.

I look at Reuben Cohen and say, "Well, it looks as though we've been deserted Reuben."

"Yes, it appears so pastor."

We sit in a prolonged awkward silence staring at each other for a while, until I break the silence with, "Do we have some things to discuss Reuben?"

"Yes, we do."

"Do you wish to do so in private?"

"I do."

"Shall we go to my office?'

"I believe that to be best."

Eve walks by and I thank her for the fine meal, and her excellent rendition of the hymns played on the organ. Cohen and I leave for my office.

I take a seat behind my desk, and Cohen sits opposite me. I intentionally remain silent. I want him to speak first. I feel deep down this conversation will pertain to the birth of Israel.

Cohen says, "I think that the Lord may have sent you here for more than your sermons pastor."

"You think so?"

"I do. May I ask you if you have heard of the "White paper" doctrine?"

"I have not."

"It is a British proclamation that restricts the immigration of Jews back into their ancient homeland of Palestine."

"Although I haven't heard the decree called "White Paper," I am aware of the current British sentiments in that regard."

"Then I ask you, have you heard of an organization called the Haganah?"

"I have heard their name mentioned. They fought against an Arab insurrection here in Palestine recently. Have they not?"

"Yes. One of their leaders, a man named David Ben-Gurion, has summed up their objectives in one sentence. He announced. "We shall fight the war against Hitler as if there is no "White Paper", and we shall fight against the "White Paper" as if there is no war." They attempt to solve the problem of reuniting all Jews back to Palestine through peaceful means, however a satellite group of them called the "Etzel" is focused on using military force against all whom would deter that immigration."

"Why are you sharing this information with me Reuben. I'm just a poor American pastor assigned here by my supporters."

"Because I have reason to believe that you are more than that sir."

"Why?"

Cohen laughs and says, "Right now, let's use an American expression, and just say "A little bird told me so."

"And who might that little bird be?"

"I think I shall divulge that at a later date pastor, however, allow me to ask if you are a Zionist?"

"I am in favor of the Jewish people being restored to their ancient and historic homeland. Yes, you could call me a Zionist."

"Will you meet with me in the future regarding that subject? I would like to introduce you to one of my friends."

"Yes, I will Reuben."

We stand, shake hands, and he says, "I will contact you."

"I add, "Lord willing."

CHAPTER 84

(May 8th, 1945)

On Tuesday morning I am awakened by our church bell loudly clanging! I run out of the parsonage, still in my pajamas, into the church, and peer up the stairs leading to the belfry. Between the clanging of the bell I holler, "Hey Joe what's up!?" I get no answer, so I climb the stairs and when I arrive at the top, I see Joe still ringing away. When I look below at the streets, cars are jammed up, and their driver's are blowing their horns! People are running and shouting everywhere! Joe stops yanking the bell's rope, runs to me, grabs me in a bear hug, and says, "Oh, Pastor Greene the war is over! Germany has surrendered! The war is over sir! It is over!" We grab hands, start laughing loudly, and commence to dance in our elevated perch above the city. Then I realized that I already was told the war would end on this date. I just forgot it was May the 8th.

Joe and I descend the stairs, and race out of the church to take part in the celebration. Ecstatic people are shouting, singing, and drinking from bottles of wine. An older woman carrying a case, comes by and hands us a bottle of merlot. Joe takes it from her, uses his Swiss army knife to remove the cork, looks at me impishly, smiles, and takes a long swallow from the bottle. Then he hands it to me with a questioning look upon his face, and I say, "For my stomach's sake Joe!" I raise the bottle and take two long gulps!

The celebration continues for most of the day, until broken up by British soldiers on horses.

Joe and I go back into the church and are greeted by Naomi and Eve. We grab each other and laugh. Naomi says, "Praise the Lord it is over!!! I say, "let's thank the Lord for this happening." Joe prays his thanks, followed by Eve, and Naomi, and I close with, "Precious Lord we are thankful you have chosen to end this terrible conflict between men, here and in Europe. I pray Lord that the confrontation that still exists in the Pacific will soon come to an end as well. In thy name we ask this amen." As I close in prayer the telephone rings. Joe answers it.

"It Is for you pastor. Mr. Reuben Cohen is on the line."

"I'll take it in my office Joe."

As I lift the receiver to my ear, I take a pen and notepad from my desk. I expect I'll need to write an address down. I answer, "Hello, this is Pastor Greene."

Cohen says, "Praise God! This is a wonderful day, is it not pastor?"

"Yes, it is Reuben. What may I do for you?"

"You have said that you would meet with me and a friend about the Zionist movement. We would like to confer with you about that subject pastor."

"Alright, where, and when?"

"I will meet you at the "Solomon Hotel" in Bethlehem, this coming Monday, the 14th, at 2:00 p.m. Is this date satisfactory for you?"

"It is. How do I find the hotel?"

"Bethlehem is a relatively small-town pastor. It is on the city's main thoroughfare. You will see its sign."

"I'll be there Reuben. Can you divulge any particulars about this meeting?"

"There are big ears on the phone system here in Palestine pastor. Let us refrain from speaking of any issues over the wires."

"Goodbye until then."

"Until then pastor. Goodbye."

CHAPTER 85

Today is the Sabbath, and I must go to the alley to examine if any further communications have been sent to me. I call Joe on the intercom to tell him to hail me a taxi. He says, "That will not be required pastor."

"Why Joe?"

"Meet me outside the parsonage sir."

"Alright Joe."

When I meet him, he is leaning against a purple car and smiling like the cat that ate the canary.

"Well, what do you think pastor? This is a 1940 Ford Deluxe convertible coupe. I bought it from a cousin of mine who has a dealership in Tel Aviv. He sold it to us at an excellent price sir!"

"Wow," I say. "That's certainly a beauty Joe." I'm thinking that maybe something a little more subdued would have been in order, but I say, "Thank you Joe. You certainly outdid yourself. I absolutely love it." And I actually did!

Let's take it for a spin pastor."

"Absolutely, let's go!" I climb in the driver seat, Joe takes shotgun, and we speed off." As the wind blows through my hair, I feel the exhilaration and joy that a fine machine can create. As I recall my younger years in my dad's '30 Ford, I feel, God forbid, that Ace Walker is living again.

We laugh and drive outside the city as I put the accelerator flush to the floor; Henry Ford's V8 accelerates rapidly. We speed for a time then turn back to the church. As we're driving back, I say, "I never expected such a nice car for the money I gave you Joe."

"You deserve it pastor."

I turn to look at him and ask, "You know Joe, I've been meaning to ask you, how did you receive that scar on your face."

"Before Pastor Davies hired me here at the church back in '36, I was employed by "Rabin and Sons" clothing store in Tel Aviv. I was simply a janitor, but occasionally they asked me to serve as a night watchman. One evening, near midnight, two thieves broke into the store to rob it. I confronted them with my nightstick. When I flashed my torch on them one ran from the building, but the other attacked me with his knife, and slashed me on my forehead. I managed somehow to avoid additional cuts from his blade, and I struck him heavily on his head. He fell to the floor unconscious. I called the police, and when they arrived, they took him away. Believe me pastor I was thankful to the Lord that I had not met with further injuries. Mr. Rabin later honored me with a dinner and also gave me a small raise in pay. The newspaper said I was a hero but believe me I was very frightened during that encounter."

"You're a brave man Mr. Ben-Hur."

"No, I was just doing my job."

When we arrived back at the parsonage I let Joe out, and told him, "I've a couple things I need to do Joe. I'll be back in a about three hours. Please tell Eve I'll dine out this evening and not to prepare any food for me."

"Yes sir."

Wanting to change into something fresher, I proceed straight to my residence, and to my surprise, I find the door unlocked. When I cautiously walk in, I see Naomi sprawled out on the sofa. Instead of wearing her regular maid's ankle-length dress, apron, and hat, she is wearing a very short purple silk robe; and I believe that is all that she is wearing......when she sees me, she hurriedly jumps to her feet!

"Oh, Pastor Greene, you surprised me! I was just bringing you a little snack of dates, and other fruits. I hope you do not mind."

"Well then, you'd be wrong Naomi. I do mind. What would it look like if somebody came by and found you and me in my apartment together! And what are you wearing?"

"Pastor please allow me to explain. When you first arrived here, I found you most handsome. I admit I have strong feelings for you, and thought you may have been lonely, and wished some female company; in order to relieve stress......you know.

"No, I don't know! I have no desire to complicate my life right now with any romance! This is the last time you will make any advances towards me. Do you understand Naomi?!"

Tears burst from her eyes as she races out of the building.

Upon arriving at the Hussein market, I park a long way from the alley's entrance. I don't want people associating my car with me. I am being cautious and prefer to walk there incognito. When I remove the star brick, I find another envelope. I can't help but wonder as to who or how these envelopes are placed there. As I go back through the alleyway and enter the street in front of the market, I have not seen one person. I climb into my new car and hear the muezzin as he begins singing the "Adhan" from his minaret tower. I cautiously look around and open the envelope. It reads:

Take the knife with you
When you go to the
Meeting with
Mr. Reuben Cohen

I go to dinner at an Arabic restaurant called "Fattoush", and dine on lamb chops, hummus, and a Fattoush salad. I then returned to the parsonage.

At Sunday morning's worship service, I am pleased to see three more attendees. I preach the sermon from First Corinthians, give the invitation to be saved, and as usual go to the front door to thank each congregant for their attendance. My new participants stop at the door to meet me, and they introduce themselves as Mr. and Mrs. Abelman and their son Caleb. Mr. Abelman is an extremely big man. My guess would be about 6' 7", 300 lbs., completely bald, and sporting a large bushy moustache. I ask them to come again.

Tomorrow should be an interesting day. I am excited, but also tentative, about meeting Reuben Cohen and his friend.

CHAPTER 86

Monday morning after breakfast I proceed down to the cellar to retrieve the Levitical knife from the strongbox. The stairs leading down are both steep and long. When I flip on the light switch, I can make out a human body lying on the cellar floor! My first thoughts are, please Lord, don't let it be Joe! When I go down to check, I find it is a strange man, and his head is at an odd angle to his body. He has broken his neck. I feel for a pulse, and there is none. I return upstairs to get Joe. He comes when called, saying "Yes pastor?"

"Joe call the police, there is a dead man lying at the foot of the basement stairs!"

It takes an hour for the police to arrive. They introduce themselves as corporals Smith and Webster. I take the two British policemen down to the basement and stand aside while they examine the body. Joe comes down to join us.

Smith says, "Tis' obvious that this bloke slipped and fell down this long flight of stairs, hit the hard cement floor headfirst, and broke his neck Pastor Greene."

I said it may have been Dee."

Webster asks, "What did you say sir?"

"I said it may have been Dumm."

"Oh yes, it surely was dumb sir," says Smith. Do either of you know this man?"

I say, "I don't do you Joe?"

"I do not know him, but I think I remember seeing him at the stables when you first came into Jerusalem sir."

Webster says, "It is apparent that this bloody fool broke into the church with the intention of robbing it and had this accident. Do you store many valuables in those boxes or in that strongbox pastor?"

"There is really nothing of value down here officers," I say.

Webster adds, "We need to check all of the containers. He may have had an accomplice that got away with something."

I add, "That won't be necessary."

Smith says, "We insist sir. This is the protocol for an investigation such as this. I am sure that you wish to know if anything is missing."

I glower at them for a minute, and with a stern face, I say very slowly, "That…will…not…be…necessary…. you…will…not…open…any… containers…in…this…cellar… will… you?"

Both Smith and Webster become frozen as figurines. Their faces have a blank stare, as if they are hypnotized. Without looking at me, and gazing somewhere at the wall behind me, Smith says, "Quite so sir. It is not necessary." And they both continue to appear frozen.

"I want to thank you both for your expediency in this matter, and if you would please, have this body removed from our premises gentlemen."

"Righto sir, and cheerio sir," says Smith.

After an ambulance arrives taking the body, and the police leave, Joe asks me, "How did you persuade those coppers to stop their investigation sir? They both became as stone statues."

"I really didn't do anything Joe; the whole thing was "Dumm". Now if you'll excuse me, I have a long ninety-mile drive to Bethlehem."

As I arrive in Bethlehem, I am amazed that I'm actually in the place of Jesus' birth. My mind dwells on that as I search for the Solomon Hotel. I find it easily and when entering into the lobby I see Cohen lounging on a sofa and reading the "Jerusalem Post". He stands to greet me, and we shake hands. He says, "Welcome to Our Savior's place of birth Pastor Greene."

"Thank you Reuben. My father was here once, and I've always wanted to visit."

"Some other time we could go for a tour pastor, but alas, we have other business to conduct today. Follow me please."

He heads to go out the door and I stop him. I say, "I thought you said the meeting would be here in the hotel?"

He answers, "No I did not sir. I said that I would <u>meet</u> you here at the hotel. We have to drive to the location of our meeting."

"Before we go, I'd like to talk to you."

"Pertaining?"

"Is there a café here in the hotel?"

"Yes, would you care for a coffee before we leave?"

"Yes."

When we are seated, I ask Reuben, "Are you a member of the Haganah organization Reuben?"

He doesn't answer, instead he says, "Let me tell you some things about myself pastor. I was born in northern Palestine in the small town of Nahariyaa. It is on the Mediterranean Sea close to the Lebanese border. Our home was a distance of seven kilometers from the village. It was in fact very isolated. My family was of modest means since my father Abraham was a fisherman, and my mother Batsheva a teacher. I had two younger sisters, the older was Bayla, and the younger was called Jovia. They were just thirteen and nine years of age. I had a very happy childhood pastor. I would at times accompany my father on his boat to catch fish. It truly was a family that loved each other. When I was eighteen my father sent me to Haifa for college. Haifa was in close proximity to our home, and I would bus between home and school quite often to visit them. In my senior year, only three months before receiving my teacher's degree, I went home for a visit. What I found upon my arrival was horrific! Our animals, such as the cows, some chickens, and our only horse were slaughtered! I ran into the house and there I discovered my entire family butchered as well! Blood was everywhere, and yet all of our possessions remained intact. Nothing was stolen. The police informed me later that week, that they had apprehended a man who confessed to be a part of a group of Muslim Lebanese terrorists that murdered my family. They were murdered Pastor Greene simply because they were Jewish and lived too close to the Lebanon border."

"I'm so sorry Reuben. What a horrible thing to happen!"

"Yes, and since that time I have lived with that horror every single day of my life, over and over again. I hated God for allowing that to happen and I hated the Muslims more. I was bitter my entire life from that point until I met Pastor Davies. He explained through the scriptures that I must forgive. He told me that my hate was destroying my own self. It wasn't until I became a Christian that I opened my heart to God and forgave. So, to answer your question pastor, yes, I am a member of the Haganah. It is my sincere desire that Israel shall rise again, and Islamic terrorism be abolished. I also believe that you are an instrument of God sent to us for that purpose. Now we must leave or be late."

I follow him outside and a black Mercedes-Benz sedan is waiting for us. Cohen says, "Get in please pastor." We both climbed into the back of the car, and I was shocked to see the driver. It is my new congregant, the huge Mr. Abelman behind the wheel. He says, "Nice to have you with us pastor."

I am somewhat puzzled and return his greeting. Then Cohen says, "I am sorry pastor, but this will be necessary until we reach our destination." He places a black bag over my head in order to blindfold me. I say, "Really Reuben is this necessary?"

He answers, "Again, I am regretful, but my friend insists."

I know that we are leaving the city when traffic and other noises cease, and even with the Mercedes' fine suspension we are being jolted by the rough terrain we are traversing. I nervously ask, "Where are we going?" Instead of an answer Cohen says, "We are almost there pastor."

When we stop, I see an RV type camper parked in the middle of nowhere. Cohen and I exit the sedan, and our chauffeur Abelman does also while shouldering an automatic rifle. He comes over to me and says, "I must frisk you pastor."

When he feels the knife sheathed under my jacket, he does nothing. I know he must have felt it, but he acts as if it's non-existent. I credit Dumm and Dee for that, then I glance at Cohen and say, "You're starting to make me nervous now Reuben."

"You have nothing to fear," he says.

We enter into the RV, and a man wearing a Jewish Army uniform with an eyepatch over his left eye is sitting at a table. Cohen says, "Commander Dayan sir, let me introduce you to Pastor David Greene. Pastor Greene this is my colleague Commander Moshe Dayan."

"Dayan says, "It is a pleasure to meet you Pastor Greene. Do you prefer to converse in Hebrew or in English?

"Your choice sir."

"Then allow me to practice my English pastor."

"As you wish commander."

Although not of my faith, Reuben claims you are a true believer."
"Yes, I believe that Jesus is the Jewish messiah."

"Unfortunately, that is the brunt of the matter. Is it not? We will agree to disagree then. Please have a seat pastor. You are probably most curious as to why I desired to meet with you, especially under these strange and trying conditions."

"Then you would be correct sir."

"Then let me elaborate. I am a leader in the Haganah Pastor Greene. Reuben tells me that he has mentioned the name of our group to you. Has he not?"

"Yes, he has."

"We in our organization feel the importance of knowing who enters Palestine.

We therefore have, what you would call scouts, which are posted at various entry points within today's so called "British Mandate". One such scout noticed your entry into our country at the "Muhammed-ed-Dhib" stables and auction. After all pastor, an American riding upon a camel into Jerusalem from the Sinai desert dressed as a Bedouin was very curious to us. When we discovered that you were the new pastor at the Grace Christian Church, we were even more puzzled and intrigued. Coincidentally, and to our delight, a recent convert to your religion, Mr. Reuben Cohen was attending services there. Now you know the why of our query, therefore please tell us who you are."

"I am indeed a Christian missionary assigned to serve at "Grace" church. I have, however, some intelligence that has been related to me that may prove to be vital to your endeavors commander."

"What news does that intelligence pertain to?"

"It pertains to your Zionist movement, and to the birth of the new nation of Israel."

"In what way would it influence the new Israel to materialize?"

I pause for a long time, look back and forth from both Cohen and Dayan, and announce, "I have the means to finance all of the weaponry and needed infrastructure for the new Israel!" ……. My interrogators are speechless. Then Moshe Dayan leans forward, rest his elbows on the table, stares at me with his one eye, and says, "How are you able to fund all of this. That amount would be in billions of U.S. dollars!"

"Yes, but I have more revenue than billions."

Dayan laughs and says, "Your story sir seems fantastical. What proof do you have?"

I remove the knife from my jacket and lay it on the table in front of Dayan. He remains silent as he fondles it. He continues to examine it and then says, "I have seen artist's renditions of these. There would have been no photographs, because the article I read said they were ancient. Is this what I think it is?"

I answer, "If you think that the knife is of Levitical origin and is thousands of years old you would be correct."

"Do you have validation of this?"

"How would that be possible?"

"Without provenance I would be highly suspicious."

"May I make a suggestion commander?"

"You may."

There are a number of antiquities dealers in Jerusalem. In fact, a member of my church a Mr. Stephen Clemens is a distinguished antiquities dealer. I will leave you the knife and would suggest that you take it to him and have it dated and appraised."

Dayan says, "Even it is highly valuable, it could not possibly fund the birth of a new nation."

"Please listen to me carefully sir. Although I can't relate to you by whom or how I have this knowledge. But I am cognizant of......I have the maps to......I have the clues to the location of sixty-three caches of treasures that would yield funds of an incalculable worth! I speak of trillions of dollars!"

Dayan looks at me nonplussed. He is speechless.

I wait for him to speak again but he doesn't, instead he remains silent and deep in thought. Finally, he says, "What are your personal financial desires in this possible enterprise Pastor Greene?"

I have no desire to gain financially. I am a confirmed Zionist Commander Dayan. I wish all proceeds realized in this venture to be used solely for the new state of Israel. I will however have some suggestions to the Haganah, as to the coordination of how and when these treasures are to be excavated and recovered."

"By informing me of that my good pastor, I wish to believe both your honor and integrity. I will keep this knife and present it to a few of our more prolific leaders of the Haganah. We will discuss what you have told me. If they concur, Reuben will contact you about it. I must ask you again, who or by what means have you discovered this treasure?"

'I insist sir, that I am not able to discuss those issues. If we are to continue in this endeavor to recover this fortune, I must never be asked that question again. I assure you that is a subject I shall never divulge, not even under the penalty of torture or death. Your members must know that they are not allowed to ask me anything pertaining to that, or I will withdraw my assistance, and forget that this meeting has ever happened."

"As you wish pastor. Do you require a receipt for the item?"

"I do not. I have been told to trust you implicitly."

"By whom?"

"By Jehovah God himself!"

"Which again speaks of your......what is the word......oh yes, veracity."

"I assure you commander, very few people have the courage of my convictions."

"Until we meet again, "Shalom."

"Shalom!"

Reuben and I leave and go to the car. As we enter Abelman is already at the wheel. Reuben snickers and says, "So you are just a poor American pastor sent to us by his supporters huh?"

"And what do think I should have told you back then?"

"I think, nothing else pastor…… nothing else." He then puts the hooded blindfold on me again.

When we arrive back in Bethlehem Abelman says, "If you allow me to have the keys to your car pastor, I shall park it with our Mercedes in a parking area that is secure."

"Then how will I return to Jerusalem?"

Reuben Cohen answers, "You will not return this evening. I have reserved a room for you here at the "Solomon", and we will dine together tonight."

I agree, and decide I'll notify Joe later using the hotel's phone.

CHAPTER 87

(June 2nd, 1945)

I t has been a month since my meeting with the Haganah; and it seems that things go back to being normal again at the church, which is at least in the minds of Joe, Eve, and hopefully Naomi. But the game has begun! I'm positive that Moshe Dayan believes my account of the vast fortune awaiting the Zionist movement. I also think of Charlie Company and all of my friends. I wonder where they are, and how thrilled they were with the end of the war against Germany. I receive news of the continuing saga against the Japanese in the "Pacific Theater of War" through the "Jerusalem Post" and, when I can get it, the "Philadelphia Inquirer". It is amazing to know certain things about the future. Now that Roosevelt is dead, and Harry S. Truman is president of the United States, I know that he will drop, what America's scientists have coined as their new weapons of mass destruction, the Atom bomb, on the Japanese cities of Hiroshima and Nagasaki. I remember Brother Elijah telling me the date would be in August, only two months from today.

Most of all, and to my mind the best of all, is that our church has grown to forty-one members. Fifteen coming forward to confess Christ during the invitation. Most of the increase being British soldiers, but six Jews have accepted Christ as their messiah. It is interesting to me that Mr. Abelman and family have never returned to church after their first visit.

Then finally after our July the third Sunday service, Reuben Cohen approaches me and says, "May we talk in your office pastor?"

"Certainly Reuben," I say.

In my office Reuben informs me, "I'll be brief and to the point pastor."

"Good Reuben, because brevity is the soul of wit, and wit is the brevity of levity. Will I be smiling at good news?"

"Yes, I think you shall, because a meeting has been scheduled. There is a small airstrip just to the west of Jerusalem. Are you familiar with it?"

"Yes, I have seen planes both landing and taking off from that area."

"I and Mr. Abelman will meet you there at 8:00 a.m. this coming Monday morning. We will be taking a short flight to Eilat, near the port of Aqabah. There we will board a boat."

"Good Reuben, we will travel then. Travel can bring out anything in a man......especially sea travel."

"Was that a joke pastor?"

"Only if you thought so Reuben."

On Saturday I retrieve another envelope from my mysterious alleyway brick. It reads:

Advise Haganah that it is imperative

that Bedouin Sheik Hussein Mohammed ali abu yussef

Be contacted in the Sinai.

Suggest that he may help with excavations and transport

of all goods. Take the bowl and candlestick with you. The

malakis will accompany you.

Beware of Amos Friedman.

The plot thickens. Now I am to involve the Arabs. I am somewhat concerned by that, because I have no experience with them, except the one time encounter I had with a group of thieves in the desert. But I know one thing. My coming experience with them will make me either better or bitter. I decided to do some research into this Sheik. I need to know more about him.

The next day I set off to the offices of the "Jerusalem Post". Upon my arrival, I encounter a young lady at the reception counter. "Hello, I am Pastor Greene from Grace Christian church. Is it possible to peruse some past editions of your newspaper. I am hoping to read any article pertaining to a Sheik Hussein Mohammed ali aba Yussef?"

She smiles, and in perfect English says, "Yes sir. Past editions are on the second floor. They are filed in chronological order. You may find information about a Sheik in the Arabic section of our press.

As I go to the second floor I pass by the press room, and enjoy the smell of ink, and the pounding noise of the press. It is a nostalgic reminder to me of past times. I then proceed to the second floor, and remove a binder dated 1945. I look through the Arab section in each of several newspapers and find nothing. I pull out another binder dated May of 1944 and find what I'm looking for. The Sheik's name is on page 48. I began reading in Arabic of course, a synopsis of the Sheiks history. I then I come across a quote of his that reads:

"Is it not written in the Koran, that the ties of neighbors are as dear as those of relations. Our friendship with the Jews goes back many years. We felt we could trust them, and they learned from us too." After reading this quotation of his, I thought it somewhat strange that he expressed a degree of empathy for the Jewish people. After all they have been enemies for centuries, ever since Abraham banished his son Ishmael

and his mother Hagar into the desert and retained his wife Sarah and their son Isaac. It is interesting to note that the account of Abraham taking Isaac up onto the mount to sacrifice him unto Jehovah; has the exact same account in the Koran as Abraham doing the same thing as sacrificing Ishmael to Allah. I leave satisfied with the knowledge of which version is correct.

It's D-day. I'm going to meet with the heads of Haganah. When I arrive at the airstrip, I discover it to be a packed dirt runway, and a single building serving as both hangar and office. The wind is blowing heavily, and sand is being swept across the airstrip and into my face as I walk from my car to the domed hangar. I have to press down the fedora I'm wearing onto my head. I enter the barn-like structure and put my briefcase containing the two antiquities on the counter. Abelman and Cohen walk over to the counter. Abelman ignores me but Reuben says, "We may, I am afraid, be delayed because of these high winds pastor."

"We have no alternatives do we Reuben," I ask.

"No, we do not. We could not possibly drive to Eilat and still be able to meet the boat on time."

"Let us pray for these winds to subside," I say. Then I look at my watch. Only ten minutes pass and the strong gusting winds come to a halt. It is now perfectly still. Reuben looks astonished at me and says, "Whenever I need something pastor, I will certainly come to you about it first!"

I say, "The Lord answers prayer Reuben!"

We endure a rather turbulent flight on the small six passenger aircraft for only two hours before landing in Eilat.

A short taxi ride takes us to the "King Saul Marina" on the Gulf of Aqaba.

"Reuben exclaims, "There she is, the "Red Pearl".

I see a beautiful white yacht moored to the dock. It is flying the red flag with white cross of Switzerland as its country of origin.

Longshoremen are scurrying everywhere to prepare her launch. When we board the gangplank, we are greeted by a man in a white Swiss naval uniform. He says, "Hello gentlemen. I am Urs Fankhauser, the first mate on this ship. Captain Gruber and I welcome you aboard the "Red Pearl". We wish for you to enjoy your cruise down through the Gulf and into the Red Sea. Anything that you need, or wish will be provided for you. You need only to ask. This is Hans, He will show you to your cabins. Good day gentlemen."

After being escorted to my berth, I ask Hans, "How do I find the ship's café Hans?"

"It is on the top deck sir, overlooking the water." He stands in anticipation.

I say, "Oh yes, I'm sorry, and hand him a tip."

"Thank you, sir."

I take a walk around the ship's perimeter in order to familiarize myself with my new accommodations. The entire vessel exudes luxury. I say out loud, "Well Dee, well Dumm, I would wager you never hobnobbed in a place this nice before." Then I think of heaven and say, "Well maybe you have, maybe you just have!" When I enter the café and bar area, I see Reuben sitting alone at a table in the far corner. The "Andrew Sisters" are singing about "Rum and Coca-Cola" on the jukebox. I sit down at Reuben's table, and he points at the bar, and says, "Look over at the bar pastor and you will see four attendees of tomorrow's meeting. I think you already know the man with the eye patch, but on his left is the leader of the "Jewish Zionist Movement", David Ben-Gurion. On Dayan's right is Dr. Chaim Weizmann. He is the head of the Haganah, and a biochemist famous for developing a method of turning acetone into cordite. Cordite is an explosive propellant, which was used successfully in WWI. He is an enigma, in that he has pure Jewish blood, and yet is an agnostic. He shuns the Jewish religion, wanting nothing to do with it. Next to Weizmann is Yitzak Rabin, commander of the

Yishuv. The Yishuv were the only Jewish residents of pre-war Palestine. They numbered only 25,000 people.

I am to inform you that our deliberations will begin at 2:00 p.m."

A waiter comes to our table asking, "May I serve you a drink gentlemen?"

I answer, "Yes, I'll have a Coca-Cola with ice please."

Reuben asks, "Do you have any "Seven-up?"

"We do sir."

"A tall one please,"

"As you wish sir. I should let you know we will be serving leg of lamb for our fare this evening."

When our drinks come, Reuben and I decide to take them to the stern of the ship. We watch the port disappear behind us.

I ask, "Have you heard anything about what the Haganah is deciding?"

"No, I have not seen Moshe Dayan or any other Haganah of importance since we last went to Bethlehem. I want you to know however that Abelman told me that a high official in the "Etzel" will be in attendance."

I say, "Isn't that the terrorist branch of Haganah?"

"Yes, it is, and our friend Abelman is an associate of theirs."

"I want you and your colleagues to know, and I say this emphatically...... that I will not be part of any violence!"

"I believe they wish this also pastor, however, even though you made yourself perfectly clear to them that you would not divulge pertinent information about who your supporters are, do not be surprised if the issue comes up again."

"I promise you Reuben. I will walk out."

CHAPTER 88

I'm enjoying the cruise in the Red Sea and wish that Ruth could be here sharing this with me. As the ship moves slowly through the water, I admire my surroundings. The beauty of the Lord's creation never ceases to stir my soul. Why I was so blind to this before, and for so many years, remains a mystery to me. His handiwork is easily visible for all to see.

Reuben and I walk to the meeting room at the appointed time. Abelman is guarding the door. He nods at us and allows entry. As we stride in, I see Dayan, Ben-Gurion, Weizmann, Rabin, and another person, unknown to me, seated together on the same side of a table. Reuben makes introductions but excludes the one person I don't know. Moshe Dayan says, "Please be seated Pastor Greene. Our esteemed leader of the Haganah. Mr. David Ben-Gurion will speak for us initially concerning this matter."

I say, "It is an honor to meet you sir."

Ben-Gurion says, "And I you Pastor Greene. Allow me to say you have been the main subject of this committee for some time now. We are anxious to further discuss the knife you so kindly gave to our brother Moshe. But I will ask our only true scientist here, Dr. Weizmann, to deliberate on our findings.

Weizmann starts with, "Pastor Greene, we have done much research on the item in question. After consulting with experts in the fields of archeology, the study of antiquities, and metallurgy, they have all confirmed that the knife is not a replica but rather a very old genuine instrument that possibly could have been used by the Jewish Levitical priesthood for the sacrificing of animals. The gold and jewels alone should verify its worth in money, but its real worth would be estimated as much more valuable because of its age and historical value. We went a step further in analyzing this item. I personally flew to the University of Chicago in America, and presented the item for testing in a new science that they are developing called "Radio-Carbon-Dating". This is a new science being developed to calculate the age of any archaeological finding. Quite frankly sir, it astonished me that their test results confirmed that this knife is at least 3,000 years old. I have been told that you know the locations of sixty-three caches of huge amounts of this treasure. Is this true?"

I answer, "Yes, it is sir." I stand and open my large briefcase, take out the bowl and candlestick, and set them on the table. "These are further proof of my findings!"

Mayhem breaks out as they all start shouting at once, and rush together to examine the two articles! It takes a while before Ben-Gurion can calm and quiet his cronies. "Gentlemen please! Let us continue in an orderly fashion!

Things start to settle down and Mr. Yitzhak Rabin asks, "What is your proposal Pastor Greene?"

"As I have already related to Reuben and Commander Dayan, I wish to show you where all of this fortune may be found. I wish none of it for myself. I wish the entire riches, except for a small stipend, be used for the birth of a new Israel."

Ben-Gurion says, "Obviously pastor we are ready to proceed in recovering this wealth. What is your proposition?"

I point at the unknown man, knowing he is a member of Etzel and say, "Before I expound upon my proposition, I wish that gentleman to be excluded from this meeting."

"What!? This is preposterous! I insist on staying! I shall not be treated like this!"

Ben Gurion says, "I am sorry Josef, but we have no choice in this matter. Call in Abelman to escort Josef out please." Abelman steps in and assists the irate Josef out.

When all things settle, I explain, "All of the treasure should be recovered by means that would allow a cautious, secretive, and secure withdrawal. Therefore, a large contingent of your men racing into the Sinai with motor vehicles and helicopters would be counterproductive."

Dayan says, "What do you suggest then? How should we proceed?"

"All our efforts should appear to be just a large caravan of Bedouin Arabs moving through the desert regions. Would this not appear as a normal customary occurrence?"

Yitzhak Rabin says, "Yes it would pastor. You also said, and I shall use your own words sir, that a small stipend would be excluded from our revenues. Where would that money go?"

"I have done some research into a Bedouin Sheik named Hussein Mohammed ali abu Yussef. I know the tensions and animosity that exist between your two cultures; however, I have read a statement by him in the Jerusalem Post that suggests he may have some sentiment for your cause of a new Israel. I propose that I meet with him. If he will accept a stipend of the treasure, as I mentioned before, he may be persuaded to provide both the camels and men to aid us in the recovery of the riches. We will also, of course, have our own armed personnel along in the operation. I wish you to sell the three items I have given you, and then make me aware of the amount of monies that you have received. I will then offer those funds to the Sheik in exchange for his assistance in recovering all of the sixty-three treasures."

Ben-Gurion scrutinizes the reaction of his peers, laughs, and says, "If what you say is true sir, then the mythical "King Solomon's Mines" may not be a myth at all, but rather a reality! The novelist Sir H. Rider Haggard who wrote the book of the same name would be flabbergasted, even if their locations differ geographically, they are on the same continent! How do you believe that we should first proceed?"

"After the sale of the three items, contact Reuben here, inform him of the amount received in American dollars, and he and I will travel to meet the sheik. I think we'll be able to negotiate an arrangement with him allowing us to recover all of the caches secretly."

Reuben says, "We will?"

"Yes Reuben, we will. Don't be a pessimist. A pessimist is a man who complains about the noise when opportunity knocks."

CHAPTER 89

On August 6th, the bomb called "Little Boy" is dropped upon Hiroshima, Japan. Three days later "Fat boy" falls on Nagasaki. Japan surrenders unconditionally on the 2nd of September. Nearly 250,000 people are killed by the blasts. I wonder how the new "Commander in Chief" Harry Truman can sleep nights. But I read in the "Post" that he believes that those two bombings ultimately will save another million lives by instantly ending the Pacific war.

A week after the Japanese surrender Reuben Cohen shows up at my door. Instead of being dressed in his usual suit he is dressed casually, wearing dungarees and a white tee shirt. He remains his handsome self with his long black hair wet and swept back. I invite him in, and we settle in the living room.

I ask, "Coffee Reuben?"

"Yes please."

"Cream and two sugars?"

"Yes."

I set both cups on the table.

"Am I to assume we have information from the Haganah?"

"You assume correctly pastor. The proceeds from the sale of the three antiquities netted 188,000 dollars."

"Excellent, now we can make plans for our journey."

"When will we leave?"

"First, we must find where Sheik Hussein's village is. Being a nomadic tribe, they move from one place to another, sometimes covering an area of hundreds of square miles."

"How do you propose we do that pastor?"

"We could ask questions at the Ahmed Hussein's stables. Certain Bedouin tribes occasionally visit there."

"That would be hit or miss."

"I agree, however we may get their approximate whereabouts and then hire a plane to scout their exact location by air."

"Why do I fear going on this venture pastor? I hear that these Arab tribes are fearsome. I hear they love to behead their adversaries! We will be armed with weapons; will we not?"

Laughing I say, "We'll need no weapons Reuben. The Lord will be with us. Have faith Reuben. Have faith. Tomorrow we'll go to the stables and start our inquiries."

"I am afraid I have classes for tomorrow and the next few days pastor. I also must schedule some vacation time in order to accompany you on this journey so I am afraid you must go there alone."

"Very well I will."

(The next day in Jerusalem)

The stink of the stables is evident when I approach it, but it reminds me of the Shashani stables and Ruth; therefore to my nostrils, it's a pleasant odor. I ask inside where I can find Nabob, and am told he's in a corral with a number of animals wearing a blue rope tagged with his name and my information on it. When I walk over to the fence, he sees me and grunts, brays, and bellows, as he runs towards me. I pet him and give him an apple. He nestles my head and slobbers it thoroughly.

I laugh and say, "Hello Nabob my good friend. Do you think you're up for another trip?" As I give him another apple, an old Jewish man walks over and asks, "Are you taking the animal out today?"

"No, I'm not. I wish to talk with any Bedouins that are either here or camping near here. Do you know of any?"

"Yesterday a group came through here. They watered and fed their camels and then proceeded in a southerly direction sir. It is all I know."

"Thank you. Is Ahmed in the office?"

"He is sir."

I leave Nabob and the man and enter the stables office. Ahmed Hussein is behind the counter asleep in a chair. Flies are buzzing around his head. I ring the bell on the counter, and he wakens frightfully waving his hands in the air in a blind attempt to swat the flies, and shouts, "By Allah what is it?!"

"Sorry to disturb your nap Mr. Hussein. Do you remember me?"

"I do. You board camel here, no?"

"I do sir. I've been told that a few Bedouins passed through here yesterday, would you know of their current whereabouts?"

"You are American pastor, no?"

"I am."

"They took Najib road to the south. If you have a motorcar you may find them."

"Thank you, Mr. Hussein."

Before you go. You must pay next two months board, no?"

I pay him, jump in my Ford, and drive on the southerly road. This Najib road ends in the desert in about ten miles. When I reach that point, I exit, take my binoculars, and walk to the highest point nearby. I start my scan of the area and see some tents and a fire about a mile to the west. "Looks like I have a long hot walk in the desert's sun," I

409

say to nobody. Then grabbing my canteen, I head towards the camped Bedouins. When I approach their encampment, I greet them in Arabic.

"A-salaam alikam alleh waberkateh."

One man stands and says, "A-salaam alikam."

(The conversation is translated into English)

"I wish not to interrupt you, but I would like to ask a question of you sir."

He looks at me warily and says, "What is it you wish to know English?"

"I have some monies from the bank in Jerusalem for Sheik Mohammed Yussef of Tuba. Do you know where he may be found?"

"For twenty English pounds I may have knowledge."

I pay him and he looks at me suspiciously and says, "I do not charge enough. I shall have twenty more for this information."

I think that I may need some help from my two invisible friends, in order not only to prevent me from paying him another twenty, but to make sure he is telling me the truth, and not fabricating a false location of the sheik. I give him my best stare and say, "You have enough now. You will not lie to me. You will give me the truth of the sheik's location." Immediately the Arab turns rigid and straight. His arms are plastered straight to his sides. There is no movement from him except his mouth when he utters, "The sheik is near Al Qosimah."

I say nothing else, turn, and head back to my car. About halfway back I look, and he is still frozen. I have the information I need. The sheik is in the Sinai near a village called Al Qosimah.

CHAPTER 90

After this week's Sunday service, I noticed a new visitor to our church about to leave. I recognize him from his picture that occurs occasionally in the "Jerusalem Post". It is Gershon Harry Agron editor of the newspaper. I rush around some worshippers to catch him before he leaves. I shout, "Mr. Agron, Mr. Agron, I want a word with you sir!"

He stops and says, "I am so sorry pastor. I have an appointment in a few minutes. I enjoyed your sermon, and if you wish to discuss something with me, please just stop by and see me at the paper. You won't even need an appointment. Drop by any time at your leisure. But you must excuse me now. I really must go."

And after he leaves, I say to myself, I'll do just that sir, I'll just do that. I've had some thoughts lately about how our local newspaper could help contribute to the growth of our church.

Reuben stays after the service at my request. I have invited him to lunch, and to tell him of my success in finding the location of the sheik. We go to a corner of the fellowship hall and Naomi, who appears to remain angry for my booting her out of the parsonage, serves us Eve's delicious sea bass.

"I have been told that the sheik is encamped near a tiny village in the Sinai called Qosimah."

"Just how much do you trust this information David?"

I was somewhat surprised that he addressed me as "David," because this was the first time he has done so. However, we are becoming close friends and I'm pleased that he had. I say, "Reuben I'm not one- hundred percent sure, but based on how I received this information, rather than from whom I did, I'm rather confident we'll find him there. I do believe that we should charter a plane for reconnaissance purposes to that area."

"No need to charter a plane we just need to borrow one."

"What do you mean?"

"I have a British pilots license, and my Uncle Judah is the owner of that small airstrip we have recently used. He has a brand-new Cessna 190 I have been dying to fly.

This is Cessna's new plane just introduced this year." I am certain he will allow us its use."

"Well, if the door to opportunity does not open to polite knocks....... kick it in! That's great Reuben! Looks like you're a man of many talents. Maybe, just maybe, we'll do more than reconnoiter, maybe we could land the plane near them! We could get lucky and avoid riding camels for weeks! You know Reuben, luck is the idol of the idle. Let's be prepared to land that plane! But first you must go to the Haganah and request a portion of the gold; say about 20,000 dollars."

"That may be difficult."

"All things are possible with the Lord."

We lift off the next week with maps and gold in hand. Reuben seems confident behind the yoke of the Cessna. As I peer down at the desert below, I recall my trip along that area months ago. Two hours later we are hovering over the village of Qosimah's supposed location. I say to Reuben, "This place is probably only an oasis with a few small buildings. We need to fly low and crisscross the region."

Ten minutes later Reuben exclaims, "There it is to my left!" He banks the aircraft and I see it below. "Look to the west Reuben there's a number of tents erected close together. We buzz the village at an elevation of only two hundred feet and find an area of the desert below us void of dunes and vegetation. Reuben circles the spot twice and says, "I believe I can land there David." He circles the area again and heads into the wind to land the plane. I hold my breath. When we touch down, the aircraft shakes violently from the rough terrain, but we finally come to a stop safely. I say, "Nice job Mr. Lindbergh!"

The sun is extremely hot as it unmercifully beats down upon us. We shoulder our backpacks and head out to find the Bedouin encampment. "How far do you think we are from those tents David?"

"I'm not sure. But they're in this direction," I say.

Then over a rise a dozen men on camels come racing down towards us. Their swords are drawn and they're waving them over their heads! They halt their animals directly in front of us, and their leader says in an Arabic dialect, "Death to all infidels!"

I answer him in his dialect, "We are friends of the Bedouin people, and have gifts for your majesty the sheik!"

Reuben, although petrified with terror, thinks only to ask, "When did you learn the Arabic language David?"

I answer, "It is a gift from God Reuben."

"Do you think they shall cut our throats?"

"Have faith my dear Reuben. Have faith. Faith is the substance of things hoped for, the evidence of things not seen. The Lord is with us."

I look at the men and say, "We wish an audience with his majesty."

"You shall have your audience infidel, and with your heads upon poles."

The men surround us, take our packs, and tie our hands behind us, while their leader marches us towards their camp.

When we arrive, I see one very large tent surrounded by at least another hundred smaller ones. We are taken to a clearing before this large shelter, and made to sit on the ground. A bonfire is before us.

413

Three men walk out of the main tent. The one in the middle is wearing a purple turban with gold necklaces, and gold rings upon his fingers. He orders, "Ahderhem elly al-Khaimah." (Bring them into the tent.) We are taken into the tent, and I'm stunned at the décor. Expensive rugs cover the floor and draperies hang on each wall. Large cushions are scattered around in a circle, and we are told to sit on one. The man wearing the purple turban says in English, "Who are you and why have you invaded our home?"

I answer, "I am Pastor David Greene of Grace Christian church in Jerusalem. My friend is Mr. Reuben Cohen a teacher of children. We have come to give a great gift to his majesty Sheik Hussein."

"I am he. Why do the English wish to give gifts to Bedouins?"

I explain, "It is the Jewish people not the English who come bearing gifts your majesty."

"Why?"

"If you would please untie us I wish to explain all things to you."

"Ezala roibtihm." (Remove their ties)

I rub my wrists, and say, "Thank you your majesty. I must say that you speak very good English."

He sits on a cushion, folds his legs underneath him and says, "When as a boy an Englishman visited our tribe to study us. He became good friends with my father, and he taught me the language as well."

"My friend and I am honored to meet with you, great one."

"Tell me more about the gift you bring Pastor Greene."

It is more of a recompence for something the Jewish wish for you to do for them sir."

"By Allah it is true. There is nothing new under the sun. What is it they wish English?"

"They wish to employ your services "Most high one". We have selected you, your majesty, because of what you had printed in the

414

Jerusalem newspaper. They were your words sir, saying it is good to be friends with your neighbors. The Jewish people wish to recover a large number of objects that their ancient ancestors have hidden in the Sinai. They wish to do so secretly."

"Where are these objects?"

"They are in sixty-three different locations. They wish for you to provide at least seventy men and camels, and this venture may take up to three months duration, in order to recover all of these objects."

"And what gift are the Jewish willing to give to our people for such a service?"

"They will award you with 150,000 American dollars in gold. Understand your majesty this will not be in currency but in gold bullion."

"This is most interesting Pastor Greene. I will confer with my men about this matter. I wish you to know that our people have this saying, "I am against my brother, my brother and I are against my cousin, and my cousin and I are against the stranger." This unfortunately is our "Hierarchy of loyalties." We by nature are the most skeptical people. Tonight, you will be our guests; there will be food and dancing and also the ceremony of Bisha 'a. We have prepared a tent for you. Now my man Mushaa will accompany you there. Please note pastor you will be guarded. You are to remain in your confines until such time as we bring you to our festivities."

I say, "As you wish your majesty", and we are escorted to our quarters.

Reuben says, "Well I thank the Lord we are not dead yet."

I say, "I have told you more than once, oh unbeliever, the Lord is with us. Would you please stop complaining. Maybe we'll enjoy the night's events."

Later that evening the man called Mushaa ushers us from our shelter to the Sheik's main pavilion. As we enter, the sheik waves us over by him and the five veiled women seated by him. He greets Reuben and me with, "Al Salam". These are my wives. Since you are foreigners, and not wise in our customs. I should inform you that it is considered impolite for you to look at them. There is a severe penalty for doing so. I advise you to refrain."

"Please be seated food will be served. Have you men had Bedouin fare before?"

"Reuben answers for us, "No your highness."

"You will find it is quite delicious. First, we shall have "Qahwa ziyada." In your tongue it is sweet coffee. You may have three cups. The first is for the soul, the second for the sword, and the third because you are my guests. We then will eat bread with goat, and haleeb, which is camel boiled in its mother's milk. Dates and berries from the desert will also be served. Please enjoy gentlemen."

"Reuben whispers to me, "I do not know if I can eat the haleeb!"

I whisper back, "You better or you will upset him!"

After long meal seconds are being offered. I smile and say, "No thank you your majesty, does not the Koran speak of moderation?"

"It is wise to do so. Does not your bible speak of this also?"

"It does your majesty."

The sheik then claps his hands and commands. "Daa al-rags yebda!" (Let the dancing begin.) Women dressed moderately in long colorful dress and veiled faces dance slowly onto a wooden laid platform in the center of the pavilion tent. He instructs us, "This is the Al-rags-al nasai. It is a most beautiful dance of the virgins."

It is indeed a rhythmic flowing movement of the women in a synchronized choreography. It is totally unlike the naked lustful movements of the belly dancing I witnessed in Cairo. I look over at Reuben and he is smiling.

When the women finish, the sheik claps his hands again and says to me, "This is my favorite dance pastor. It is a tribal sword dance. It is the "Raqsa al-saif"! it is a battle!"

Bare chested men come racing out by an accompaniment of a loud and fast crescendo of Arabic drums and flutes. They wave their long, heavy, curved scimitar swords over their heads, and mimic fighting a mock battle with each other. They leap to heights I never thought possible. Then they stop in a heartbeat, face the sheik, kneel, and bow to him. Sometimes it's funny how we think, because while they were dancing, I thought of my old Alma Mater the U. of Delaware's basketball team, those perennial losers could have used one or two of these guys on their team!

As the men exit the makeshift stage a man walks onto it by himself. The sheik says to me, "This is the "Mubesha". He is a holy man. This Mubesha is the 13th in a long line of Mubesha's from the same family. It is a great honor to be one, and its office is passed down from father to son."

"What is his purpose," I ask.

"Allow me to find the words in your tongue......He is a judge, a holy judge."

"I see. Will there be a trial this evening?"

"Yes. A man was said to have stolen two goats from another man."

Just then two men come walking onto the platform, and each stop on opposite sides of the Mubesha. Next four men come walking in carrying a large metal vase and set it down in front of the judge (the Mubesha). They leave and next a young man carries in a table with a metal object lying on it. He places it next to the vase.

The sheik explains to Reuben and me, "The men on the left of the Mubesha is the accused, and the man on his right is the accuser. Again, he has said that the accused is a thief, and has stolen from him two goats. What will happen now is interesting." The sheik stands, and translated to English, he says, "Light the fire!"

The young man lights the contents of the vase and flames shoot upward. I am mesmerized by the theatrics of this. Next the Mubesha takes the object from the table and holds it up into the air for all to see. It is an elongated spoon. He then offers prayers to his god Allah, and the entire audience bows down prone to the ground. I elbow Reuben suggesting that we'd better do the same. When he finishes his prayer, all sit back to watch. The Mubesha judge lowers the spoon over the flames from the vase and holds it there for a long time. When he removes it from the fire the spoon end can be seen glowing red hot. Then of all horrors, the accused man opens his mouth, and the Mubesha inserts the molten spoon into his mouth and presses it down upon his tongue. The accused man screams as the Arabic judge continues pressing the spoon down. The sheik then interrupts Reuben and me and says, "Now judgement shall be pronounced. If the accused man's tongue is scarred, he will be pronounced guilty. If not, he is innocent."

We wait for the judgement to be passed. The judge inspects the accused's tongue. He turns to render the verdict. In a loud voice he says, "Ine mozannab!" (He is guilty!) The accused screams and starts to run but is blocked from escaping by men in the audience. The two men who initially brought in the vase detain him, and remove him from the scene.

I ask the sheik, "What will his punishment be?"

"Thieves will have a hand severed. It is the law."

Reuben whispers to me, "This is barbaric!"

"I agree Reuben, but this is their way. It is their culture."

The sheik looks at me and says, "We have talked about your proposition Pastor Greene. It has been decided in our tribal council that we require a sign from Allah himself. If you agree to participate in the "Bisha' a" and be found innocent of any lies, we will agree to provide the men and animals for your Jewish friends. If not, we will sadly decline."

Reuben stands and looks at me in panic, "You will do no such thing David! This whole scenario is repulsive!"

I answer, "Unfortunately Reuben we have no alternative." I glance at the sheik and say, "Since my God is greater than your god, I accept your testing."

The sheik is highly angered. He glares at me and says, "What you say is blasphemy pastor! Is not your God Jesus?"

"He is."

"We know of your Jesus. He is spoken of in our holy book the Koran. He is considered a minor prophet. Certainly, he is not greater than the most holy of all, the prophet Mohammed."

"Mohammed is dead your majesty. My Jesus is alive!"

"Very well, we shall see then. If you are found truthful and also not a blasphemer, we shall aid in your friends' recovery of the ancient objects they desire. I also will be persuaded to hear more about your Jesus. Let the Bisha 'a begin!"

Reuben shrieks, "No David, no! You cannot participate in this devilish thing!"

"Relax Reuben. I have told you the Lord is with us." And then I walk down to the Mubesha. I pray silently to myself, "Oh Holy Spirit grant me peace as I do this thing. You have saved your servant Daniel from the lion's mouth, and his three friends from the burning fire. I ask you to save me from this agony. All honor is now upon you Lord."

Their judge places the spoon into the fire again. He waits until it is burning hot. I open my mouth and he places the instrument of torture onto my tongue. I stiffen and cringe. Immediately I feel its heat in my mouth. I feel no burning sensation on my tongue. I feel no pain. Tears of joy come from my eyes, and I praise the Lord my God, as the judge retains the spoon upon my tongue. Then he finally removes it. I kneel and thank the Lord for His great power and glory! The judge inspects my tongue and jumps back in a panic. He takes a while to calm himself, and then pronounces, "Ine bare." (He is innocent!) The crowd of Arabs are in turmoil. They look towards their leader for guidance. The sheik gets up off his cushion and announces, "So be it, it is done!"

When I return to my place next to the sheik and his wives, he smiles at me and says, "We will go to my quarters now pastor." He claps his hands once again and the entire flock of Arabs exit the pavilion. "Follow me please." Reuben and I arise to follow him, and he stops us, looks at Reuben and says, "Only the pastor may come Mr. Cohen." Reuben looks at me with anxiety and we part ways. The sheik's wives leave him, and he and I are alone in a small, draped corner of the main tent. We again rest on cushions, and he is the first to speak, "Your God is very persuasive Pastor Greene. I wish to know more of Him. In all the lives of my ancestors none has been so brave as you. The Mubesha has never witnessed a tongue that was never scarred a little. By Allah you have amazed me."

"Not by Allah your majesty, but by my Lord Jesus."

"You almost persuade me; however, I wish to know more of your God."

"Of course, your majesty. I have brought with me a satchel containing two gifts for you. If you would send a servant to bring it to me, I shall give them to you."

The sheik claps his hands, and a young man enters. He gives him orders to retrieve my satchel. When he returns, I open it, and before giving him its contents, I ask, "Does this mean you will provide the caravan and men to aid in the retrieval of the Jewish antiquities?"

"I will pastor. Of a certainty, I will."

Then this is for you sir. I hand him a New Testament that has been translated into Arabic. "This will tell you all about my God. My wish is that he will be yours as well." He takes the book and is obviously gratified. Then I hand him sixty, one-ounce gold bullions valued at 20,000 American dollars. He smiles again, and says," I am most pleased pastor. When do we begin this effort?"

"I must first return to the Haganah council and receive their instructions, then I'll return here and provide you with maps and further orders."

"That will be a joyous event for me when you return. May I ask if you are married pastor, or does your religion prohibit a pastor to be wed?"

"No, I may marry, but I am not."

"I have seven daughters, and none are married, may I give you two, or even three to wed?"

I am taken aback and don't want to insult the sheik, so I say, "I am honored by your majesty's generous offer, however I am a man of few words and usually a few words to a wife are never sufficient. I am not quite ready for marriage sheik; possibly in the future, but I must politely decline at this time."

"You are indeed a wise man pastor. Perhaps when we meet again you will reconsider."

"Perhaps."

"Do you wish to remain with our people here for a time?"

"No, your majesty, I must return to Jerusalem tomorrow with the good news of our agreement."

"Then I shall meet with you upon your return."

"I thank you most gracious one."

CHAPTER 91

The next morning as Reuben and I enter the Cessna 190, he says, "What you did back there in that ceremony David is the bravest thing I have ever witnessed."

"As I've told you Mr. Cohen, what I did was not based on my bravery, but rather on my abiding faith in our Lord. He's your Lord also is He not?"

"He is, but I believe I need to grow more in the faith. I do not believe that I could have done what you did."

"As your pastor I would advise you to "Trust in the Lord with all your heart." Now Let's get this new toy of your uncles off the ground."

"If we can. This sand is very soft here."

"That's alright I'll just pray then."

Reuben pushes the throttle full forward, and our aircraft starts to gain speed. It takes longer than the usual time required to gain the rotate speed of 65 knots. When we achieve it Reuben pulls on the yoke, and we get airborne. He wipes his brow, and shouts, "Hallelujah we did it!"

After elevating to 4,000 feet, I take a goatskin bag containing Bedouin coffee, open the top, and pour me and Reuben each a cup. I hand him one and say, "Here, courtesy of the sheik."

"Thank you, David. By the way, I've been meaning to ask you about the H in your middle name. For what does it stand?"

I chuckle and ask, "What would you like it to stand for?"

"What?"

"You heard me. For what would you like it to stand?"

"Well, it certainly must be a name of someone who was very brave. Let me think......I know, it is Horatio. As in the famous, courageous, and heroic naval officer "Captain Horatio Hornblower"."

"Horatio it is then."

"You're kidding me. I guessed right?"

"Reuben, let's just say it's Horatio and leave it at that."

"Sometimes David I think I still don't know who you really are!"

We land back in Jerusalem, I get in my Ford convertible, and as I drive to my church my mind replays the events of the past two days. I think to myself, that's history, and I start to focus on my plan I've had pertaining to the newspaper. Joe is waiting for me as I pull into the driveway.

He greets me with, "Welcome home pastor, I hope you've had a pleasant trip."

"I must say Joe it was very interesting." Naomi and Eve ran out to greet me. Naomi kisses me on the cheek, jumps back startled and says, "Oh I am most sorry for that sir. I do not know what I was thinking. Please forgive me."

"Naomi I will never forgive someone for giving me a welcome home kiss; It's good to see all of you."

Joe says, "I shall get your bags sir."

I take a much-needed shower, eat a sandwich that Naomi brought me, and head straight to the "Jerusalem Post. The same girl is behind the reception desk. I snicker, "Would you inform Mr. Agron that pastor David H. Greene wishes to see him? The H in my name stands for Horatio." (Sometimes I get too full of myself!)

"Yes sir. Please be seated sir."

After only five minutes I'm ushered in to see the editor, Mr. Gershon Harry Agron. He stands behind his desk and offers his hand. We shake and he says, "Please have a seat pastor." I do and he asks, "I must admit it has been a long time since I've been to church, and I somewhat enjoyed your service. Have you come to see me in order to shake more of my agnostic dust off of me?"

"I would love to do that Mr. Agron, but that's not why I came."

"Please call me Harry. Then pray tell, what purpose does this meeting serve?"

"I have had some experience in the newspaper field and I'm familiar with the power of the press. I think that your paper could possibly aid me in the growth of my church."

"By all means pastor, we accept all advertising."

"I really wasn't thinking of placing an advertisement in your paper Harry."

"What do you wish then?"

"I want to write a weekly column for you."

"Pertaining to?"

"The Christian message. I want to quote various scriptures and add some commentary to a blog I would title "The Christian Voice"."

"You should be aware pastor that most of our readers are Muslim or Jewish."

"I realize that, but certainly you could see the value of conveying Jesus' message to your readers. You are an American, aren't you?"

"Yes, I was born in Russia, but my citizenship is American."

"Isn't a good portion of your readers British executives and soldiers?"

"A portion, yes."

"What day of the week is your highest circulation?"

"That would be on the Sabbath. Saturday is our largest circulation."

"Then I would ask you Harry, if you would publish a Saturday column written by me entitled "The Christian Voice"? I trust that it would increase your circulation as well as add to my congregation."

"Are you expecting any renumeration?"

"None. My rewards would be measured in the increase of my church."

"Then why not pastor...... why not?"

"Excellent! I want to thank you very much. When is the deadline for the Sabbath paper?"

"Thursday at 5:00 p.m."

"Then our business is completed Harry. I'd like to see you in church again."

"From time to time you may see me there pastor."

"May God bless you. Have a pleasant day Harry."

"And you pastor."

We shake hands again and I leave.

The next week I write my first blog:

"THE CHRISTIAN VOICE"

"Hello and welcome to a new column in the Jerusalem Post

Entitled "The Christian Voice"

I am pastor David Greene of "Grace Christian Church". This new article

Will be published weekly on every Sabbath day. The Lord has said, "Faith

cometh by hearing, and hearing by the word of God."

It is the purpose of this column to share select scriptures with you for your edification and joy. Our church is

located at 881 Mesilat Yesharim St. here in Jerusalem, and our congregation of believer's welcomes you to our

10:00 a.m. worship service.

Today's scripture is from Proverbs 18:10. "The name of the Lord is a strong tower: the righteous runneth into it and is safe."

"Shalom"

Pastor David H. Greene

CHAPTER 92

The next week Reuben and I are to meet with the Haganah once again in Eilat at on the "Red Pearl." As we drive to his Uncle Judah's airstrip he says, "My uncle has given us permission to use his Cessna again. This time we will not need to charter a flight to Eilat. Any advice this time?"

"No Reuben, although advice is interesting, if you take it, you can make the same mistakes everybody else does."

We land in the seaport and find that the "Red Pearl" is moored and waiting for us. We board and I'm shown to the same cabin I had previously occupied. I've often found that the best sleeping pill is simply reading a good book in bed, so I open up Rudyard Kipling's "Captains Courageous". I fall asleep on page fifteen.

I'm awakened in the morning by knocking on my door. Reuben says, "Hey, you've overslept. We will just have time for a quick breakfast before our meeting. Hurry up and get dressed."

"I wasn't sleeping Reuben, I was hibernating."

"Hibernating or not, hurry up we've got to go!"

"I'm coming! I'm coming!"

After a breakfast of kippers and eggs, we walk into our meeting room with Ben Gurion and cronies present. Morning salutations are exchanged, and as I sit in my seat It feels like an interrogation box on a witness stand.

The questions start with Ben Gurion asking, "I understand from Mr. Cohen that you met with the sheik in the Sinai Pastor Greene, however he refused to inform me of the results of that meeting. Were we successful in soliciting his help?"

I can't help myself and say, "No we did not sir, and he also pilfered your twenty grand from us."

Moshe Dayan jumps from his seat and accuses me with, "This is an outrage! Did you take that money for yourself!"

I laugh and say, "Relax commander, I just thought I'd have a little fun. The truth is money is always changing hands ……and people. In this case it did change hands, and it changed into the sheiks. He has agreed to provide us with the men and camels needed to transport the antiquities to wherever you desire. Of course, that would include your offer of an additional one hundred and thirty grand to be placed in his coffers. That's right I said only another one-hundred and thirty thousand. I saved you thirty-eight thousand dollars."

Dr. Weizmann laughs and says, "I am positive that we appreciate you humor pastor. But before you give our beloved Dayan a heart attack, I wish you to refrain in doing so please."

I continue, "I'm sorry and I shall do so. Sheik Hussein is more than willing to aide us in our endeavors, as long as the additional monies are paid. We must now formulate the logistics of our enterprise. I believe that we need at least two dozen men of the Haganah dressed as Arabs, mounted on camels, mimicking a caravan of Bedouins, and are prepared to meet the sheik's entourage of seventy men in the valley of Acor. It is only about thirty miles from Jerusalem, and it is where I found the first cache. I will lead this caravan, and only this one. When the first treasure is exhumed, I will give your appointed leader the clues to the remaining locations. I must ask now who that leader will be."

Ben-Gurion says, "We shall take a break now for refreshments and decide who will be in charge of the expedition. Our meeting will resume in two hours gentlemen."

Reuben and I drink pomegranate juice on the bow of the ship, and he says, "There is one man in this meeting I do not trust. He is Amos Friedman. You will see him not on the dais but sitting alone to the left of it. Today he is wearing a grey suit with a black yarmaka on his head. He is a little man with a grey mustache, and he will be constantly smoking a cigarette."

"I noticed him earlier. Some men smoke between meals, others eat between smokes. I also have reason not to trust him."

Reuben asks, "Why don't you trust him?"

"Let's just say I've been warned."

"By whom?"

"Of whom, I would prefer not to say."

"Fair enough; but you do realize David that I need to watch over you."

"Believe me Reuben, there are already two that do."

"Oh yeah......who?'

"Now that's a Dum question."

An hour later Ben-Gurion calls the meeting to order. "We have decided that Major Levi Zats should lead our foray into the Sinai. He has commanded men in the Jewish brigade during the war. We find him most capable."

Major Zats stands and says, "Pastor Greene, when one cache of the sixty-three is discovered how many Bedouins will be needed to transport that load to the location that we have decided upon?"

"Let me ask first where you intend to carry them?"

Zats turns to face a large map of the Sinai region. With a pointer he says, "After a certain treasure has been disentombed, we propose to

429

carry it to a wasteland totally void of people. Pointing on the map he explains, "This vast wilderness between Nuweibaa and Dahab right on the Gulf of Aqaba seems perfect to me. We will have a launch stationed there to transport the goods to the "Red Pearl". She will be anchored in close proximity to the shore. After all the antiquities have been brought aboard, and safely secured in the ship's hold, we will sail to the destination that we have selected. Our leader Mr. Ben-Gurion has decided that the treasure's final destination shall not be disclosed to anyone outside this group of men sitting here on the dais."

I answer, "That place of embarkment, in my mind, seems a reasonable objective, therefore I believe that a caravan of two dozen Bedouins and their camels, plus two Jewish soldiers of the Haganah should be sufficient to convey the articles of one cache. I also volunteer Mr. Reuben Cohen to procure all of the Bedouin attire needed for the Haganah men. Also, and with your permission, he and I shall meet with Sheik Hussein in one week. Reuben and I will at that time describe our plans, as well as rewarding him with half of the remaining money that you have agreed upon. The balance of funds will be paid to him upon completion of the venture."

For the first time in the session Dr. Chaim Weizmann chimes in, "We must set the date for this exposition. When do you propose that will be pastor?"

"Today is the 10th of July. I shall tell the sheik we'll rendezvous with him on the 24th of this month in the valley of Acor. This will allow Reuben and I enough time to go and meet with him, and also allow you sufficient time to organize your men and equipment. You will need shovels, picks, and possibly some explosives. I think it also imperative that everyone that is a part of this expedition be trained in riding and the handling of camels. I'd suggest that can be arranged at the "Muhammed ed-Dhib" stables west of town. We will depart three days before our scheduled meeting with the Bedouins to allow for travel time, and to organize our encampment. Water is available there, but we'll need other provisions. Cohen will coordinate our activities and communications with you beforehand."

Ariel Sharon, who was quiet during all the proceedings adds, "We are most thankful to you pastor. Success will ensure the new state of Israel, but may I ask how you initially came upon this discovery?"

I look at him with a dour expression, say nothing, and walk out the door.

CHAPTER 93

(Berlin)

As Lieutenant Andrew Harrison drives the crew of "Thumper" for the first time onto the streets of Berlin, he views German citizens walking along buildings that once were prominent and proud. Now they are nothing but rubble, being demolished by American bombers, and are only a reminder of what they once were. He looks at their faces. They are defeated, downtrodden, and impoverished. Their once great Fuehrer Adolf Hitler, having committed suicide in a bunker, is only an insipid remembrance in their minds. Men, women, and children are seen scavenging amongst the annihilated structures. All flags, swastikas, and other Nazi paraphernalia have already been removed and destroyed. There is no longer any indication that their regime existed. Paddy shouts, "And we'll be a sayin' goodbye to the bloody 3rd Reich!" They stop "Thumper" at the newly established American command center, a sign above indicating it is "The Hotel Edelweiss". The five men exit their tank, and Andy says, "This is it guys. We're to report here. I understand General Patton is furious that the British and Russians beat him here. He's always despised Montgomery."

They enter along with a contingent of Charlie company and are stopped at a desk with an inscription on a sign saying, "Incoming Personnel". A sergeant is sitting behind the desk, stares at them, and orders, "Form a single line soldiers and remove your dog tags for my inspection. We need a headcount and also must assign your billets. Chow is served in this hotel's restaurant and the mess is now open. Because of limited space, food may be taken to your assigned rooms. You will be quartered five or six to a room. Beds have been removed and cots have been added to accommodate you. There is a mandatory briefing scheduled outside in the rear of this building in a large courtyard starting at 1400 hours and every other hour until the last one at 1800 hours. All personnel must attend for indoctrination. You will be given room keys along with your time to attend the briefing. The line moves forward as the soldiers check in.

Andy says, "Let's get rid of our duffels. We're on the seventh floor."

When they enter in and inspect their accommodations Ski says, "Man this is sure better than tents. Hey, look guys we even have a balcony!"

Joe suggests, "Let's settle in and go down and get some food. I'm sick to death of K-rations. Oh, how I would love a bowl of clam chowda' now."

"Good luck with that," says Fowler, "I'll settle for a plain old hamburger."

A courier comes in their room and asks, "I'm looking for MSgt. Patrick O'Brien. Is he here?"

"I'm O'Brien."

"Sergeant, I have a message here from the Congress of the United States. It says they are awarding you the "Medal of Honor"!

Andy takes the letter and reads it. He looks at his friend and says, "Well congratulations you old potato head, congratulations!" They all gather around Paddy with hugs of delight!

At 1500 hours the five men go to the indoctrination. A major Donahue walks up on a freshly constructed stage and begins:

433

"Welcome to Berlin soldiers! Thanks to you this evil of "fascism" has been defeated! But before we are discharged, we still have a job to do. Our president Mr. Truman, the Russian dictator Joseph Stalin, and the prime minister of Great Britain, Mr. Winston Churchill while together in Potsdam, have ordered what is called the "Berlin Declaration". This declaration has decreed that Berlin will be divided into three sectors. The American sector, the Russian sector, and the British sector. Each will convene to maintain peace within their sectors.

You will now become policemen, and here are your rules of engagement.

The major turns to a large blackboard behind him and reads from it.

1. The American sector is cordoned off with blockades on each street confining our sector. No personnel are to leave our sector, unless having written orders to do so.

2. You are ordered to patrol your assigned area of our sector only, and you will destroy any evidence still existing from the Nazi regime.

3. You will not fire your weapons at any German citizen unless first fired upon.

4. You will conduct yourselves in the manner of a humane American soldier, while aiding any civilian that requests your help, or that you find in danger.

5. There will be no fraternization with members of the other allied nations. Any soldier or groups of soldiers that violate any of these rules will receive article thirteens for misconduct and possible time in the brig.

You will be given a copy of these rules. If there are any questions you have concerning them, make a query to your company's NCO in charge. You are dismissed."

The men leave the briefing and Andy says, "I sure wish we were heading straight home guys, but it looks like we've got some more work to do."

Ski says, "Yeah now it looks like we're in a police union......" Amalgamated Copper".

Little did they know that they would be sent home in six months and discharged.

CHAPTER 94

(In Jerusalem)

I have a reoccurring dream now. Ruth and I are on horseback riding to Joshua's Grove again. We arrive and lie by the brook in embrace, not in naked lust, but filled with love and joy. I touch her smiling face and kiss her softly on the lips. We gaze into each other's eyes in the wonderment of our tender affection for one another. I relish the warmth of our bodies enfolded together......and then I awaken. My love for her will never ebb. I miss her so. I also miss Luke's grin as he cleans a stall, young Ishmael's happy eagerness, Jacob's mentoring, Elijah's wisdom, and even Samuel's admonishments. Most of all I simply miss Shashani, and though I am absent from there I am happy and content in serving my Lord.

Today Reuben and I will launch the Cessna from Jerusalem and he asks, "Do you notice the difference, David?"

"You mean the skis with smaller wheels underneath them?"

"Yes, oh observant one."

"Great idea Reuben."

A voice from behind me says, "My idea, certainly not his," says his Uncle Judah. I think they will function as superb landing gear on soft sand. You men have a safe journey."

"Thanks for the use of your plane Judah." Then we take to the skies.

We find the Bedouin encampment easier this time and Reuben is thrilled with the performance of our skis upon landing. It doesn't take long before we are welcomed by a group of men on camels including the sheik himself.

"Welcome back Pastor Greene and Mr. Cohen. We our most happy about your return. We have prepared, what you would call in the English, a great extravaganza!"

"It is good to see you again your majesty. I have good news!"

The next three days are spent in celebration with dancing and food. Once again, much to our chagrin, we are forced to partake in the "haleeb", the camel meat boiled in its mother's milk. I also am offered again three of his daughters to wed. But most importantly I relate to the sheik the plans for the expedition, and the date and place of our proposed rendezvous in the valley of Acor. He is paid his stipends of gold and then he tells me.

"I would like you to know pastor, that I have found your bible most interesting. May I ask, is it possible that we may continue to communicate through the mail? I have many questions for you.

"Of course, your highness, and I also plan on seeing you again in your camp; wherever it may be.

We take off from the sands of the Sinai, this time rather smoothly, because of our new skis.

Four days have passed and today I will meet our entourage at the El-Dhib stables. Reuben and the team's leader Major Levi Zats ride over to me. When I go to retrieve Nabob, he excitedly runs to me. I ask him, "You ready to go big fella'?" He grunts and brays enthusiastically. The major says, "Lead the way pastor." And Nabob and I head to the front of the caravan of the two dozen Haganah soldiers. Then I noticed in passing that Amos Friedmann is in the group. He is the one I'm told to beware of. I shall watch him closely.

It's interesting, or maybe a better word would be gratifying, to know the future. I have already heard from Elijah his prophecy proclaiming Israel to be reborn a nation again in only three more years. I know without a doubt that this group of men will succeed on this trip, and yet I'm still cautious about what we will encounter.

We should arrive in the valley of Acor in my estimation in another two to three hours. Reuben rides aside me and says, "This heat is killing me David. I absolutely hate this desert."

"We'll be there shortly Reuben. "Remember, "God has put the firewood there, but that every man must gather and light the fire."

"Was that a quote from the poet Keats?"

"No Reuben, "The Lone Ranger".

"Who?"

The Lone Ranger......" Kemosabe".

"What?"

"Never mind, you'd never understand."

As we enter a rise in the landscape and start to descend into the valley, I see about twenty men on horseback. I am startled and wonder who they are and how long they have preceded us. There is only one reason they would, out of the blue, be here, and that is to beat us to the treasure. They evidently knew where we would be heading to find it, however not when. The only way that could have happened, would be if there's a traitor amongst us, and I have a sneaky suspicion of just who that conspirator is. Major Zats rides up beside me and asks, "Who in the hell are they pastor?"

"I haven't a clue who they are sir, but there could only be one reason why they're here, and that's to grab the treasure before us."

Zats says, "Let's take a run at them! I will lead the charge!" He turns on his mount to inform the others, runs back to the front, and commands "CHARGE!"

The soldiers all kickstart their camels and race towards them. The horsemen then start firing their rifles at our charge, and the Haganah soldiers start to return fire. The camels are startled by the gunfire, and some begin to hesitate and buck. Reuben and I remain behind since we have no weapons. Two of our men are thrown from their animals onto the desert floor. One is Amos Friedman. As the battle continues three of our adversaries are shot off their horses. Then I see the little Friedman running away from the skirmish as fast as his short legs will carry him. I command Nabob "Down Nabob" and he obeys. I mount, give him chase, and in a short time I reach him and tackle him to the ground.

He screams and says, "I have done nothing wrong. Get off of me!" Reuben hurries and jockeys his camel over, and helps me restrain the man. I break off a heavy branch of a tree and warn him, "Stay right there on the ground Amos or I'll bludgeon you with this!"

Our group of professional soldiers run the intruders back towards Jerusalem while killing three more. They then ride back to Reuben and me. They all dismount, and Major Zats with two of his soldiers contain Friedman with ropes around his arms and legs. The major highly irate, glowers at the restrained man and says, "You set this up didn't you scumbag."

Friedman shakes his head and shouts in denial, "No major. I swear, I do not know who they

were."

"Someone within our company did, and I trust every one of these men. They have fought beside me in many conflicts. Everyone but you. I told Ben-Gurion you would have no value to us on this expedition, but he relented and insisted you join us. He said you could identify some of the antiquities and would document their findings." He unholsters his pistol and aims it at Friedman's head. "Tell me the truth or I will most certainly put this bullet through your skull right now!"

Friedman in a panic shouts, "I swear! I swear! I had nothing to do with this!"

I exclaim, "No major don't. Don't kill him. I think I can measure his veracity."

"How?"

"Order a couple of your men to start a fire."

"What?"

"Just start a fire."

As two of his men follow his orders, I go to Nabob and take a spoon out of my pack. They bring our suspect to the fire, and I kneel to heat the spoon.

"Bring him here and have him kneel. We'll find the truth the Bedouin way." Once the small ladle is hot, I look at him and say, "I am going to press this hot spoon upon your tongue. If you're telling the truth your tongue will not scar. If it does, you're guilty. Open your mouth!"

Friedman is terrified. He cries, "This is cruel! This is barbarous! You cannot subject me to this!"

"Either open your mouth, or I'll push this into your eye. Which one do you prefer?"

He quickly opens his mouth, and then cries out, "I did it! Oh God I did it! I am so sorry. Please get that thing away from me!" Then he bows his head down and sobs like a baby.

I say, "Don't kill this man. I'll not have his death on this trip. Keep him restrained and away from his mount. He'll walk behind us in this heat."

We then continued on our journey. Reuben says to me, "That was nuts David, but I loved it!"

I answer, "Oh Reuben, in this world you have to be a little crazy or you'll go nuts." He laughs as we proceed on our quest.

In about another hour, I see the stone hovel in the distance. When we arrive at it, I begin to give orders. "This is it men. Grab your shovels and a pick. Remove all the sand and debris from the opening. You'll find a wooden cellar door." Once cleared they open it. I see no spiders crawl out. "Give me a flashlight. Major you and Reuben follow me down. When we attain the floor of the cellar, I tell Reuben, "Take the pick and hack against this wall." As before it easily crumbles away, and I lead the two through the tunnel to the treasure room. "Here it is in all of its glory!"

Reuben and the major gawk in amazement at the heap of precious gold, silver, and jewels!

I say, "Major my job is done here." Then I handed him the list of the sixty-two other clues that I deciphered. "Here's the list where you may find the others."

The major says, "Thank you for your service to Israel Pastor Greene. May our God bless you greatly."

"May I ask major, what will you do to Amos Friedman?"

"I have given this some thought and have decided that on our first trek to the Gulf of Aqaba we shall leave him by himself somewhere in that vast wasteland. Let us see if he can find his way back to civilization."

"You realize that he will probably die out there."

"So be it."

As we exit the cellar, I see the long parade of Bedouins on camels moving single file through the saddle on the mountain I had once crossed before. I smile as they ride to us. They lower their animals, dismount, and the sheik himself comes to greet me. We grin at each other and shake hands.

"Major Levi Zats allow me to introduce you to his majesty Sheik Hussein Mohammed ali abu yussef. Your majesty this is the leader of our quest Major Levi Zats."

Zats bows his head and replies, "I am honored your majesty."

The sheik answers, "It is my honor and pleasure to meet you major."

That evening after the tents are erected, our cooks begin to serve us dinner. I tell the sheik, "I apologize your majesty, we have no "haleeb. I hope you find our beef stew to your liking. I and Mr. Cohen have completed our part in the mission here and we will be leaving in the morning."

"I wish to thank you pastor once again. You have brought great wealth to my people. Through your benevolence their lives will prosper."

He grins and says, "I hope to have your company again Pastor Greene. Have you reconsidered the offer of my daughters?"

"I have not your highness."

"Then it is, hatti nultaqi morra akhra."

I answer, "Yes, until we meet again sir."

CHAPTER 95

Four months have passed, and on one Sabbath day I take my usual weekly trip to the marketplace, and my brick wall in the alleyway. I have received my first message since returning from the Sinai.

It reads:

All goods safely on ship.

The angels have left you

To guard it.

"I'm truly thankful Lord."

The "Christian Voice" has brought a few more people into our church. Some would think it is out of curiosity, but I've a mind to believe it is the Father bringing them to his Son. Men can only bring the message; it is the Holy Spirit that convicts them of their sins unto repentance. We now number eighty-three in our congregation.

Later that week Reuben comes to the parsonage. He tells me, "We must talk."

"Let's go."

In my quarters I ask, "Something to drink Reuben?"

"I'll have a coke if you have one."

I bring them out. "Glass?"

"No."

"What's on your mind?"

"I have been informed by the Haganah that all of the goods are in the "Red Pearl's hold and is on its way to a destination that they will not disclose. Do you have any concerns about its safety?"

"Absolutely not, and I have already received this news."

"Now how in the world would you have received this news?"

"The Lord himself told me my good friend."

"Say David, would you like to take the Cessna up again? This time for just a little joy ride?"

"Yes, I believe I would, that is if I can pick the area of joy to ride."

"Alright, where to?"

"Let's fly over the Sinai again. We can buzz the Bedouins, and also there is a particular place I'd enjoy flying by."

"Fine by me. I'll meet you at the airfield tomorrow at noon."

"We're on good buddy!"

That evening, I got an idea, and I sit down to write a letter.

Dear Ruth: I don't know if this letter will find you, but I miss you and want you to know I love you very much. I think of you every day.

One day we will meet again in the presence of our Savior. I am also ready to walk with you in his kingdom here on earth with our new sinless bodies. Please say hello to Ishmael and Luke. If you do receive this letter, I wouldn't mention it to Jacob or Samuel. It could anger them. Elijah probably will already be aware that I sent it to you anyway. Again, I'll say I love you.

Until we meet once more my love,

Hiram

I say to myself, "I don't know if this will work but I'm going to give it a try." I go to the church's basement where I once saw an old croquet set. I take one ball; a red one, and I saw it in half. I hollow out a portion of its center and put the letter inside. Then I glue it back together, put a dab of glue on a small piece of paper on which I write the name of "RUTH" and paste it on the ball. Then I pray that the Lord will allow me to do what I'm planning.

When I meet Reuben at the airfield he is all smiles. "Let's get this thing in the air David!" I climb aboard and we take off. "Remember You said we'll go where I want."

He laughs and says, "Okay kemosabe!"

"What did you say?"

"I said OKAY kemosabe! I found a book about the Lone Ranger. You sparked my interest."

I laugh and tell him, "Head straight into the Sinai and let's fly low over the sheik's tribe."

We're both enjoying the flight. The stress of our foray into the desert to retrieve the first cache of treasure is finally fading away. "Look at 5 o'clock Reuben."

"I see it David. It's the sheiks encampment. I'll take it down to 100 feet and wave my wings as we buzz them."

We zoom over the Bedouins and they wave at us from below. "That was fun," my pilot says. "Where to now?"

"Head southwest for about an hour."

"What are we looking for?"

"A circle of mountains with a cloud covering over them."

"I don't know if you have noticed David, but there is not a cloud in the sky."

"They will be there. They'll be sunk slightly below the range's peaks."

Then I see the mountain range...... at least I think it's them.

David says, "Well I don't believe it. There are thick clouds covering this entire range of mountains. There must be a large lake there to evaporate that much moisture upwards. How did you know that?"

"I've been in this area once before."

"Aha! Is that where you came from when you first rode Nabob into Jerusalem?"

"You're close David. You're close. Now fly straight over that cloud formation until our plane is almost into it!"

As Reuben pilots the plane over the center of the valley that I know is below, I open my window and drop the red ball out. He says, "What did you just throw out?"

I pray forgive me Lord and I lie, "The rest of my sandwich. It didn't taste good."

"Where to now my strange navigator?"

"Let's head straight east to the gulf and fly up the straits of Aqaba. Then we'll head home."

"Roger that." He banks the Cessna and we're off.

Then I ask him a question that has been on my mind; no, not just about Reuben only, but about all of the worshippers in our church. I ask him, "Have you ever been baptized Reuben?"

"No, I have not David."

"I think it's time to discover how many of our church members haven't been. Once a person accepts Christ as their Lord, it's good to make one's profession public. In fact, Jesus said believe and be baptized. It is faith only that forgives sins, but one needs to announce it to the world. I'll research this next Sunday."

CHAPTER 96

The next time I sit down to write the "Christian Voice" I decide to put in a message that should really peak the Jewish community's curiosity and puzzlement. In our blog I write the entire chapter of Isaiah fifty-three:

"Who hath believed our report? And to whom is the arm of the Lord revealed?

For he shall grow up before him as a tender plant,

And as a root out of dry ground: he hath nor form or comeliness: and when we shall see him, there is no beauty that we should desire him.

He is despised and rejected of men; a man of sorrows and acquainted with grief: and we hid as it were our faces from him; he was despised, and we esteemed him not.

Surely he hath borne our griefs and carried our sorrows: yet we did esteem him stricken, smitten of God and afflicted.

But he was wounded for our transgressions, he was bruised for our iniquities: the chastisement of our peace was upon him; and with his stripes we are healed.

All we like sheep have gone astray; we have turned everyone, to his own way; and the Lord hath laid on him the iniquity of us all.

He was oppressed and he was afflicted, yet he opened not his mouth: he is brought as a lamb to the slaughter, and as a sheep before her shearers is dumb, so he openeth not his mouth.

He was taken from prison and from judgement: and who shall declare his generation? For he was cut off from the land of the living: for the transgression of my people was he stricken.

And he made his grave with the wicked, and with the rich in his death; because he hath done no violence, neither was there any deceit in his mouth.

Yet it pleased the Lord to bruise him; he hath put him to grief: when thou shall make his soul an offering for sin, he shall see his seed, he shall prolong his days, and the pleasure of the Lord shall prosper in his hand. He shall see the travail of his soul and shall be satisfied: by his knowledge shall my righteous servant justify many: for he shall bear their iniquities.

Therefore, will I divide him a portion with the great, and he shall divide the spoil with the strong; because he hath poured out his soul to the death: and he was numbered with the transgressors; and he bare the sins of many, and made intercession for the transgressors."

"I must ask our readers of whom is the prophet speaking of? Who is this sacrificial lamb that has borne the sins of many?

For the answer to that question, we ask you to meet with us

At "Grace Christian Church", 881 Mesilat Yesharim St., Jerusalem

May God bless you!

I am Pastor David H. Greene

The next Lord's Day the Holy Spirit moved fifteen new people to attend our services, and I read this chapter of the book of Isaiah for their ears. I follow with Jesus said, "I am the way, the_truth, and the life, no one cometh to the Father but through me."

When I give the invitation to come forward and accept Christ as Lord and Savior, eight new souls come forward to confess Him for the forgiveness if their sins! Nine our Jewish! I thank you Jesus!

CHAPTER 97

(One day in Shashani)

The boy Ishmael comes running excitedly towards the Shashani stables. He falls, picks himself up, and continues his race. He enters the barn out of breath and attempts to cry out loud, but cannot due to his breathlessness. Luke sees him and says worriedly, "What is wrong Ishmael? What is wrong? Calm down and tell me!"

Ishmael gasps and says, "Where is Sister Ruth? Where is she?!"

"She is in her office."

The boy turns from him and runs to the stable's office with Luke following him. When bursting in Ruth stands up from her desk and says, "Well my goodness Ishmael what is the rush? Are you alright?"

Luke tells him, "Now calm down boy. Calm down."

"Look Sister Ruth. Look......look what I found!" And he hands her a red ball.

"Why it's just a red ball Ishmael, that is all it is." "But look. It has your name on it!"

She rotates the ball in her hands and says, "Oh my, yes it does."

Luke says, "May I see it Ruth?" And she gives it to him.

Luke asks, "Where did you find this ball?"

He answers, "Out in the stable's pasture. It was just lying there!"

Luke examines the ball and says, "I see it was once cut in half, you can see glue around the cut that is holding it together." He puts the ball on Ruth's desk and says, "I shall be right back. I need a screwdriver and hammer." When he returns, he proceeds to pry open the ball. In just a short time he's successful. "Look there is a paper inside! He starts to unfold the paper but stops, "The ball did have your name on it Ruth," he says.

Ruth takes it from him unfolds the letter, sits back down, and reads. In only a few moments she begins to cry, and then gives the letter back for them to read.

They both read it and Ishmael jumps up and down in happiness, as Luke is simply bewildered. He asks, "But how? "How?"

CHAPTER 98

(In Jerusalem)

A t our next worship service I ask, "I would like to see how many of our members who wish to be baptized. Would you step forward to join me up by the podium please."

Twenty-eight people stand, come forward and gather around me. "God bless you. It's the Lord's desire that all saved people, all born again Christians, be baptized. The simple truth of the gospel is that a man is justified by faith alone. Ephesians 2:8 & 9 expounds, "For by grace are ye saved. Through faith; and that not of yourselves: it is the gift of God" not of works, lest any man should boast." Yes, the scriptures say no man or woman can boast or brag about how good they were on this earth, or by how many good deeds they've done, that would earn them their right to enter heaven. Because the good book says, "For all have sinned and come short of the glory of God." And it also says, "All of our righteousness is as filthy rags". That gift of God spoken in Ephesians is the gift of His Son dying on the cross. Our acceptance of His gift grants us the forgiveness of our sins, and our salvation. Although baptism does not remove sins, it is imperative for us to give a public proclamation of our faith. In baptism we die to ourselves; that is the going under the water, and our resurrection; the rising up from the water, proclaiming we are dead to ourselves and alive unto Christ." Jesus himself was baptized by his cousin John the Baptist in the Jordan river. I'm therefore going to charter a bus and take these our beloved brothers and sisters to the Jordan river for baptism. I will inform you this week as to the date. Again, may God bless you and keep you. That concludes today's service." Eve plays the organ to the hymn of "How great

thou art".

In three weeks, our bus takes the twenty-eight and me to the Jordan river where Jesus was baptized. We all don white robes. As I enter the water I'm reminded of my baptism during "Immersion" in Shashani. I call the first person in, and Dr. Archibald McLeish, his wife Annette, and their little daughter Patricia come into the Jordan as a family. The doctor says, "Patricia first pastor. I hold her back and ask, "Have you accepted Christ as you Lord and Savior?"

She answers, "Yes pastor."

"Then my sister I baptize you in the name of the Father, and of the Son, and of the Holy Ghost." I dunk her under the water and raise her up again. Everyone present shouts, "Hallelujah."

Then the remainder of the saved are baptized except for one.

Reuben walks down into the water. We hug and we are filled with tears of joy. I baptize him, we all enjoy a picnic lunch by the Jordan, and I thank the Lord for the wonder of his love, for He first loved us even before we loved him.

CHAPTER 99

Jerusalem 1948

Jerusalem has become a powder keg ready to explode. Britain has declared that their "Mandate" over Palestine will end. Jews and Arabs are constantly engaged in local battles. On the 18th of March, the United Nations reported that it has been unable to arrange a truce.

The president of the U.S., Harry S. Truman writes, "I think the proper thing to do, and the thing I have been doing, is to do what I think is right and let them all go to hell." It is obvious to Congress that the White House wants to ignore the situation in the Mideast.

But on the 25th of March Truman addresses the UN security council proposing a UN trusteeship of Palestine. He says, "Unfortunately it has become clear that the so called "Partition Plan" (Dividing Palestine into two separate Jewish and Arab states) cannot be carried out at this time by peaceful means. Unless emergency action is taken, there will be no public authority in Palestine capable of preserving law and order. Violence and bloodshed will descend upon the Holy Land and large-scale fighting will occur."

In secret behind closed doors of the oval office at the "White House", Truman tells his "Chief of Staff, John R. Steelman", that he wants nothing further to do with the situation in the Mideast.

Back in Jerusalem at a Haganah council meeting, their leaders gather together to discuss the current situation. Their leader, David Ben-Gurion addresses Yitzak Rabin, Chaim Weizmann, Ariel Sharon, and Moshe Dayan. He tells them, "We must seek a meeting in Washington with President Truman. He must be convinced that our only hope, our only solution, is to have him recommend that Israel will become its own independent nation. I have requested many times to meet with him and have been denied. I have asked an American to help us with this dilemma, and his plane will arrive here tonight. This man will be instrumental to our cause.

Also, our member Reuben Cohen is good friends with Pastor Greene. Contact Cohen and inform him that we wish to speak with the pastor."

CHAPTER 100

"Come on in Reuben the door is open." He knocks again. I put down the newspaper I was reading and say, "I'm coming, "Hold your camels." I open the door and say, "Sorry I thought it was unlocked."

He steps in and says, "I thought the expression was "hold your horses."

"Not in Jerusalem, only in Wyoming.

I've been reading in the Philly Inquirer a friend of mine is receiving the Medal of Honor."

"That's great David."

"What's up?"

"The Haganah, that's what's up. They want to meet with you."

"Why?"

"I don't know. They wouldn't tell me."

"When?"

"Tomorrow."

"Where?"

"They said they would meet you at "the King David Hotel" at 3:00 p.m."

"Give them a message for me."

"What about?"

"Tell them I'll meet them, but they owe me one."

"What do you think they owe you?"

"None of your business "Oh inquisitive one"."

"Alright…… What do you have to eat?"

"Just go to the fridge and help yourself."

Reuben does and comes back with a sandwich. What is in this?"

"It's a ham sandwich Reuben."

He hands it to me and says, "You know I shouldn't eat this."

I say, "My good friend you are a Christian now. Are you still paying attention to the old Levitical laws about food? If you remember, St. Peter was shown by the Lord in a vision on that Joppa roof top that those dietary laws are now defunct under this dispensation of grace."

"I still feel odd about eating pork."

"Take a bite!"

He does and says, "Wow! This is delicious."

"Do you see what you've been missing?"

Reuben sits down and between bites says, "I don't know for sure David, but I think they want to send you on another mission."

"This ought to be good! I wonder for what purpose and where they want to send me. Well, I guess I'll find out tomorrow. By the way, what are you doing the rest of tonight?"

"Nothing."

I hear a Bogie and Bacall movie called "Key Largo" is playing at the British Fort's outdoor screen. Want to go?"

"Only if you buy the popcorn."

******

The next day I meet with the Haganah council. As usual they sit me in front of a long table with six of their members behind it. I know them all except for a man sitting in the middle next to Ben- Gurion. On the other side of Ben-Gurion is Dr. Chaim Weizmann. He is an old man now and nearly blind. He speaks first, "Thank you for joining us today Pastor Greene. I believe that you know everyone here today except for the gentleman sitting next to Mr. Ben-Gurion. This is Mr. Edward Jacobson of Kansas City, Missouri. Mr. Jacobson, I would like to introduce you to Pastor David Greene, a fellow American of yours, and pastor of Grace Christian church here in Jerusalem. Pastor Greene has been a great supporter of our Zionist movement and was instrumental in our efforts to produce the great wealth now in our possession that I have told you about.

Pastor Greene, Mr. Jacobson, Is great friends with the President of the United States, Mr. Harry Truman. They fought together side by side in World War I. They were also business associates being partners in a haberdashery in Kansas City. As you probably know I have gone to Washington to see Mr. Truman about reversing his decision on supporting the UN plan to divide Palestine into two states. However, he refuses to discuss this issue with me. We have, therefore, solicited Mr. Jacobson's aid. He has flown here to discuss all matters pertaining to our desire for the new state of Israel. He has volunteered to go to Washington to speak to his good friend the president, about supporting the new nation of Israel. We wish for you to accompany him."

I ask, "Why? How can I help?"

We in our organization are forever grateful for your achievements that provided the financial support for our newly proposed nation. Mr. Jacobson feels that you may help convince his friend that we indeed have these funds."

"You realize that I cannot reveal to anyone how I knew that the treasures were there."

"Yes, and that will not be necessary."

"I will accompany Mr. Jacobson to Washington if you do two things for me."

Then Ben-Gurion speaks up, "What do you wish for us to do pastor?"

"First, I need some funding to expand my church. Due to our increase in worshippers, it's becoming too small to accommodate them all. Second, I have a friend who is receiving "The Congressional Medal of Honor" at a ceremony in the White House on the 12th of April. I want an invite to that ceremony."

Jacobson stands, walks around the table shakes my hand and says, "Rest assured Pastor Greene this will be arranged!"

On the drive home, while contemplating going back to America; I've decided that it's time for a long vacation. I'll call the missionary Joel Stevens, who's supporters have positioned him in Haifa, to conduct our Sunday services and write a proverb in the "Christian Voice" each week. After I turn into the church I call Joe, Eve, and Naomi for a meeting and explain that I'll be leaving for about three weeks. I tell them, "I want to visit some old friends that I haven't seen for a long time."

CHAPTER 101

As Jacobson and I board a DC 3 for our long flight to Washington he tells me, "Harry and I have been best friends for decades now. He usually listens to what I have to say, but lately he has been very sour on the subject of Palestine. My friend told me that he has become increasingly irritated by lobbying from Zionists and has issued instructions that he didn't want to see any more of their spokesmen."

I ask, "Then why do you think we'll be able to make any difference in the current situation?"

"Because he has never said no to me."

"Why then, am I really going along with you?"

"To assure him of the Zionist's newfound wealth."

The plane lands in D.C. and we taxi to the "White House."

Jacobson holds a letter signed by the president that allows us entry into its gates. Secret Service personnel are everywhere. We are met by Truman's chief of staff John Steelman at the door. He greets us with, "Welcome gentlemen. The president is anxious to see you Mr. Jacobson."

Within an hour we are ushered into the "oval office", and Mr. Truman is standing behind his desk as we enter.

Truman says, "Hello Eddie you old buzzard, it's damn sure good to see you!" Jacobson walks around the desk and hugs the president. He says, "Good to see you too Harry!"

"And who's this gentleman?"

"Please let me introduce Pastor David Greene. He's an American Harry. He pastors a church in Jerusalem."

The president says, "It's a pleasure to meet you Pastor Greene. Any friend of Eddie's is a friend of mine. Please be seated men. May I offer you something to drink?"

We both decline.

Jacobsen says, "Harry I was disappointed that you didn't help Chaim Weizmann in regard to the Jewish State. I know your hero is Andrew Jackson. I have a hero too. He's the greatest Jew alive. I'm talking about Dr. Chaim Weizmann. You putting him off isn't like you Harry. I want you to listen carefully what Pastor Greene has to tell you."

I explain, "Mr. President I am representing "The Jewish Zionist Organization". Its leaders wish to inform you that they have been blessed by God in receiving an almost incalculable wealth. I have been involved in them receiving these funds, and I can verify truthfully that these new found riches are worth more than the entire coffers of the United States Treasury and England's combined. I have seen it myself. We wish to inform you that this new wealth will assure their stability in becoming a new sovereign nation. If you will support the section of the United Nations "Resolution 181" which supports the creation of a new Jewish state, Israel will be not only a friend to the U.S. but will be the only true democratic country in the middle east."

The president leans back in his chair, looks back and forth at each of us and asks me the same question that I have heard once before. He grins and asks, "What in the hell did you do? Then he laughs and says, "Did you actually find "King Solomon's Mines?"

I answer, "Yes…… Mr. President it was something like that."

Jacobson says, "Harry you can't put this off any longer. The UN is going to put it to vote. Let us go back and tell those Jewish dignitaries that you will support them to become a new nation."

President Truman removes his glasses, leans forward resting his elbows on the desk, and says, "You know Eddie I could never say no to you. I'll support your damn resolution. Now you can't say no to this. He picks up the phone and orders, "Wilma bring in the "Schenley" whisky and a few cokes......and hurry!"

After leaving the "White House" I tell Jacobson, "Your friend is quite a character." Jacobson says to me, "Now you know why I coined the phrase "Give 'em hell Harry!"

CHAPTER 102

Edward Jacobson returns to Palestine, and I remain in D.C. My accommodations are at the "Washington Hilton", and I have a splendid view of the "Washington Monument" and "White House". Tomorrow I'll witness the greatest honor an American soldier can receive. And this "Medal of Honor", will be given to a great friend of mine. He is none other than MSgt Patrick Michael O'Brien!

More than anything I wish I could hug him afterwards in congratulations and attend the dinner in his honor. But that's impossible. I am dead to this world. I'm sure I'll also see Andy, Ski, and Joe at the ceremony, so I must disguise myself. In preparation for this I rented a Hassidic Jew wardrobe including wig, beard, and hat at a downtown Halloween store. I'm confident that this disguise will hide my presence, but being still somewhat nervous about it, I buy a pair of black horn-rimmed sunglasses.

The day finally comes, and the press and invitees are flowing into the east wing of the white house.

I'm intentionally coming in near the end of the crowd. I make my way to the rear of the room with sunglasses on, attempting to be as inconspicuous as possible. Then I'm a bit taken aback because who walks in but my old boss Mr. John Jacob's and his wife. Oh no I gasp; they are followed in by my old fiancé Irene and her new husband Xander Bascombe. I should have known that the "Philadelphia Inquirer" would have a contingent witnessing a hometown boy's achievements. The honoree's family and friends are seated next, and then I see Andy carrying his son Brian and holding Becky's hand. Ski, and Joe follow them, and they take their seats. I really can't explain how I feel. I guess I'm just filled with mixed emotions. Part of me wants to run up to them all and say, "Look! I'm alive! I want to embrace my friends, and kiss Irene one last time! Then President Truman with his staff enter the room and all stand. He goes to the podium and thanks everyone for attending this honorable ceremony. He then explains the history and the requirements of valor needed for congress to award the medal of honor to a person in the military. No one really notices me, the Hassidic Jew, sitting in the background.

Then Paddy comes in wearing his dress blues, smiling, and looking the part of the hero that he really is. I'm so thrilled for him I break down crying. People stand again and give him a thunderous applause. He nods at them and walks to the president. Mr. Truman greets him with a big smile and shakes his hand. Then an army chaplain gives an invocation, and then an "Eulogy". He speaks, "Sergeant O'Brien has requested that I read the names in honor of four men, friends of his, that have died during action. They are Michael Collins, Benjamin Shields, James Huston, and Hiram Walker. These men have given the ultimate price of their lives in the defense of their country!"

I gasp as my throat chokes up.

Then President Truman starts. He reads from a paper of all the heroic efforts, above and beyond the call of duty that has brought MSgt Patrick Michael O'Brien to this moment, including leading (what was called a suicide squad) to blow up a bridge on some river in Germany called the Neckar. Then he says, "It is my great pleasure and honor Master Sergeant O'Brien to award you with the highest symbol that can be given for bravery that America can bestow on a service member of our military "The Medal of Honor". With that said he places the medal around Paddy's neck! The crown stands and applauds again, flashbulbs go off from press photographers, my old friends and Paddy's family go up to greet the hero. Kate Smith in person, accompanied by a small army band, starts singing "God Bless America". I simply remain hidden in the back bawling like a baby but with happy tears.

As the ceremony ends and the audience begins to leave for the awards banquet, I remain seated in the rear of the east wing. Occasionally someone would glance towards me. However, when Irene files by she looks at me and stops suddenly. She stares straight at me. She doesn't move. She just stands there and stares. Finally, her husband says something to her, and she continues on, but she looks back over her shoulder at me again as if she knows it's me. I'm horrified until she exits the room. Paddy and my buddies are in such a celebratory mood they don't even glance in my direction. I wait until the wing is vacated by all and go to my car. My thoughts trouble me; for as much as I enjoyed seeing my friends, it leaves me in a deep state of depression because I have not been able to participate nor celebrate with them. I am dead to this world, but alive again unto Christ!

CHAPTER 103

I stay two more days in Washington. I visit the Lincoln Memorial and the Smithsonian Institute still in disguise as a Hassidic. Then I board a train, sans costume, to York, Pennsylvania. I realize I have some unfinished business there, and I pray to the Lord that he will give me the ability, the courage, and the power to do what I must do.

My recollections of my friend Roger Sutcliffe have never been erased from my mind. I have often thought of him, especially while in prayer during my days in Shashani. I realize I must see him again because there is something I must do for him.

I arrive by taxi at the "Williamston's Mental Hospital" just outside of York. When I enter, I ask for the doctor who may be treating Roger Sutcliffe.

A nurse behind the information desk asks me, "Are you a relative sir?"

"No ma'am I'm in the clergy, my name is Pastor David H. Greene. Mr. Sutcliffe is a very good friend of mine."

She says, "Dr. Redding is Mr. Sutcliffe's doctor. I'm not sure if I can contact him right now. Do you have an appointment with Dr. Redding?"

"No ma'am I don't. However, I have travelled a long way. I have flown in from Jerusalem and it is vital that I see him."

She answers, "I must see some identification, Pastor."

I hand her my British driver's license, and she says, "Please have a seat Pastor Greene. It may take a while to contact him. I know that he is on duty, and currently he's on his rounds. I'll wave you over when I reach him."

"Thank you." As I examine my surroundings I'm pleased with the conditions in this hospital. Contrary to the filth and stench of "Byberry" this facility is clean. The floors are shining with wax, no debris of any kind is evident anywhere, the air has a faint and clean medicinal odor to it, nurses and staff wear white, spotless, starched uniforms, and everything appears organized. I take a seat in a waiting area and watch the staff perform their duties.

About ten minutes later the receptionist waves me over to her counter.

"I have contacted Dr. Redding and he says he'll be right down to meet with you." "Thank you nurse."

"You're most welcome sir."

As I lean against the counter a man with a stethoscope around his neck approaches me. I ask, "Are you Dr. Redding?"

"I am sir. I understand from nurse Owens that you wish to see me about Mr. Roger Sutcliffe, am I correct?"

"Yes, I'm Pastor David Greene from Jerusalem, and Roger and I were very good friends at one time."

"I am afraid pastor, that Roger may not even recognize you."

"Nevertheless, I need to see him."

"Then follow me please. The rooms for the criminally insane are all on the basement floor of this establishment. No elevators have been installed for going down there, so we must use a flight of stairs."

I continue to observe the conditions of the hospital as I walk with the doctor. Doors to patients' rooms are closed, and the ones open display comfortable living conditions. Staff are scurrying everywhere. I view an open area where patients are eating, and another where activities are being conducted by staff for the residents. We then descend into the basement until stopped by a barred partition with a security guard sitting behind it. Dr. Redding says, "Open the gate for us please Lester."

We enter the criminally insane ward and Redding says, "Please let me explain our "Modus Operandi"on this ward. Some of the rooms only have beds and nothing else. They are padded for the patient's protection. In others there are tables, lamps, and a chest of drawers for their use. Those would be for patients that are cognizant of their surroundings and understand why they are here. We do have instances where rehabilitation occurs amongst our patients. Our psychiatric staff excels greatly here at "Williamston". Unfortunately, there are some of our institutionalized that seem to be without hope. Mr. Sutcliffe is one of them."

We continue down a hallway and stop at a door with a small window and a slotted opening to permit food to be placed through it. Dr. Redding says, "This is Roger Sutcliffe's room."

I peek through the small window and see Roger sitting in a corner, staring at nothing, and sucking his thumb. I say to the doctor, "I must go in to see him."

"That is impossible pastor! It would be too dangerous! He most certainly will do you harm!"

"I assure you Dr. Redding no harm will come to me."

"I'm afraid I cannot allow that sir."

"May I remind you doctor that I am the clergy. If you deny me entry you are violating Mr. Sutcliffe's religious rights. I then would have no alternative except to contact his attorney. Eventually a judge would decide this matter and allow me entry based on this patient's first amendment rights. I will also report this matter to the "Philadelphia Inquirer". I'm certain that you wish no negative publicity to affect your institution."

He looks at me soberly and says, "Very well sir. But I must put two guards outside the door as you enter."

"As long as they can't oversee or hear what happens inside this cell I concur."

"As you wish Pastor Greene. But I will have you sign a release form that exempts the hospital from any harm coming to you." Redding takes a walkie-talkie from his pocket and orders, "Lester I need a hospital release forum and two security guards at cell eighteen immediately." When they come, I sign the form, and they open the door and slam it shut.

Roger lifts his head to look at me. He smiles. But it is not a congenial smile. It is a nasty evil grin. It has the look of death in it. Then he says, no ......better words would be he growls in a deep raspy voice, "Well if it isn't Ace Walker. Long time no see Ace!" Then he laughs demonically. He points at me with his left hand and resumes his fiendish cackling. The laughter is deafening in the cell. He...... no, not he...... it...... says, "You are now called Pastor David Greene! And he shrieks with more laughter. "What have you to do with us you follower of Jesus? What do you wish from us, you who have talked to the prophet Elijah?"

I ask it, "Who are you?"

"We are the same. We are named "Legion" for we are many! We are the same as in Jesus' day, you pig eater!" Then more demonic laughter.

I take a small bible from my pocket and read from Mark 16:17, "And these signs shall follow them that believe; in my name they shall cast out devils; they shall speak with new tongues." I point at the thing that was Roger and order, "In the name of God the Father, and of His son Jesus, and of the Holy Spirit, I command you to depart from this man!" The thing shudders and says, "No! No! No! No!"

Once again, I command it, "Hihilem mahaish hazeh (leave this man" in Hebrew)!" The thing then screams in anguish, as I command the words again, "In the name of Jesus of Nazareth be gone from him!"

Roger falls prone to the floor. He dizzily shakes his head, looks up at me, and says, "Ace...... What am I doing here?"

I walk over to him and help him stand. I embrace him and say, "It's a long story Roger. It truly is a long story."

We go and sit together in a corner, and for the next hour I explain the past events of his life to him. During my narration, his face frequently grimaces questioningly.

"I say, "Roger I'll have the psychiatrists give you a thorough examination now. I will also have your attorney contact you in order to appeal your sentence. You certainly did not kill those women; however, it will be difficult to believe not only your exorcism, but that it was a host of demons that murdered them. I will help with any correspondence that you need from me including my appearance in any court demanding my presence."

He says, "I can't believe this Ace. I just can't believe it."

"You must do one thing for me though Roger."

"You must never use the name of Hiram (Ace) Walker again. He is dead Roger! You must now refer to me as Pastor David Greene. You cannot ever tell anyone, and I mean anyone, that you have seen Ace Walker. Do you understand?"

"Yes, I do."

We pray together and I leave.

On the way back to my hotel I thank the Lord for Roger's deliverance, and when in my room, I write a long correspondence to Roger's attorney and to the staff of psychiatrists at "Williamston Mental Hospital", explaining Roger's previous condition.

I am ready to return to Jerusalem.

CHAPTER 104

(Tel Aviv 14ᵗʰ of May 1948)

D avid Ben-Gurion stands from a balcony at the Tel Aviv Museum with a loudspeaker in his hands. A huge throng of people gather below as he gives this proclamation, "Ladies and gentlemen today is a monumental day in the history of the world! Today the United Nations with the support of thirty-three of its member nations voted yes for the new nation of Israel. The last and deciding vote was made by President Truman of the United States of America. LADIES AND GENTLEMEN THIS EDICT HAS PROCLAIMED "ISRAEL" AS ITS OWN SOVERIEGN NATION!!

The thousands of the new citizens of Israel, gathered below the balcony, erupt in in cheers as the nation's new white flag with its "Blue Star of David" centered in its middle is hoisted high above the building! The shouting with joy, the hugging, the kissing, the mayhem continues for hours. Never in the history of the world has a nation been completely vanquished, its people dispersed throughout the earth, and then after three-millennia it becomes its own country again; its own sovereign nation!

A short time later the government of the new country elects its leaders. Dr. Chaim Weizmann is elected as its first president. David

Ben-Gurion is sworn in as its first prime minister. Regional and city officers are elected, and the new government is formed.

But the hating antisemite Arab nations are incensed. They are completely in turmoil. Their only desire is the complete the final annihilation of Israel. War that has constantly been waged, has accelerated into a coalition of the Arab states planning the destruction of the new nation. Only God's miracles are saving the nation. Then in 1956 Egyptian President Abdul Nasser, in a historic stance against Israel, blocks access to Israeli ships from passing through the Suez Canal, and blocks Israel's southern port of Eilat. The Israelis', in retaliation, invade the Egyptian Sinai Peninsula, and capture Gaza, Rafah, and Al- arish while taking thousands of prisoners. They then occupied the east of the Suez Canal thus ending the conflict.

CHAPTER 105

(Grace Christian Church 1956)

Years have gone by, and the leaders of the new Israel, as promised, constructed a new entire building for us. The Lord has added a total of two hundred and forty-seven members to our church. As I sit in my office and develop my next sermon for Sunday, I thank the Lord for protecting and preserving our buildings from the turmoil of the wars and bombings that have surrounded us.

For years now, during Sunday worship services, Joe has sat near the front door with a shotgun lying across his lap. When he began doing this, I told him, "Joe you really don't need to bear arms during services. The Lord will protect us."

He said, "I know pastor, but this is for backup!"

I smile and tell him, "You know Joe, I once thought exactly the same thing in a cave years ago."

As I continue to pen my sermon, I think to myself, "I surely have friends in high places. I'm intimate with not only the president of the U.S., the president and prime minister of Israel, but most importantly with my Lord and Savior. The highest one of all.

I have been pastoring here at "Grace Christian" for going on ten years now, I'm thirty-six years old, and I'm starting to get an itch. No, it's not only an itch but a heartfelt desire to satisfy a question that has been nagging at me since the birth of Israel. I finish my sermon and take letterhead and pen. I begin to compose a letter that reads:

Dear sirs: I am Pastor David H. Greene of "Grace Christian Church" in Jerusalem, Israel. I wish this letter to serve as my introduction.

The Lord has appointed me here to serve for almost ten years now.

Recently I have prayed if He wishes for me to continue this path.

He has both open and closed doors for me in answering my question.

And in obeying Proverbs three, I have not leaned unto my own understanding, but I trust in Him.

He has answered my question in a number of interesting ways. I shall not at this time share them with you unless you request that I should.

At this time, I wish to vacate my position here at "Grace Christian", and pursue where I believe He is sending me, I strongly feel that He has a teaching mission for me.

I therefore am inquiring if any person within the fellowship of your, "Independent Christian Missions Organization", would be led by the Lord to serve here in the Holy Land.

I am most anxious to hear from you.

our address is 881 Mesilat Yesharim St.

Jerusalem, Israel

Yours in Christ,

David H. Greene

I address the envelope and plan on taking it to post tomorrow.

Two months pass before a receive a letter of reply from the "Christian Missions Organization."

They answer:

Dear Pastor Greene:

Thank you for your request to fill the pastorate at

your church in Jerusalem. We indeed have a young man from Liverpool,

England that has a desire to move to Israel.

His name is Edward Wilson, and he has been led by the Lord to

serve in the holy land. He is fluent in the Hebrew language and is anxious to hear from you.

Please contact us via mail once again and inform us as to what date you would wish him to

arrive.

Very truly yours, Donald Mahler

I write back to Mr. Mahler at his "Missions" office informing him to have Edward Wilson to replace me on the 15th of April. A week later I receive their reply of confirmation but am somewhat saddened by the thought of leaving the church. I have loved my flock here while engaging daily in the Lord's work.

I decided it was time to have a meeting with my staff, and one morning I called them into my office. I explain that I'm leaving the church, and I feel the Lord is drawing me to another location to teach. Joe is stunned, and both Naomi and Eve start to cry. I tell them how much I appreciate what they have done for me and the church. We embrace and Eve demands to have a going away dinner for me. She says, "You must say goodbye to everyone pastor, and I'll prepare your favorite meal of sea bass."

I say, "Thank you Eve. You should plan the dinner for the 17th of April. Your new pastor Mr. Edward Wilson will be here on the 15th and that will also be a good time for everyone to meet him."

Four days later as I go to my kitchen to find a snack, I hear a knock on my door.

A voice behind the door says, "It's Reuben."

"Come on in brother. What are you up to tonight?"

As of yet, I haven't told him about my leaving Jerusalem, and I think that tonight will be the right moment to let him know.

"I met a new girl, and I am taking her to dinner tonight. I thought you might want to join us."

"Anybody I know?"

"I don't think you have met her yet David. She's a new teacher at my school. She's an American from the state of Delaware."

"Really, what town is she from?"

"I believe she told me Louie. Is there a Louie Delaware?"

My heart skips a beat. "No, it's a small state. There is no Louie. Do you mean Lewes Delaware?"

"Yes, that's it, Lewes Delaware."

I'm thinking this is getting too close to home. "What's her name?"

"It's a Polish name I believe. Her name's Sylvia Jankowski."

My mind is racing. Then I think, Oh no! Wasn't the first baseman on our team named Jankowski? Yeah, it was Jankowski...... Don Jankowski!

He had a sister too; a cute little thing. I remember she was a couple of years younger than Don, but I don't remember her first name. This is scary. This would be too coincidental; I have to be careful here.

"So, like I said, why don't you come along with us tonight? I'll introduce you."

"Not tonight Reuben. I have some things to clear up here at the church."

"Well, that's your loss then. That's why I stopped."

"Sorry pal. Maybe I'll meet her another time."

"See you later then."

Reuben leaves, and I never mention my coming departure.

My farewell dinner is in three days. I call in the staff and tell them, "I'm sorry but something has come up and we have to cancel my dinner. I have composed a farewell address to the church, as well as an introduction to Pastor Wilson. I wish for you to read it Joe, at our next service."

All three of my staff complain about this. And again, I apologize.

On the evening of the 13th, two days before the new pastor is to arrive, I get out my old Bedouin clothing and backpack and prepare for my journey. I'll leave tomorrow morning.

When I awake in the morning I write a note to Joe, telling him that I had an unexpected situation and had to leave early without saying goodbye. I told him I would leave the Ford at the stables where we first met.

I know this is harsh but I'm afraid that I might have to encounter a meeting with Sylvia Jankowski. I feel the Lord tugging at me to hurry and leave.

CHAPTER 106

I reach the stables, park the car, and go into the office. I give the keys to the attendant on duty, and tell him, "I wish to take out my camel Nabob. Do I owe you any money for his boarding?"

"No, you up to date," he says in broken English.

As usual when Nabob sees me, he immediately gallops over, and I give him an apple. I ask him, "Well boy are you ready for maybe… …I say maybe…… one last long trip?" I lead him out of the corral and mount him. He starts all of his camel's braying. I mount him, and command, "Go Nabob, Go!" We then head directly towards the Sinai. This time I don't have to give any directional commands to Nabob. He seems to know where we're going, and he is anxious to return to his home stable. Once again, I am "David Greene of the Sinai"!

CHAPTER 107

Tired of waiting to introduce his new girlfriend to me, Reuben brings her to the parsonage. He knocks on the door and a man answer that he does not know.

The new pastor asks, "Yes, how may I help you?"

"We're here to see Pastor Greene. Who are you may I ask?"

"I am Edward Wilson the new pastor here at "Grace Church". I am afraid that Pastor Greene is not here."

"Really! Well, I suppose it is nice to meet you pastor, but do you know where David is?"

"I have no knowledge as to where Pastor Greene has disappeared. It was strange that he did not meet with me upon my arrival. It is customary to introduce a new pastor to his congregation. Instead, he had the maintenance man, Mr. Ben-Hur to read an introductory message to the flock. I say, it was most unusual. Please, why don't you both come in."

"Oh, excuse me, I guess we didn't introduce ourselves. I'm Reuben Cohen and this is my friend Miss Sylvia Jankowski. We both teach at the middle school here in Jerusalem. Sylvia has just arrived here from America not long ago."

Sylvia says, "Nice to meet you pastor."

"And I you as well. Won't you be seated please. Perhaps you would relish a cuppa?"

I say, "A what?"

"I am sorry Mr. Cohen, but on occasion, my English colloquialisms hamper my communications with the non-English. I should ask would you care for tea?"

Sylvia answers, "Yes please. If it's not too much trouble."

"Nonsense, I shall ring Naomi."

I say, "I have to say that I'm somewhat concerned about David. We've become great friends and have shared some amazing adventures together. It's not like him to go off somewhere and not tell me he was leaving."

Naomi arrives with a tray of tea with milk, lemon, and sugar."

"Thank you, Naomi,", Pastor Wilson says.

The three of us doctor our tea as preferred, and Sylvia looks at a framed picture on a lampstand. She puts down her cup, stands, and walks over to it. "Is this your photo Pastor Wilson?"

"No, it is not. It seems that Pastor Greene took all of his possessions with him, but alas, forgot that photograph."

She picks it up, looks at both men, and says, "This man in the picture next to you Reuben who is he?"

"Why that's David. My uncle Judah took that photo of us before one of our flights over the Sinai," I answer.

She exclaims, "No it can't be! I know this man! This is Ace Walker!"

"Who?" I ask.

Sylvia continues, "The man in this picture with you is Ace Walker. Well Ace was his nickname; his first name was really Hiram. He's from

Rehoboth Beach, Delaware! I would know him anywhere. My brother Donald and I were classmates with him at the University of Delaware!"

Reuben says, "You must be mistaken Sylvia."

She says, "No I'm not. He played with my brother on the baseball team. I had a huge crush on him at the time, but he never paid any attention to me. He always called me "little bit".

I stand up and look at the picture with her and say, "Maybe it's just a strong resemblance."

"That would be uncanny unless he has a twin brother!"

"David never said to me that he had any siblings."

She regresses and says, "Well maybe it isn't. I heard he died in the war in '43. He was a war correspondent for the "Philadelphia Inquirer". Wow, it sure does look like him!"

I stare at the photo with her and think to myself, Well David, I always have said, I don't really know who you actually are. You shall ever remain a mystery to me! But most of all you were my best friend. I have a suspicion that I shall never see you again. Go with God my brother. Go with God!

CHAPTER 108

(In the Sinai)

On the third day of our journey, I come to what was the second oasis on my first trip through this area. Nabob and I water, and rest.

The next day I can see in the distance Mount Sinai where Moses received the "Ten Commandments" from God. Then I pass closely by The Monastery of St. Catherine's at the foot of the mount. I tell Nabob, "We're almost there my friend!" As we travel another thirty miles or so, Nabob gets jittery. He bucks and brays. Then he takes off at a gallop. I try to slow him down, but it's of no use, he simply races ahead, paying no attention to my commands. Then I spot the cave and my mount halts suddenly in front of it. I dismount and lead Nabob into the cavern. I humbly kneel on the ground and pray. "Lord your will be done and not mine." I kneel in silence for a long period of time before I ask aloud, "Your humble servant asks dear Lord for you to open the gate." Then in the solitude of the cavern a grinding noise can be heard. The boulder is scraping against the rocky ground. It is moving. The gate is open. I cry, stand, and say "Thank you my blessed Savior!" Then Nabob and I enter into the paradise of Shashani once again!

I have only one question. Will the gate be open for you?

THE END

Epilogue

It is interesting to note what happens in the future to our main characters.

Andrew Harrison goes back to school and eventually received his "Doctorate in Chemical Engineering". Upon his graduation he accepts a position with "The Dupont Company". He and Becky have two daughters, in addition to their son Brian.

Joe (Sox) Knight returns to Boston and starts a seafood restaurant featuring "The Best Clam Chowda in Boston". He marries a girl from Charlestown and is the season ticket holder of two seats at Fenway Park.

Patrick (Paddy) Michael O'Brien remains in the army, fights in the Korean war, receives an additional "Purple Heart" and a "Bronze Star" to add to his "Silver Star", and "Medal of Honor". He continues his service after thirty years, at the rank of "Command Sergeant Major" of the 2nd Artillery Division.

Matthew (Ski) Laskowski returns to East St. Louis, Illinois and opens a gas station. He marries a mail- order bride from France, and they have four sons.

Reuben Cohen, after a long two-year engagement, marries Sylvia Jankowski. They move back to his home in Haifa and start a new children's school there.

As for me, my wife Ruth, and Nabob, we live happily in Shashani waiting for the Lord's return.

FACT VS. FICTION

Fiction

Of course, being a work of fiction, the characters don't really exist, except for the noted actual political leaders of the Haganah, the presidents and officials of countries, the actual military generals noted, and actors and singers mentioned.

I am sorry to say that Shashani is fictional!

I, the author, have taken some liberties as to the location of some battles in WWII.

No one knows what really happened to the treasures that were once in either Solomon's or Herod's temples.

Fact

All scripture is from the King James Version of the Bible.

It was indeed Mr. Edward Jacobson's close relationship with President Truman that encouraged him to vote for the new nation of Israel.

The Essenes were an actual sect of the Jews as were the Pharisees and Sadducees. They have been credited with the writings of the Dead Sea Scrolls.

The Dead Sea Scrolls were indeed discovered where and when as written in the story, after the fictional account of Pastor Greene's findings.

The Copper Scrolls are fact. The clues to the treasure in the Valley of Acor are actually written on one copper scroll. And there are indeed clues written to 63 other treasures. The author encourages the readers to use their favorite search engine (Wikipedia recommended) to discover more information about the Copper Scrolls.

Treasure hunters have actually searched for these antiquities for decades now and no one has found any of these historical articles of silver and gold.

OR HAVE THEY???

www.ingramcontent.com/pod-product-compliance
Lightning Source LLC
Chambersburg PA
CBHW071131130626
46553CB00004B/1329